RCW

Reconciling Human Existence with Ecological Integrity

Reconciling Human Existence with Ecological Integrity

Science, Ethics, Economics and Law

*Edited by Laura Westra, Klaus Bosselmann
and Richard Westra*

publishing for a sustainable future
London • Sterling, VA

First published by Earthscan in the UK and USA in 2008

ISBN 978-1-84407-565-2

Typeset by Domex e-data Pvt. Ltd, India
Printed and bound in the UK by TJ International, Padstow
Cover design by Michael Fell and Susanne Harris

For a full list of publications please contact:

Earthscan
Dunstan House
14a St Cross Street
London EC1N 8XA, UK
Tel: +44 (0)20 7841 1930
Fax: +44 (0)20 7242 1474
Email: earthinfo@earthscan.co.uk
Web: **www.earthscan.co.uk**

22883 Quicksilver Drive, Sterling, VA 20166-2012, USA

Earthscan publishes in association with the International Institute
for Environment and Development

A catalogue record for this book is available from the British Library

Library of Congress Cataloging-in-Publication Data has been applied for

The paper used for this book is FSC-certified.
FSC (the Forest Stewardship Council) is an
international network to promote responsible
management of the world's forests.

Mixed Sources

Product group from well-managed
forests and other controlled sources
www.fsc.org   Cert no. SGS-COC-2482
© 1996 Forest Stewardship Council

This book is dedicated to the laureates of the Right Livelihood Award, and all those, named and unnamed, who have given their lives – including those who have made the ultimate sacrifice of life itself – for the cause of global ecological integrity, social justice and peace

Contents

PART I – OVERVIEW: FOUNDATIONS OF ECOLOGICAL INTEGRITY

PART II – ECOLOGICAL INTEGRITY AND BIOLOGICAL INTEGRITY: THE INTERFACE

PART III – ECOLOGICAL INTEGRITY AND ENVIRONMENTAL JUSTICE

Contents

PART I – OVERVIEW: FOUNDATIONS OF ECOLOGICAL INTEGRITY

PART II – ECOLOGICAL INTEGRITY AND BIOLOGICAL INTEGRITY: THE INTERFACE

PART III – ECOLOGICAL INTEGRITY AND ENVIRONMENTAL JUSTICE

PART IV – ECOLOGICAL INTEGRITY, CLIMATE CHANGE AND ENERGY

PART V – FUTURE POLICY PATHS FOR ECOLOGICAL INTEGRITY

List of Boxes, Figures and Tables

BOXES

FIGURES

TABLES

Foreword

Humanity has undergone an explosive change from just another species on the planet to a dominant force that is altering the biological, chemical and physical features of the planet on a geological scale. It has happened so suddenly that we are only now beginning to understand the ramifications of our increased numbers, technological prowess, consumption and global economy.

Ecology and economics are based on the same root word: *eco*, from the Greek word *oikos*, meaning home. Ecology is the study of home while economics is its management. Ecologists study the conditions and principles that govern life's ability to flourish. Economics should operate within those conditions and principles to be sustainable. But we have elevated economics above ecology by virtue of the fact that our leaders place economic growth before such issues as climate change, deforestation, habitat destruction, decline of fisheries, toxic pollution and concern about future generations. Thus, our leaders argue that action to reduce greenhouse gas emissions must be tempered by the need to maintain economic growth. This is ultimately suicidal.

Sustainability is bandied about in a token way as corporations and governments 'greenwash' themselves. In the scientific discussions of this book, we see what the context, conditions and principles of sustainability are as well as the outlines of the path towards a genuinely sustainable future. We must wake up and recognize that, without regard to the integrity of all ecological systems, we are allowing ourselves and our governments to wantonly plunder our only home, Earth. Evidence of the consequences of catastrophic harms is shown throughout this book and everybody needs to act on its message to avert expanding harms on a massive scale.

David Suzuki

Preface

Ecological Integrity and the Inspiration of the Great Lakes Water Quality Agreement

Jack Manno

The first time I met Dr Laura Westra, the originator of the Global Ecological Integrity Project, in the early 1990s, we were at a meeting discussing the implementation – or lack thereof – of the Great Lakes Water Quality Agreement (GLWQA) between Canada and the US. At that time she had already begun to organize the forum of scientists and scholars that became the Global Ecological Integrity Group (GEIG). The GLWQA was widely regarded as a success, and, indeed, a model of an international environmental agreement, because of how the two governments had effectively responded to the lower lakes' eutrophication crisis, the excessive algal growth that fouled shores, reduced water clarity to historic lows and compromised the habitat of fish and other aquatic organisms. However, by the early 1990s the Great Lakes institutions were mired in controversy and inaction over how to address the significantly more complicated, and to some more urgent, policy challenge posed by a steady flow of new evidence linking a broad range of wildlife health effects and, increasingly, similar human health effects to exposure to toxic chemicals in the Great Lakes environment, most significantly PCBs, Dioxin and other chlorinated organic compounds either directly produced by or the by-products of industry and agriculture. Theo Colborn at the World Wide Fund for Nature was pulling together threads of evidence from wildlife and human health studies and making a compelling case that the common theme in the accumulating data was chemical disruption of endocrine functioning, the body's chemical messaging system, that was eroding the vitality, and in some cases the viability, of exposed organisms. This degradation of the health of whole populations was just as important as, and perhaps more important than, any cause–effect linkages between any specific exposure and individual illness. Arguably it was the very definition of a decline in biological integrity.

In Article II of the GLWQA, the Parties, the US and Canadian Governments, agreed that their purpose in signing the agreement was 'to restore and maintain the chemical, physical and biological integrity of the waters of the Great Lakes basin ecosystem'. Westra and her colleagues were asking important questions related to the substantive meaning of integrity and what an official statement of purpose in the GLWQA (and a number of other legal and policy documents worldwide) demands of those who commit their governments or agencies to the restoration and maintenance of integrity. Inspired by my participation in the United Nations Conference on Environment and Development (the 1992 Earth Summit) in Brazil, I was particularly interested in the economic system dynamics that subverted environmental goals (see Chapter 17) and I joined GEIG and its cutting-edge transdisciplinary exploration of integrity by philosophers, legal scholars, ecologists, biologists, planners and others with a shared commitment to systems thinking.

At the time, it seemed critically important to clarify and defend the commitment to integrity as stated in the GLWQA. In 1992 the International Joint Commission (IJC), the binational organization established in 1909 by the Boundary Waters Treaty and given oversight responsibilities for the GLWQA, released its Sixth Biennial Report (IJC, 1992), its review of progress under the agreement. In it, spurred by activists from Greenpeace and supported by scientists like Dr Jack Vallentyne, the Canadian Co-Chair of the IJC's Science Advisory Board and the limnologist most often cited for clarifying the role of phosphorus pollution in eutrophication, the US and Canadian Commissioners made the remarkable recommendation that 'the Parties, in consultation with industry and other affected interests, develop timetables to sunset the use of chlorine and chlorine-containing compounds as industrial feedstock' (IJC, 1992). In so doing the commissioners were following the logic of the agreement's commitment to integrity. The regulatory processes in both countries, based as they were on a one-by-one, chemical-by-chemical assessment of potential exposure and harm and a presumption of safety, or innocence until proven guilty, had clearly failed to protect the lakes from what was appearing to be devastating and potentially irreversible pollution. Being highly reactive, chlorine forms powerful chemical bonds that tend to persist in the environment, and the use of elemental chlorine in manufacturing often leads to a variety of unintentional chlorinated by-products. Chlorinated organic compounds, such as PCB, Dioxin, DDT and Dieldrin, dominated the IJC's list of priority pollutants. While governments slowly dealt with the toxic chemicals they knew were present and harmful, new compounds were continually entering the Great Lakes environment untested, unregulated and unmonitored. All living things in the Great Lakes were sure to encounter and to ingest substances that their ancestors had never encountered. Stored in their genetic inheritance were no mechanisms evolved by selecting those least susceptible to this kind of chemical assault (DePinto and Manno, 1997).

Thomas Jorling drafted the US Clean Water Act and is often credited with the insertion of the statement that 'The objective of the Act is to restore and maintain the chemical, physical and biological integrity of the nation's waters.' Later, as assistant administrator for water at US Environmental Protection Agency (EPA) headquarters, Jorling served as the US Chair of the IJC Water

Quality Board. He wrote about integrity in his influential article 'Incorporating ecological principles into public policy':

> *The intellectual roots of this perspective are found in the study of evolution. The objective of this concept is the maximum patterning of human communities after biogeochemical cycles with a minimum departure from the geological or background rates of change in the biosphere. Framed another way the objective is to move from linear pathways in the movement of matter and energy to circular pathways.*
> (Jorling, 1976, p142)

From this perspective, which is at the heart of the US Clean Water Act and the GLWQA, the widespread release into the environment of a stew of chlorinated organic compounds represents an assault on the chemical and biological integrity of the waters of the Great Lakes.

But politically the recommendation was a disaster. In his book *The Making of a Conservative Environmentalist*, Gordon Durnil, the US Co-Chair of the IJC at the time of the chlorine controversy, later wrote about his transformation from a political operative who helped deliver the state of Indiana for the campaign of the first President Bush to someone who recommended the most radical pollution prevention programme in the history of the commission. The chemical industry responded quickly and reached into the White House to influence incoming President Clinton to ensure that the 'next lot of commissioners will not be as green as the current bunch' (Durnil, 1995). The IJC never recovered. Following the 1987 amendments to the GLWQA, the US and Canadian government agencies created a Binational Executive Committee to coordinate the Great Lakes programme and began a long period of relative disengagement with the IJC. Much like with the US Clean Water Act, what still has not been effectively tackled, or not, in fact, even discussed, are the real policy implications of a governmental commitment to ecological integrity such as that made in the GLWQA. That was the question with which GEIG began.

Whatever the political or indeed the scientific merits of the IJC recommendation on chlorine, it represented an attempt to urge the Canadian and US Governments to seriously consider the implications of their commitment to integrity. As in the US Clean Water Act, the integrity-centred purpose of the GLWQA defined it as a responsibility-based agreement unlike entitlement-based water quality approaches of the past focused on protecting the most monetarily significant *uses*. Thomas Jorling wrote about how the new 1972 Clean Water Act marked a clear departure from earlier policy:

> *Under the earlier programme, the basic assumption was that the biosphere, and in particular the water component of the biosphere, was to be, and in fact existed to be, used ... The measure of water quality*

under pre-1972 US law was to be its 'beneficial use'. The new programme has a different underpinning. It assumes that man is a component of the biosphere and that the relationship we seek to achieve with the environment is what some have called harmony. (Jorling, 1976)

Elsewhere he was quoted as saying:

The 1972 Act ... provides an opportunity, if we use it, to look at the structure and functioning of human communities as elements in the overall biosphere and make judgments about the life-support requirements of those human communities. This is a tall order. Yet it is the direction in which we must move; it is the legacy of the concept of ecological integrity. (Regier and France, 1990, p4).

The Great Lakes ecosystem is one of the great natural wonders of the world. It is hard to overstate its importance. Consider this. Of all the water in the world, 97.5 per cent is salt water; only 2.5 per cent is fresh. Nearly three-quarters of that 2.5 per cent is stored in glaciers and polar ice caps. Almost all the rest is deep underground, or locked in soils as moisture or permafrost. Only 0.3 per cent of the world's fresh water is surface water found in rivers or lakes. Thus only 0.007 per cent of the world's water is fresh surface water and nearly a fifth of that scarce and precious resource is stored in the Great Lakes of North America. One out of every three Canadians and one of every ten Americans takes their water from the Great Lakes.

By the late 1960s the degradation of the Great Lakes was obvious by sight and smell. Routine algal blooms choked the oxygen out of the central basin of Lake Erie. Populations of non-native prey fish, primarily alewife, exploded following the dramatic decline in large predator fish due to overfishing and bioconcentrated dioxin pollution. The fish washed up, rotted, and their dried and windblown carcasses collected into rows on the shore. The Cayahoga River caught fire. The resulting public outcry led to political pressure for environmental action. Among the results was the GLWQA.

The GLWQA, signed first in 1972, was a major milestone in the history of international environmental agreements. In its preamble it recognized the clear links between population and economic growth and water pollution. In 1978 it was renegotiated and revised to include a new emphasis on toxic chemical pollution and express its purpose to restore and maintain the chemical, physical and biological integrity of the waters of the Great Lakes basin ecosystem. It established clear, ecologically based principles and goals, promising to eventually virtually eliminate persistent toxic chemicals through zero discharge of persistent, bioaccumulative toxic substances. The agreement institutions were built on the principle and assumption that participants from both countries did not serve as representatives of their nations' or agencies' interests but rather served the welfare of the ecosystem and the people in it. The IJC Water Quality and Science Advisory Boards were populated equally by Canadians and Americans. Appointees were expected to 'represent' not their agencies or their national interests but the interest of the lakes, using their best professional judgement. The agreement set goals and objectives, but the means to achieve these ends were left to each country.

Over the years, Great Lakes management has shifted away from the responsibility-based concepts embedded in the language of the GLWQA and its ecological purpose of integrity, and towards a much more rights- and entitlement-based implementation.

Once every two years during the first two decades of the GLWQA, the IJC held a public meeting during which the governments were expected to report on progress towards achieving the objectives of the agreement. By the mid-1980s, these meetings were drawing upwards of 2000 people, many of them citizen activists driven by concern over the growing evidence of chemical contamination and insisting that their governments carry out their responsibilities under the agreement. By the 1990s, the US and Canadian Governments had initiated a new biennial meeting, known as the State of Lakes Ecosystem Conference (SOLEC), outside the IJC and GLWQA institutional framework. For these conferences the governments commissioned a range of experts to report on the environmental status of the lakes using a broad range of indicators, most of which were use-related. The US EPA and Environment Canada resisted calls by the IJC and others to relate their indicators and reporting data directly to their commitments under the GLWQA.

These examples illustrate an ongoing trend of moving away from a responsibilities-based approach to water management to a use-based or entitlement-based approach. They also correspond to a move away from the objective of restoring and maintaining ecosystem integrity. GEIG began with the question of what responsibilities governments have when they commit to ecological integrity. The GLWQA was one of the inspirations for that question. Over the years we have expanded our question from the meaning of ecological integrity to questions of what kinds of laws, policies and international institutions will make it most likely to achieve the goal of restoring and maintaining ecological integrity in ecosystems around the world, including especially the global ecological systems that make planet Earth inhabitable.

The GLWQA is being reviewed, evaluated and, perhaps, renegotiated in the 2007–2010 period. There are a number of ways that will help return the framework to one built around a set of clear responsibilities with means for concerned citizens to hold governments accountable. These include:

• mechanisms for representation of First Nations and Native Communities on the IJC as sovereign partners along with the US and Canada;

- regular reporting on progress in achieving the objectives of the agreement, with indicators directly related to specific commitments;
- provisions for citizen petition for redress for harms to the environment;
- regular updating of key provisions, ecosystem objectives and priority pollutants; and
- indicators of ecological integrity developed for each lake and the connecting channels.

The US Clean Water Act of 1972, with its requirement that governments subject their actions to environmental impact assessment, a requirement too often ignored or made *pro forma*, assigns a particular and constant form of environmental responsibility to government. This language and the commitment to the 'chemical, physical and biological integrity of the nation's waters' asserted a trust responsibility based on ecological principles that 35 years later we are still, with increasing urgency, trying to fulfil. This has been part of the task of GEIG.

REFERENCES

DePinto, J. and Manno, J. (1997) *Proposed Chlorine Sun Setting in the Great Lakes Basin: Policy Implications for New York State*, Monograph 11, Donald Rennie Monograph Series, Great Lakes Program, University at Buffalo, Buffalo, NY

Durnil, G. (1995) *The Making of a Conservative Environmentalist*, Indiana University Press, Bloomington, IN

IJC (International Joint Commission) (1992) 'Sixth biennial report under the Great Lakes Water Quality Agreement of 1978', International Joint Commission

Jorling, T. (1976) 'Incorporating ecological principles into public policy', *Environmental Policy and Law*, vol 2, pp140–154

Regier, H. A. and France, R. L. (1990) 'Perspectives on the meaning of ecosystem integrity in 1975' in C. J. Edwards and H. Regier (eds) *An Ecosystem Approach to the Integrity of the Great Lakes in Turbulent Times*, Special Publication, Great Lakes Fisheries Commission, Ann Arbor, MI

Acknowledgements

This book celebrates fifteen years of the Global Ecological Integrity Group. However, it originated in the thought of many scholars, far more than the wonderful sampling available in the following chapters. Our work includes that of the many thinkers and researchers who participated in fifteen years of meetings and conferences all over Europe and North America. It is their research, their special expertise that helped each one of us to better understand and make the connections between different disciplines that comprise our work on integrity.

Among the early origins of the concept of ecological integrity was a small monthly Christian farmers' journal, extolling the importance of the 'integrity of creation', and the obligation we all shared to respect it. To further explore this insight, Laura Westra received an original grant from The Social Sciences and Humanities Research Council of Canada (SSHRC). This grant was followed by subsequent grants in support of a small group that eventually evolved into a worldwide network of scientists, philosophers, social scientists, economists, and lawyers, united in their search for ecological integrity.

As editors, we want to acknowledge our deepest thanks not only to the authors of this book's chapters, but to all the participants in our meetings through the years. Every one of them has been a source of inspiration, companionship and collective success. The fact that today we can think of ecological integrity as the conceptual foundation for a just, sustainable world is owed to this network of diverse and committed scholarship.

We are delighted about the celebration of the first fifteen years of integrity scholarship and look forward to ongoing interaction. To continue to track our progress, we intend to design some guiding principles based on ecological integrity. These will eventually be available on the website at www.globalecointegrity.net. Other resources relevant to the group's research are: www.climateethics.org (Don Brown), www.ecohealth.net (Colin Soskolne), www.footprintnetwork.org (William Rees) and the Earth Charter (Ron Engel and Brendan Mackey).

We want to especially thank commissioning editor Michael Fell and production co-ordinator Hamish Ironside of Earthscan, who worked with us. Both manifested their excellent professional abilities without losing their warmth and patience for our lack of technological expertise. Warm thanks are also due to Luc Quenneville (word processing, University of Windsor), whose outstanding expertise more than made up for our failings in that respect.

Finally, we express our gratitude to the universities that the members of our global network belong to. Their support and foresight has helped to create a space that academic work so desperately needs – that is, a space for transdisciplinary dialogue and knowledge in the search for sustainability.

List of Acronyms and Abbreviations

ATCA	Alien Torts Claims Act
BOD	biological oxygen demand
CFC	chlorofluorocarbon
CGIAR	Consultative Group on International Agricultural Research
CI	categorical imperative
CIEL	Center for International Environmental Law
COSS	cost of service study
CS	carbon sequestration
CSERA	Canadian System of Environmental and Resource Accounts
DALY	disability-adjusted life year
DDG	dried distiller's grains
DDT	dichlorodiphenyltrichloroethane
DNA	deoxyribonucleic acid
DPSEEA	driving forces, pressures, state, exposure, effects, actions
DRC	Democratic Republic of Congo
ECOSOC	United Nations Economic and Social Council
EEA	European Environment Agency
EFA	ecological footprint analysis
EFR	Ecological Fiscal Reform (Canada)
ENGO	environmental non-governmental organization
EPA	Environmental Protection Agency (US)
ESG	Ethics Specialist Group
FAO	Food and Agriculture Organization of the United Nations
FCA	full-cost accounting
FCPF	Forest Carbon Partnership Facility
GDP	gross domestic product
GEIG	Global Ecological Integrity Group
GHG	greenhouse gas
GIS	geographic information system
GLWQA	Great Lakes Water Quality Agreement
GPI	genuine progress indicator
HEADLAMP	Health and Environment Analysis for Decision-Making project
HRC	Human Rights Committee (UN)
IACHR	Inter-American Commission on Human Rights
IBI	index of biological integrity

IBRD	International Bank for Reconstruction and Development
ICC	Inuit Circumpolar Conference
ICCPR	International Covenant on Civil and Political Rights
ICESCR	International Covenant on Economic, Social and Cultural Rights
ICHRP	International Council on Human Rights Policy
ICLEI	International Council for Local Environmental Initiatives
IDA	International Development Association
IEG	Independent Evaluation Group (World Bank)
IFC	International Finance Corporation
IFPRI	International Food Policy Research Institute
IISD	International Institute for Sustainable Development
IJC	International Joint Commission
ILO	International Labour Office
ILRI	International Livestock Research Institute
IMF	International Monetary Fund
IMV	inherent moral value
IPCC	Intergovernmental Panel on Climate Change
IUCN	International Union for the Conservation of Nature
IUPN	International Union for the Preservation of Nature
LCVA	life-cycle value assessment
LETS	local exchange and trading systems
MC	moral community
MEA	Millennium Ecosystem Assessment (UN)
MIC	middle-income country
NGO	non-governmental organization
NRTEE	National Round Table on the Environment and the Economy (Canada)
OAS	Organization of American States
OECD	Organisation for Economic Co-operation and Development
PCB	polychlorinated biphenyl
ppm	parts per million
PUB	Public Utilities Board (Manitoba)
RCM	Resource Conservation Manitoba
REACH	Regulation (EC) no. 1907/2006 of the European Parliament and of the Council on the Registration, Evaluation, Authorization and Restriction of Chemicals
SAHSU	small area health statistics unit
SDN	Sustainable Development Network (World Bank)
SGIP	Specialist Group on Indigenous Peoples
SOLEC	State of Lakes Ecosystem Conference
SOHO	self-organizing holarchic open
SRES	Special Report on Emissions Scenarios (IPPC)

SSHRC	Social Sciences and Humanities Research Council of Canada
TEK	traditional environmental knowledge
TREE	Time to Respect Earth's Ecosystems
TRIPS	Trade-Related Aspects of Intellectual Property Rights
UC	universal consideration
UDHR	Universal Declaration of Human Rights
UNCED	United Nations Conference on Environment and Development
UNEP	United Nations Environmental Programme
UNFCCC	UN Framework Convention on Climate Change
UNSCCUR	United Nations Scientific Conference on the Conservation and Utilization of Natural Resources
UNESCO	United Nations Educational, Scientific and Cultural Organization
WB	World Bank
WBG	World Bank Group
WHO	World Health Organization
WTO	World Trade Organization
WWF	World Wide Fund for Nature

PART I

OVERVIEW: FOUNDATIONS OF ECOLOGICAL INTEGRITY

Introduction

Laura Westra and Klaus Bosselmann

The chapters in this part echo faithfully the first concern of the Global Ecological Integrity Group (GEIG): to define ecological integrity. Providing the background to that definition, Laura Westra (Chapter 1) describes the history and development of the group since its inception in 1992, as well as pointing to ways forward in years to come.

Despite the presence of many doubters, people who insisted on viewing integrity as a 'metaphor' rather than a measurable reality, the group decided to follow James Karr's understanding of the concept. Explaining its scientific meaning, demonstrating how and why it should be measured, Karr identifies 'ecological decline' (or disintegrity) as a 'dangerous enemy' and emphasizes the need to research and study biological indicators.

That decline, or the damage and ultimate destruction of natural areas, combined with climate change, has exponentially increased the gravity of so-called 'natural' disasters. Karr further indicates that accepted measurements such as gross domestic product (GDP), traditional policy goals such as 'growth' and accepted forms of governmental institutions all demonstrate that the current directions of our whole society are deeply flawed. Karr is the first of the representative GEIG scholars in this volume to advocate a fundamental turnaround of what we measure, what we value and what we strive to achieve.

In the next chapter, philosopher Konrad Ott revisits another of our major original concerns: the question of the value of nature. Ott takes us through the arguments of various sorts of ecocentrists, biocentrists and other non-anthropocentrists. Starting with the important position of Immanuel Kant, he explores ways to accommodate a non-anthropocentric argument with Kant's categorical imperative and Habermas's 'discourse ethics'. Reflecting on a range environmental philosophers, including Schweitzer, Jonas, Leopold, Taylor, Callicott and Westra, Ott aims for an ethical stance that can bridge humanist traditions with contemporary biocentrism. After critically evaluating those arguments, the 'demarcation problem' may be overcome with ethics centred around 'life as focal point'.

From the start, our group sought to ensure that its work reflected current legal paradigms, or showed their lacunae if there were any. Starting, as we saw in the preface, with the Clean Water Act (US, 1972) and the Great Lakes Water Quality Agreement (1978, ratified 1988), inevitably the group turned to the major international instrument that makes ecological integrity one of its basic principles: the Earth Charter. Brendan Mackey expands on the legal importance of this document in Chapter 4, and, as we shall see, the final chapter in Part V will also return to that theme.

The Earth Charter views ecological integrity as a basis and foundation of its ethical norms. It is a unique document, because it has been complied with the collaboration of people from all continents, ethnic background and religions. It is also unique in that it links explicitly private and public ethics. Yet the Earth Charter is only slowly increasing its impact, because it has not yet filtered through all society and because of its radical tenets. Nevertheless it is being adopted by communities, cities and even a number of governments, as well as international organizations such as the United Nations Educational, Scientific and Cultural Organization (UNESCO) and the International Union for the Conservation of Nature (IUCN). These endorsements, and the fact that the Earth Charter is the recognized guiding document for the current United Nations Decade for Education for Sustainable Development (2005–2014), are very significant: ecological integrity has been elevated to a principle that is debated in education, politics and law.

The last chapter in this part combines the work of two economists. For Crabbé and Manno, ecological integrity is an 'emergent public good'. Most of its component parts already represent goods that are both private and public. 'Water' and 'timber', for instance, are already considered to be 'goods', and ecosystem services are considered by some to be 'public goods' as well. The questions that must be answered, then, are how can important public goods be protected and what are the policies necessary to protect integrity itself, when its value lies only in its undisturbed wholeness, while its component parts are already considered to be public goods on their own. Considering the global nature of ecological integrity, Crabbé and Manno call for the development of new global institutional mechanisms.

Crabbé and Manno's chapter concludes Part I, showing the spectrum of different approaches to ecological integrity. In the second part, the influence of public health considerations will emerge more clearly, as will the reasons why the group turned its efforts in that direction.

1

Ecological Integrity: Its History, Its Future and the Development of the Global Ecological Integrity Group

Laura Westra

THE GLOBAL ECOLOGICAL INTEGRITY PROJECT

As we approach the 15th anniversary meeting of the Global Ecological Integrity Group (GEIG), it is perhaps time to consider how we started, where we have come from and how our group's work has developed over the last 15 years. It is also time to recall that our starting point has been ecological integrity, so that it is imperative that we recognize its continuing role through our present varied interests, all of which, in some way, manifest its centrality.

The Global Ecological Integrity Project was initiated in 1992, when I first sought support from the Social Sciences and Humanities Research Council of Canada (SSHRC). The aim of the project was to seek a thorough understanding of the meaning and role of ecological integrity, through a series of intensely focused, closed meetings to which the leading ecological scientists were invited. The meetings involved primarily scientists and some philosophers. The SSHRC eventually funded our work as long as I remained at the University of Windsor, which was up to 1999.

The expression 'ecosystem integrity' or 'ecological integrity' appeared in regulations, laws and mission statements not only in Canada and the US, but all over the world (Westra, 1994). The concept of integrity had been introduced in 1972 in the US Clean Water Act, and its use multiplied and accelerated in the years after that. The Great Lakes Water Quality Agreement (1978, ratified 1988) is a clear example of its use:

> *The purpose of the Parties is to restore and maintain the chemical, physical and biological integrity of the waters of the Great Lakes Basin Ecosystem … where the latter is defined as … the interacting components of air, land, water and living organisms including humans within the drainage basin of the St Lawrence River.* (Westra, 1994)

In most documents that refer to integrity, only the vaguest definition of the concept is available, and most of the time no attempt is made to clarify it. This is surprising, to say the least, in regard to a concept that is intended to represent the goal of legislation. For this reason, my first effort was to secure funding to examine the concept of integrity from many points of view and from the perspective of several disciplines. We used the funding we received to conduct workshops on business/business ethics, agriculture, fisheries and other enterprises. The question was, in each case, 'How do we understand ecosystem integrity and how do we define it?'

Following the series of meetings, a team comprised of two complex-systems theorists and ecologists, James Kay and Robert Ulanowicz; an ecologist, Henry Regier; a physicist and ecologist, Don de Angelis; and the author drafted a definition after careful discussion of each word and concept (Westra, 1994). This definition was later shown to conservation biologist Reed Noss and to ecologist and biologist James Karr, both of whom were largely in agreement with most of the language therein. However, aside from its use in various legal documents, little had been done to fully understand the meaning of integrity at that time.

Before we can fully comprehend its reach and its importance, we need to understand integrity fully in all its implications. The generic concept of integrity connotes a valuable whole, 'the state of being whole, entire or undiminished' or 'sound, unimpaired or perfect conditions' (Random House, 1966). We begin with the recognition that integrity, in common usage, is an umbrella concept that encompasses a variety of other concepts (Westra, 1994). The example of the blooming desert illustrates a number of the themes associated with ecological integrity:

1   The example is drawn from *wild nature*, in other words nature that is relatively unimpacted by human presence or activities. Although the concept of integrity may be applied in other contexts, wild nature provides the paradigmatic examples for our reflection and research. Because of the extent of human exploitation of the planet, such examples are most often found in those places that, until recently, have been least hospitable to dense human occupancy and industrial development: deserts, the high arctic, high altitude mountain ranges, the ocean deep, and the less accessible reaches of forest and jungle. Wild nature is also found in locations whose capacity to evoke human admiration won their protection in natural parks.

2   The rapid bloom of desert organisms illustrates in dramatic fashion some of the *autopoietic* (self-creative) *capacities* of life to organize, regenerate, reproduce, sustain, adapt, develop and evolve.

3   These self-creative capacities of life are *dynamic*. The present display of living forms and processes in the desert gains significance through its past and its future.

4   Conjoined with its past, the Chilean desert is a part of *nature's legacy*, the product of natural history. Because of the relative absence of anthropogenic impacts, the desert biota is a creature largely of 'evolutionary and biogeographical processes at that place' (Angermeier and Karr, 1994). It thus illustrates what nature is and does in the absence of the human design and impacts that dominate the built, modified and impacted environments in which we live most of our lives.

5   The events of its past and present demonstrate the capacity of desert life-forms to maintain their functions, to respond to changing conditions to evolve. If those capacities are not destroyed, we may anticipate their evolving *future realizations*. Indeed continued evolution provides evidence that these adaptive capacities have not been destroyed.

6   Desert conditions, relieved by rains at rare intervals, are themselves the products of larger regional and global weather patterns. Indeed both the biological and geoclimatic processes that lead to the blooming desert play themselves out on a stage with much larger spatial scope (Westra et al, 2000).

7   Ecological integrity is *valuable and valued*. In the case of the Chilean desert, the dramatic transformation of 'barren' desert into a vital and diverse biotic community provokes wonder and appreciation. Other ecological communities, such as reefs and rainforests, display their prolific life in a more continuous, less seasonal or episodic fashion. More generally, the kinds of processes at work in these instances give rise to the totality of life on Earth, including ourselves, and together maintain the conditions for the continuation of life as we know it. Thus natural ecosystems are valuable to and in themselves, for their continuing support of the life on Earth, for their aesthetic features, and for the goods and services they provide to humankind. Ecological integrity is thus essential to the maintenance of ecological sustainability as a foundation of a sustainable society. For these reasons, there is a growing body of policy and law which mandate the protection and restoration of ecological integrity (Westra et al, 2000).

It will be useful to trace the history of our project and the expansion and growth of the group through several periods, each of which can be characterized by a specific emphasis. Only then can we be sure to include the main aspects of our mature understanding and the full import of additional research in several directions.

Looking back, it seems that there are already three 'streams' of research that have been pursued by the group, as well as a fourth stream that is just at its inception. In the following sections I will attempt to describe and characterize these streams and the consecutive periods of our work, resulting in the collective publication, thus far (see www.globalecointegrity.net).

The first period: Scientific and philosophical analysis and definition (1992–1999)

This voyage of discovery was based on our attempts to clarify the meaning and role of ecological integrity, and it involved primarily the physical sciences and philosophical analysis. Some of the ecologists in the group, however, particularly the late James Kay and Henry Regier, eventually were not comfortable with the final version of the definition of integrity they had helped to draft. Because of the centrality of chaos theory (Goerner, 1994) and complex-systems theory (Kay and Schneider, 1994) to their position, any definition based on science was judged to be inappropriate, as too rigid perhaps, so that a sort of popular/democratic/local approach to the meaning of integrity appeared to be superior to the position we actually adopted.

Yet both James Karr's approach, based upon biology, and Reed Noss's, on conservation biology, were such that a scientific, not a consensus-based position was to be sought: local/regional decision-making, even when based upon enlightened, 'green' preferences, is not sufficient to inform the ultimate need for universality in public policy that ecological integrity requires, given the many roles it plays in many fields.

Essentially, then, there was, right at the beginning, the need to respond to no less than two attacks: one, internal, based on the altered perceptions and beliefs of two of the original voices in our group; the other an external attack based on a specific, North American understanding of ecological science, such as that of philosopher Kristin Shrader-Frechette (1995, pp125–145).

The latter indeed attempted to discredit the whole project by arguing for a 'modest approach based on case studies' and terming our approach and that of James Karr's index of biological integrity (IBI) 'untestable, definitional and based on grand theories' and on 'soft ecology' (Shrader-Frechette, 1995, p140), without considering that Karr's work itself is entirely based on scientific observation and research, as was that of Reed Noss and others in the group. Both attacks were duly noted and published in our interdisciplinary collections but, because of the misconceptions upon which they were based, they left untouched the importance and basic value of integrity and our commitment to thorough research on that topic.

Following the publication in 1998 of a volume published by Kluwer (Lemons et al, 1998) and one from Rowman and Littlefield (Westra and Werhane, 1998) that added some business ethics perspectives, and finally with the product of our group's final grant (this time from NATO in 1999), we were in a position to publish two volumes in 2000: another from Kluwer (Crabbé et al, 2000) and one from Island Press (Pimentel et al, 2000). These publications brought this period of intensive scientific investigation and analysis to a close. The group was well satisfied with the understanding and definition of integrity that had emerged.

The second period: Public health, human rights and ecological footprint analysis (1999–2002)

Both collections published in 2000 included the products of our yearly conferences up to and including 1999. But in 1998 two new and important fields were added to our areas of research: public health and the relevance of ecological footprint analysis to disintegrity. Epidemiologist Colin Soskolne joined the group and, in 1998, convened a meeting at the Rome offices of the World Health Organization (WHO), together with Dr Roberto Bertollini. Several representatives of our group were present, as well as other WHO-based scientists. This resulted in the publication of a landmark document in 1999 (Soskolne and Bertollini, 1999). It also introduced a strong addition to our group in William Rees, who was present in Rome, and who helped publicize our work through the media. Since that time, a public health component has been a regular part of our yearly meetings.

In 2000 I arranged a meeting in San Jose, Costa Rica, to promote a dialogue with the representatives of the Earth Charter, given our growing interest in and closeness to that document and its principles. Mirian Vilela, Abelardo Brenes-Castro and others from the University for Peace were present and collaborated. That meeting signified the beginning of an even closer association with the Earth Charter: its principles have figured in GEIG programmes ever since, and Peter Miller joined me in publishing *Just Ecological Integrity* (Miller and Westra, 2002), with a foreword on the development of the Earth Charter by Steven Rockefeller.

The integration of the Earth Charter indicated a corresponding shift of emphasis, already in evidence with the introduction of public health concerns, from scientific research to public policy. A further component was added in 2003 as we entered our third phase.

The third period: International law and public policy (2002–2006)

The third period is characterized by the introduction of international law and by an emphasis on human rights in that area, together with the introduction of ecological footprint analysis as basic to our concerns. Under the guidance of Ron Engel in 2003, we added the IUCN-ESG (International Union for the Conservation of Nature–Ethics Specialist Group) to our list, and our meeting in Urbino was a particularly diverse and exciting one, as the Earth Charter was also meeting there at the same time.

Richard Westra also added a political science dimension to our environmental and public health concerns. Don Brown published his *American Heat* in 2002, and the ongoing and emergent concerns with climate change became one of several emphases, together with the rights to food and water. The next two meetings, in Montreal (2004) and Venice (2005), continued to reflect these novel dimensions, and both our publications and conferences were now reported on our newly established website (www.globalecointegrity.net).

After my second PhD in Jurisprudence (2005), and with the support of grants from Health Canada (principal investigators Colin Soskolne and Don Spady) and once again the SSHRC (principal investigator William Rees), I studied law at the WHO in Geneva and published on the rights of the child and future generations: another area that became part of our research.

All these different concerns and interests were eventually to feature in a collection produced primarily by Colin Soskolne, with an emphasis on present environmental threats and on the continuing role of the Earth Charter on sustaining life on Earth (Soskolne, 2007).

The fourth period: North–South issues and indigenous peoples (2006 to present)

Since the publication of *American Heat* (Brown, 2002) and *Ecoviolence and the Law* (Westra, 2004), the importance of climate change and of pollution harms were increasingly presented at our meetings, and the work of William Rees continues to outline the harms perpetrated by the ecological footprint analysis (EFA) of affluent countries on those in the South. My own interests have also turned to the plight of indigenous peoples, and I studied comparative Aboriginal law as a post-doctoral student in Ottawa with Bradford Morse. As a co-chair of the IUCN-CEL Indigenous Peoples Specialist Group, I have also invited that group to join us at our Halifax meeting. My book on the topic, *Environmental Justice and the Rights of Indigenous Peoples* (Westra, 2007), indicates the addition of yet another important topic to our work, and that topic has been accepted by many delegates at our Halifax meeting and should persist to our next meeting in Berlin in 2008.

What maintains the cohesion of the group is the centrality of ecological integrity to each aspect of our research. And this is the main point that I would like to see emphasized in this volume: the enduring and expanding role of ecological and biological integrity in our collective work. Today the ecosystem approach is a routinely accepted position in both science and international law. The harmful role of chemicals, toxins and the by-products of industrial operations are recognized and – at least in Europe – clearly proscribed by regulatory regimes (see for instance Regulation (EC) no. 1907/2006 of the European Parliament and of the Council on the Registration, Evaluation, Authorization and Restriction of Chemicals (REACH for short)).

Climate change and other effects of Northwest countries' ecological footprint are routinely discussed in the media. But none of these problems is discussed with explicit reference to ecological integrity. Public health is equally silent on this topic. When 'harms' are admitted as part of regular global industrial corporate operation, the health specifics are excluded from consideration.

Vulnerable indigenous communities have the recognized right to 'cultural integrity', but there is little or no discussion of the fact that the latter is absolutely dependent on ecological integrity for its existence, and for the survival of all traditional communities. In addition, as William Rees emphasizes (see Chapter 17 of this volume), our inability to recognize our ecological limits puts the future survival of mankind itself at grave risk.

I propose that some invited scholars of GEIG should address the centrality of biological and ecological integrity in various aspects of their research, in order to show to some extent where we have arrived and what has persisted of our original concerns. The examples can be multiplied, but it might be best to simply allow some of those who were part of the original group, as well as others who have joined in one of the 'streams' described above, to show where and how ecological integrity and its opposite, disintegrity, play a foundational role in their current work.

BIOLOGICAL AND ECOLOGICAL INTEGRITY AS FOUNDATIONAL TO THE SUSTAINABILITY OF LIFE

The development of the work of GEIG has served to fill out gradually both the meaning of ecological integrity and the role it should play in public policy. From its original understanding as a desirable and legally defensible condition of water, its scientific reality has come to encompass both the absence of pollution, including toxic substances, and the need to protect integrity itself from modern human enterprise because of its essential role in the protection of human and non-human life (Westra, 1998).

The first period of research on integrity uncovered its role as a necessary condition for the presence of necessary services for all plant, animal and human life and for the normal functioning of ecosystems. Reed Noss recognized that not only was the condition or quality of the land necessary, but that quantity requirements were equally vital, and that quantity requirements varied according to the species to be protected. That is, large carnivores needed large quantities of wild lands in order to survive; small animals could survive in much less (Noss and Cooperrider, 1994). In addition, core areas of integrity or of wild undeveloped land also needed the protection of buffer zones surrounding them.

The *Wildlands Project* (Noss, 1992) acknowledged that land had the same requirement for integrity that was found in the Clean Water Act (1972), the Great Lakes Water Quality agreement (1978, ratified 1988) and especially what James Karr's IBI emphasized in his work on the integrity of water (Karr and Chu, 1999). The problem is that these scientific realities were never incorporated in the law, hence the connection with human rights was and still is lost. For instance, the Great Lakes Association reported yearly the 'success' of reduced amounts of various pollutants discharged into the waters of the Great Lakes, thus by-passing the mandate of 'zero discharge' that was intended to govern their policies.

Both in Canada and in the US, the laws and policies governing natural parks and other protected areas did not emphasize the necessity of drastically reducing or eliminating various discharges and effluents, in order to achieve the required protection of certain areas. Even Environmental Protection Acts, for the most part, limit their rigorous prohibitions to their preambular parts, while making repeated 'exceptions' in the body of the acts for such substances as agricultural pollutants, or the effluents of various industrial operations, all judged to be required for the 'public interest'.

In other words, the strong green sentiments expressed in the preambles or mission statements of those instruments are quickly lost, in the interest of economics, 'business as usual' and the status quo, as exceptions quickly eliminate the original express intent of these documents. These problems become acute as environmental and wildlife protection acts are not connected in any way to human rights legislation, and are viewed, at best, as modifications to the licences and permits granted to industrial operations. Hence regulatory breaches are not viewed as crimes, unless a large-scale disaster follows (Westra, 2004, Chapter 4).

But regular exposures, even in small quantities, affect the ecosystem where both plants and animals dwell, and hence the functions of the ecosystem itself. In addition, human health is also gravely affected (Soskolne and Bertollini, 1999), particularly the most vulnerable individuals (Grandjean and Landrigan, 2006) and groups (Westra, 2007). It is this realization that led the group to turn from earth and water science to epidemiology and medicine. Ecological integrity is basic to sustainability, and therefore to the survival and normal function of all life and, as the WHO confirmed in 1999, that includes humans (Soskolne and Bertollini, 1999).

The biological integrity of each plant, animal and human being depends on appropriately functioning ecosystems according to the requirements of each species. Hence the biological integrity and normal function and development of each require ecological integrity in their habitat. However, disintegrity diminishes or eliminates the capacity of ecosystems to provide normal life-support, resulting in morbidity, altered function or even DNA changes in each species. Immature and developing organisms react more strongly and the harm they suffer is correspondingly more grave than that suffered by mature organisms (Grandjean and Landrigan, 2006). This is particularly obvious when exposure to chemicals and other toxic substances is considered.

There is ample scientific evidence that demonstrates the causal connection between disintegrity and minor but regular exposures and animal and human harms (Licari et al, 2005), totally aside from the occasional but predictable disaster or major accident that may harm hundreds or thousands of people of all ages (Westra, 2006, Chapter 5; see also Chapter 8 of this volume). The presence of all these insidious ongoing harms is what convinced those who were already working on integrity that once these facts became common knowledge, the close relation between integrity and health would strongly influence both public policy and the law.

However, this desirable outcome did not materialize: environmental policies are still clearly locked in their traditional approach, in which economic and business considerations have primacy. Environmental laws are still clearly separated, even conceptually, from human rights instruments. So case law dealing with environmental torts simply does not acknowledge the public health/human rights component.[1]

At least the group moved seriously into making this connection explicit: all yearly meetings included an emphasis on the health results of disintegrity from 1999 on, and the only meeting funded by NATO took place in Budapest at the offices of the WHO. In 2000, in San Jose, Costa Rica, the meeting included a presentation by Dr Roberto Bertollini of WHO. That was also the first meeting that emphasized the fact that ecological integrity is one of the main principles of the Earth Charter. At the same time, that document expresses its total commitment to the respect for all life, for the 'community of life', including human beings.

Although it does not explicitly connect ecological integrity with human life and health, the Earth Charter acknowledges and promotes the interface between the two. Hence support for the Earth Charter has become a constant theme at our meetings and in our publications. This represents a step forward in the incorporation of public policies and law on the part of the group, although the Earth Charter remains only 'soft law' at this time.

Since 2003 the role of law, both domestic and international, also became a yearly feature at our meetings, as we joined forces with the IUCN-CEL, the Ethics Specialist Group (ESG) and, more recently, eventually also with the Specialist Group on Indigenous Peoples (SGIP). These additions significantly enlarged our horizon, as members of those groups from Africa and Asia attended the conferences and presented their research.

The impact of disintegrity on ecosystems and people in developing countries was emphasized by presentations dealing with the global South, where the sheltering effect of wealth was not available to protect individuals and communities. The need for legal considerations in fact became increasingly obvious, as to limit its reach to land and water, and perhaps to climate, is to ignore two other major effects of disintegrity: first and foremost, the impact of depleted normal function (Tamburlini et al, 2002); second the need to understand the major cause of disintegrity, that is the ecological footprint of Northwest countries (Rees and Wackernagel, 1996).

The legal component of the ecofootprint is the fact that it appropriates natural services, modifies local and regional economies, and imposes harmful trade conditions on local inhabitants, under unfair conditions that include neither meaningful consultation nor informed consent (see Chapter 13, this volume).

As human rights are clearly at issue, as is racial discrimination in the case of ethnic groups and communities, as well as unlawful appropriation of the resources necessary for survival, the lack of a unified and robust regime to deal with these issues is a grave lacuna in law. The next section will address the first consideration, that is the human rights effects of so-called breaches of environmental regulations.

ECOLOGICAL AND BIOLOGICAL INTEGRITY IN LAW

It is very hard to find any clear protection for either eco-integrity or biological integrity in legal instruments, whether domestic or international. Even the right to life may be found explicitly only in the American Convention on Human Rights as its implications for infants and for the unborn and future generations are too explicit for most modern liberal nations to accept, both in Europe and in North America.[2] Further, in any number of cases tried under the Alien Torts Claims Act (ATCA) that involve indigenous communities attempting to fight the encroachment of corporate operations, the claimants' narratives address their 'right to life' regularly.

Often these narratives and the experts presenting the case of the indigenous groups refer to Article 8.1 of the European Convention for the Protection of Human Rights and Freedoms (4 November 1950, 213 U.N.T.S. 221) as one of the few legally enforceable document articles that can be cited in defence of human life and health today:

Article 8

1   *Everyone has the right to respect for his private and family life, his home, and his correspondence.*
2   *There shall be no interference by a public authority with the exercise of this right except such as is in accordance with the law and is necessary in a democratic society in the interests of national security, public order or the economic wellbeing of the country, for the prevention of disorder or crime, for the protection of health or morals, or for the protection of the rights and freedoms of others.*

Among other articles of note on this topic, Article 25.1 of the Universal Declaration of Human Rights[3] states:

Everyone has the right to a standard of living adequate for the health of himself and of his family, including food, clothing, housing and medical care and necessary social services.

And Principle 1 of the Stockholm Declaration[4] says:

Man has the fundamental right to freedom, equality and adequate conditions of life, in an environment of a quality that permits a life of dignity and wellbeing, and he bears a solemn responsibility to protect and improve the environment for present and future generations.

Several European judgements in fact accept the application of Article 8.1 to environmental cases:

Article 8 may apply in environmental cases whether the pollution is directly caused by the State, or whether the State responsibility arises from the failure to properly regulate private industry.[5]

Nevertheless, there are other related instruments that do not even attempt to face the question of environmental harms and their effects on the biological and functional integrity of human beings. Despite the abundant research available from the WHO and the medical sciences in general, describing in detail on one hand the proliferation of chemical and toxic substances in use in the last 50 years and, on the other, the results of these exposures on all organisms, including humans, somehow this intelligence has not yet filtered down to the legislators or to the judges who must decide on eventual cases that result from these exposures.

Judgements regularly state that environmental harms do not reach to the level of international law, let alone human rights law. Yet when those affected belong to a specific ethnic or racial group, I have argued, these attacks on the biological and functional integrity of individuals and groups ought to be viewed as acts of genocide, even if precedents for defining harms in this manner cannot be found in the jurisprudence of common law at this time.

With the increasing impact of climate change, too many suffer irreversible damage in too many parts of the world to simply continue to view environmental harms as separate and less weighty than human rights breaches. Regulatory regimes should proscribe all activities that cause these exposures, reversing the burden of proof regarding the harmlessness of substances, before the harms occur and the necessity for court cases arises. The ongoing effects of chemical and other industrial exposures, totally aside from expected but only occasional disasters, make it necessary to approach the problem of the interface between disintegrity and biological and functional harms in a proactive way.

The precautionary principle[6] should govern trade and economic regulations, as these harms are most often incompensable; therefore they should not be relegated to tort procedures after they occur, but the products and activities that cause them should be proscribed from the outset instead. This is perhaps the gravest difficulty faced by those who recognize the interface between ecological disintegrity and the normal life of biological organisms, including human beings.

The wide reach of industrial products and processes has increased exponentially, with the proliferation of chemicals and other toxic substances, since the Second World War (Grandjean and Landrigan, 2006). For the most part, these substances have only been tested for safety 'in house', in other words by their manufacturers, so that only repeated, cumulative harms eventually indicate their true nature: for this reason they should be eliminated, rather than just 'regulated', pending exhaustive and reliable independent proof of their harmlessness.

Since the connection between ecological integrity and the normal function and integrity of individuals is not acknowledged in law, the jurisprudence reflects this lacuna and there appears to be no end in sight for the twofold results that follow. On the one hand, prevention is not demanded in any legal instruments; on the other, the harms that occur routinely are not acknowledged for what they are, their etiology is not explicitly accepted and when cases appear in the courts, redress is limited to the economic aspects of the losses incurred, unless the results reach disaster proportions (Westra, 2006, Chapters 4 and 5; Westra, 2007, Chapters 4 and 5). Therefore we are forced to accept that, at the present time, neither ecological nor biological integrity is explicitly placed as a requirement or a condition to be respected in legal documents, or clearly defended in law.

A FUTURE FOR ECOLOGICAL AND BIOLOGICAL INTEGRITY IN INTERNATIONAL AND SUPRANATIONAL LAW?

The first step required to ensure that both ecological and biological integrity gain recognition in public policy, I believe, is to have an impartial, highly respected UN body state unequivocally their fundamental importance in a public forum. Based on its own research on various industrial exposures, this body should be the WHO. Recalling the long Odyssey forced on humankind by tobacco companies, a journey littered with dead bodies and suffering brought on by misleading junk science, one can see at least a similar lengthy battle looming ahead.

As long as cases are tried one by one when an individual or a community's health/environmental effects are grave enough to prompt them to seek redress, the judgements provide answers that remain piecemeal, mainly of interest to other lawyers or affected groups, while the cause of the harms is not disclosed openly to the public, and the harms continue undeterred and unchecked. Hence it is not this or that effect that should be recognized, or this or that specific perpetrator punished: as in the case of tobacco, it is the whole product, the whole industry that must be indicted and shown for what it is and what it does, wherever the consequences might occur. Only then there might be the hope that a convention might result, one more global and robust than the present European REACH. Such a document might rely in part on effects on the 'canaries', the 'sentinels', as the research on harms to those individuals is well established and published at this time. For Europe, it is mainly the health effects on the unborn, infants and young children, as those harms are clearly described in the literature of the WHO. For the rest of the world, the 'canaries' are also the most vulnerable groups, the indigenous populations globally, and that research needs still to be completed (Westra, 2007, Chapter 10). Public health recognizes that, once the most vulnerable populations are protected, then so are the rest of the people, hence that research is vitally important.

The next step is to incorporate this knowledge into the appropriate legal instruments, internationally and nationally. This will be a hard task, no doubt, but not an impossible one, if one recalls how other human right breaches, related to women or people of colour for the most part, have been added to or inserted into various human rights documents that did not previously include them in the last several decades.

Thus, in principle at least, once the breaches of human rights are recognized, they can be used to revise and modify present legal instruments. Some of the instruments that should be so modified include the following:

- the Declaration of Human Rights[7];
- the Convention on the Prevention and Punishment of the Crime of Genocide[8];
- the Convention on the Elimination of Racial Discrimination[9];
- the Convention Concerning the Protection of the World Cultural and Natural Heritage[10];
- the Convention on the Rights of the Child[11];
- the International Criminal Court[12];
- the International Covenant on Civil and Political Rights[13]; and
- the World Trade Organization (WTO), especially Article XX.

Once the major international human rights instruments are modified to incorporate up-to-date scientific information, the domestic legal regimes will need to reflect the changes, thus addressing the present lacunae in those documents.

Equally important would be a global version of REACH, one that no longer accepted the present exceptions and facilitations to chemical companies. Although the Earth Charter contains all the principles required to effect the changes necessary to protect health and life, it may not be desirable to transform it into a treaty to be ratified by all nations. The problem is that, with the unfolding of the required procedures, one could expect that most wealthy Northwest countries (or, at least, their governments and their industrial elites) would not accept the current language of the document, but would labour by any means to reduce or eliminate the strong, unequivocal language that characterizes it. Perhaps the Earth Charter should just remain a blueprint for morally appropriate regulatory regimes without itself becoming one of them.

Another guiding 'blueprint' for appropriate action could be found by pursuing a full understanding of and respect for the traditional lifestyles of indigenous people. These communities are presently the 'sentinels' who demonstrate the grave harms imposed by mining and other extractive industries, hence by the very substances researched by the WHO in other contexts. But their role far exceeds that of 'victims'. Their traditional lifestyles represent a 'living charter' with nature that should also be used as a template against which to measure all our present legal regimes, not to copy them blindly, but to acknowledge them as role models for the future.

GEIG is highly interdisciplinary and it also includes scholars and researchers with various levels of influence and capacity to participate in policymaking at the global level. Hence it is hard to predict whether any of the changes here advocated will be realized. One thing is assured, though: according to our various powers and abilities, the group's members will continue to struggle to see that eventually the changes are made.

NOTES

1 See, for instance, Westra, 2006, especially Chapters 4 and 5; for analysis of several Alien Torts Claims Act (ATCA) cases involving indigenous peoples, see Westra, 2007, Chapters 5 and 6.
2 American Convention on Human Rights (1969), OAS Tr. Ser./NO. 26; 111144 U.N.T.S. 123; see also Westra, 2006, Chapter 2.
3 1948, G.A. Res. 217, UN GAOR 3d Sess. At 71, UN Doc. A/810.
4 *Stockholm Declaration of the United Nations Conference on the Human Environment*, 16 June 1972, 11 I.L.M. 1416.
5 *Hatton and Others v. United Kingdom*, 37 EHRR 28 (2003) Grand Chamber Judgment; see also 34 ____(2002), Paragraph 98.
6 Or, better yet, the *post*-cautionary principle as argued by Lisa Heinzerling (Heinzerling, 2008).
7 G.A. Res. 217, UN GAOR 3d Sess., U.S.Doc.A/810(1948).
8 78 U.N.T.S. 277 (1951).
9 A.5 e(4) (1965).
10 Adopted by the UNESCO General Conference at its 17th session, Paris, 16 November 1972.
11 1990 UN Doc. E/CN.4/1989/29, in force 20 November 1990.
12 Rome Statute, in force 12 July 2002.
13 G.A. Res. 2200A, UN Doc. A/6316(1966) 999 U.N.T.S 171.

REFERENCES

Angermeier, P. L. and Karr, J. R. (1994) 'Biological integrity versus biological diversity as policy directives', *BioScience*, vol 44, pp690–697
Brown, D. (2002) *American Heat*, Rowman and Littlefield, Lanham, MD
Crabbé, P., Westra, L., Holland, A. and Ryczkowski, L. (eds) (2000) *Implementing Ecological Integrity: Restoring Regional and Global Environmental and Human Health*, NATO Scientific Publications, Kluwer Academic Publishers, Dordrecht, The Netherlands

Goerner, S. (1994) *Chaos and the Evolving Ecological Universe*, Gordon and Breach Science Publishers, Amsterdam, The Netherlands

Grandjean, P. and Landrigan, P. J. (2006) 'Developmental neurotoxicity of industrial chemicals', *The Lancet*, 8 November

Heinzerling, L. (2008) 'The post-cautionary principle', *Georgetown International Law Journal*, January, p445

Karr, J. and Chu, E. (1999) *Restoring Life to Running Waters: Better Biological Monitoring*, Island Press, Washington, DC

Kay, J. and Schneider, E. (1994) 'The challenge of the ecosystem approach', *Alternatives*, vol 20, no 3, pp1–6

Lemons, J., Westra, L. and Goodland, R. (eds) (1998) *Ecological Sustainability and Integrity: Concepts and Approaches*, Kluwer, Dordrecht

Licari, L., Nemer, L. and Tamburlini, G. (eds) (2005) *Children's Health and the Environment*, World Health Organization, Copenhagen

Miller, P. and Westra, L. (eds) (2002) *Just Ecological Integrity*, Rowman and Littlefield, Lanham, MD

Noss, R. (1992) 'The Wildlands Project: Land conservation strategy', *Wild Earth Special Issue*

Noss, R. and Cooperrider, A. (1994) *Saving Nature's Legacy*, Island Press, Washington, DC

Pimentel, D., Westra, L. and Noss, R. (eds) (2000) *Ecological Integrity: Integrating Environment Conservation and Health*, Island Press, Washington, DC

Random House (1966) *The Random House Dictionary of the English Language, Unabridged*, Random House, New York

Rees, W. and Wackernagel, M. (1996) *Our Ecological Footprint*, New Society Publishers, Gabriola Island, BC, Canada

Rees, W. and Westra, L. (2003) 'When consumption does violence: Can there be sustainability and environmental justice in a resource limited world?', in J. Ageyman, R. Evans and R. D. Bullard (eds) *Just Sustainabilities*, Earthscan, London, pp99–124

Shrader-Frechette, K. (1995) 'Hard ecology, soft ecology and ecosystem integrity', in L. Westra and J. Lemons (eds) *Perspectives on Ecological Integrity*, Kluwer Academic Publishers, Dordrecht, The Netherlands

Soskolne, C. (editor-in-chief) (with Westra, L., Kotzé, L. J., Mackey, B., Rees, W. E. and Westra, W., co-editors) (2007) *Sustaining Life on Earth: Environmental and Human Health Through Global Governance*, Lexington Books (Rowman and Littlefield), Lanham, MD

Soskolne, C. and Bertollini, R. (1999) 'Global ecological integrity and sustainable development: Cornerstone of public health', available at www.euro.who.int/document/ghc/Globaleco/ecoreps/pdf

Tamburlini, G., Von Ehrenstein, O. and Bertollini, R. (eds) (2002) *Children's Health and Environment: Review of the Evidence*, European Environment Agency (EEA) Report No 29

Westra, L. (1994) *An Environmental Proposal for Ethics*, Rowman and Littlefield, Lanham, MD

Westra, L. (1998) *Living in Integrity*, Rowman and Littlefield, Lanham, MD

Westra, L. (2004) *Ecoviolence and the Law*, Transnational Publishers, Ardsley, NY

Westra, L. (2006) *Environmental Justice and the Rights of Unborn and Future Generations: Law, Environmental Harm and the Right to Health*, Earthscan, London

Westra, L. (2007) *Environmental Justice and the Rights of Indigenous Peoples: International and Domestic Legal Perspectives,* Earthscan, London

Westra, L. and Werhane, P. (1998) *The Business of Consumption*, Rowman and Littlefield, Lanham MD

Westra, L., Miller, P., Rees, W. and Ulanowicz, R. (2000) 'Ecological integrity and the aims of the global ecological integrity project', in D. Pimentel, L. Westra and R. F. Noss (eds) *Ecological Integrity: Integrating Environment, Conservation and Health*, Island Press, Washington, DC, pp19–41

2

Attaining a Sustainable Society

James R. Karr

INTRODUCTION

For millennia, nature – specifically living systems – provided food, fibre and materials to nourish, clothe and house us. Living systems conditioned the air we breathe, regulated the global water cycle, created the soil that sustained our developing agriculture, and decomposed and absorbed our wastes. Beyond practicality, nature fed the human spirit. But the cumulative impacts of more than 6 billion humans are taking a toll on living systems. The toll is manifest, for example, in the decline of living water resources worldwide. Yet society has remained largely unaware of this decline because it perceives water only as a non-living fluid – a commodity to be consumed or used as a raw material in agriculture or industry. Because water resource monitoring has focused on chemical rather than biological indicators, degradation has persisted despite powerful laws calling for broader thinking and a broader regulatory framework.

The problem of poor or misleading indicators is not limited to ecological systems; the choice of indicators to track economic vitality and social wellbeing is also flawed. To reverse the erosion of living systems, society needs a new generation of indicators that fully reveal the state of economic, social and ecological systems. Without such measures, we will not fully perceive the erosion of Earth's life-support systems – human or non-human – and policymakers will lack the crucial foundation for informed decision-making. Still, even with better indicators, human society and life on Earth cannot be sustained without a revised worldview and concerted action on the parts of business, government and civil society at large.

WHAT HUMANS HAVE WROUGHT

The 2000-fold increase in Earth's human population during the last 15,000 years – from a few million to 6.6 billion as of October 2007, and growing – is the result of human ingenuity and a rich biosphere. Ingenuity gave humans an edge, allowing them to efficiently exploit the rich variety of their surrounding environments and associated living systems. During this period, human natural history changed from that of a social, patch-disturbing hunter-gatherer (Rees, 2000) dependent on materials produced by nature to that of a techno-creature able to extract living and non-living resources in support of the agricultural and industrial metabolism that enabled modern society. In effect, humanity has prospered thanks to what it has taken from Earth's ecosystems. That taking permitted the 2000-fold increase – a huge rise considering humans' large body size – making us the most influential species in history. Humans now occupy an extraordinary geographic area and influence an even larger area because of proliferating technology and increasing rates of resource consumption and waste generation.

Although society still views these trends with pride, overharvest of natural resources, the spread of society's waste and humanity's ability to exploit energy (especially in fossil fuels over the past 1000 years) have distorted the biosphere in ways that threaten human wellbeing (Figure 2.1). Among the disparate corollaries of these distortions are rising asthma rates, food insecurity, depleted fisheries, changing climate, stress syndromes from overcrowding or the pace of modern life, mounting numbers of environmental refugees (for example, 250,000 displaced from New Orleans by Hurricane Katrina), and increasing disparities between the rich and the poor. In the last 40 years of the 20th century, for example, the gap between the percentage of global gross domestic product (GDP) controlled by the richest fifth of the population and the percentage controlled by the poorest

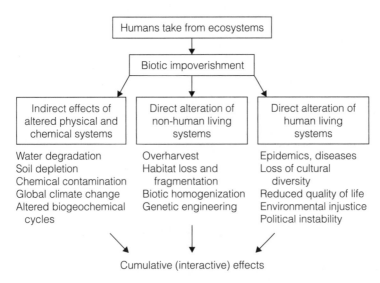

Figure 2.1 *The many faces of biotic impoverishment, resulting from humans taking from Earth's ecosystems*

Source: Modified from Chu and Karr (2001)

fifth widened, reaching a ratio of 80 to 1 by 2000 (Hart, 2005). And this widening gap is likely to lead to socio-political unrest around the world. Because a healthy biosphere is a prerequisite for healthy humans and for societal wellbeing, humanity can ill afford to ignore the consequences of actions that degrade Earth's living systems.

THE LESSONS OF HISTORY

Distortion of the biosphere is not just a 20th-century phenomenon or a by-product of European advances in the last 500 years. Urbanization, population growth and the accumulation of capital, or wealth, have distorted nature worldwide for at least 5000 years (Chew, 2001; Hughes, 2001). The archaeological record has revealed that numerous societies did not live in harmony with nature (Redman, 1999), often with serious social and health consequences for rulers as well as peasants (Fagan, 1999 and 2000).

These disharmonies only accelerated through the 20th century, a period when human consumption grew at unprecedented rates (Table 2.1). In ancient Rome, the wealthy used slaves, a direct subjugation of members of the current generation, as an inexpensive energy subsidy. Most 21st-century humans recognize slavery as repugnant. Yet according to McNeill (2000), modern global citizens in 1990 consumed the per capita equivalent of 20 full-time energy slaves; for the rich, the number was much higher. That is, the rich in the new millennium practise de facto slavery through excess energy use. They indirectly subjugate today's powerless as well as future generations, who will have to contend with legacies such as global climate change and environmental contamination. I suggest that the modern energy subsidy from fossil fuels is as

Table 2.1 *Ecological changes in the 20th century expressed as growth in consumption: The scale of human activity*

Item	Increase factor	Item	Increase factor
World population	4	Marine fish catch	35
Urban population	14	Cattle population	4
Global economy	14	Pig population	9
Industrial output	40	Horse population	1.1
Energy use	16	Forest area	0.8
Coal production	7	Irrigated area	5
Carbon dioxide emissions	17	Cropland	2

Source: Adapted from McNeill (2000)

morally repugnant as the slavery practised in Roman times. As McNeill (2000) explains, the 20th-century effects of people on the planet will overshadow the importance of socio-political events like the world wars, the rise and fall of communism, or the spread of mass literacy. Woodbridge (2004) suggests that in our preoccupation with the war on terrorism, we have lost sight of a more dangerous enemy – ecological decline.

As more historians and geographers reflect on the collapse of past societies, two lessons for our own times emerge as particularly important: first, recent ecological history and socio-economic history make full sense only if seen together (Diamond, 1997 and 2005; McNeill, 2000; Hughes, 2001); second, although humanity did not begin as a global species, it is global now (Clark, 2001). Globalization has its roots in the past, and it is as much an ecological, demographic and technological phenomenon as it is economic and political. At least five rounds of globalization can be identified (Karr, 2007):

1   hunter-gatherers spread to all the major continents;
2   plants and animals were domesticated, and agriculture evolved independently in several regions;
3   packages of domesticated species spread from these centres of origin;
4   technology proliferated and spread throughout the world, eventually culminating in industrialization; and
5   economic globalization and industrial capitalism arose.

Each round of globalization has made humans more efficient at taking from Earth's ecosystems, to the point where we must now add a sixth round, which is a direct consequence of the first five – globalization of environmental challenges.

Since living organisms first emerged from the primordial soup, success – defined as becoming an ancestor – has been determined by an ability to mobilize a continuous flow of resources. Those most effective at this activity often changed the environments in which they lived and have been labelled 'ecosystem engineers'. The first photosynthetic prokaryotes changed the Earth's atmosphere by releasing oxygen, for example; land plants and animals formed soils; beavers built dams and altered the flow of rivers, creating countless wetlands. Today, humans are the dominant ecosystem engineers, monopolizing 40 per cent of annual terrestrial plant growth, 35 per cent of the ocean's continental shelf production and 60 per cent of accessible fresh water (Pimm, 2001).

One attribute makes humans unique among all ecosystem engineers: humans alone are capable of recognizing the threat imposed by their own natural propensities. Will we be able to move beyond our past to protect the interest of future generations?

An important step in making such a transition to the future will be recognizing that the search for solutions did not originate with 'progressive Western Enlightenment philosophies and their associated rationalization processes' (Chew, 2001, p157). A sense of caring for the environment and recognizing the role of human agency in threatening that environment can be traced back at least to Mesopotamia and South Asia 4500 years ago. Writings from those times reveal an awareness of biodiversity and of the relationships among living things. They reveal knowledge of natural order in the biosphere and of the consequences of disrupting it. Well before ecology the science emerged in the modern world, humans observed and understood many of the core lessons of that science. Contemporary debate by modern philosophers, ethicists, scientists and citizens concerned about the future simply extend these discussions (Leopold, 1949; Orr, 1992 and 1994; Rolston, 1994; Westra, 1998; Pimentel et al, 2000). The need for an ethical compass – such as the Earth Charter (www.earthcharter.org) – to constrain the behaviour of human society has never been more critical. Environmental laws offer secular evidence that we acknowledge limits and responsibilities; implementing those laws, however, tests our will (Karr, 2001).

WATER RESOURCES AND BIOLOGICAL INDICATORS

Water and associated resources illustrate the pervasive and devastating nature of human distortion of living systems. In 1995, for example, 80 countries containing 40 per cent of the world's population had water shortages that crippled their agriculture and industries. In 2006, heat and a severe drought left 18 million people in 15 of China's provinces short of drinking water and 2.5 million hectares of cropland damaged (*Shangai Daily*, 2006). Detailed studies of two Midwestern US rivers show that 67 per cent of fish species from the Illinois River and 44 per cent of species from the Maumee River have become rarer or have disappeared since 1850 (Karr et al, 1985). Centuries to decades ago, harvestable populations of many freshwater fishes disappeared in many regions, and fish in rivers of the Amazon basin and Southeast Asia are rapidly following them into oblivion. Some of the world's most productive marine fisheries (for Atlantic cod, large whales and other mammals) and freshwater environments (the Laurentian Great Lakes and African Rift Lakes) are so depleted that harvest has been prohibited.

From the devastation of Indonesia's Banda Aceh by a tsunami in 2004 to the destruction of the US Mississippi delta wetlands and New Orleans by Hurricane Katrina in 2005, the effects of natural events are made infinitely worse by legacies of damage and destruction to coastal wetlands and forests. Since 1925, for example, Louisiana has lost 770,000 hectares of barrier islands and coastal marshes, and the coastline in some regions has receded by up to 24km. With compaction and the lack of sediment deposition without new flooding, 73km^2 of delta sink beneath the waves each year. Both Banda Aceh and New Orleans have contributed to the global flow of environmental refugees caused by the collision of human abuse of natural systems with nature's own extreme events.

The same lesson arises repeatedly: water bodies and landscapes linked to them continue to be degraded by the activities of humans. One cause of this continuing degradation is that the patchwork of programmes (legal, scientific, engineering and political) designed to protect water resources has not been successful at preventing continuing damage.

In the mid-1970s, my own research expanded from a focus on tropical forest birds to include stream fish. Although I began with an interest in stream ecology, I quickly came to view water resource problems as a specifically biological challenge, not a plumbing problem that could be resolved by simple engineering or political solutions. Thus, for more than 30 years, I have advocated the use of biological monitoring to sample the biota of a place and biological assessment to evaluate the biological condition, or 'health', of places on the basis of those samples.

This effort has led to two advances. First, my colleagues and I demonstrated that human influences on aquatic living systems fall into five major classes: physical habitat alteration, modification of seasonal flows, addition of both chemical and biological pollutants, changes in energy sources, and shifts in biotic interactions (Karr, 1991; Angermeier and Karr, 1994; Karr and Chu, 1999). This observation helped reveal the futility of an approach that focused only on the goal of making water cleaner. Second, given the choice of measuring all influences on water resources or of directly measuring the condition of the biota – which includes the prime witnesses, and victims, of environmental change – we took the next logical step into biological monitoring and assessment (for brevity, bioassessment) and developed an index of biological integrity (IBI).

This multimetric index directly assesses the condition of a water body in biological, as opposed to chemical pollutant, terms. Since IBI was first proposed (Karr, 1981), literally hundreds of technical papers, many special issues of journals and numerous books have been written on the importance of bioassessment. The following list summarizes seven foundations of bioassessment (see Karr, 2006, for a detailed discussion of each of these points):

1 Water bodies throughout the world are not healthy.
2 Legislative mandates to correct the situation are clear.
3 Implementation programmes that focus narrowly on clean water or some conception of optimal habitat for a few favoured species have limited success.
4 Biological measures make the best primary measurement endpoints.
5 Selecting measures of biological condition that provide clear, easily interpreted signals is key to monitoring and assessment success.
6 Success also depends on rigorous sampling design and carefully formulated procedures.
7 Communicating the results of bioassessments with the public and policymakers fosters policies to benefit water resources and the people who depend on them.

The development and tuning of IBI over the last 25 years defined a formal process for selecting indicators (called metrics) to include in the index. The process also rigorously defined an appropriate benchmark, or standard, against which places should be assessed, just as a doctor compares the temperature of a human patient with the norm of about 37°C. Most researchers now agree that a natural system standard, referred to as 'reference condition' (Hughes et al, 1986), has biological integrity – that is, the characteristics embodied in the parts (genetic diversity, species, communities) and processes (hydrology, demography, interspecific interactions, energy flow, nutrient dynamics) of nature's legacy in a region. Protecting integrity involves protecting the living systems' capacity to regenerate, reproduce, sustain, adapt, develop and evolve (Westra et al, 2000). Ultimately, protecting the health of living systems requires biological metrics to measure biological condition as a divergence from integrity.

The IBI approach to metric selection is modelled after toxicologists' use of dose–response curves to understand the effects of chemicals on individual organisms. Instead of a chemical dose in a laboratory experiment, however, the 'dose' is the level of human activity – a human disturbance gradient – in a watershed where biological attributes exhibit quantitative changes in value across that gradient. In short, the goal is to identify specific biological measures that reflect how living systems change in response to human actions (Figure 2.2).

Graphically, changes in biological condition along a biological condition gradient stem from changes in human activities along a human disturbance gradient (see Figure 2.2). The IBI is based on empirically defined metrics because such metrics:

1   are biologically and ecologically meaningful;
2   increase or decrease as human influence increases;
3   are sensitive to a range of stresses;
4   distinguish stress-induced variation of human origin from natural and sampling variation;
5   are relevant to societal concerns; and
6   are easy to measure and interpret.

After a number of such metrics are defined by their empirical relationship with the human influence gradient, they can be integrated into an IBI. The resulting IBI will be strongly correlated with the human influence gradient. Implicit in this relationship is the reality that the condition of living systems varies continuously with human influence (see Figure 2.2). Such a conception of biological evaluation is more appropriate than the typically simplified regulatory designation of water bodies as 'impaired' or 'unimpaired'. As a result, using an IBI, scientists and managers can express biological condition (or ecological health) with greater precision and on a continuous scale.

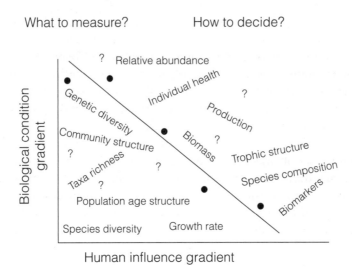

Figure 2.2   *Dose–response curves of biological condition with respect to a gradient of human influence: Foundation for selecting appropriate metrics for bioassessment*

Source: After Karr and Chu (1999)

Notes: Almost any biological attribute can be measured, but only certain attributes provide reliable signals of biological condition and therefore merit integration into a multimetric index. Success in bioassessment is tied to choosing appropriate metrics from the profusion of attributes that could be measured.

In the US Pacific Northwest, for example, benthic IBIs (B-IBIs, which monitor streambed invertebrates) show the healthiest streams as supporting an ecologically rich assemblage of invertebrates (high native taxa richness, abundance of predators, and many long-lived and intolerant taxa, among other characteristics). As human influence increases, salmon and most stoneflies disappear, and the B-IBI drops below 35 out of 50. When the B-IBI drops below 20 out of 50, cut-throat trout largely disappear, and only the most tolerant mayflies and caddisflies are present. These and other shifts in the biota, and the progressively declining IBIs that quantitatively summarize those shifts, are associated with a variety of human land uses, from protected parks through suburban and urban development, which also vary continuously in their effects.

The development of the IBI was an explicit response to the need for improved protocols to track the health of river biota. The approach has now been used to examine the effects of human activities in a broad range of aquatic and terrestrial environments (Karr, 2006).

BEYOND BIOLOGICAL INDICATORS

Humans are attuned to a rich variety of indicators (Table 2.2). Some are important for understanding individual health (for example, cholesterol level), while others emphasize other dimensions of wellbeing for individuals (annual income, ratio of expenditures to income) and nations (GDP, index of leading economic indicators).

Nations should be compiling information to reflect the status of and trends in economic, social and ecological wellbeing; such indicators should drive policymaking. But, alas, some indicators are more mythology than fact (for example, personal horoscopes based on planetary alignment), while others leave out so much that they mislead by distortion. Weaknesses in GDP, for example, are widely recognized (Cobb et al, 1995; Davidson, 2000), even if certain politicians pretend the weaknesses do not exist. In his 1999 State of the Union address, US President Bill Clinton proclaimed that the nation was in the 'longest peacetime expansion in history' (Rowe and Silverstein, 1999). But no one asked what was expanding, and the President didn't tell; this wonderful news went without challenge. As Rowe and Silverstein note, many things are expanding – from waistlines to medical bills, from debt to traffic. The monetary and health costs of obesity illustrate the problem. Each year the food industry in America spends US$700 billion on advertising to compel Americans to eat more industry products. And each year Americans spend US$32 billion on diet and weight-loss programmes; they undergo 110,000 liposuctions at a cost of about US$2000 each. The health consequences of this state of affairs include rising incidences of childhood obesity and type II diabetes. Yet the monetary value of all this consumption and healthcare go into the GDP, along with the assumption that it increases the nation's wealth. In fact, the cost of healthcare should be subtracted.

Table 2.2   *Examples of classes of indicators used by human society,*
with selected indicators in each class

Indicator class	Indicator examples
Individual health	Temperature, cholesterol level, blood chemistry, weight
Economic: Individual	Income, stock profile, ratio of expenditures to income
Economic: Business	Number of items manufactured or sold, profit per item
Economic: National	Index of leading economic indicators, GDP, inflation rate
Social	Crime, literacy, suicide, poverty rates, education
Technology	Automobile gas mileage, raw material recycled
Planetary alignments	Horoscope
Biological	Largely ignored historically; IBI and other indexes today

GDP measures the economy's throughput – the amount of money changing hands – but it fails on several counts as a measure of societal wellbeing. First, it ignores important aspects of the economy, such as income distribution, unpaid work and the black market. Second, it does not valuate non-monetary contributions to human fulfilment, such as health, education, freedom, security and peace. And third, it omits social and environmental costs such as pollution, resource depletion, cancer and crime. GDP simply does not measure the state of Earth's ecosystems. Perhaps most perversely, GDP counts social and environmental costs – like those associated with excessive food consumption – as benefits. Other economic indexes, such as the Dow Jones industrial average, the index of leading economic indicators or the consumer price index, are similarly limited as measures of societal wellbeing.

GDP, like so many of the other indicators used by modern industrialized society, implicitly gives permission to escape responsibility for actions. It tacitly endorses unsustainable values and lifestyles that distort social systems and disrupt ecological health. Two hundred years of using such indicators has produced a society that values what it measures rather than measuring what is valuable. Biotic impoverishment is an alarming by-product of our indicator choices.

Although social indicators have so far not been a high priority, efforts to produce social indicators measuring human wellbeing are gaining ground. Beginning in the 1970s, at least eight European nations formalized 'national social health reports'. Other nations (for example, Canada, Hungary, Turkey and Australia) joined these countries in the 1980s and 1990s. In 2002 the ruler of Bhutan mandated production of a 'gross national happiness' report.

The US still does not participate with the nearly 20 other countries explicitly mandating systematic evaluation of social wellbeing. Public concern in the US about the inability to monitor public human services the way the nation monitors financial markets stimulated development of a social index of leading indicators (Miringhoff and Miringhoff, 1999; Stille, 2002). This social index combines 16 measures of social health, including child poverty, teenage suicide rates, average weekly wages, homicide rates, health insurance coverage and alcohol-related traffic deaths. When aggregated at state levels, such indexes reveal variation among US states, with Iowans suffering the least (73 out of a maximum 100) and New Mexicans the most (scoring 21). Three indicators in particular – child poverty, high school completion and health insurance – were bellwethers of overall social health (Stille, 2002). The Miringoffs' study showed that although gross domestic product had increased by 92 per cent over the preceding 30 years, Americans' social health had declined by 29 per cent, because problems such as child poverty, lower average wages, youth suicide rates and health insurance coverage had all worsened.

In his book titled *The Wellbeing of Nations*, Robert Prescott-Allen (2001) developed and applied an index to track human wellbeing for 184 nations. His human wellbeing index includes measures of health, population, household wealth, national wealth, knowledge, culture, freedom and governance, peace and order, household equity, and gender equity. The patterns observed by Prescott-Allen are not encouraging. Only three countries – Norway, Denmark and Finland – are rated as good. The distribution of other countries is disappointing but not surprising: fair (34), medium (52), poor (51) and bad (40).

These social indicators reinforce the view that use of conventional economic indicators may harm the non-economic dimensions of human society. Both social and non-human biological indexes paint a very different picture from the one based on GDP. Our planet develops over time without growing, and our economy must adopt a similar pattern of development, without growth in throughput (Daly, 1991). Econometric indicators should reflect that reality. One effort to improve such econometrics is the index of sustainable economic welfare, which adjusts for negative impacts on natural capital, for wealth disparities across classes, for the effects of pollution, and for other long-term social and environmental damage (Costanza et al, 1997). The world needs more such comprehensive indicators.

ALTERING CURRENT TRAJECTORIES

Human society faces a paradox (Karr, 2007). Despite unprecedented advances in science and technology over the last two centuries, threats to human and non-human living systems worsen. How can we be smarter and more knowledgeable yet blind to so many of the lessons of this knowledge? How can we continue to observe social and ecological degradation and not take definitive action to reverse these trends?

Clearly, one reason for our ignorance is the tendency to use indicators, like GDP, that allow us to overlook serious long-term trends. Another obvious reason is the tendency to assume that the human economy is separate from the environment and free from biophysical constraints. This assumption is grounded in an expansionist perspective (Rees, 2002), which assumes the environment is the source of an unlimited supply of resources and a sink for an unlimited quantity of wastes. Expansionists have faith that human ingenuity always has provided and always will provide creative solutions to all challenges faced by society. In reality, the Earth, a finite body, does not continue to grow, so neither populations nor their material consumption can continue to grow forever. A steady-state (as opposed to expansionist) perspective more accurately reflects the reality of a finite Earth.

Many people use a Venn diagram to illustrate the relationships and need for an integrative understanding of ecological, social and economic dimensions of wellbeing (Figure 2.3, left). In this conception, the goal becomes understanding the small central area of overlap. But this conception is as flawed as the expansionist perspective. A more realistic alternative (Karr, 2007) arrays social,

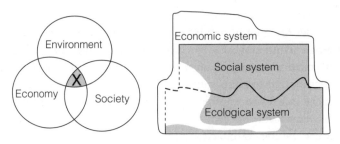

Figure 2.3   *One flawed and one realistic depiction of the relationships among natural, social and economic systems*

Source: Modified from Karr (2007)

Notes: Left: Relationships among the three key components of Earth systems – natural, social and economic – are often inappropriately depicted with a Venn diagram. Right: These relationships are more appropriately depicted as a layer cake. Human economies (the icing) are shown here eroding the underlying social and ecological systems, threatening the foundation and sustainability of those systems. Indicators of economic vitality, social wellbeing, and human and ecological health are needed to understand the true condition of Earth's systems.

economic and ecological systems in three interdependent dimensions, like the layers of a cake (Figure 2.3, right). The economic system is the top layer, supported by the social system. Both are supported by the bottom layer, Earth's ecosystems. The preoccupation with growth in the economy has allowed society to overlook social inequities and depletion of natural capital, which are in reality the uncounted costs of growth and a threat to the very foundations of society.

ATTAINING A SUSTAINABLE SOCIETY

Society cannot come to grips with the global ecological challenges it faces without coordinated thinking and action. We cannot achieve a sustainable society without a revised worldview – one that acknowledges and embraces our dependence on the rest of life on Earth. We cannot even attain a sustainable human society without assessing and communicating the impacts of human actions on ecological health, social wellbeing and economic vitality.

In the US, we have shifted in the last half century from being a 'can-do' nation to being one that cannot afford basics such as living-wage jobs, quality education, healthcare, safety nets for the poor or environmental protection (Korten, 2006). Paradoxically, this shift is happening as economists conclude that the nation as a whole is getting richer.

Guilty parties in the blame game are everywhere. Capitalism's obsession with economic growth and creating wealth benefits a small proportion of the population while everyone bears the social and environmental costs. Government fails to enact laws (or does not enforce existing laws) designed to protect human and non-human living systems. Worse yet, the growing power of international corporations co-opts the powers of government and subverts democracy (Reich, 2007). As democracy withers, disparities between the haves and have-nots worsen, and the larger life-support systems of Earth that sustain human society are irreparably damaged.

So what can we do? Rather than emphasizing the inherent evil of any of the three primary sectors – business, government and civil society – we must recognize the failure of all to think and operate in the interest of human wellbeing. For too long, society at large has denied the effects of the churning human industrial metabolism on Earth's living systems. We all need to recognize these effects and act together; otherwise, all will perish.

Throughout the last three centuries, visionaries from Alexander Humboldt, George Perkins Marsh and Frederick Law Olmsted to Aldo Leopold and Rachel Carson have led the way in identifying the local, regional and planetary effects of human activity. All were natural scientists who acted on their scientific knowledge and, through their writings, inspired others to act. Rachel Carson's work, in particular, embodied the effective merger of ecology the science and ecological thinking. She was fascinated with the intricacies of life, particularly with understanding the connections between the physico-chemical world and the biological world (Lear, 1998). She had a deep anxiety about the future and a reverence for life. She was concerned that public ignorance and apathy were the greatest obstacles to quality decision-making in society, and, as a result, she was determined to write to inform the public, to overcome that ignorance and apathy.

Perhaps the most important event of the last few decades has been the spread of this understanding and concern to all corners of society: to citizens (the Earth Charter), business leaders (Paul Hawken and Stuart Hart), economists (Robert Reich and Herman Daly), philosophers (Holmes Rolston, Laura Westra and Baird Callicott), politicians (Al Gore and Mikhail Gorbachev) and religious leaders (His Holiness Bartholomew I and Pope John Paul II). But now modern society has reached an important fork in the road; if we fail to change course, the future appears increasingly bleak. In his book *Capitalism at the Crossroads*, Stephen Hart (2005) calls for a new brand of capitalism to 'become the catalyst for a truly sustainable form of global development'. This new capitalism would take into account the entire human community of 6.6 billion people, as well as the host of other species with which we share this planet. Pollution by industry, Hart notes, is 'waste and poor management'. Hart suggests that multinational corporations cannot thrive if they pursue greater profitability while ignoring their workers' lives or while degrading the environment. He concludes that short-term profit cannot trump long-term sustainability if business is to continue well into the 21st century. While increasing shareholder value, a sustainable global business undertaking would 'simultaneously raise the quality of life for the world's poor, respect cultural diversity and conserve the ecological integrity of the planet for future generations'.

But a sustainable human society on a living planet cannot be attained by the energies of business alone; business, government, non-profits, multilateral agencies and an active citizenry must all engage to hasten the essential transitions. The goal of sustaining Earth's living systems must be seen as a continuing transformation, as a collective, uncertain and adaptive transition, not an endpoint to be accomplished (NRC, 2000). Robert Reich (2007) explores how citizens and government have been complicit with business and industry in recent decades as democratic capitalism has morphed into global capitalism and, most recently, supercapitalism. (All this follows the collapse of socialism, communism and fascism.) Consumers benefited from the proliferation of goods, and investors benefited from growing profits. As capitalism became more narrowly responsive to citizens as purchasers of goods, however, it grew less responsive to what citizens needed as expressions of the common good. And so we find ourselves with a vibrant, growing economy that cannot keep pace with fundamental societal needs.

Real democracy, that is, a real government by the people, is key to the future. Democracy needs the active participation of both government and citizens. Through government, citizens participate in choosing among crucial trade-offs associated with common multidimensional goals: economic vitality, social wellbeing, human health and ecological health. Protecting wellbeing in these crucial dimensions requires us all to sacrifice some benefits as consumers to achieve too long neglected social and ecological ends.

Like Rachel Carson a half century ago, ecologists and other scientists today have a special role to play in creating a sustainable society. They should at a minimum inform the general public about the relevance and importance of their work (Bazzaz et al, 1998). They should also lend their technical and scientific expertise to the many others concerned about ecological decline (such as the thousands who participated in developing the Earth Charter). In one far-reaching effort, for example, more than 2000 authors and reviewers contributed their knowledge and creativity in compiling the Millennium Ecosystem Assessment (2005), a path-breaking international evaluation that hopes to meet decision-makers' needs for scientific information on the consequences of ecosystem change for human wellbeing and on the options available to respond to undesired changes. Similarly, the Intergovernmental Panel on Climate Change has cautiously, but definitively, moved into the policy arena. And many other individual scientists working in business, government and civil society have been speaking and writing quietly about these issues for decades.

As David Korten (2006) notes in his recent book, if we are successful, 'future generations may look back on this time ... as the Great Turning'; if we fail, they will see this time as a continuation of the 'Great Unraveling'.

ACKNOWLEDGEMENTS

This chapter was first presented as the 1999 Rachel Carson Memorial Lecture hosted by the School of Forest Resources and the Department of Agricultural Economics and Rural Sociology at Pennsylvania State University. Revisions were presented at the 2002 annual meeting of the Association for Public Policy Analysis and Management in Dallas, Texas, and as a plenary lecture at the 2005 meeting of the Società Italiana di Ecologia in Turin, Italy. The ideas advanced here were also tuned by my participation in several meetings of the Global Ecological Integrity Group. Special thanks to Laura Westra for her leadership of the group; to the above organizations for challenging me with their lecture invitations; and, as always in the last 15 years, to Ellen W. Chu for her continuing editorial insight.

REFERENCES

Angermeier, P. L. and Karr, J. R. (1994) 'Biological integrity versus biological diversity as policy directives', *BioScience*, vol 44, no 10, pp690–697

Bazzaz, F. A. and 19 others (1998) 'Ecological science and the human predicament', *Science*, vol 282, no 5390, p879

Chew, S. C. (2001) *World Ecological Degradation: Accumulation, Urbanization, and Deforestation, 3000 B.C.–A.D. 2000*, Altamira Press, Walnut Creek, CA

Chu, E. W. and Karr, J. R. (2001) 'Environmental impact, concept and measurement of', in S. A. Levin (ed) *Encyclopedia of Biodiversity*, vol 2, Academic Press, Orlando, FL, pp557–577

Clark, R. P. (2001) *Global Life Systems: Population, Food, and Disease in the Process of Globalization*, Rowman and Littlefield, Lanham, MD

Cobb, C., Halstead, T. and Rowe, J. (1995) 'If the GDP is up, why is America down?', *Atlantic Monthly*, vol 276, no 4, pp59–78

Costanza, R., Cumberland, J., Daly, H., Goodland, R. and Norgaard, R. (1997) *An Introduction to Ecological Economics*, St Lucie Press, Boca Raton, FL

Daly, H. E. (1991) 'Boundless bull', *Orion*, vol 3, summer, pp59–61

Davidson, E. A. (2000) *You Can't Eat GNP: Economics as if Ecology Mattered*, Perseus, Cambridge, MA

Diamond, J. (1997) *Guns, Germs, and Steel: The Fates of Human Societies*, Norton, New York

Diamond, J. (2005) *Collapse: How Societies Choose to Fail or Succeed*, Viking, New York

Fagan, B. (1999) *Floods, Famines and Emperors: El Niño and the Fate of Civilizations*, Basic Books, New York

Fagan, B. (2000) *The Little Ice Age: How Climate Made History, 1300–1850*, Basic Books, New York

Hart, S. L. (2005) *Capitalism at the Crossroads: The Unlimited Business Opportunities in Solving the World's Most Difficult Problems*, Wharton School Publishing, Upper Saddle River, NJ

Hughes, J. D. (2001) *An Environmental History of the World: Humankind's Changing Role in the Community of Life*, Routledge, New York

Hughes, R. M., Larsen, D. P. and Omernik, J. M. (1986) 'Regional reference sites: A method for assessing stream pollution', *Environmental Management*, vol 10, no 5, pp629–635

Karr, J. R. (1981) 'Assessment of biotic integrity using fish communities', *Fisheries*, vol 6, no 6, pp21–27

Karr, J. R. (1991) 'Biological integrity: A long-neglected aspect of water resource management', *Ecological Applications*, vol 1, no 1, pp66–84

Karr, J. R. (2001) 'Protecting life: Weaving together environment, people and law', in R. G. Stahl, Jr, R. A. Bachman, A. L. Barton, J. R. Clark, P. L. deFur, S. J. Ells, C. A. Pittinger, M. W. Slimak and R. S. Wentsel (eds) *Risk Management: Ecological Risk-Based Decision-Making*, SETAC Press, Pensacola, FL, pp175–185

Karr, J. R. (2006) 'Seven foundations of biological monitoring and assessment', *Biologia Ambientale*, vol 20, no 2, pp7–18

Karr, J. R. (2007) 'Protecting society from itself: Reconnecting ecology and economy', in C. L. Soskolne (ed) *Sustaining Life on Earth: Environmental and Human Health through Global Governance*, Lexington Books, Lanham, MD, pp95–108

Karr, J. R. and Chu, E. W. (1999) *Restoring Life in Running Waters: Better Biological Monitoring*, Island Press, Washington, DC

Karr, J. R., Toth, L. A. and Dudley, D. R. (1985) 'Fish communities of Midwestern rivers: A history of degradation', *BioScience*, vol 35, no 2, pp90–95

Korten, D. C. (2006) *The Great Turning: From Empire to Earth Community*, Kumarian Press, Bloomfield, CT, and Berrett-Koehler, San Francisco, CA

Lear, L. (ed) (1998) *Lost Woods: The Discovered Writing of Rachel Carson*, Beacon Press, Boston, MA

Leopold, A. (1949) *A Sand County Almanac*, Oxford University Press, Oxford, UK

McNeill, J. R. (2000) *Something New Under the Sun: An Environmental History of the Twentieth-Century World*, Norton, New York

Millennium Ecosystem Assessment (2005) *Our Human Planet: Summary for Decision-Makers,* Island Press, Washington, DC

Miringoff, M. L. and Miringoff, M. L. (1999) *The Social Health of the Nation: How America Is Really Doing*, Oxford University Press, New York

NRC (National Research Council) (2000) *Our Common Journey: A Transition toward Sustainability*, National Academy Press, Washington, DC

Orr, D. W. (1992) *Ecological Literacy: Education and the Transition to a Postmodern World*, State University of New York Press, Albany, NY

Orr, D. W. (1994) *Earth in Mind: On Education, Environment, and the Human Prospect*, Island Press, Washington, DC

Pimentel, D., Westra, L. and Noss, R. F. (eds) (2000) *Ecological Integrity: Integrating Environment, Conservation, and Health*, Island Press, Washington, DC

Pimm, S. L. (2001) The *World According to Pimm: A Scientist Audits the Earth*, McGraw-Hill, New York

Prescott-Allen, R. (2001) *The Wellbeing of Nations: A Country-by-Country Index of Quality of Life and the Environment*, Island Press, Washington, DC

Redman, C. L. (1999) *Human Impact on Ancient Environments*, University of Arizona Press, Tucson, AZ

Rees, W. E. (2000) 'Patch disturbance, ecofootprints, and biological integrity: Revisiting the limits to growth (or why industrial society is inherently unsustainable)', in D. Pimentel, L. Westra and R. F. Noss (eds) *Ecological Integrity: Integrating Environment, Conservation and Health*, Island Press, Washington, DC, pp139–156

Rees, W. E. (2002) 'Globalization and sustainability: Conflict or convergence?', *Bulletin of Science, Technology and Society*, vol 22, no 4, pp249–268

Reich, R. B. (2007) *Supercapitalism: The Transformation of Business, Democracy, and Everyday Life*, Knopf, New York

Rolston, H., III (1994) *Conserving Natural Value*, Columbia University Press, New York

Rowe, J. and Silverstein, J. (1999) 'The GDP myth: Why "growth" isn't always a good thing', *Washington Monthly*, vol 31, no 3, pp17–21

Shangai Daily (2006) 'Drought leaves 18 million thirsty in China', *Shangai (China) Daily*, 20 August

Stille, A. (2002) 'With the index of leading economic indicators, a social report card', *New York Times*, 27 April

Westra, L. (1998) *Living in Integrity: A Global Ethic to Restore a Fragmented Earth*, Rowman and Littlefield, Lanham, MD

Westra, L., Miller, P., Karr, J. R., Rees, W. E. and Ulanowicz, R. E. (2000) 'Ecological integrity and the aims of the global integrity project', in D. Pimentel, L. Westra and R. F. Noss (eds) *Ecological Integrity: Integrating Environment, Conservation, and Health*, Island Press, Washington, DC, pp19–41

Woodbridge, R. (2004) *The Next World War: Tribes, Cities, Nations, and Ecological Decline*, University of Toronto Press, Toronto, Canada

3

A Modest Proposal of How to Proceed in Order to Solve the Problem of Inherent Moral Value in Nature

Konrad Ott

INTRODUCTION

To me, the very idea of living in integrity does not refer to specific states of certain ecosystems, but to a human way of life with and within nature that is grounded in all the reasonable arguments by which the universe of discourse in environmental ethics is constituted. The ideal of moral persons who have comprised the universe of environmental discourse completely and profoundly entails a *eudaimonistic* (*eudaimonia* meaning related to a good and flourishing human life), a *political* and a *moral* dimension of personhood. In the *eudaimonistic* dimension, we find many culturally shaped biophilic values (aesthetic, recreational, transformative, heritage, bioregional and the like), which have impacts on the virtues and attitudes of such persons. Thus such persons are mostly 'naturalists' in lifestyle, adopting most of the virtues Philip Cafaro recommends in his writings on environmental virtue ethics.[1] The virtue of voluntary simplicity is at the core of such a lifestyle. In the *political* dimension, such persons will engage in environmental policies, such as nature conservation, restoration ecology or the mitigation of climate change. In this chapter, I remain silent on environmental policymaking, focusing on (meta-)ethical problems.[2]

In the *moral* dimension, such persons will accept a specific set of obligations with regard to natural beings. This set augments the set of obligations in the inter-human ethics. Clearly, there is an ambiguity in the term 'with regard to', because obligations can be either direct or indirect (in Kant, '*Pflichten gegenüber*' as distinguished from '*Pflichten in Ansehung von*'). This ambiguity will be resolved in the next section. Moral obligations presuppose some beings that have to be respected for their own sake. The phrase 'for their own sake' is related to the category of inherent moral value (synonym: intrinsic value). The class of beings 'having' inherent moral value (IMV) is defined as the 'moral community' (MC). For instance, one can have a direct moral obligation (synonym: duty) to a human or to a non-human being with regard to his, her or its natural environment which provides a livelihood for this being.

The moral dimension is related to the problem of attributing IMV to natural beings. Therefore, the so-called demarcation problem (Sober, 1995) is conceptually entailed in the overall ethical idea of living in integrity. This problem is about *attributing* the category of IMV to certain beings from the moral point of view. For convenience, I dub it 'the IMV problem'. It is a general ethical problem which has been addressed in the field of environmental ethics for several reasons. One reason is the widespread intuition among environmentalists (Butler and Acott, 2007) that it is necessary, prudent, mandatory, wise or simply 'good' to overcome anthropocentrism. The IMV problem has attracted and absorbed much intellectual energy in environmental ethics. A solution would mean progress in this field of enquiry.

It is not true that modern ethics in general has favoured anthropocentrism. Jeremy Bentham,[3] Jean-Jaques Rousseau[4] and Arthur Schopenhauer have favoured sentientism, giving IMV to all beings that are able to experience mental states of pleasure and pain. Albert Schweitzer's ethics of 'reverence for life' (1923) is, at least, biocentric. The following solutions have been proposed in recent literature: IMV to persons, humans, sentient animals, living organisms, ecosystems or any real beings. These solutions come in specific variants (egalitarianism versus gradualism) and in different ethical shape (consequentialistic versus deontological).[5] Of course, all ethicists have *argued* in favour of a specific solution.[6] We find multiple comments, rejections, rebuttals and the like. Nevertheless, there is neither convergence nor reconciliation, but rather 'camps'. Thus scepticism has become widespread as to whether the IMV problem can be solved and, moreover, what kind of reasoning should count as a contribution to a 'reasonable' solution. Does, for instance, the IMV problem allow for 'baseline' solutions which define some baseline as mandatory (say sentientism) and give leeway of personal choice to all options beyond that baseline? Biocentrics, ecocentrics and holists must oppose such a baseline solution since it suggests that any position beyond the baseline is based in metaphysical worldviews or doctrines. Such solutions might be acceptable in the realm of environmental policies, since they constitute practical convergence among environmentalists in Bryan Norton's sense, but they are not acceptable in environmental ethics proper. Some ethicists argue that we should leave the problem open, accept pluralism and different solutions at different times and places (Birch, 1993), downplay the demarcation problem for practical purposes (Norton, 1991), rely on pragmatic multi-criterial approaches (Warren, 1997), redesign the demarcation problem as a problem of self-esteem (Wetlesen, 1999), and so forth. These are proposals of how to cope with an unresolved moral problem, but not resolutions in themselves.

In this chapter, I *presume* that progress in solving the IMV problem is within reach. I *assume* that the epistemic anthropocentrism of all ethics is compatible with any substantial solution of the IMV problem. Under this presumption and assumption, I *propose* some methodological proceeding and some substantial arguments which shall, I hope, come close to a reasonable solution for the time being.

FRAMINGS AND PRELIMINARY SUPPOSITIONS

I wish to distinguish between two broad categories of moral status:

1   *inherent moral value*; and
2   *protective goods* which are to be conserved (preserved, restored) with regard to the broadly understood welfare interests of some or all members of the MC.[7]

A natural being which is not regarded as being a member of the MC is, therefore, by no means without protection. Nature conservation can rely on the second category of moral status to a great extent. It would be begging the question to argue that it is an unfair discrimination against natural beings to put them 'only' in this second category. Natural beings, as far as we know, do not mind under which category they are protected; only moral agents owe each other reasons in this respect. Of course, there are conceptual differences involved in both categories of moral status. Protective goods can be compared, ranked, substituted against each other and weighed, while IMV constitutes strong moral standing.[8] This is often seen as an advantage of attributing IMV to natural beings, since the process of weighing goods might be biased in favour of human economic interests, as is, indeed, very often the case. Nevertheless, this preliminary advantage of attributing IMV comes at a price. Moral claims of members of an enlarged MC will come into different kinds of conflicts. If the extension of the MC is large, the problem of weighing goods re-emerges as moral conflict within the enlarged MC. Thus the stronger moral status of IMV should not bias us against conceptual frameworks in environmental ethics which rely on both categories.

The IMV problem should not be confused with the question of which parts of nature human societies mostly rely on. There is strong empirical evidence that human systems rely deeply on beings (such as convective belts, clouds, plants, micro-organisms and plankton) that are different from the natural beings that are *prima facie* candidates for MC membership (for example whales, dolphins, apes and elephants). Recognizing the embedding and reliance of human systems is different from attributing IMV. The concept of living in integrity has to address both questions without confusion.

Gary Varner's (1998) distinction between *practical* and *ethical* holism is helpful at this point. Leaving metaphysical approaches aside, ethical holism is either ecocentrism (Callicott, 1980; Johnson, 1991; Westra, 1994) or pluralistic holism (Gorke, 2003 and 2007). Practical holism is about sustainable, cautious and wise use of the 'land'. I deeply endorse practical holism. In our 'Greifswald' variant of Daly's concept of strong sustainability (Ott and Döring, 2004), we have made some proposals of how to apply practical holism to different components of natural capital (fisheries, forests, climate systems and agriculture). 'Natural capital' is a broad concept which refers to a nested set of protective goods, for instance soils, mires, rivers and lakes. Under this perspective, projects in restoration ecology can be regarded as investments in natural capital. A 'land ethics' can be based on practical holism, which can be specified to concepts of 'wise use' and 'adaptive management'. Thus supporters of practical holism can agree to the second-order principles of ethical holism, such as embracing complexity, applying the precautionary principle and seeing our activities as in a buffer zone (Westra, 1998, Chapter 9).

ANALYSIS

The IMV problem is a relational one: On the one side there are ('exist') different kinds of beings X (adult humans, human foetuses, genes, organs, species, ecological systems, rocks, molecules, stardust, raindrops, clouds and the like). Some existing beings have quite sharp boundaries (organisms), other have fuzzy ones (ecosystems). To attribute 'existence' to beings is logically different from attributing specific features. Existence is denoted by '$\exists$'; a feature is denoted by 'f'. In the following, I use the term 'feature' instead of 'property', because 'property' suggests a commitment to an Aristotelian substance-accidence ontology which I wish to avoid. The term 'feature' is used in a way that is (or should be) compatible with different approaches in ontology.[9] The proposition 'There exists a being X with some features f' is denoted by '$\exists X f(a, b, c \ldots)$'. Similar beings can be comprised to sets, classes, types or (natural) kinds. The type–token relation applies within the demarcation problem: if IMV is attributed to a certain type it must, *ceteris paribus*, be applied to all tokens of that type. This type–token relation can be formalized in schemes of inference as practical syllogism. Most environmentalists suppose an ontology which is more richly textured than a physicalistic ontology in a Quinean sense. Arne Naess, among others, has criticized the ontology of physicalism which only addresses the 'night vision' (Fechner: '*Nachtansicht der Natur*') of nature (1989, p53). Therefore we should assume an ontology that is as 'rich' as the natural and cultural world we live in. By philosophical intuition, I have no preference for 'desert landscapes' (Quine) in ontology.

On the other side of the relation we find the ethical notion of IMV which is part of our moral language game. This notion means that any being X which 'owes' ('has') such IMV has to be respected morally for its own sake. This notion implies that moral agents have at least one (but probably more than one) direct moral obligation against X. Such direct obligations might be obligations against causing harm, making suffer, killing, impairing interests and the like. Both sides of this relation must be combined into specific moral validity claims. Any proposal of how to solve the demarcation problem must entail such claims. The general formula (scheme) is $\exists Xf(a, b, c \ldots) \Leftrightarrow IMV$. In this scheme, the arrow means 'IMV should be attributed to X (from the moral point of view)'. Moral claims can be accepted or refused. The core of the IMV problem is about how to justify such specific relations by giving reasons. The formula must therefore be enlarged by reasons R which can justify the claims being made:

$$(1) \qquad R(r, s, t \ldots) \rightarrow (\exists Xf(a, b, c \ldots) \Leftrightarrow IMV).$$

Formula (1) means this: it follows from some reasons R that the claim $(\exists Xf(a, b, c \ldots) \Leftrightarrow IMV)$ is valid and should be accepted by all moral agents. The thin arrow, $\rightarrow$, is to be understood in a less rigid sense of 'making $(\exists Xf(a, b, c \ldots) \Leftrightarrow IMV)$ acceptable in moral discourse'. We can never derive the attribution of IMV from a neutral description of features without committing a naturalistic fallacy. Reasons R must entail some assumptions about morally relevant features. The reasons R must refer to the empirical features $f(a, b, c \ldots)$ via patterns of argument that bridge the gap between empirical features and moral considerability without committing a naturalistic fallacy. I restrict myself to two patterns of reasoning, but there might be more than just two. If there, *first*, is a moral rule (norm) of action N that (a) is regarded valid in human ethics (I rely on the proposal made by Gert, 1966) and (b) can be applied to certain non-human beings because of their features, then there is a reason to believe that those beings are to have IMV. Since at least some moral rules can, obviously, be applied to non-humans (norms against killing and causing pain) there is *prima facie* moral considerability beyond humans. If, *second*, some basic ethical notions (like the notion of interest) can be applied to some natural beings, there are more reasons to believe that there is moral considerability beyond humans. Formula (1) can thus be augmented. The more complete scheme, which indicates how solving the IMV problem should be performed in ethics, can be given as:

$$(2) \qquad (R(r, s, t \ldots) \rightarrow C) \rightarrow (\exists Xf(a, b, c \ldots) \Leftrightarrow IMV).$$

The formula '$R(r, s, t \ldots) \rightarrow C$' means that reasons R result in a criterion C. Since a criterion C must not be arbitrarily chosen or be given by definition, it must be derivative to substantial reasons. Reasoning about morally relevant features is decisive, while the criterion the reasons establish is nothing but a kind of convenient shorthand. If the reasons are sound, the criterion C may function as criteria do. They include some entities in the MC while excluding others. If one distinguishes between logical and moral discrimination, a criterion C for membership in the MC that rests on reasons R is, as such, not morally discriminating. Superficial rhetoric might falsely suggest that any kind of exclusion from the MC is, as such, morally repugnant.[10] But this is misleading. Any criterion discriminates in some respects between different entities. This is the logical (or conceptual) meaning of discrimination (from the Latin *discrimen, discriminare*). Discrimination in a moral sense means, in the human sphere, an unfair treatment. In cases of moral discrimination, a difference of treatment rests on differences in certain features (for example skin colour, sex, age or religion) which do not justify such different treatment from the moral point of view. This does not imply that all criteria being used in morals are morally repugnant. There are many moral or legal rules and many standards of distributive justice which discriminate between different groups of persons in a way which seems perfectly adequate from the moral point of view (for example special care for disabled people). Even if one believes that species membership does not justify different treatment (rejection of 'speciesism'), one is not committed to the claim that any discrimination is morally repugnant in itself. If no criterion of IMV is self-evident, it simply does not follow that any criterion must be arbitrarily chosen, as Morito (2003, p327) suggests. Such general accusation of arbitrariness rests on *non sequiturs*. If the previous argument is sound, to exclude beings from the MC is not repugnant in itself.

PROBLEM-SOLVING IN ETHICS

The language game that surrounds the concept of a problem is a pragmatic one. Problems are something to which, in principle, solutions can be found. Even if it is argued that a problem P hasn't got a solution so far, it is still presumed that there is or might be some solution to be found. We face problems in everyday life and search for solutions. Sometimes we succeed, sometimes we fail. Scientific disciplines specialize in different kinds of problem-solving. A scientific problem might find the one best solution (truth) or, as in technology or in hermeneutics, there might be several satisfying solutions. Ethics addresses moral problems in search of solutions. Discourse ethics assumes that for moral problems a solution can be found if a moral discourse is performed according to a set of rules and without scarcity of time. A 'one best solution' implies that other proposals are false (wrong or misleading), while a 'first best solution' implies that other proposals are less good. I suppose that there might be a first best solution to the IMV problem which, perhaps, might be surrounded by some satisfying solutions. Any first best solution is a solution *for the time being*, since we cannot know whether better solutions might be proposed at some point in the future.[11]

There are widely accepted standards among experts in science and technology that define good or satisfying solutions. The standards for resolving philosophical and ethical problems are far less clear. If standards are uncertain or contested, one might rely on paradigm cases of reasonable problem solution in philosophy and in ethics. Paradigm cases in the history of ethical reasoning are arguments against torture, arguments against slavery, arguments in favour of '*ius in bello*', arguments that children have rights against their parents, arguments against the discrimination against women, arguments about informed consent in research on humans, and so on. If we adopt a set of such paradigm cases, we may feel encouraged that the IMV problem can be among an enlarged set. Only if a huge number of serious attempts to solve the demarcation problem in moral discourse fail might one feel entitled to shape the demarcation 'issue' as a 'topic' which can be addressed differently by different peoples and cultures. This is clearly a default option.

Problem-solving is performed according to *methods*. The original Greek meaning of 'method' is about how to proceed in order to resolve a problem.[12] 'The claim provides the method' (Brennan, 1977, p90). With regard to the IMV problem, there are two *routes of proceeding*. The first one is the 'extensibility route', which has been the mainstream route in environmental ethics. This route starts from a class of beings which are assumed to 'have' IMV in our common human ethics (persons or human beings) and one considers reasonable enlargements of the MC on this route. The other route is less familiar, but has been proposed by some ethicists, for example Thomas Birch and Martin Gorke. It is the 'route from outside' since, under this methodological approach, one has to argue why some entities should *not* be regarded as members of the MC. On this route, the IMV problem is not about inclusion but about exclusion from the MC.

If the notion of method is taken seriously, the choice of the route should not be begging the question. That is to say, if there is a sound first-best solution to the IMV problem at all, we should reach it on both routes. If both routes converge towards some focal point, we have reason to believe that we are coming close to a satisfying solution to the demarcation problem. *Both routes must be viable.* If a way is not viable at all, there is no way.

We can take some equipment with us on both routes. Thought experiments of the 'last person' and 'Whom would you save?' conflicts and the concept of deontic experience (Birch, 1993) are helpful tools or, say, touchstones. Taken in isolation, however, none of them is decisive for problem solution. Taken in isolation, the thought experiment of the 'last person' (Routley, 1973; see also Carter, 2004) and the 'saving dilemmas' (see Michael, 1997) can clarify which solution of the IMV problem one has already adopted. If one believes that the last person should not destroy plants, one has adopted a biocentric solution. If one believes that one newborn human baby and not five adult dogs should be saved from a burning house, one has rejected the position that the life of all sentient beings is of equal moral value. But no tool gets rid of some 'if'; both tools are simply useful touchstones for the coherence of an environmental ethics. 'Saving conflicts' face the problem that they can be varied without limits (for example one blind and deaf dog against twenty flowers and a collection of shells).

A parallel holds for presumptive deontic experiences (Birch, 1993). Whether experiences that have been perceived as deontic by someone should count as genuine deontic experiences for all moral agents remains an open question. Taken in isolation, the concept of deontic experience bears, as Birch sees clearly, the moral hazards of self-deception and, worse, of fanatics. The concept of deontic experience entails some story-telling. Thus the stories (narratives) that express deontic experiences must be interpreted by a community of moral persons which take them as *presumptive disclosure* of IMV but not as ultimate 'moral truth'. For instance, Birch's example of focusing rocks in a situation of sportive climbing wasn't convincing to me as a genuine deontic experience. Taking rocks, river flows, stormy waters, snow fields and the like into close account in situations of hiking or sailing entails a sense of 'respect' for nature which, to my own intuitions, is clearly non-moral.[13] This rejection opens a common debate about how to interpret such 'deep' experiences with nature. The experiences of observing dying fleas under the microscope (Arne Naess), facing a dying wolf in a situation of hunting (Aldo Leopold) and perceiving a herd of hippopotamuses in an African river at sunset (Albert Schweitzer) are more appealing to my own intuitions as being deontic ones. They clearly support sentientism and zoocentrism. The experience of 'healthy' land in Northern Mexico (Aldo Leopold) supports, in any case, practical holism, but it might also support ecocentrism.[14]

Those touchstones, in addition to moral intuitions and to the two patterns of reasoning given in the previous section, can be used on both routes in order to reach a reflective equilibrium in our moral belief system. Before walking the two routes, here comes a checklist of our problem-solving equipment:

- intuitions;
- applicability of well-established moral rules to certain beings;
- applicability of a broadly defined notion of interest to certain beings;
- the thought experiment of the 'last person';
- interpretations of 'saving dilemmas'; and
- stories about deontic experience with nature.

TAKING THE ROUTE FROM INSIDE

Let us start 'from inside' with the famous Kantian argument in favour of human dignity ('*Würde*', '*Selbstzweck*'), which is equated with inherent moral value by Kant. Kant's argument supposes the categorical imperative (CI). To Kant, the CI is the one and only 'matter' which has dignity in itself. IMV is derivative to the CI. Humans, taken as natural beings, have no dignity. Only if humans are taken as moral persons are they supposed to be free and autonomous beings, since freedom is *ratio essendi* of morality, while morality is *ratio cognoscendi* of freedom. Autonomy is moral freedom. Fulfilling preferences, natural inclinations and desires can never make humans free since they stem from external stimuli. Only because humans are, in principle, capable of making use of the CI by asking themselves whether their maxims are suited to found common moral and legal institutions, are they persons and, as such, beyond the causal chain of nature.

Only because persons have access to the realm of moral reasoning do they participate, as moral agents, in the dignity of the CI. Thus, according to pure practical reason, the notion of dignity can be applied only to reasonable beings (*Vernunftwesen*). This seems to be incompatible with any solution to the IMV problem except rigid anthropocentrism.

In his '*Metaphysik der Sitten*' (Tugendlehre, §17), Kant addresses the problems of destroying natural beauty and of how to treat sentient animals. As it is well known, Kant argues that destructiveness against natural beauty and cruelty against sentient animals is morally wrong since it affects the moral character of persons for worse (the so-called '*Verrohungs*' argument). Barantzke (2006) has, in a fine and balanced analysis, argued that Kant's argument does not rest on questionable psychological assumptions. A non-cruel treatment of animals is a perfect moral obligation that a moral person has against himself. A non-cruel treatment of animals rests, in daily life, on sentiments such as empathy and gratefulness, but it should be regarded as a binding obligation against oneself in ethics. Nevertheless, the argument remains, in the end, anthropocentric. Decisive for Kant's anthropocentrism is his claim in the previous paragraph (§16) that anybody who believes that there are moral obligations with respect to non-humans commits a fallacy similar to the amphibolies in the *Kritik der reinen Vernunft*. This argument deserves close attention with regard to the IMV problem. If it fails, the route 'from inside' is viable in a Kantian paradigm of ethics. If this is the case, Kantians are not restricted to Kant's anthropocentrism.

Kant opens §16, saying that, according to pure practical reason ('*nach der bloßen Vernunft zu urteilen*'), humans have moral duties only with respect to fellow humans or other reasonable beings (if there are any). Given Kant's premises, this is true. Any argument in favour of moral duties against natural beings cannot rest on *pure* practical reason. But why should it rest on pure reason? Why not give more leeway to arguments which are 'impure' since they rest on some assumptions a posteriori. At this point, Kant argues that any idea ('*Vorstellung*') to have a moral duty against non-human beings must rest on an amphiboly. In his *Kritik der reinen Vernunft*, Kant defines an amphiboly as confusion between the transcendental and the empirical use of reason. Kant's argument against obligations towards natural beings is a *non sequitur*. If an argument in favour of moral duties against natural beings must be 'impure', and if conceptual amphibolies might occur in the field of theoretical reason, it does not follow that any such impure argument in ethics must rest on confusion.

One is entitled to speculate about Kant's profound motivation to remain on anthropocentric grounds. At the end of transcendental analysis, Kant makes use of a metaphor. To Kant, the 'land of pure reason' (*Land des reinen Verstandes*) is an island which is surrounded by a vast and stormy ocean where fog and melting ice suggest land where there is none. Transcendental analysis has mapped this island and, by doing so, contributed to its overall security against the ocean outside. Kant warns us against embarking upon the ocean and he recommends that, before embarkation, one should consider closely whether one should better remain safely on the well-established island of reason. This fear of embarking onto the ocean (*der Sitz des Scheins*) might be in the background of Kant's unwillingness to accept 'impure' arguments in favour of obligations against natural beings. Kant warns us against but he does not prohibit such embarkation. Kant himself didn't embark. He felt comfortable and safe with his argument in §17.

This being accepted, an argument in favour of a non-anthropocentric solution of the IMV problem is still within reach as being an impure but unconfused argument about morally relevant features of natural beings (according to formula (2)). Such an argument should not deny or reject Kant's transcendental argument in favour of the dignity of moral agents. If this is accepted, Kantians can endorse morally relevant features which are not sufficient for attributing dignity, but are sufficient for IMV. If this argument is sound, the way 'from inside' has been opened beyond anthropocentrism. This is of paramount relevance to discourse ethics (see next section).

This solution comes at a price. In a Kantian paradigm, one has to divide the moral community into subclasses: (a) moral agents with dignity, (b) human beings without (actual or potential) personhood, and (c) non-human beings having morally relevant features. In subclasses (b) and (c), the problem occurs that personhood and such features might come in degree. Obviously, this opens a sphere of conflicts within the MC and a field of conflicts and weighing between protective goods and members of (b) and (c). Whether a Kantian can sacrifice a human foetus for a masterpiece of art remains open. The price of this solution seems acceptable since any environmental ethics needs a basic conception for conflict resolution which can meet different types of conflicts.

DISCOURSE ETHICS AND THE DEMARCATION PROBLEM

Angelika Krebs has argued that discourse ethics is committed to anthropocentrism. Krebs relies on an anthropocentric definition of morality given by Habermas (1986). At a closer look on the overall argument, Habermas gave this definition from an evolutionary-anthropological perspective. From this *genealogical* perspective, the essential function of morals is to protect the overall integrity of vulnerable human beings. Krebs downplays the genealogical perspective and concludes from the definition itself that discourse ethics won't find any pathway out of anthropocentrism. To me, Habermas's genealogical definition of morals was never intended to be the final comment of discourse ethics to the demarcation problem. As we know from Hegel, origins should not be identified with final solutions. In my own writings (Ott, 1998a), I propose to

draw a distinction between the core of discourse ethics and a set of applications which constitute a concept of morality. The IMV problem does not belong to the theoretical core but to this set of applications. The core of discourse ethics has to be justified by reflexive (transcendental) arguments. In the field of applications, different patterns of argumentation can be used to solve specific moral problems. There is no requirement that arguments that refer to the IMV problem must be transcendental ones. Thus the core of discourse ethics is compatible with non-anthropocentric solutions of the IMV problem.

Habermas himself has modified his position in recent years. At the end of his *Erläuterungen zur Diskursethik* (1991), he argues that cruelty against animals is, by intuition, morally wrong and that humans can interact with higher animals in ways that have moral implications. He also argues that aesthetic experiences can make us aware of the *Unantastbarkeit* ('being sacrosanct') of natural beings. In some aesthetic experiences, parts of nature disclosure themselves as if we should keep our hands off and treat them with care and respect. Such 'strong' aesthetic experiences seem to come close to deontic ones. To Kantians, the problem remains whether such closeness rests on confusion between morals and aesthetics.[15] Habermas leaves this open.

In his *Zukunft der menschlichen Natur*, which deals with bioethical issues, Habermas argues that autopoietic systems, as organisms, deserve a caring treatment (2001, p83). The closer an organism comes to the human life-form, the more there emerges empathy with the vulnerability of organisms and a certain kind of respect. To Habermas, this morally relevant empathy has its roots in the sensitivity of the human body. This pattern of argument comes close to some reverence for life.

The discourse ethicist Micha Werner (2003, pp54–77) has presented a nuanced argument to overcome anthropocentrism which I present in a nutshell: if persons agree in discourse that they should treat each other with care and respect even if some of them should lose all the features that are constitutive for personhood but remain sentient, then there are no valid moral reasons to treat natural beings which are sentient, but will never become persons, without that care and respect. If one agrees with this argument (as I do), the question remains open whether it can be extended to biocentrism. Why shouldn't persons make a similar agreement for such cases which might be unable to experience pleasure or pain, but are alive and able to perceive something. Under such an agreement, Werner's argument holds for all living beings which have, to use a Whiteheadian term, prehensions.[16]

To sum up, it is a myth that discourse ethics is committed to anthropocentrism. Discourse ethicists have come close to the edge of biocentrism. Expressiveness and having prehensions are perceived as candidates for morally relevant features. Moreover, the route from inside still remains open beyond this solution. Discourse ethicists are willing to check reasons that justify the attribution of IMV to species, ecosystems or physical entities. Discourse ethicists can also 'change horses' and take the other route.

TAKING THE ROUTE FROM OUTSIDE

The viability of the Kantian route beyond anthropocentrism has been demonstrated. Thus the second route should not be less viable than the first one. Let's imagine now that moral persons who have accepted the arguments of the previous sections are now taking the route 'from outside'. Let us assume these persons are adopting a perspective of universal consideration (UC), as has been proposed by Thomas Birch (1993). They also adopt a spirit of generosity as a general attitude which allows all natural entities to disclose of their genuine values, if there are any, to moral agents. UC is a relationship between humans and natural beings. UC supposes a moral sense on the side of the human *and* a potential for value-disclosure on the side of natural beings. I can hardly imagine such disclosure without some ontological involvement. Therefore, UC must take into account the ontological distinctiveness of different natural beings. This implies that UC presupposes a richly textured ontology right from the start. Resulting from UC, specific proper attitudes towards different kinds of being are emerging, such as awe, aesthetic appreciation, cultural significance and moral respect.

These people adopt Birch's distinction between universal consideration and moral considerability. UC does not imply that one has to attribute IMV to each and every being. These moral agents are familiar with the IMV problem. Thus, they are, on the one hand, somewhat sceptical about criteria for IMV, since criteria *might* be biased or arbitrarily chosen. On the other hand, they keep the general analysis in mind (see 'Analysis' section above). Thus they do not overlook the crucial distinction between logical and moral discrimination and they are aware of conceptual confusions between 'fascination', 'appreciation', 'awe', 'reverence' and 'moral respect'. Contrary to Birch, these persons do *not* suppose that (a) any criterion must be mistaken, that (b) the demarcation problem must be 'kept open' (for how long?) or that (c) there are different (equally satisfying?) solutions at different times and places (which implies cultural relativism). Those suppositions undermine the search for a solution and cast doubts on the viability of the second route. The route from outside is a freeway if moral persons perform UC by going all the way down together, exchanging reasons, stories and experiences. Such common UC will, in any case, deepen our relationships with nature. But performing UC can (and even should) sharpen our sensibilities with regard to the attribution of IMV.

The way from outside can be more rigidly conceived than Birch did (Gorke, 2003 and 2007). To Gorke, moral persons, first, have to take the 'route from outside'. This (presumptive) way starts with an ethical holist's basic claim that 'all beings have equal IMV until convincing reasons allow for an exclusion of certain beings'. An initial *burden of proof* falls on persons who wish to exclude beings from the MC. Whoever wishes to deny the basic proposition must justify against its proponent that he or she is not reasoning arbitrarily.[17] Any criterion whatsoever can be said to be arbitrary. The meta-ethical *prima facie* principle by which arbitrariness is to be judged is *ontological parsimony*. Gorke claims that this principle is fair as a rule of discourse about the IMV problem. I remain sceptical on this point, because the principle is not balanced by other principles and is specified to the following decisive rule: 'the less parsimonious, the more arbitrary'. Under this rule, any substantial reason looks more arbitrary than the holists claim.[18] To me, this looks more like a well-built trap than a viable pathway. Thus I can endorse the UC way, but I do not wish to be trapped. If a way is not viable at all then there is no such way. Thus, I prefer the UC route.[19]

As we go together all the way down performing UC, we face, first, the problem of whether it is legitimate to exclude *technical devices* from the MC.[20] Checking common intuitions against our equipment (see 'Problem-Solving in Ethics' section above), the following result seems about to emerge: Would we really mind if the last person destroyed some artefacts? If someone saved their PC with all their data instead of a sentient animal, should they apologize? Personally, I cannot remember a deontic experience with technical devices. In my writings on an ethics of technology, I have argued against pseudo-moral attitudes towards the technical sphere (Ott, 2005a, p639). Non-living technical artefacts have no interests which have to be considered. No moral norm can be applied to them. Thus the exclusion of technical artefacts from the moral community seems well justified.[21]

Going further, the persons face natural entities such as sand, rocks, feathers, bones, exuviae, fallen leaves, animal hairs or feathers. Why shouldn't we argue that, say, a fallen leaf does not own any morally relevant features? Again we can make use of our tool-kit. Moral persons would not blame the last person for crushing fallen leaves. They would not perceive any conflict in saving situations (one living bird against many fallen leaves). Stories that include deontic experiences with such entities are rarely to be found and should be interpreted with scrutiny. All things considered, the persons would hold that such entities should be excluded from the MC.[22] The same results hold, or so I wish to claim, for genes and organs such as kidneys.[23]

At the next step, we face nested *biotic communities*, which are dubbed 'natural wholes', 'ecosystems' or simply 'land'. Attributing IMV to natural wholes is by no means trivial.[24] Ecosystems are entities that are partly constructed by scientists and are partly real nested entities. In some ecosystems, such as mires, the reality aspect seems to dominate, while in other systems, such as meadows and grasslands, the constructive aspect seems to be decisive. Both aspects change by degree. Morally relevant features, if there are any, have to be found in the reality aspect of ecosystems, since features of epistemic models seem to be morally irrelevant.

It is open for debate whether Aldo Leopold himself has proposed ecocentrism. Callicott argued in his *Triangular Affair* that Leopold's famous prescription – 'A thing is right if it tends to preserve the integrity, stability and beauty of the biotic community. It is wrong when it tends otherwise.' – should be taken as a supreme moral principle (1980, p320). Later, Callicott revised his original ecocentric approach into a concentric-circle model which is not *ecocentric* at all any more and comes, in his practical consequences, close to practical holism (Callicott, 1987). New readings suggest that Leopold restricted this prescription to the context of land use and nature conservation (Meine, 1988 and 2004). Restricted to questions of sustainable land-use strategies, the Leopoldian principle is quite appropriate and doesn't face the threat of ecofascism. Therefore a Leopoldian land ethics could be based also on practical holism and strong sustainability.

Johnson's (1991) overall argument to justify ecocentrism supposes (a) that a distinction between 'strong' and 'weak' interests can be made, (b) that organisms have weak interests, (c) that weak interests are sufficient for the attribution of IMV, and (d) that ecosystems can be paralleled with symbiotic life-forms. The first premise is quite reasonable: a 'strong' interest requires that a being itself takes an interest in something; a 'weak' interest requires that it can be claimed that something is or is not in the interest of a being (for example water is in the interest of a plant). The concept of weak interest has been adopted as a pattern which may bridge the gap between empirical features and IMV (see 'Analysis' section above). Even (b) seems acceptable. The ethical claim (c), that weak interests are sufficient for IMV, already implies biocentrism. Taking the route from inside, we have reached the edge of biocentrism, but biocentrism has not been adopted yet. The next step, (d), is biologically contested. To Johnson, lichens are 'something like a small closely knit ecosystem' (1991, p163). This claim has been stated by Tehler (1996, p217) thus: 'Lichens are not organisms. Lichens are small ecosystems.' But Tehler's claim has been rejected by Schöller (1997, pp69ff), who argues that the organic aspects in lichens are predominant. For the time being,[25] I adopt Schöller's point of view, rejecting the crucial assumption (d) which paves Johnson's pathway to eco-interests. If one wishes to defend Johnson's argument, all steps except (a) deserve a closer look. If we cannot suppose biocentrism, the overall argument fails right from the start.

LIFE AS FOCAL MEETING POINT AND ZOOCENTRISM
AS A NEW OPTION

The Kantian and discourse-ethicist route has reached the edge of biocentrism while the route from outside has reached the same edge. The first and the second routes meet at ontological concepts like 'teleological structure' (Taylor, 1986), 'representational goals' (Agar, 2001) or, as Whiteheadians would say, 'having prehensions', and at the ethical concept of weak interests. If this is the case, biocentrism seems a focal meeting point from both routes. If so, Frankena (1979) underestimated biocentrism. Biocentrism is open for hypothetical investigation, since no route implies a commitment to biocentrism so far. If such hypothetical reasoning does not result in an agreement, Kantians can restrict themselves to sentientism while ecocentrics can search for arguments in favour of morally relevant features of natural wholes (such as, perhaps, 'ecosystem health').

This focal point of life is highly complex in itself ontologically, reaching from animals to plants, fungi, bacteria and – at the edge of life – viruses. We can distinguish ontological subclasses according to the vast biological kingdoms. Biocentrism claims that all living beings belong to the MC, irrespective of to which kingdom of life they belong. Biocentrism has been always conceived as an 'all-or-nothing' approach. Why not think of reasons and criteria that draw a distinction inside the realm of life that is not the distinction being made by sentientism?

Ethical justifications for biocentrism are given in Schweitzer (1923), Taylor (1986) and Agar (2001).[26] Schweitzer's concept of reverence (*Ehrfurcht*) for life is ambiguous because it mixes up fascination, awe and moral respect under a religious and even mystical framework. To Schweitzer, life, as phenomenon, is a kind of mysterious wonder which biological science is unable to explain. The attitude of awe is appropriate to the wonderful phenomenon called 'life'. Schweitzer closes the remaining gap between awe and moral respect by suggesting that awe requires reverence, and reverence entails moral respect. At this gap, there is either a *non sequitur* or conceptual confusion (Ott, 2005c, pp63ff).

Paul Taylor's biocentric outlook is one worldview among many. Personally, I find this worldview neither convincing nor appealing.[27] And to the question of whether one should choose this outlook for epistemic reasons, I would suggest the answer is no. On the one hand, in Taylor's situation of ideal decision-making between competing worldviews, the only decisive criterion for choosing the biocentric outlook is the criterion of 'reality awareness' (1986, pp164–166). On the other hand, reality awareness is a crucial part of the biocentric outlook itself (1986, p120). If it is taken as the decisive criterion, Taylor's reasoning is circular (or begging the question).

Once upon a time, I made an insufficient attempt to argue in favour of the moral relevance of teleological structures (Ott, 1993), following Hans Jonas's *Organismus und Freiheit* (1973). In the face of sharp criticism (Krebs, 2000), I adopted Krebs' dichotomy between (a) genuine teleology, which is restricted to actions and intentions, and (b) functional teleology, which is morally irrelevant.[28] Thus, I regarded sentientism a satisfying solution of the IMV problem. Since I wished to leave some room for the many biophilic and, perhaps, biocentric intuitions about teleonomic, autopoietic and negentropic structures, I endorsed the solution Jon Wetlesen (1999) proposed. To Wetlesen, biocentric attitudes can be part of a concept of self-esteem. Under such a concept, the borderlines between biophilic and biocentric attitudes might remain fuzzy. 'Deep' environmental humanism in combination with biophilic/biocentric attitudes, practical holism and (gradual) sentientism seemed to me a satisfying position in environmental ethics.[29]

The question remains whether the distinction between genuine and functional teleology is a complete dichotomy implying *tertium non datur*. If it is not, third options remain within reach. Therefore concepts such as 'prehension', 'representational goal' or 'biopreference' (Agar, 2001) might perhaps replace the 'classical' teleological argument.[30] Such replacement could modify the extension of the MC beyond sentientism. Consider now the very difference between higher animals (even spiders, ants and beetles) and other forms of life. Higher animals are 'centred' or 'centralized' in ways plants and fungi are not.[31] This organization makes such animals aware of the events in their surroundings. The performance of such animals against their environment is completely different to plants' reactions. Such experiencing awareness can be dubbed 'prehension'.[32] A position that argues that IMV should be attributed to all prehensive animals can be dubbed 'zoocentrism'.[33]

Let us hypothetically test this unfamiliar position. Under this position, the last person should not voluntarily kill beetles or ants. All other things being equal, one should save a beehive instead of a piece of grassland. My personal deontic experience goes as follows. Hiking in some remote Swedish woods, I was considering the IMV problem and suddenly wondered why I should draw the line of moral considerability between the sentient small frogs on the one hand and the many ants, spiders, bees and dragonflies on the other. Why should it be morally wrong to kill the frog but morally permissible to kill spiders, ants and dragonflies?

Prehensions can be claimed as being sufficient for having interests. It is, in some ways, bad for prehensive beings themselves if they are killed. There is harm being prehended even if there might be epistemic doubts whether there is pain being felt. If, for instance, a beetle or a flea is drowned in poisonous chemicals, it shows strong reactions of being harmed. The moral rule of not harming others applies. Moreover, zoocentrism could be brought into a reflective equilibrium with recent developments in discourse ethics (see 'Discourse Ethics and the Demarcation Problem' section above).[34] I do *not* claim that zoocentrism *is* the final solution of the IMV problem. At the moment, it is nothing but a hypothesis that I wish to entertain further. If it fails, returning to sentientism is an easy and safe step back to Kantians. Returning to biocentrism is a step back on the route from outside. Probably, other environmental ethicists will not agree with this hypothesis but will consider closely the idea that the line of moral considerability should be drawn somewhere inside the kingdom of life.[35] I won't mind taking a closer look into the kingdom of life.

ACKNOWLEDGEMENTS

Thanks to Tanja von Egan-Krieger, Workineh Kelbessa Golga, Martin Gorke, Mitja Hörning, Barbara Muraca and Laura Westra for helpful comments.

NOTES

1 Recent 'green' interpretations of Nietzsche's (politically dangerous) concept of *Übermensch* are, interestingly enough, very close to such virtues (DelCaro, 2004). See my comment on Cafaro's book (Ott, 2005b).

2 Having been a member of the German Environmental Advisory Council from 2000 to 2008, most of my ideas, objectives and strategies in environmental policymaking are to be found in the reports of the council at www.umweltrat.de.

3 To Hare, Singer and other utilitarians, sentience has always been the clear cut-off point of moral considerability. See Hare (1987).

4 'As they (sentient beings) share something of our nature through the sensitivity with which they are endowed, one will judge that they too ought to participate in natural right, and that man is subject to some sort of duties towards them.' (Second Discourse, quoted in Lane and Clark, 2006, p67).

5 There are, for instance, consequentialist biocentric approaches (R. Attfield) and right-based approaches of sentientism (T. Regan). I wish to leave all variants aside for a moment in order to focus on the core of the IMV problem.

6 If so, all ethicists that presume to contribute to the demarcation problem *ipso facto* subscribe to some rules of sound argumentation.

7 Each category constitutes a class of beings which might be divided into subclasses according to more specific distinctions.

8 If one dislikes such weighting of protective goods, one can define a certain subclass of 'first-order high rank goods' which are protected against weighing. Niagara, the Grand Canyon, biodiversity hotspots, the Great Barrier Reef and other places could, or so I hope, fall in this class.

9 My overall approach clearly rests on a cognitivistic discourse-oriented approach in meta-ethics which is neither 'subjectivistic' nor 'objectivistic'. I neither rely solely on intuitions nor do I believe in moral facts.

10 Birch, sometimes, seems to equate logical and moral discrimination. This equation is warranted by Birch by some background assumptions about the imperialistic project of civilization which I don't find very convincing.

11 This also implies that nobody can look as a future historian onto our contemporary moral debates in environmental ethics, already 'knowing' that a moral evolution is driving us towards ethical holism.

12 Walzer (1987) distinguishes the ethical methods of discovery, invention and interpretation. This distinction does not seem of much help with regard to the IMV problem. I leave those methods aside. Some helpful remarks about the method of ethical enquiry are to be found in Brennan (1977), especially Part II.

13 Wiggins (2000, p26) has argued rightly that this sense of respect means that nature is, in such cases, a dangerous force to be reckoned with.

14 For closer analysis of the concepts of ecosystem health, see the contributions in the special issue of *Environmental Values* (1995, vol 4, no 4). To me, 'ecosystem health' is a metaphor which can be analysed under a concept of resilience. One should not take the metaphor literally.

15 As I have argued elsewhere, closeness is different from confusion (Ott, 1998b).

16 The concept of prehension should be understood as 'being aware'. There might be, as in beetles, ants or spiders, basic kinds of awareness without sentient feelings. Thanks to Barbara Muraca for clarifying this point.

17 Arbitrariness is taken as a manifestation of an egoistic attitude which is incompatible with the moral point of view.

18 Ontological parsimony is not a criterion of moral truth and, therefore, should not work as such a criterion in an ethical theory.

19 The method of a phenomenology of nature (Böhme, 1997) can be applied to UC.

20 Gorke includes devices in the MC, since exclusion would rest on an arbitrary criterion that makes a distinction between natural and artificial beings. Since the distinction between the natural and the artificial comes in degrees in our culturally shaped landscapes and in the murky realm of 'bio-facts' (Karafyllis, 2003), the exclusion of some hybrid beings (such as genetically modified plants) would be arbitrary. And, eventually, everything is made of some natural stuff and thus participates in the IMV of material existence. Thus, on the first layer of ethical holism, plastic spoons and pieces of toilet paper have equal IMV as persons.

21 From the perspective of practical holism, there are many sound reasons why humans should restrict themselves in transforming natural beings into technical artefacts or energy resources. We should, for instance, restrict cutting woods for producing paper.

22 This, of course, leaves open many ways to protect beautiful rock formations, collect feathers, enjoy playing with sand on the shore, and the like.

23 In this chapter, I remain silent on the moral status of species. This problem needs another paper, or even a book.

24 Sometimes it is argued that ecocentrism is an approach in environmental ethics which is more close to ecological science than, say, sentientism. If one takes a closer look at recent developments in ecology which cast doubts on concepts like stability or equilibrium, one becomes critical about this claim.

25 As a philosopher, I cannot resolve this controversy about the ontological status of lichens.

26 I remain silent on Nicholas Agar's sophisticated biocentric approach, which requires close reading and comment.

27 It is beyond the scope of this chapter to explicate this claim more closely with regard (a) to the concept of freedom that unites humans and other living beings to a 'community of life on Earth' and (b) to the rejection of human superiority which rests on the concept of 'judgements of merit'.

28 To argue that functional teleology is a morally relevant feature would face a *reductio*, because functional teleology can be found in technical devices.

29 This stance even allows for the claim that there is prelingual expressiveness in living beings. In certain ways, natural beings articulate themselves. But, as Vogel (2006) rightly argues, those kinds of expressive articulation are not part of discourse. At the very best, interpretation might be possible.

30 Agar's method, if not his result, is well compatible with such a solution: we look for features which can be 'properly described by conceptual descendants of our ancient value-anchoring theory' (Agar, 2001, pp96–97). Agar himself seems sceptical about biocentrism in the case of micro-organisms.

31 A classical phenomenological analysis has been given by Plessner in his *Die Stufen des Organischen und der Mensch* (1927).

32 Such basic awareness is not synonymous with sentience, which requires a system of nerves. Prehensions are more than reactions to biochemical signals, which can be found also in plants, but they do not presuppose consciousness (as sentience does).

33 This option emerged in recent debates with Tanja von Egan-Krieger, Barbara Muraca and Lieske Voget. The original idea is theirs.

34 Such zoocentric position would pay the Kantian price of dividing the MC into subcategories: (1) persons, (2) humans devoid of personhood, (3) sentient animals and (4) prehensive animals. The broad category of protective goods supplements this interpretation of the MC.

35 At this point, Agar's concept of representational goals and the Whiteheadian concept of prehensions should be compared. See Agar (1995).

REFERENCES

Agar, N. (1995) 'Valuing species and valuing individuals', *Environmental Ethics*, vol 17, no 4, pp397–415

Agar, N. (2001) *Life's Intrinsic Value*, Columbia University Press, New York

Barantzke, H. (2006) 'Tierethik, Tiernatur und Moralanthropologie im Kontext von §17, Tugendlehre', *Kant-Studien*, vol 96, no 3, pp336–363

Birch, T. (1993) 'Moral considerability and universal consideration', *Environmental Ethics*, vol 15, no 4, pp313–332

Böhme, G. (1997) 'Phänomenologie der Natur – Ein Projekt', in G. Böhme and G. Schiemann (eds) *Phänomenologie der Natur*, Suhrkamp, Frankfurt, Germany, pp11–43

Brennan, J. M. (1977) *The Open-Texture of Moral Concepts*, Macmillan Press, London

Butler, W. F. and Acott, T. G. (2007) 'An inquiry concerning the acceptance of intrinsic values theories in nature', *Environmental Values*, vol 16, no 2, pp149–168

Callicott, B. (1980) 'Animal liberation: A triangular affair', *Environmental Ethics*, vol 2, no 4, pp311–338

Callicott, B. (1987) 'The conceptual foundations of the land ethic', in B. Callicott (ed) *Companion to a Sand County Almanac*, University of Wisconsin Press, Madison, WI, pp186–220

Carter, A. (2004) 'Projectism and the last person argument', *American Philosophical Quarterly*, vol 41, no 1, pp51–61

DelCaro, A. (2004) *Grounding the Nietzsche Rhetoric of Earth*, DeGruyter, Berlin

Frankena, W. K. (1979) 'Ethics and the environment', in K. E. Goodpaster and K. M. Sayre (eds) *Ethics and Problems of the 21st Century*, University of Notre Dame Press, Notre Dame, IN, pp21–35

Gert, B. (1966) *The Moral Rules*, Harper and Row, New York

Gorke, M. (2003) *The Death of our Planet Species*, Island Press, Washington, DC

Gorke, M. (2007) *Eigenwert der Natur*, Habilitation Thesis, University of Greifswald, Greifswald, Germany

Habermas, J. (1986) 'Moralität und Sittlichkeit', in W. Kuhlmann (ed) *Moralität und Sittlichkeit*, Suhrkamp, Frankfurt, Germany, pp16–37

Habermas, J. (1991) *Erläuterungen zur Diskursethik*, Suhrkamp, Frankfurt, Germany

Habermas, J. (2001) *Die Zukunft der menschlichen Natur*, Suhrkamp, Frankfurt, Germany

Hare, R. M. (1987) 'Moral reasoning about the environment', *Journal of Applied Philosophy*, vol 4, no 1, pp3–14

Johnson, L. E. (1991) *A Morally Deep World*, Cambridge University Press, Cambridge, UK

Jonas, H. (1973) *Organismus und Freiheit*, Vandenhoeck and Ruprecht, Göttingen, Germany

Lane, J. H. and Clark, R. (2006) 'The solitary walker in the political world: The Paradoxes of Rousseau and deep ecology', *Political Theory*, vol 34, no 1, pp62–93

Karafyllis, N. (2003) 'Das Wesen der Biofakte', in N. Karafyllis (ed) *Biofakte*, Mentis, Paderborn, Germany, pp11–26

Krebs, A. (2000) 'Das teleologische Argument in der Naturethik', in K. Ott and M. Gorke (eds) *Spektrum der Umweltethik*, Metropolis, Marburg, Germany, pp67–80

Meine, C. (1988) *Aldo Leopold: His Life and Work*, University of Wisconsin Press, Madison, WI

Meine, C. (2004) *Correction Lines: Essays on Land, Leopold, and Conservation*, Island Press, Washington, DC

Michael, M. (1997) 'Environmental egalitarianism and "Who do you save?" dilemmas', *Environmental Values*, vol 6, pp307–325

Morito, B. (2003) 'Intrinsic value: A modern albatross for the ecological approach', *Environmental Values*, vol 12, pp317–336

Naess, A. (1989) *Ecology, Community and Lifestyle*, Cambridge University Press, Cambridge, UK

Norton, B.G. (1991) *Toward Unity among Environmentalists*, Oxford University Press, Oxford

Ott, K. (1993) *Ökologie and Ethic*, Attempto Verlag, Tübingen, Germany

Ott, K. (1998a) 'Über den Theoriekern und einige intendierte Anwendungen der Diskursethik', *Zeitschrift für philosophische Forschung*, vol 52, no 2, pp268–291

Ott, K. (1998b) 'Naturästhetik, Umweltethik, Ökologie und Landschaftsbewertung', in W. Theobald (ed) *Integrative Umweltbewertung*, Springer, Berlin, pp221–246

Ott, K. (2005a) 'Technik und Ethik', in J. Nida-Rümelin (ed) *Angewandte Ethik*, Kröner, Stuttgart, Germany, pp568–647

Ott, K. (2005b) 'On taming Nietzsche for environmental ethics', *Nietzsche-Studien*, vol 34, pp441–457

Ott, K. (2005c) 'Ehrfurcht vor dem Leben und "grüne" Gentechnik – Versuch einer Verhältnisbestimmung', in G. Schüz (ed) *Leben nach Maß – Zwischen Machbarkeit und Unantastbarkeit*, Lang, Frankfurt, Germany, pp55–73

Ott, K. and Döring, R. (2004) *Theorie und Praxis starker Nachhaltigkeit*, Metropolis, Marburg, Germany

Plessner, H. (1927) *Die Stufen des Organischen und der Mensch*, DeGruyter, Berlin

Routley, R. (1973) 'Is there a need for a new, an environmental ethics?', in Bulgarian Organizing Committee (ed) *Proceedings of the XVth World Congress of Philosophy*, Sophia Press, Sophia, Bulgaria

Schöller, H. (1997) *Flechten*, Senckenberg, Frankfurt, Germany

Schweitzer, A. (1923) *Kultur und Ethik*, Beksche Verlagsbuchhandlung, Munich

Sober, E. (1995) 'Philosophical problems for environmentalism', in R. Elliott (ed) *Environmental Ethics*, Oxford University Press, Oxford, UK

Taylor, P. (1986) *Respect for Nature*, Princeton University Press, Princeton, NJ

Tehler, A (1996) 'Systematics, phylogeny and classification', in T. H. Nash (ed) *Lichen Biology*, Cambridge University Press, Cambridge, UK, pp217–239

Varner, G. (1998) *In Nature's Interest?*, Oxford University Press, New York

Vogel, S. (2006) 'The silence of nature', *Environmental Values*, vol 15, pp145–171

Walzer, M. (1987) *Interpretation and Social Criticism*, Harvard University Press, Cambridge, MA

Warren, M. A. (1997) *Moral Status*, Clarendon, Oxford, UK

Werner, M. (2003) *Diskursethik als Maximenethik*, Königshausen and Neumann, Würzburg, Germany

Westra, L. (1994) *The Principle of Integrity*, Rowman and Littlefield, Lanham, MD

Westra, L. (1998) *Living in Integrity*, Rowman and Littlefield, Lanham, MD

Wetlesen, J. (1999) 'The moral status of beings who are not persons: A casuistic argument', *Environmental Value*, vol 8, pp287–323

Wiggins, D. (2000) 'Nature, respect for nature and the human scale of values', *Proceedings of the Aristotelian Society*, New Series, vol C, part 1, pp1–32

4

The Earth Charter, Ethics
and Global Governance

Brendan Mackey

BACKGROUND

We stand at a critical moment in Earth's history, a time when humanity must choose its future. As the world becomes increasingly interdependent and fragile, the future at once holds great peril and great promise ... The choice is ours: form a global partnership to care for Earth and one another or risk the destruction of ourselves and the diversity of life. Fundamental changes are needed in our values, institutions and ways of living. (The Earth Charter, Preamble)

The Earth Charter is not alone in expressing deep concern about the state of Earth's environment, the connectedness of our ecological, social and economic challenges, and the need for global reform in support of a more just, sustainable and peaceful world.

There has been a plethora of international ethical statements and commitments over the last decade or so in relation to issues of environment and development. Examples include the Rio Declaration (UN, 1992a), the World Summit on Sustainable Development Political Declaration UN, 2002), and the various ethical principles (such as the precautionary principle) contained within legal instruments such as the United Nations Framework Convention on Climate Change (UN, 1992b). Given this, what is the added value to global governance of a civil society document such as the Earth Charter?

The relevance of the Earth Charter is further challenged by the prevailing geo-political situation. Multilateralism appears on the wane as the guiding principle of international relations. National self-interest is apparently on the ascendancy and threatens to reverse the remarkable progress made in redefining international relations since the formation of the United Nations. Yet the globalization of human endeavour continues unabated, with all its intended and unintended consequences. Economic globalization is proceeding largely unfettered by environmental and social responsibilities. International affairs are increasingly dominated by militaristic responses, at least on the part of some national governments. A lack of international cooperation is evident in the area of environment and sustainable development, as witnessed by the failure of the 2002 World Summit on Sustainable Development to agree on targets and timetables for meeting commitments made at the 1992 Rio Earth Summit.

From an environmental and social justice perspective, current world trends are deeply worrying and point to the need for a significant improvement in global governance. The Millennium Ecosystem Assessment reports (MEA, 2005) provide rigorous scientific assessments of the extent to which current patterns of production, consumption and reproduction are ecologically unsustainable. The UN Millennium Development Goals (UN, 2000) provide a clear reminder of the extent of human deprivation in the world today and that poverty alleviation remains our greatest human development challenge. Global governance is needed that promotes a balance between, among other things:

- the legitimate rights of nations to self-determination and to safeguard national self-interest;
- the benefits that flow from efficient economic systems;
- the need to maintain environmental life-support systems and stem the loss of natural heritage values and traditional human–nature relations; and
- the imperative obligation to alleviate poverty and provide all with life's essentials.

The Earth Charter can play a vital role in advancing the global governance structures, instruments and processes needed to secure a more just, sustainable and peaceful world. The case in support of this claim hinges on the proposition that if global governance is to advance, there must be a global moral community that calls for and supports the next generation of global governance mechanisms. There needs to be a strong international community of people in all regions and cultures of the world that seek to have their national interests balanced with a commitment to the wellbeing and security of all. The root causes of global insecurity are now so interconnected that this commitment must be comprehensive and extend to future generations and other life-forms with whom we share Earth as home.

There are four reasons why the Earth Charter can contribute to this critical task of building the necessary global moral community in support of advancing global governance for a more just, sustainable and peaceful world: first, the Charter's inclusive drafting process and subsequent uptake; second, the Charter's explicit attempt to link personal ethics with public ethics; third, the increasing currency given to the primacy of values in national and international affairs; and fourth, the prominence given in the Charter to the ecological integrity imperative.

DRAFTING PROCESS AND UPTAKE

The Charter's capacity to influence global reform processes is a function of the validity of its claim to be a world ethic of shared values and universal principles. In addition to the validity of this claim in theory, Dower (1998) argued that for a world ethic to be a social reality its values and principles need to be accepted by a significant number of actors in the world and established in influential international organizations. The evidence in support of the Earth Charter's claim to be a valid world ethic can be found in both the story of its drafting and its subsequent uptake and applications. A brief review of the Earth Charter's history is therefore necessary (see also ECIS, 2006).

The Earth Charter was conceived in a recommendation from the report of the World Commission on Environment and Development, *Our Common Future* (WCED, 1987), and born out of disappointment with the compromised ethical vision of the Rio Declaration from the 1992 Earth Summit. To advance the idea of a 'people's' Earth Charter, a group of eminent civil society leaders were invited to form an Earth Charter Commission and a small secretariat created in Costa Rica with assistance from the Dutch and Costa Rica Governments. An international drafting team was formed, chaired by Steven Rockefeller, at the time Professor of Religion at Middlebury College in the US. However, the final authority for the text lay with the Earth Charter Commission.

The drafting process involved three main stages. First, a review was made of values and principles articulated in existing international treaties and declarations such as the Rio Declaration and universal ethical declarations such as the World Charter for Nature (UN, 1982). A draft charter was then examined at the 1997 Rio+5 non-governmental organization (NGO) meeting attended by around 500 civil society representatives. The text was extensively revised from these consultations to produce 'Benchmark Draft II'.

The Earth Charter Commission then embarked upon an ambitious global consultation process to give the document the broadest possible exposure. Over the next four years the document was considered by groups from different sectors in over 40 countries, along with regional consultations. In parallel, international meetings of various expert groups considered drafts of the document. The Charter was redrafted dozens of times in response to the incoming recommendations and comments received from all regions of the world. The global consultation process ended when the Commission launched the Charter in a special event at the Hague Peace Palace in 2000.

The Earth Charter's values and principles are organized around the four pillars of 'respect and care for the community of life', 'ecological integrity', 'social and economic justice', and 'democracy, non-violence and peace'. These four major themes contain 16 major and 61 supporting principles, which are preceded by an introductory section, the Preamble, which summarizes the document, and are followed by a concluding comment called 'The Way Forward'. The document can be found online at www.earthcharter.org.

Since the Earth Charter was launched, an international initiative has developed, facilitated by the secretariat in Costa Rica. The Charter has been endorsed by around 14,000 organizations, along with some national governments (for example Mexico). The Earth Charter has been used in various educational programmes in many of the world's regions and formed the basis of a Type II educational partnership at the 2002 World Summit on Sustainable Development. The Charter has been endorsed by UNESCO and the International Council for Local Environmental Initiatives (ICLEI), among others with an international dimension (ECIS, 2003).

The Earth Charter has been presented and debated at numerous international conferences, for example the 2004 IUCN Bangkok World Conservation Congress. In November 2005 a major international conference was held in Amsterdam, sponsored by The Netherlands Government called Earth Charter +5. An extensive literature now exists about the Earth Charter which pays further testimony to its international reach (ECIS, 2004; Corcoran et al, 2005).

LINKING PRIVATE AND PUBLIC ETHICS

The second argument in support of the Earth Charter's potential to influence global governance is the link it provides between private and public ethics. Previous international ethical declarations, such as the World Charter for Nature and the Rio Declaration, were drafted and negotiated as government-to-government documents, identifying the principles to be followed by and the responsibilities of national governments. However, a characteristic of the global sustainability challenge is the diversity of agents in all sectors and at all levels who must be involved – as sustainability is everyone's business. In addition to the advocacy of international organizations, modern electronic communications is facilitating the connectivity between local and national organizations on global governance issues. Individuals and communities are better informed about globalization and are more able to network in order to advocate reform.

The intergovernmental nature of documents like the Rio Declaration dictates their format and language, and limits their relevance to non-national governmental agents. But declarations of shared values and principles are needed with a purpose, format and language relevant to individuals and organizations, as well as governments at all levels. The Earth Charter was specifically drafted as a 'peoples' charter' rather than an intergovernmental agreement. The Charter does not specify who is responsible for giving effect to each principle. While some might think this feature of the document a limitation, it has the advantage of making the Charter relevant to everyone in every sector.

VALUES AND PUBLIC POLICY

The third reason for the Earth Charter's role in global governance reform processes is based on the proposition that it provides a vehicle to address a major impediment to sustainability, namely the clash of value systems and the lack of a share ethical framework for their peaceful resolution.

The rise of the political influence of neo-conservative political agendas in the US has revived public debate about values, their cultural basis and their role in public policy. Lakoff (2005) argued that neo-conservative values are defined by a specific set of reinforcing views on, *inter alia*, economics, government, education, nature, regulation, rights, democracy and foreign policy. More liberal-minded politicians and voters have been taken by surprise by the explicit reference to value systems of neo-conservative political parties and their success at the electoral ballots.

The success of neo-conservative politics in the US has spilt over into other conservative governments, such as that of Australia, where similar 'values wars' are now being argued in the public domain. For example, Peter Costello, the Australian Treasurer under the previous government led by John Howard, was reported as saying in a speech that 'radical Muslims needed to assimilate and accept Australian values, or move to another country' (NINEMSN, 2006). The use of 'values' language has now become commonplace in Australian politics. Where neo-conservative-influenced governments are winning the values war it is not because they have more powerful logic or better-constructed arguments. Rather, it is because they have succeeded in reframing the political debates in terms of their values system.

The influence of neo-conservative values on global governance can be seen in a shift in foreign policy and strategy as many nations retreat from universal multilateral negotiations. International agreements between select nations are being negotiated outside the UN system. For example, the Australian Government under Howard refused to ratify the Kyoto Protocol it helped negotiate under the UN Framework Convention on Climate Change (UNFCCC). Rather, it negotiated with US and selected governments a global climate change agreement outside the UNFCCC, the Asia-Pacific Partnership on Clean Development and Climate (McKibbin, 2005).

The philosophical basis for a rejection of universal multilateralism lies in the concepts that:

1 The nation state is the only valid foundation of culture, values, moral responsibility and law.
2 The responsibility of governments is to their citizens and not to citizens of other nation states (nor non-human life).
3 The only loyalty their citizens can possess is to their nation state (Dower, 1998).

Neo-conservatives argue that we have gone too far down the road of global governance, as human culture and values are grounded within the nation state. From this perspective, there is no global society, culture and morality, and therefore no social reality that can be used to justify global ethics and strong democratic global governance mechanisms.

The cosmopolitan ethic of the Earth Charter is based on a different worldview to that of the neo-conservatives (which reflects an extreme libertarian dogmatism). However, it is important to stress that the Earth Charter ethic is not an anti-free-market ethic. Rather, it explicitly recognizes the positive contributions of markets, calling for market corrections of various kinds such as internalizing the full social and environmental costs of production in the price of goods and services. Nor is the Earth Charter in any way 'anti-personal freedoms'; quite the opposite, as it expands upon and champions universal individual rights. However, it does present the view that personal liberties, while necessary, are insufficient to bring about the global conditions necessary for the flourishing of human wellbeing and life generally. Personal freedoms can only flourish in a supporting social and ecological environment where global obligations are recognized and the need accepted for collaboration to address shared problems.

THE ECOLOGICAL INTEGRITY IMPERATIVE

The fourth argument in support of the Earth Charter's potential international influence stems from the extent its ethic draws upon a scientific perspective of ecological integrity. It is only since the 1972 Stockholm UN Conference on the Human Environment that global environmental concerns have been on the international policy agenda (UNEP, 1972). That meeting also set a precedent for the use of scientific-based information about the state of the global environment to inform dialogue and negotiations around international agreements.

Modern, industrialized societies have an odd relationship with science. On the one hand, people are happy to enjoy the material benefits that flow from technological innovations. New technologies are generally now adopted without question and few pause to query the science underpinning their development and ongoing operation. So long as the product delivers the desired service, the scientific understanding upon which the technology is based is taken for granted. We travel around Earth's atmosphere strapped inside metal cigar-shaped jets, kilometres high, at mind-boggling speeds, without doubting for one second the physics of flight and aero-engineering.

However, a different attitude emerges when application of the same scientific methodology provides information challenging the status quo and confronting people with uncomfortable facts about the state of Earth's environment and the impact of human activities. Evidence of severe global environmental degradation is dismissed as inconclusive, and the messenger declared an emotive scaremonger.

Nonetheless, there is now a raft of authoritative scientific assessments of the state of Earth's environment and life-support systems (MEA, 2005; WMO-UNEP, 2006). Indeed, the world's nations have in recent years acknowledged the significance of the situation and signed various international treaties concerning climate change, loss of biodiversity and desertification (UN, 1992b; CBD-UNEP, 1992; UN, 1994). However, deep political scepticism remains about the scientifically based urgency of the ecological imperative faced by humanity.

Perhaps the scepticism around scientific environmental assessments partly reflects ignorance. Contemporary scientific understanding about the co-evolution of Earth's life-support systems has yet to be integrated into educational curricula at any level – with only a handful of courses dealing with such themes evident at the university level. Indeed, many people still deny biological evolution, let alone scientific understanding of cosmology. Consequently, there is a general level of ignorance about the scientific basis to human–nature relations, the dependency of human health and wellbeing on the continued functioning of natural processes, and the capacity of human endeavour to alter global environmental conditions.

In drafting the Earth Charter ethic, in particular the 'ecological integrity' theme of Section II, scientific-based understanding about the Earth system and associated ecological and evolutionary processes were drawn upon in the formulation of its values and principles. Scientific-based understanding can profoundly alter our perception of the world and our place in it. How humans value the natural environment is influenced by scientific understanding of Earth's life-support systems. Knowledge about the ongoing process of biological evolution and the origins of the human species affects how we perceive and value other species. Meeting the challenges of global governance in the 21st century demands a world ethic that is informed by the realities of our ecological situation. The Earth Charter is uniquely placed in this respect.

WHY THE EARTH CHARTER MAY FAIL

I have suggested four reasons why the Earth Charter can contribute to global governance reform. However, all four arguments can be challenged in ways that could cause the Earth Charter to fail to meet its potential.

Regarding the first argument, while the Earth Charter has achieved considerable international recognition, there is a long road to travel before the Earth Charter ethic can claim to be a significant influence on the value systems dominating global governance. A useful analogy is the Universal Declaration of Human Rights (UN, 1948), which after 60 years has now reached a point where its ethic does significantly influence national and international policies and programmes. Herein lies a guide to the long-term effort needed before the Earth Charter can substantiate its claim to be a global social reality.

The second reason can also be challenged, as there are critics who reject the Charter's ethic on philosophical grounds, either with respect to specific principles or *in toto*. The Earth Charter ethic calls for, among other things, restraint in consumerist lifestyles and a recommitment to the UN Charter and non-violent means (for example Principle 16c: 'Demilitarize national security systems to the level of a non-provocative defence posture, and convert military resources to peaceful purposes, including ecological restoration'). The Charter challenges policies that promote uni- and bilateral approaches ahead of multilateralism in addressing global problems. Consequently, we can predict that governments of a neo-conservative persuasion may be predisposed to view the Earth Charter with scepticism. In any case, many national governments will remain cynical about the role of ethics in international relations, accepting them only up to the point where they are useful and convenient. National defence advisers will no doubt continue to promote foreign policy that assumes an ongoing state of 'war readiness' (Machiavelli, 1531; Hobbes, 1651; Dower, 1998).

Those of an anarchistic philosophical persuasion may view any mechanism related to 'global governance' with great suspicion, and see initiatives like the Earth Charter as merely reinforcing the existing flawed system and therefore being part of the problem. Critical postmodernists may also be suspicious of documents like the Earth Charter that attempt to articulate universal perspectives on the grounds that however well intended such documents are, they will inevitably reflect dominant, Western values at the expense of local cultural diversity. The Earth Charter could also be dismissed by deep green (Naess, 1989) environmentalists as being too human-focused. Conversely, social justice advocates may find the Charter's attempt to couple human and nature concerns as unhelpful. Pragmatic civil society members, hardened by years of activism in international forums, may agree with the Charter's values and principles but dismiss the Earth Charter on the basis that the 'era of declarations' has come and gone, and more time should not be wasted on such things which merely serve to divert scarce resources from more urgent and practical problems.

Perhaps the critics are right and we have already gone too far down the path of globalization and more action is needed at the local community level. Is the only necessary principle that of subsidiarity? Has not the era of declarations passed and the priority now shifted to realpolitik and reaching agreement with achievable concrete targets and time lines? Why focus on even more unenforceable (para)legal instruments when there is scope to implement innovative market-based approaches? In any case, why should the international community take any notice of a civil society declaration like the Earth Charter?

The above criticisms and concerns illustrate the point that there are many philosophical and practical impediments to the Earth Charter being substantially accepted across sectors and being broadly embraced as a universal world ethic linking civil society and governments at all levels together with business and industry.

CONCLUSION AND RECOMMENDATIONS

Perhaps we should not expect too much from a world ethic produced by a civil society initiative. On the other hand, the Earth Charter remains a compelling concept and its text a commendable attempt at an integrated world ethic. Even if the Charter's future as a social reality is limited, it will be for many an aspirational document and a checklist of what remains to be achieved in all sectors and at all levels of government towards a more just, sustainable and peaceful world.

It is hard to predict the future of global governance. International relations may simply continue to stagger forth as they have for the last few years, to varying extents involving and being guided by UN-related processes. Non-multilateral agreements are of concern if they are at the expense of strengthening the United Nations. This is the course promoted by the Earth Charter in its concluding section, 'The Way Forward':

> *In order to build a sustainable global community, the nations of the world must renew their commitment to the United Nations, fulfil their obligations under existing international agreements, and support the implementation of Earth Charter principles with an international legally binding instrument on environment and development.*

To advance global governance, the values system upon which the current political realities are built must change. As a 'cosmopolitan' ethic, the Earth Charter does not seek to replace the diversity of values in different cultures with a new 'mono-ethic'. Rather, as a cosmopolitan ethic it articulates shared values and principles that coexist with more culturally specific values. A critical mass is needed of people in nations throughout the world who have integrated into their value systems the principles of world ethics such as those articulated in the Earth Charter. When this happens, there will be a strong global moral community whose worldview acknowledges universal obligations to promote the flourishing of the entire community of life and the equitable sharing of the good things of life for present and future generations. This global moral community will demand the democratic and just global governance mechanisms needed to protect and advance these shared values and universal obligations.

Of course, we have the foundations of global society, world ethics and international law in the great work the UN has promoted since the end of World War II, together with the efforts of earlier endeavours such as the International Labour Organization (ILO, 1919). But the next generation of global governance mechanisms is now needed to meet the challenges of the 21st century. In the long term, the growth of a global moral community which respects diversity and includes all life and future generations in the sphere of its moral concerns is an essential prerequisite and foundation for global governance reform.

In the short term, the Earth Charter can continue to serve as a source of para-legal principles for national governments to draw upon when drafting and negotiating new global governance mechanisms. Specifically, the Earth Charter could be used as a reference document for negotiation of a new UN-based international legally binding instrument on environment and development. Finally, the use of the Earth Charter in formal and informal education will remain a fundamentally important and ongoing contribution to the global reform process.

REFERENCES

CBD-UNEP (1992) 'The Convention on Biological Diversity', Convention on Biological Diversity and United Nations Environment Programme, www.biodiv.org/default.shtml, accessed 3 March 2006

Corcoran, P. B., Vilela, M. and Roerink, A. (eds) (2005) *Toward a Sustainable World: The Earth Charter in Action*, Kit Publishers, Amsterdam

Dower, N. (1998) *World Ethics – The New Agenda*, Edinburgh University Press, Edinburgh

ECIS (2003) 'Earth Charter Initiative Biannual Report 2002–2003', Earth Charter International Secretariat, San Jose, Costa Rica, www.earthcharter.org/files/resources/Biannual%20Report.pdf, accessed 3 March 2006

ECIS (2004) 'Selected bibliography of books, essays, papers, magazines and newsletters related to the Earth Charter', compiled by Claire Wilson and Betty McDermott, Earth Charter International Secretariat, San Jose, Costa Rica, www.earthcharter.org/Files/Resources/ Bibliography2.Pdf, accessed 3 March 2006

ECIS (2006) 'The Earth Charter Handbook', Earth Charter International Secretariat, San Jose, Costa Rica, www.earthcharter.org/resources/index.cfm?pagina=categories_display.cfm&id_category=79, accessed 23 February 2006

Hobbes, T. (1651) *Leviathan*, 1963 edition edited by R. Tuck, Cambridge University Press, Cambridge, UK

ILO (1919) 'International Labour Organization', www.ilo.org/, accessed 3 March 2006

Lakoff, G. (2005) *Don't Think of an Elephant*, Scribe Publications, Carlton North, Australia

Machiavelli, N. (1531) 'Discourses', cited in P. Bondanelli and M. Musa Harmondsworth (eds) (1979) *The Portable Machiavelli*, Penguin Books, London

McKibbin, W. (2005) 'Climate pact a good beginning', *Australian Financial Review*, 1 August

MEA (2005) 'Reports of the Millennium Ecosystem Assessment', various reports available at www.millenniumassessment.org/en/index.aspx, accessed 23 February 2006

Naess, A. (1989) *Ecology, Community and Lifestyle*, Cambridge University Press, Cambridge, UK

NINEMSN (2006) 'Don't ostracize hardline Muslims: Abbott', NINEMSN News, 27 February 2006, http://news.ninemsn.com.au/article.aspx?id=88387, accessed 3 March 2006

UN (1948) 'Universal Declaration of Human Rights', United Nations Organization, www.un.org/Overview/rights.html, accessed 3 March 2006

UN (1982) 'World Charter for Nature', United Nations Organization, www.un.org/documents/ga/res/37/a37r007.htm, accessed 3 March 2006

UN (1992a) 'Rio Declaration on Environment and Development', report of the United Nations Conference on Environment and Development, Rio de Janeiro, 3–14 June 1992, Annex I, United Nations Organization, www.un.org/cyberschoolbus/peace/earthsummit.htm, accessed 3 March 2006

UN (1992b) 'United Nations Framework Convention on Climate Change', United Nations Organization, http://unfccc.int/2860.php, accessed 3 March 2006

UN (1994) 'United Nations Convention to Combat Desertification', United Nations Organization, www.unccd.int/, accessed 3 March 2006

UN (2000) 'Millennium Development Goals', United Nations Organization, www.un.org/millenniumgoals/, accessed 3 March 2006

UN (2002) 'From our Origins to the Future: Johannesburg Declaration on Sustainable Development', World Summit on Sustainable Development, Johannesburg, United Nations Organization, www.un.org/esa/sustdev/documents/WSSD_POI_PD/English/POI_PD.htm, accessed 5 March 2006

UNEP (1972) 'Report of the United Nations Conference on the Human Environment, Stockholm 1972', United Nations Environmental Programme, www.unep.org/Documents.multilingual/Default.asp?DocumentID=97&ArticleID=, accessed 3 March 2006

WCED (1987) *Our Common Future*, report of the World Commission on Environment and Development, Oxford University Press, Oxford, UK

WMO-UNEP (2006) 'Intergovernmental Panel on Climate Change', World Meteorological Organizations and United Nations Environment Programme, www.ipcc.ch/, accessed 3 March 2006

5

Ecological Integrity as an Emergent Global Public Good

P. J. Crabbé and J. P. Manno

INTRODUCTION

Globalization has meant opening markets worldwide to free trade in goods and services. Cross-border transactions also involve investment, travel, communication, entertainment, insurance, migration and more. However, not all interactions among economic agents go through the market and deal with goods and services. As market interactions increase globally, unintended non-market interactions among economic agents, externalities in economic parlance, increase *pari passu*. These externalities can be positive or negative or both according to the issues. The goods and services involved in these externalities may be intangible and are then more of the nature of conditions, such as enhanced security. For example, the quasi-universal availability of banking machines improves travel security around the planet but, at the same time, increases the level of global travel, which may have negative environmental effects. Avian flu, a negative externality (it is not transmitted through market transactions), has worldwide relevance; so has the quasi-eradication of smallpox, a positive externality. Economic development increases opportunities while accelerating the burning of fossil fuels and the build-up of the concentration of greenhouse gases in the atmosphere. Many risks increase with globalization. For example, the decline of biodiversity worldwide leaves us more exposed to diseases, whether affecting plants, animals or humans. Security issues, whether financial or environmental health- or conflict-related, are global but cannot be resolved through markets or through markets alone. Neither the costs nor the benefits of externalities are reflected in the prices or profits of market transactions. The speed at which these non-market interactions occur has also greatly increased. We need policies and non-market institutions to complement the markets and manage these externalities issues in a timely fashion through preference-revealing and political bargaining not only for efficiency but also for fairness. If the scale of these externalities can be managed, those affected most by them should have a say in their regulation and provision according to the principle of subsidiarity or of fiscal equivalence. The principle of subsidiarity means that regulations and actions should be implemented at the lowest level of administration possible, presumably closest to the citizens concerned, in other words the stakeholders. The principle of fiscal equivalence says that those who benefit from the externalities should be the ones who contribute the resources needed for their management (Kaul and Mendoza, 2003). Numerous international institutions have been created to handle externalities, including heightened risks. Many more institutions are on their way.

A public good shares many economic properties with positive externalities, but a public good is typically recognized as such and policies are adopted to encourage a deliberate level of provision. The question investigated in this chapter is whether ecological integrity, as an emergent property of an ecosystem, is a public good and, in the affirmative, to what extent policies can influence its provision. If ecological integrity is a public good, and one that has been in decline in critical ecosystems around the world, then deliberate mechanisms, cooperative or incentive-compatible, are required to provide the conditions necessary for its protection and restoration. Some public goods are intentionally created to enhance the opportunities and reduce the risks associated with globalization. These include systems of communication and finance and governance institutions, systems of negotiation and decision-making deliberately created to regulate and enhance the flow of market goods and services worldwide that, through economic, social and political positive feedback, further increase the global flow of market goods and services. Examples are international and non-governmental organizations such as the World Trade Organization (WTO), the International Monetary Fund (IMF), the Intergovernmental Panel on Climate Change (IPCC) and the International Union for the Conservation of Nature (IUCN). These institutions are often set up for the purpose of managing and allocating global public goods (and bads), whether or not their leaders and participants see their mission in those terms. Many of them are designed to address the harms associated with globalization. This is particularly true of global environmental institutions whose mission is to protect and restore public goods associated with the global commons, the Earth's oceans, atmosphere and hydrological cycle, whose conditions determine the habitability of the planet. For the past 15 years, the Global Ecological Integrity Group (GEIG) has been grappling with the question of the relationship between ecological integrity and human habitability (see, for example, Crabbé, 2000; McMichael and Kovats, 2000; Miller and Ehnes, 2000; Pimentel et al, 2000).

Ecological integrity is an ecosystem property, in other words a property of the entire ecosystem or of the system structure of ecosystem relations which is not shared by its components. Ecological integrity is an emergent property of a self-organizing ecosystem, in other words a property that spontaneously connects its macro-properties with its micro-properties. For example, the resilience of the forest as a macro-property may be connected with the age composition of the forest component tree species, a micro-property.

The questions investigated in this chapter are: whether ecological integrity, as an emergent property of a complex system, should be considered a global public good; how scientific knowledge of the state of ecosystem integrity affects how and how much it is valued; and whether being a global public good enhances the protection of ecological integrity or whether it places it further at risk. The answer to the final question depends on the relationship between the goods (private or public) provided by ecosystem components (for example water, timber or whales) and the ones provided by the ecosystem services. If the benefits provided by the whole (ecological integrity and other emergent properties and associated services) exceed the benefits of the parts (natural resource products), ecological integrity has a better chance of remaining intact (of being provided at a sufficient level), unless the benefits provided by the parts are private ones while the benefits of the whole are public and not supported economically and politically by policy. Those interested in protecting and restoring integrity can learn from how some global public goods are effectively provided by institutions and policies while others are not. How does the fact that a global public good is also an emergent property of systems have an impact on its provisioning? What policies need to be put in place to protect and sustain ecological integrity?

ECOLOGICAL INTEGRITY AS AN EMERGENT PROPERTY OF A COMPLEX SYSTEM AND AS A GLOBAL PUBLIC GOOD

Ecosystems are complex dynamic systems whose component variables interact non-linearly across a range of spatio-temporal scales and which are subject to stochastic disturbances such as climate variability (Chee, 2004). Humans benefit from ecosystems through the latter's goods and services. Ecological goods and services are the conditions (intangible goods and services such as resilience, health, ecological integrity and biodiversity) and processes through which natural ecosystems and the species that compose them sustain and fulfil human life (Daily, 1997). These conditions and processes encompass the delivery, provision, production, protection and maintenance of these goods and services (Daily, 1997). They impact the provision of inputs to production processes and human welfare either directly or indirectly through the regulation of natural processes (Nunes and van den Bergh, 2001). Ecological goods and services are economically valued by their total economic value, i.e. the sum of their use value (direct benefits), non-use value (indirect benefits) and existence value. Because ecosystem goods and services may be interdependent, economic valuation may lead to sub-additivity (leading to double counting by counting essentially the same service twice) or super-additivity (as an outcome of services' and processes' interaction, a form of emergent value, a value assigned to the system structure, independently of the value of its components and their addition) (Chee, 2004).

Ecological integrity is defined here, following Karr and Dudley (1981), as 'the capacity of an ecosystem to support and maintain a balanced, integrated, adaptive community of organisms having a species composition, diversity and functional organization comparable to that of similar, undisturbed ecosystems in the region' (cited in Carignan and Villard, 2002). Ecological integrity, like resilience and, sometimes, biodiversity, is a concept that applies to an entire ecosystem; it is, therefore, a system property. It is a difficult abstract concept, still little understood (Nunes and van den Bergh, 2001). This system property is called 'emergent' if it relates spontaneously the system components (their micro-properties) to the system macro-properties. It is an abstract concept that can be associated with a wide range of benefits to society. For example, a leaf from a tree may not have the property of ecological integrity, while an entire forest can. This does not mean that the leaf cannot have some form of integrity (without which it is no longer a leaf), but it cannot have ecological integrity unless one characterizes a leaf as an ecosystem in its own right (i.e. including its insect population and its predators).[1] As another example, resilience, as a macro-property of an ecosystem, say a forest, is the outcome of the arrangements of and interactions among the micro-properties of its ecosystem components, say trees, shrubs, fauna and so forth. Resilience is the capacity of a system to maintain its characteristic patterns, structures, function and rates of processes despite perturbations (Carignan and Villard, 2002).

Biodiversity, on the other hand, can be defined as a property of the component species of an ecosystem, for example species richness or the diversity function, or by a property of the ecosystem, for example species evenness, the distribution of species, which is an emergent property. Heal calls biodiversity a commodity because it provides utility directly (Heal, 2004).[2] Biodiversity provides or enhances ecosystem productivity, insurance, knowledge and ecosystem services. Brock's measure of biodiversity as 'the value of characteristics or services that an ecosystem provides or enhances when managed optimally' is an emergent property as well (Brock and Xepapadeas, 2003). If resilience is positively correlated with biodiversity, valuing biodiversity is a proxy for valuing resilience. If biodiversity is affected by an environmental driver, it is on the environmental driver one should focus attention, in particular if the driver is subject to management, for example in the case of water (Knowler, 2007). Biodiversity value arises from the total of values arising from species and genetic diversity, values associated with natural areas and landscape diversity, benefits from ecosystem functions, and non-use values stemming from biodiversity.

An emergent property of a system often, but not always, has the economic properties of a public good if it is considered valuable by economic agents.[3] A forest, for example, may have greater economic value than the sum of the values of its components if it is a resilient ecosystem endowed with many interdependent ecological services (timber, wildlife, water and nutrient storage, etc)[4] (Chee, 2004). Often this greater economic value will be apparent to society as a whole, but not to an individual who is unable to appropriate it, in other words to exclude others from its benefits (see Costanza et al, 1997; UNEP, 2005); moreover, to have the property of 'pure' public good, the emergent property must be 'non-rival' in consumption, thus my enjoyment or appreciation of the integrity of an ecosystem and its associated services should not diminish their availability to others at zero cost, in other words it is not exhaustible. Some ecosystem services, such as the carbon sequestration of a forest, are neither excludable nor exhaustible. I am unable to exclude anybody from the benefits of carbon sequestration; the benefit I derive from carbon sequestration does not impinge upon – is non-rival with – its consumption by others. This is precisely the definition of a pure public good: a good or service which is neither excludable nor exhaustible. Since this property is available to everybody on the planet and all generations, one can therefore rightly speak of it as a global public good (Kaul et al, 1999). On the other hand, some ecological functions of the forest, such as timber provision, are excludable and rival in consumption. Ecological integrity is, therefore, a macro-combination of inter-related public and private ecological goods and services, many of which are themselves public goods that interact with other ecosystems, providing what economists call externalities if these interactions affect human beings positively or negatively. Ecological integrity is, therefore, a public good. It is the (super-additive) compact of private and public ecological goods and services. To put it in ethical terms, ecological integrity has a good of its own, which is not reducible to the sum of the benefits derived from its ecological goods and services.[5] The features of a public good are largely institutionally determined because these, non-exclusivity, for example, depend upon specific definitions and allocations of property rights and the perceived value and availability of the good or service. For example, elementary school education is not rival in consumption when it is available to all but becomes rival when it is not (Kaul and Mendoza, 2003).

Since an individual will be expected to underestimate the value of a public good, pure public goods are not good candidates for production or supply by private firms or individuals, who are unable to charge a price for them. In the case of global public goods, a similar argument may be made for countries as economic actors, as well as for private firms or individuals. Since the private sector (or collection of sovereignties) may underestimate the social value of (global) pure public goods, the former will produce or supply too little of the good for the benefit of (global) society. Therefore (global) pure public goods ought to be supplied by governments (or international institutions) that have the ability to charge taxes to pay for the provision of the public good, for example to pay for conservation measures and other measures to protect and restore ecological integrity (Davies and Slivinski, 2005). International institutions do not have taxation power, however. Therefore, individual countries acting in consort with others in international agreements will necessarily be responsible for the provision of environmental public goods, most significantly ecological integrity.

This is not the whole story, though, because the level of provision of public goods depends upon people's preferences for many other public goods, such as security, public health and financial stability, and because, in democratic societies, the level of provision of a public good depends upon political bargaining. This applies in the international sphere as well.

SCIENTIFIC ASSESSMENT OF ECOLOGICAL INTEGRITY

Ecological integrity, in order to have economic value, must be known to exist in an ecosystem and, therefore, must be scientifically[6] assessed. The resulting scientific information, furthermore, must be made public. In other words, ecological integrity depends upon knowledge generation that is also endowed with public good features.

Considering how information about ecological integrity is also a public good, we can use the same logic to address how such information can best be provided. Information about ecological integrity may be generated by public authorities (for example the government) or by private ones (for example private universities or consulting firms). A government may contract out the scientific studies or produce them on its own; it may decide how much information to make public and to whom this information will be released and at what price. If the information is provided entirely privately, the question arises about whether this activity should be regulated (Davies and Slivinski, 2005).

Meteorological information is an example of scientific information that has private value: the government providing meteorological information is able to exclude people from accessing it by charging a price for it. However, the information remains inexhaustible: the information provided to my neighbour does not decrease the information available to me. Once the raw meteorological information is massaged into a service designed for a specific customer or category of customers (for example farmers), it remains inexhaustible but becomes excludable. Some people have argued that raw meteorological information should be nearly freely available to all because no private providers would be able to charge a price which allows them to recoup the large cost of production of meteorological information (large supercomputers, etc); the only price that could be charged would be the additional cost of dissemination of the information to an additional individual (for example paying for a hard copy of the forecast). Special groups of customers or firms provided with targeted information can be charged the price of massaging the information, since targeted information would not be worth producing if customers were not willing to pay for it (Davies and Slivinski, 2005). A group of customers or firms could derive a private benefit from knowing the state of ecological integrity of an ecosystem. This could take the form of existence value for individuals or of insurance for firms. Ecological integrity is, in some cases, a proxy for biodiversity or, more precisely, for the presence of an indicator species whose benefits can be appropriated. Organizations whose members value certain species, or those who harvest from the wild, are interested in protecting the ecological integrity that sustains certain habitats. There is at least one example of a private business – ICValue Inc., founded by Orie Loucks, an ecologist associated with the Global Ecological Integrity Project – that sells information to environmentally responsible individual investors and green investment firms about the impacts of corporate practices on ecosystem integrity (see www.icvalue.com/).

Scientific information, including information about ecological integrity, can be made available in the form of raw data, or the information can be processed and targeted for interpretation and use by specific customers. The provision of raw data is often a basic service provided by the government free of charge (except for the cost of dissemination to an additional customer), while the provision of processed information requires more specialized, value-added services for which a charge corresponding to the customer willingness to pay can be levied. Typically, the provision of public goods, such as environmental information, by private agents is insufficient because it is subject to a market failure: the benefits of the good or service cannot be captured by adding up the quantities of the good or service consumed and selecting the price to which this aggregate quantity corresponds on a market demand curve for the good or service in question. This is why pure public goods are provided by governments according to citizens' preferences and political bargaining. The provision of targeted information by a private company may lead to a natural monopoly if the unit cost of the information provided decreases with the amount of information provided.[7] Therefore, the private unregulated firm would be able to charge an inordinately high price to its customer (Davies and Slivinski, 2005).

Information about ecological integrity is valuable because it reduces collective risks, in other words it has insurance value. Knowing the state of ecological integrity of a given ecosystem, or for global ecological integrity as a whole, allows ecosystem users or governments to take appropriate actions which could protect or restore ecological integrity. Knowledge about the loss of integrity enables forecasts and the issuance of warnings about degraded future states of the ecosystem. These warnings are useful to specific users, who benefit from the ecosystem goods and services sustained by ecological integrity (Davies and Slivinski, 2005).

If raw data relevant for assessing ecological integrity is an intermediate good that is used in the production of targeted information, a price should be charged for the raw information corresponding to its opportunity cost. The opportunity cost is the total cost of producing the raw information if there is a single user. If there are several, the opportunity cost is the cost of dissemination since nobody can effectively be excluded from the information (Davies and Slivinski, 2005).

The consumption of public goods may also generate externalities, in other words may confer benefits or costs to other individuals. For example, knowing that the ecological integrity of an ecosystem has been degraded may induce people to move to another ecosystem, thereby increasing the value of the latter's services. These are called pecuniary externalities and do not affect the argument, since increasing the gains of producers decreases the welfare of consumers, each cancelling the other.

On the other hand, if knowing that an ecosystem has been degraded leads to me having to decrease my extraction activities from an ecosystem, this reduced activity benefits others, though the benefits are not necessarily equal to the cost I incurred by reducing my extractive activity. These are benefits that are not automatically compensated for by my losses. These are truly (technological) externalities. If a public good confers positive externalities, the provider may charge less for the public good or improve its quality to encourage its dissemination (Davies and Slivinski, 2005).

Raw data and processed information are not independent. The more data there is, the more valuable and the cheaper the targeted information because the latter becomes more reliable. In turn, the higher the demand for targeted information, the more raw data will be supplied since the latter has become more valuable. Targeted information does not have to be provided by private firms necessarily, even if they are more efficient than public firms in doing so, because there may exist economies of scope in providing jointly raw and processed information (it may be cheaper to do so) since the inputs are common to both types of firms (Davies and Slivinski, 2005).

The provision of information about ecological integrity may create problems related to the asymmetry of information. A farmer, having been informed by some government programme that his fields provide socially valuable ecosystem services, may have the incentive to exaggerate the cost of his unmonitored conservation measures (or 'best management practices') in order to obtain government compensation. This is called a moral hazard problem: the farmer has an incentive to distort the information he alone possesses. Moreover, if only farmers whose fields have been environmentally degraded are eligible for restoration subsidies, incentives may be created to allow ones' fields to degrade. This is called an adverse selection problem. Only the worse risks participate in the government programme.

Governments could provide forecasts about the state of ecological integrity of an ecosystem. If this forecast depends upon information privately owned by an individual, this individual may have an incentive not to reveal the information that the ecosystem is in poor state because a prospective buyer may attach much importance to ecological integrity (for example Nature Conservancy). If the information is inexpensive to acquire, only ecosystems with substantial ecological integrity will be acquired if the seller is not concerned about reputation. If the information is expensive to acquire, the buyer will take his chance and buy the available ecosystems, discarding the bad ones if he believes ecological integrity is a dominant feature. If he believes the reverse, no ecosystem will change hands. If reputation matters, the seller has a stronger incentive to hide the truth. If information is expensive to acquire, he may lie about the state of ecological integrity and the buyer may be unable to identify the state of ecological integrity (Stoneham, 2003; Sheriff and Osgood, 2007).

DOES THE QUALITY OF GLOBAL PUBLIC GOOD ENHANCE ECOLOGICAL INTEGRITY?

One problem with ecological integrity is that, though it has clear social value, there exists no current accepted means to measure it and express it, resulting in its perceived value being effectively rather low (Carignan and Villard, 2002; Antrobus and Law, 2005). One way to express the importance of ecosystems whose integrity remains largely intact is to protect them as special areas by granting them status as parks, usually though not always public. In these cases, their economic value is often enhanced by tourism. The emergence and growth of the ecotourism sector is one way that the economic value of ecosystem integrity has been able to be made manifest. Since biodiversity is often (although not always) positively correlated with ecological integrity, another approach to valuing integrity is to link it to efforts to value biological diversity and associated goods and services.

Ecological integrity provides at the same time ecosystem services, often public and distant, and natural resource products, usually private and local. It requires trade-offs between socially relevant but poorly known values and local ones, more easily appropriated, which can be better measured. The social value of ecological integrity may be best assessed scientifically and communicated both to the beneficiaries, which may be distant, even global, and locally to those most dependent on ecosystems to provide the resources for their livelihoods. The local values can then be enhanced by a levy (for example on ecotourism), which stands as a proxy for the social value of ecological integrity. Local incentives to protect ecological integrity would then amount to compensating local communities for their conservation efforts (Perrings and Gadgil, 2003). This requires establishing local property rights, whether private or communal or some mix of the two.

If a government would like private landowners to take measures to protect ecological integrity, it may subsidize them to do so. This subsidy may turn out to be expensive, because a private landowner might in any case undertake the measures without the subsidy or with a much lower one than the one being offered. It is therefore important, for a government that has a limited budget to devote to ecological integrity, to find out how much a landowner would be willing to devote to ecological integrity protection. A simple contingent valuation exercise will not do, since the landowner may have an incentive to lie about the true cost of the conservation measure on his land in the hope, for example, of receiving a subsidy which exceeds the cost of the measure (Chee, 2004). It is, therefore, important to design mechanisms such as certain types of auctions in which there is an incentive for the landowner not to lie. The landowners who bid the lowest price for the measure as compared with its environmental benefit would get the government subsidy for the environmental measure to be undertaken. Moreover, since shoring up ecological integrity requires a minimal area of land (for example a biosphere reserve), the mechanism requires that there be benefits in aggregation, in other words that neighbouring landowners have an incentive to bid the lowest price for the measure in such a way that it enjoys sufficient scale to protect ecological integrity. This is a recent subject of environmental economic research on institutional mechanisms (called reverse auctions) which lead private property owners to implement public goods on their land at minimum cost for the public purse (Stoneham, 2003). These institutional mechanisms can be tested in the laboratory and are the subject area of a field called experimental economics. Examples of application of this methodology can be found in the US in the Conestoga watershed in Pennsylvania for phosphorus; in Australia in the BushTender and EcoTender programmes in the state of Victoria for various environmental objectives, including biodiversity protection; and in Canada in the Pilot Emission Removals, Reductions and Learnings (PERRL) programme for greenhouse gas emission reduction (DAA Stratégies and CIRANO, 2007).

CONCLUSION

The social value of ecological integrity may be far higher than the value (or sum of values) of its components, but the only way to establish it is to assess it through scientific research and ensure that the information provided is targeted mainly to local users of the ecosystem, even if global public goods must be provided internationally by the principle of subsidiarity or fiscal equivalence. Yes, externalities, including increased risks, go hand-in-hand with globalization, but so does institutional cooperation, which determines ultimately which good is public and how much of it must be provided through preference-revealing and political bargaining in order to insure against these new risks. Their cost can be kept low by designing institutional mechanisms which are truth-revealing and provide incentives to protect ecological integrity at the scale required.

In conclusion, we have looked at the economic implications of ecological integrity as an emergent property of ecosystems, a macro-property fundamentally responsible for the continued provision of a number of critically important ecosystem services. Ecological integrity clearly meets the criteria of a global public good. And being a global public good, it will only be protected and restored through the deliberate development of global institutional mechanisms to create economic value through information and cost-effective compensation for local conservation. These will have the most likelihood of success if they are designed with full understanding of the dynamics of both emergent properties and global public goods within the appropriate institutional context.

NOTES

1   As is often the case in the systems approach, an emergent property depends very much on how the system considered is being defined.
2   See Brock and Xepapadeas (2003) for an overview.
3   All emergent properties are not necessarily global public goods, however. For example, a Pareto distribution is an emergent property of a whole slate of social system phenomena, but it is not a public good; it does not per se provide any benefit. Some global public goods, such as national security, are not necessarily emergent properties of a system, but are more like membranes, component parts of a system that function in biological systems to mediate relations with other systems and the external environment.
4   The pure theory of public goods determines that their allocation is optimal when the sum of the marginal willingness to pay for one more unit of the good equals the marginal cost of producing one more unit of the good. This is known as the Samuelson condition (Chee, 2004).
5   Some ecosystems may produce public bads as well, such as when the ecosystem is a hotbed of parasites such as vector-borne malaria (Perrings and Gadgil, 2003).
6   We use the word science broadly to encompass social sciences as well as soft system approaches.
7   This will occur if the production of targeted scientific information is capital-intensive.

REFERENCES

Antrobus, G. and Law, M. (2005) 'Towards an economic evaluation of biodiversity', www.iwlearn.net/abt_iwlearn/events/ouagadougou/readingfiles/essa-freshwater-valuation.pdf

Bar-Yam, Y. (2004) *Making Things Work*, Knowledge Press, Cambridge, MA

Brock, W. and Xepapadeas, A. (2003) 'Valuing biodiversity from an economic perspective: A unified economic, ecological and genetic approach', *American Economic Review*, vol 93, pp1597–1614

Carignan, V. and Villard, M. A. (2002) 'Selecting indicator species to monitor ecological integrity: A review', *Environmental Monitoring and Assessment*, vol 78, pp45–61

Chee, Y. E. (2004) 'An ecological perspective on the valuation of ecosystem services', *Biological Conservation*, vol 120, pp549–565

Costanza, R., d'Arge, R., de Groot, R., Farber, S., Grasso, M., Hannon, B., Limburg, K., Naeem, S., O'Neill, R. V., Paruelo, J., Raskin, R. G., Sutton, P. and van den Belt, M. (1997) 'The value of the world ecosystem services, *Nature*, vol 387, pp253–260

Crabbé, P. (2000) 'A complex systems approach to urban ecosystem integrity', in P. Crabbé, A. Holland, L. Ryszkowski and L. Westra (eds) *Implementing Ecological Integrity: Restoring Regional and Global Environmental and Human Health*, Kluwer, Dordrecht

DAA Stratégies and CIRANO (2007) *Utilisation des Enchères Inversées pour la Promotion de Pratiques de Gestion Environnementale sur les Terres Privées [Using Reverse Auctions for*

Promoting Best Environmental Practices on Private Lands], Environment Canada, Ottawa, Canada

Daily, G. (ed) (1997) *Nature Services: Societal Dependence on Natural Ecosystems*, Island Press, Washington, DC

Davies, J. B. and Slivinski, A. (2005) 'The public role in provision of scientific information: An economic approach', www.ssc.uwo.ca/economics/centres/epri/

Folke, C., Carpenter, S., Walker, B., Scheffer, M., Elmqvist, T., Gunderson, L. and Holling, C. S. (2004) 'Regime shifts, resilience and biodiversity in ecosystem management', *Annual Review of Ecology, Evolution and Systematics*, vol 35, pp557–581

Heal, G. (2004) 'Economics of biodiversity: An introduction', *Resource and Energy Economics*, vol 26, pp105–114

Karr, J. R. and Dudley, D. R. (1981) 'Ecological perspective on water quality goals', *Environmental Management*, vol 5, pp55–68

Kaul, I. and Mendoza, R. U. (2003) 'Advancing the concept of public goods', in I. Kaul, P. Conceiçao, K. Le Goulven and R. U. Mendoza (eds) *Providing Global Public Goods*, Oxford University Press, Oxford, UK, pp78–111

Kaul, I., Grunberg, I. and Stern, M. A. (eds) (1999) *Global Public Goods: International Cooperation in the 21st Century*, Oxford University Press, Oxford, UK

Knowler, D. (2007) 'Valuing ecosystem services associated with biodiversity in the black fly–livestock system of South Africa', paper presented at Ottawa Canadian Resources and Environmental Economics (CREE) Conference, October

McMichael, A. J. and Kovats, R. S. (2000) 'Strategies for assessing the health impacts of global environmental change', in P. Crabbé, A. Holland, L. Ryszkowski and L. Westra (eds) *Implementing Ecological Integrity: Restoring Regional and Global Environmental and Human Health*, Kluwer, Dordrecht

Miller, P. and Ehnes, J. W. (2000) 'Can Canadian approaches to sustainable forest management maintain ecological integrity?', in D. Pimentel, L. Westra and R. F. Noss (eds) *Ecological Integrity: Integrating Environment*, Island Press, Washington, DC

Nunes, P. A. and van den Bergh, J. C. (2001) 'Economic valuation of biodiversity: Sense or nonsense?', *Ecological Economics*, vol 39, pp203–222

Perrings, C. and Gadgil, M. (2003) 'Conserving biodiversity: Reconciling local and global public benefits', in I. Kaul, P. Conceiçao, K. Le Goulven and R. U. Mendoza (eds) *Providing Global Public Goods*, Oxford University Press, Oxford, UK, pp532–555

Pimentel, D., Westra, L. and Noss, R. F. (eds) (2000) *Ecological Integrity: Integrating Environment, Conservation, and Health,* Island Press, Washington, DC

Sheriff, G. and Osgood, D. (2007) 'Climate forecasts and livestock disease disclosure: A shepherd's dilemma', paper presented at Ottawa CREE Conference, October

Stoneham, G. (2003) 'Auctions for conservation contracts', *Australian Journal of Agricultural and Resources Economics*, vol 47, no 4, pp477–500

UNEP (2005) 'Millennium assessment', www.millenniumassessment.org/en/index.aspx

PART II

ECOLOGICAL INTEGRITY AND BIOLOGICAL INTEGRITY: THE INTERFACE

Introduction

Laura Westra and Klaus Bosselmann

James Karr discusses ecological integrity by referring to 'biological integrity'. Laura Westra, on the other hand, in her earlier work has distinguished biological from ecological integrity (Westra, 1994) and, later, 'macro-integrity' from 'micro-integrity' (Westra, 1998). The latter is intended to define ecosystem integrity, while the former refers to the integrity of the component parts of ecosystems, including human organisms.

Ecological integrity cannot persist, even in a wild area, if the plant and animal life whose habitat it is are affected by either pollution or climate change, or both, so that their interdependence is equally affected, and the ecosystem becomes incapable of providing the services it would otherwise provide.

Hence the arguments leading from ecological integrity to public health are more than the acknowledgement of the ad hoc results of disintegrity. Despite the possibility of protecting some organisms from the effects of disintegrity, at least temporarily, macro-integrity (the integrity of ecosystems) is necessary for micro-integrity (the health and normal function of all organisms that form part of the system). Conversely, unless the component parts of the system have normal function and each organism's integrity has not been altered or violated, that habitat itself cannot claim to possess integrity.

This part combines ecology and philosophy with public health through research with the scientists and the work of the WHO (Soskolne and Bertollini, 1999). Although Prue Taylor's main concern is not public health, her chapter on 'ecological human rights' provides both the rationale and the bridge for the passage from environmental ethics and ecology to law and governance.

Taylor reviews GEIG's contributions to finding the appropriate balance between 'rights' and 'responsibilities'. She shows how the initial focus on public health has shifted to a broader concept of ecological health, allowing a direct dialogue with environmental policy and law. The development of environmental law, at national and international levels, has always been accompanied by an ecological critique questioning its fragmented, anthropocentric design. From an ecological perspective, the human rights approach to environmental protection is important, but incomplete if not balanced with responsibilities. The emergence of environmental rights over the last 20 years clearly indicates a 'greening' of human rights. However, even more significant is the jurisprudential debate surrounding ecological limitations of human rights, in particular property rights.

In the next chapter, Colin Soskolne completes and justifies the movement from eco-integrity to public health. Eco-epidemiology is a term applied to ecological influences on human health. It is a sub-specialty of epidemiology, unifying molecular, social and population-based epidemiology in a multi-level application of methods aimed at identifying causes, categorizing risks and controlling public health problems. Soskolne emphasizes the importance of measuring health effects. Traditional epidemiological measures and indicators do not suffice: the story that emerges when either the wrong or not enough things are measured is counter-intuitive and does not support the findings of the WHO in 'Global ecological integrity and "sustainable development": Cornerstones of public health' (Soskolne and Bertollini, 1999). Hence, Soskolne argues for the need to expand and enrich the field of eco-epidemiology, to include more sensitive measures, and to extend that research to wider regional boundaries.

In the final chapter in this part, Beumer, Huynen and Martens discuss these issues in an overview that examines the historical understanding of humans in nature through various perspectives. The authors also emphasize the role of declining biodiversity, as the true 'canary in the mine', arguing that the increasing disappearance of keystone and other species should alert us to the fact that integrity is fast disappearing, and that the results can be observed in the increase of new (and returning 'older') infectious diseases and in the skyrocketing number of cancers and emotional and intellectual disabilities, as 'the world's ecosystems reach to the micro-levels of our physiological cells and of our cognitive and emotional condition'.

In addition, global change carries within it a strong element of injustice as, at least temporarily, the poor, indigenous people, and the unborn and children are the most vulnerable to these harms, hence the most gravely affected. These facts are acknowledged in Part III, which discusses the interface between ecological integrity and human rights.

REFERENCES

Soskolne, C. L. and Bertollini, R. (1999) 'Global ecological integrity and "sustainable development": Cornerstones of public health – A discussion document', European Centre for Environment and Health, Rome Division, WHO, www.euro.who.int/document/gch/ecorep5.pdf

Westra, L. (1994) *An Environmental Proposal for Ethics: The Principle of Ecological Integrity*, Rowman and Littlefield, Lanham, MD

Westra, L. (1998) *Living in Integrity: A Global Ethic to Restore a Fragmented Earth*, Rowman and Littlefield, Lanham, MD

6

Ecological Integrity and Human Rights

Prue Taylor

INTRODUCTION: THE 'RIGHTS' VERSUS 'RESPONSIBILITIES' DEBATE

One of the recurrent themes of debate within the Global Ecological Integrity Group (GEIG) has been the correct balance between 'rights' and 'responsibilities'. This debate was a particular feature of meetings held in 2004, 2005 and 2007, reflecting an interesting range of papers on law, ethics and the interface between them.

There is common agreement within GEIG that the exercise of legal 'rights', such as those to land and natural resources, has led to large-scale ecological degradation. This is because natural resources are viewed, almost solely, as economic factors of production. The law serves this utilitarian purpose by protecting the exercise of these 'rights' from interference by others in the exercise of their 'rights'. As a result, natural resources, and interconnected ecological systems, receive only indirect protection, to the extent to which another's 'rights' are interfered with. In other words, ecological systems receive no direct legal protection in recognition of a range of values beyond human utility. Potential conflict or competition between 'rights' delivers little. These deficiencies are further exacerbated because, from a moral perspective, legal rights are exercised from within a dominant anthropocentric ethical framework that does not respect nature or recognize its intrinsic value. As a consequence there is no over-riding sense of a 'moral responsibility' that would limit, or constrain, the exercise of legal rights.

What, then, should the appropriate response be to this situation? This is the central question of debate.

One option is the further development and use of legal rights, in particular human rights. This can be achieved in a variety of ways. It could be done, for example, by strengthening pre-existing human rights to life, health and an adequate standard of living. A related option is to strengthen procedural and constitutional environmental rights. More progressive efforts involve the creation of a dedicated human right to a healthy environment and/or legally enforceable rights for nature. A number of papers, delivered by GEIG members, have argued the advantages of these rights-based approaches (Soskolne, 2008). In recent years, Laura Westra's work has demonstrated the valuable contribution that can be made by strengthening the human rights (Westra, 2004) of the most vulnerable human beings, particularly the rights of children (including the unborn) and indigenous peoples (Westra, 2006 and 2007). The contributions by scholars from African states have also been formative in understanding the value of constitutional rights, particularly in impoverished communities.

As a counterbalance to this rights-based approach, other GEIG members have delivered papers that offer legal and ethical critiques and analysis. Some of these papers have argued that, in addition to offering only indirect and limited ecological protection (for the purpose of meeting goals of human health and wellbeing), these rights-based responses reinforce the anthropocentric value system that is at the root of ecological degradation. This alternative view has generally triggered lively discussion among participants and consideration of alternatives to the rights-based approach. What we need is *not* more legally asserted and protected 'rights' to the environment, which will foster more conflict over entitlements. What we need is more emphasis upon the adoption and exercise of 'moral responsibility' towards all life (including non-human life).

The need for, and the source of, a strong sense of 'moral responsibility' has often been the subject of work by GEIG members. This, in part, reflects the strong influence of the Earth Charter. Ron Engel's chapter in this book is illustrative. His chapter is about the realization of a sacred covenant between humans and all life. Engel argues that a sacred covenant or agreement is the source of universal responsibility for the present and future wellbeing of humans and the larger living world. In 2007, a paper by Jack Manno pointed to the strengths of a responsibility rather than a rights focus. The specific context was an agreement between the US and Canada for the protection of the Great Lakes. A responsibility focus emphasized that the purpose of the agreement was to work together in the best interest of the Great Lakes themselves. In comparison, a rights focus would encourage the nation states to fall back into the habit of asserting sovereign interests to utilize the lakes. Manno argued the need for agreements consistent with an indigenous peoples' view that responsibility is an honour and the greater the responsibility, the greater the honour (Manno, 2007).

Building upon this ethical understanding, some (but not all) GEIG members argue that human moral responsibility should also be implemented in law. This would give legal recognition to the reality that all rights are exercised within both a social context and a finite ecological context. There are a number of ways of achieving this legal implementation. International agreements, containing provisions for the protection of environmental rights, could include articles creating collective and individual state responsibility for the protection and restoration of the ecological basis of all life. This would extend responsibility well beyond the level needed to protect the exercise of environmental human rights and recognize the intrinsic value of nature. Adequate accountability and enforcement mechanisms would also be required. At the municipal level, constitutional reform could include parallel articles imposing constitutional responsibilities upon states to protect the ecological basis of all life. An alternative means of creating legal responsibility would be through the development of trustee or stewardship concepts. These concepts, if adopted, would have the power to transform nation states from mere protectors of national interests to stewards or guardians of global and territorial ecological systems (Brown, 2001).

What all these examples of implementation of legal responsibility have in common is that they focus upon the nation state as the holder of responsibility. What then of the individual rights holder? How could legal responsibility be attributed to them? This is where the concept of 'ecological human rights' becomes significant (Bosselmann, 1998 and 2001; Taylor, 1998a). This is a concept that reframes human rights by placing ecological restrictions or constraints upon their exercise. By taking this approach, ecological human rights can make two important contributions to the rights and responsibilities debate.

First, no new rights to the environment are created, for the benefit of either humans or nature (nature's rights). Instead, the exercise of pre-existing human rights is subjected to restrictions in a manner that legally implements moral responsibilities. As these moral responsibilities are owed to all life on Earth, the level of ecological protection required extends beyond that necessary to provide exclusively for human health and wellbeing. And second, the ecological human rights approach takes neither an exclusively legal nor an exclusively moral approach, but acknowledges the important interaction between the two. Ecological human rights are a legal tool that can promote and reflect the broader societal changes that must occur in order for humanity to revalue nature. In other words, legal reforms such as this are but one means to an end, and not an end in themselves.

In addition to making a contribution to the rights and responsibilities debate, ecological human rights are an important legal implementation of the 'ecological integrity' concept. As other chapters in this book illustrate, GEIG's work has been pivotal in developing the ecological paradigm of human health. This paradigm recognizes that the Earth's ecological systems and human health are interdependent and interactive entities. But the work of GEIG goes beyond linking the ecological health of ecosystems, their role as determinants of human population health and understanding the human behavioural drivers of degradation. 'Ecological integrity' is a concept that values the whole, the entire and the undiminished. It includes the descriptor of good health, but goes beyond this to include the 'self-creative capacities of life to organize, regenerate, reproduce, sustain, adapt, develop and evolve itself' (Pimentel et al, 2000, p11).

Crucially, 'ecological integrity' also includes a multidimensional and reprioritized valuing of nature: it 'signifies that the combined functions and components of whole natural systems are valuable for their own sake; their life-support functions; their psycho-spiritual, scientific and cultural significance;

and the goods and services they provide' (Pimentel et al, 2000, p11). As noted above, ecological human rights place additional constraints (ecological protection) upon the exercise of human rights. In doing so, there is acknowledgement of human interests (for example health and wellbeing), but there is also recognition of the intrinsic value of, and the value in the provision of life-support services for, all life. As will be seen below, the notion of constraint can be implemented through express articulation of legal responsibilities or duties owed to nature and humanity. In this way, moral obligations can be given legal form and significance within the theory of human rights.

Having introduced the rights and responsibilities debate within GEIG, and the core idea of ecological human rights, this chapter proceeds by describing, in more detail, the justification for this approach. This is followed by a discussion of how ecological human rights can be created. The final section considers some legal precedents. The primary focus is international human rights, rather than regional and national human rights developments (Bosselmann, 1998 and 2001). Further, this chapter does not address debate around the notion of 'nature's rights', which has been referred to as a strong-rights-based approach (Taylor, 1998a). Rather, the focus here is on the implementation of intrinsic values, a so-called weak-rights-based approach (Redgwell, 1996, p73).

AN ECOLOGICAL CRITIQUE OF HUMAN RIGHTS

The ecological critique of human rights is a part of the broader discussion about the ethical relationship between humanity and nature. In particular, it is part of the debate about the anthropocentric underpinnings of current law and the need for the law (and society at large) to transform to reflect an ecocentric ethic. The arguments for and against this transformation are covered in a growing body of literature and need not be repeated here. What are of particular importance here are the limitations of human rights law and how these limitations could be overcome so that the law implements an ecocentric ethic.

In general terms, international human rights theory is characterized by a progression of social, political and economic developments, starting with the liberal philosophies of the 17th and 18th centuries and later embracing the socialist revolutions of the 20th. From today's perspective of grave concern for the Earth's ecological systems and for human survival (current and future), one of the common features of the different theories of human rights is a basic 'ecological blindness' (Taylor, 1998a). They are all primarily concerned with theorizing various aspects of human relationships: individuals vs. the state, individuals vs. individuals, and individuals vs. the collective or human society. In other words, their focus has been the development and legal expression of individual and human social ethics. Given the conditions and challenges of the last three and a half centuries of human history, this focus is fully understandable.

Nature, for its part, has largely been a peripheral consideration and treated either as the subject of fear, which needed to be conquered, or as a storehouse of useful resources. As a consequence, human rights theory developed without recognition of human dependence upon, and vulnerability to, ecological change. In addition, it developed without any understanding of the complex interactions between ecosystems and the physical environment, which provides the basis for all life on Earth.

From an ethical perspective, human rights developed without any moral concern for non-human life. In sum, the growing catalogue of 'freedoms from' and the more positive 'rights to' existed in a vacuum, isolated from concern for ecological integrity. Landmark documents of the time illustrate this point: the Charter of the United Nations (1945), the Universal Declaration of Human Rights (1948) and the two 1966 international human rights covenants that followed the Universal Declaration – the International Covenant on Civil and Political Rights (ICCPR) and the International Covenant on Economic Social and Cultural Rights (ICESCR) – are all silent on the linkages between human rights and ecological systems.

In the last 30 to 40 years, humanity has begun to acknowledge the impact of environmental degradation on human health and wellbeing, on other life, and on Earth's life-support systems. Legal responses have included a growing body of national and international environmental law, drawn up for the purpose of protecting collective human wellbeing. However, it is only more recently that the interdependence between *individual* human rights and environmental protection has been recognized. Greater environmental awareness has made it increasingly obvious that environmental quality is an essential precondition to the enjoyment of many existing international human rights, such as the right to life, the right to health, the right to property and the right to an adequate standard of living. Thus, in 1972, the Stockholm Declaration stated that 'both aspects of man's environment, the natural and the man-made, are essential to his wellbeing and to the enjoyment of basic rights – even the right to life itself' and that 'man has the fundamental right to freedom, equality and adequate conditions of life, in an environment of a quality that permits a life of dignity and wellbeing' (Preamble and Principle 1).

The growing understanding of the interdependence between human rights and environmental conditions has given rise to two related, yet distinct, responses in law. Human rights law has begun to change to expressly recognize the factual connection between respect for human rights and environmental conditions. The overall objective is to make it much clearer that environmental damage, or the threat of environmental damage, can trigger a human rights violation. Environmental law, on the other hand, has begun to consider human rights law as one potentially useful legal tool for the achievement of environmental protection objectives (Shelton, 1991). The primary distinction between these legal responses is in their different priorities. Human rights law prioritizes human welfare; environmental law does not necessarily prioritize human welfare, but sees it as an important component of broader concern for ecological systems.

At present, there are essentially three emerging trends evident in human rights law. All are intended to better integrate human rights law and the environment. Collectively these trends are referred to here as 'environmental human rights'. The paragraphs that follow give a brief summary of these trends, as evident in international law. This provides a background for understanding the ecological critique that follows.

Reinterpretation of recognized human rights

As noted above, the Stockholm Declaration expressly identified the challenge that environmental degradation poses to existing human rights. This led to a number of efforts to reinterpret, or reformulate, substantive human rights to incorporate standards of environmental quality. This represents an attempt to 'green' existing rights. The United Nations Convention on the Rights of the Child provides an example of growing environmental awareness by linking the right to health with environmental quality. It provides that measures to protect a child's right to health should include the provision of clean drinking water and nutritious food, 'taking into consideration the dangers and risks of environmental pollution' (Article 24). As regards litigation, there are definite indications that severe environmental degradation will be treated as causing a violation of existing human rights, in particular the right to life. A line of cases, heard by various human rights tribunals, have noted that state failure to protect citizens from environmental deprivation can raise serious issues about state obligations to protect human life. In addition to the right to life, environmental degradation has been recognized by commentators and tribunals as violating rights to health, privacy and family life, property, suitable working conditions, adequate standards of living, and culture. Environmental harm may also violate the unique (and often more comprehensive) rights of indigenous peoples (Westra, 2007; see also Inuit Case, Petition of the Inuit Circumpolar Conference of 2005, in Smith and Shearman, 2006).

Despite these developments, there is uncertainty about how substantive human rights, such as the rights to life and health, will be interpreted in an environmental context. However, a range of cases demonstrate a growing tendency to use human rights doctrine for protection and redress. There is also a certain willingness on the part of human rights tribunals to apply human rights doctrine to cases that involve environmental degradation. This may be partly due to the fact that no new theory is involved, but just a more literate interpretation of pre-existing rights that expands state obligations. There is certainly a growing body of authoritative science to support this more literate interpretation (UN MEA, 2005; IPCC, 2007).

The use of human rights actions are more suited to some environmental harms than others. Harm caused to individuals due to direct exposure to a pollutant (such as radioactive waste), for example, is likely to raise few problems (Port Hope Case). In contrast, severe, large-scale pollution causing multiple direct and indirect harms, due to multiple acts and omissions, will be much more difficult to litigate. For these reasons, emerging climate change litigation, based upon human rights violations, will be a real test case (Smith and Shearman, 2006). Commentators have recently noted that causation (the link between harmful activities and resultant harm) will be easier to establish in the case of harm to property than harm to life and health. This is because of the complex web of interacting variables that can affect human health, making it difficult to satisfy legal standards of proof (Smith and Shearman, 2006, p165).

Procedural environmental human rights

A number of proposals exist for the reformulation and expansion of existing political and civil rights in the context of environmental protection. The objective is to use existing rights to political participation and information to create a set of procedural guarantees, or a kind of environmental due process, upon which individuals and groups can rely. In essence, procedural regimes would require a right to prior knowledge of actions which may have a significant environmental impact (together with a corresponding state duty to inform), a right to participate in decision-making and a right to recourse before administrative and judicial organs. While these suggestions involve an expanded understanding of existing participatory rights, and could therefore have been described under the category of reinterpreted rights considered above, they are generally given their own category. This may be because a specialist body of law is emerging around participatory rights in an environmental context. This development is, in part, attributable to Agenda 21 and the Rio Declaration, both of which were adopted at the 1992 United Nations Conference on Environment and Development (UNCED).

Agenda 21 recognized that 'one of the fundamental prerequisites for the achievement of sustainable development is broad public participation in decision-making' (Paragraph 23.2). Principle 10 of the Rio Declaration articulated procedural environmental rights in more detail:

> *Environmental issues are best handled with participation of concerned citizens at the relevant level. At the national level, each individual shall have appropriate access to information concerning the environment that is held by public authorities ... and the opportunity to participate in decision-making processes. States shall facilitate and encourage public awareness and participation by making information widely available. Effective access to judicial and administrative proceedings, including redress and remedy, shall be provided.*

The momentum created at UNCED has resulted in the incorporation of procedural environmental rights in a number of subsequent multilateral and bilateral treaties. Such rights are also evident in a number of national constitutions. One of the best-known and influential treaties to emerge is the Aarhus Convention (2001), which created an extensive range of procedural environmental rights that have influenced legal development throughout Europe and beyond.

A dedicated environmental human right

One of the most progressive arguments in the context of human rights norms and environmental protection is the view that international law has evolved to recognize a human right to a decent, healthy or sustainable environment. A related view is that it is time for international law to give express recognition to such a right, in a human rights document. A recent development is illustrative: in February 2007 an appeal was adopted at a conference bringing together non-government organizations, senior United Nations officials and the French Head of State. This appeal stated that:

> *To promote environmental ethics, we are calling for the adoption of a Universal Declaration of Environmental Rights and Duties. This common charter will ensure that present and future generations have a new human right to a sound and well-preserved environment.*
> (Paris Appeal, 2007)

Since the 1972 Stockholm Declaration, which drew a connection between the environment and human rights, a number of international documents have emerged which recognize a dedicated environmental human right. Some selected examples are illustrative of the general trends.

In 1994, the United Nations Special Rapporteur on Human Rights and the Environment (Ksentini Report) released a report that recognized the link between environmental protection and human rights protection. The report noted that serious environmental harm can violate existing human rights, and that recognition and implementation of procedural rights are crucial to both human rights and environmental protection. However, the Rapporteur then went further to find that an environmental human right has already been recognized at national, regional and international levels. She wrote that recognizing and operationalizing the right to a healthy environment 'should make it possible to go beyond reductionist concepts of "mankind first" or "ecology first" and achieve a coalescence of common objectives of development and environmental protection'(Ksentini Report, 1994, p3). A draft Declaration of Principles on Human Rights and the Environment included two interesting principles: Principle 2 states that 'all persons have the right to a secure healthy and ecologically sound environment', and Principle 5 provides that 'all persons have the right to freedom from pollution, environmental degradation, and activities that adversely affect the environment and threaten life, health, livelihood, wellbeing or sustainable development within, across or outside national boundaries' (Draft Declaration of Principles, 1994).

Following on from this work, in 1999 the Bizkaia Declaration on the Right to the Environment was produced under the auspices of UNESCO and the UN High Commissioner for Human Rights. Article 1 recognizes that 'everyone has the right, individually or in association with others, to enjoy a healthy, ecologically balanced environment [which] may be exercised before public bodies and private entities'. The Preamble of this Declaration is also significant because it collects evidence of an emerging right to environment in, for example, the Stockholm and Rio Declarations, regional recognition of the right to environment, a UN General Assembly Resolution, and recognition of the right in national constitutions.

At the international level, the recently adopted UN Declaration on the Rights of Indigenous Peoples gives important recognition to the unique environmental rights of indigenous peoples (for example Principles 25, 26, 29, 31 and 32). Regionally, the two most significant agreements are the African Charter on Human and Peoples' Rights (a right to a general satisfactory environment favourable to development – Principle 24) and the Protocol of San Salvador. The Protocol recognizes the right to a healthy environment and requires states to promote the protection, preservation and improvement of the environment (Articles 11 and 2).

These international and regional documents are generally reflective of national developments. A 2005 survey noted that of around 193 countries in the world, 117 have national constitutions that mention the protection of the environment or natural resources. Of these, some 56 explicitly refer to a right to a clean and healthy environment and 97 to a duty of government to prevent environmental harm (Mollo et al, 2005). This trend seems to have begun in the 1970s, as virtually every constitution revised or adopted since has addressed environmental issues (Kiss and Shelton, 1991). Two of the most frequently cited constitutional provisions are those from the Brazilian and Portuguese constitutions. The Brazilian Constitution provides that 'everyone has a right to an ecologically balanced environment, which is a public good for the people's use and is essential for a healthy life. The Government and the community have a duty to defend and to preserve the environment for present and future generations' (Article 225). The Portuguese Constitution is also notable because, in addition to granting individual rights, it imposes corresponding duties upon both individuals *and* government authorities. It provides that, 'Everyone shall have the right to a healthy and ecologically balanced human environment and the duty to defend it.' The Constitution then specifies the duties of the State, including 'promot[ing] the rational use of natural resources, safeguarding their capacity for renewal and ecological stability' (Article 66).

However, even acknowledging these developments, the standard view of international law scholars is that no independent right to the environment currently exists in a form that provides sufficient certainty as to its content, scope and enforceability. Even when express rights exist (as noted above), they are often considered aspirational, expressing national goals and intents, rather than legally enforceable rights. For this reason, reinterpretations of existing rights, as previously described, are more often relied upon to provide surrogate protection against environmental harm.

The ecological critique

The sections above gave an overview of trends to integrate environmental protection and human rights theory. The primary intention is to protect human interests, and to use legal action to put pressure on governments and corporations to change their policy and practice. A related intention is to use litigation to raise and focus public awareness of environmental issues. These are important and laudable goals. However, the importance of an ecological critique is that it helps identify some of the limitations inherent in these approaches to the use of human rights. The importance of ecological human rights (as described below) is that they are an effort to overcome these limitations.

There is real concern among many commentators over the inherent anthropocentricity of environmental human rights (Redgwell, 1996). To some, the very existence of environmental human rights reinforces the idea that the environment and natural resources exist only for human benefit and have no intrinsic worth. Furthermore, these rights create a hierarchy, according to which humanity is given a position of superiority and importance above, and separate from, other members of the natural community (Birnie and Boyle, 2002, pp257–258). More specifically, the objectives and standards applied are human-centred. Humanity's survival, living standards, health, aesthetics and continued use of resources are the objectives. The state of the environment is determined by the needs of humanity, not the needs of other species, or the ecological significance of the complex interactions between species and the physical environment that provide the life-support systems of all life. An example is useful here. In 1987 the German Federal Administrative Court noted that 'the law cannot provide for the health of ecosystems per se, but only in so far as required to protect the rights of affected people' (Bosselmann, 2001, pp94–97).

The human-centred character of an environmental human right leads to a philosophical tension between deep and shallow ecologists. As a result of this tension, some commentators wholly reject human rights proposals (Giagnocavo and Goldstein, 1990; Gibson, 1990), while others offer compromise positions (Shelton, 1991; Nickel, 1993; Taylor, 1998b).

Those who condemn the human rights approach raise several concerns. First, anthropocentric approaches to environmental protection are seen as *perpetuating* the values and attitudes that are at the root of environmental degradation. Second, anthropocentric approaches deprive the environment of direct and comprehensive protection, as *human* life, health and standards of living are likely to be the aims of environmental protection. Thus the environment is only protected as a consequence of, and to the extent necessary to meet, the need to protect human wellbeing. An environmental right thus subjugates all other needs, interests and values of nature to those of humanity. Environmental degradation or loss of ecological integrity as such is not sufficient cause for complaint; it must be linked to human wellbeing. Third, humans are the beneficiaries of any relief for infringement of the right. There is no guarantee of its utilization for the benefit of the environment, nor is there any recognition of nature as the victim of degradation. And fourth, environmental protection requires humans to initiate legal action, in other words human protest from a rights holder.

On the other hand, a number of arguments are put forward which may, to some extent, mitigate these concerns. First, it is suggested that a degree of anthropocentrism is a necessary part of environmental protection because humanity is the only species that we know of which has the consciousness to recognize and respect the morality of rights, and because human beings are themselves an integral part of nature. In short, the interests and duties of humanity are inseparable from environmental protection. Shelton argues that:

> ... humans are not separable members of the universe. Rather, humans are interlinked and interdependent participants with duties to protect and conserve all elements of nature, whether or not they have known benefits or current economic utility. This anthropocentric purpose should be distinguished from utilitarianism. (Shelton, 1991, p110)

Shelton goes on to argue that an environmental human right could be complementary to a wider protection of the biosphere that recognizes the intrinsic value of nature, independent of human needs. As Birnie and Boyle point out, however, this approach would not work 'if human claims are extracted from these broader environmental concerns and elevated to a separate or prior status as "rights" outside any process for resolving the conflicts that may result with other rights or claim' (Birnie and Boyle, 2002, p258). They see the implications of the issue as being largely structural, requiring the integration of human rights claims within a broader decision-making framework capable of taking into account, among other factors, intrinsic values, the needs of future generations and the competing interests of states. In their view, existing human rights institutions are too limited in their perspective to be able to balance these factors (Birnie and Boyle, 2002, p258).

Rolston also advocates a compromise position. He accepts the paradigm of human rights for protection of human needs for environmental quality, but also suggests the elaboration of human responsibilities for nature (Rolston, 1993). According to Nickel, human rights play a 'useful and justifiable role in protecting human interests in a safe environment and in providing a link between the environment and human rights movements' (Nickel, 1993, p282). He labels his approach as 'accommodationist', arguing that anthropocentrism is not a significant objection if 'it can be supplemented by other norms that will address other issues'. In other words, it could be seen as a useful part of 'the normative repertory of environmentalism' (Nickel, 1993, p283).

It is suggested that, in the short term, these compromise or accommodationist approaches might be useful in assisting the law to transform from an essentially anthropocentric perspective to an ecocentric perspective. However, in the longer term, the existence of a dedicated environmental human right could be seen as self-contradictory. A better option is the development of *all human rights* in a manner that demonstrates that humanity is an integral part of the biosphere, that nature has an intrinsic value and that humanity has responsibilities towards nature. In short, ecological limitations, expressed as responsibilities or duties, should be part of the human rights discourse.

THE CREATION OF ECOLOGICAL HUMAN RIGHTS

The purpose of this section is to demonstrate how ecological limitations can be introduced in a manner consistent with international human rights theory. The objective of the limitations is to implement an ecocentric ethic in a manner that imposes responsibilities and duties upon humankind and to take intrinsic values and the interests of the natural community into account when exercising human rights. In this manner, ecological limitations can qualify the exercise of basic rights and freedoms, such as the right to free use and enjoyment of property. Such limitations could apply to a number of other human rights, including the rights to liberty and freedom of expression, but the primary focus of this article is on property rights.

Boundaries of rights and freedoms

One of the most important aspects of human rights is the restriction or qualification of human rights to the extent necessary to protect the rights of others and the common interest. Generally speaking, international human rights documents employ several different techniques to define the boundaries of rights. One technique is to prescribe a right together with duties, so that the limits of the rights will be determined by the duties. Another technique is to use the concept of abuse of rights. Here the declaration of a right is followed by the qualification that one must not abuse one's rights in a way that deprives others of their rights. Finally, two of the most commonly used techniques are to prescribe general boundaries around all rights, or to prescribe specific boundaries around specific rights. Article 29 of the Universal Declaration, for example, states:

1   *Everyone has duties to the community in which alone the free and full development of his personality is possible.*

2   *In the exercise of his rights and freedoms, everyone shall be subject only to such limitations as are determined by law solely for the purpose of securing due recognition and respect for the rights and freedoms of others and of meeting the just requirements of morality, public order and the general welfare in a democratic society.*

Sieghart identifies several important and independent components of limitations. The limitation must be provided for by law, and that law must be necessary, rather than merely useful or desirable. Regarding the nature of interests which can be protected, Sieghart states that the limitation must protect one or more of a restricted set of public interests such as national security, public safety, public order, public health, public morals, and the rights and freedoms of others (Sieghart, 1985, p80).[1] Regarding interpretation of these limitations, it is recognized that they should be given a strict and narrow construction. Specifically, there is a burden to produce the exact law involved and to demonstrate its necessity and that it protects the specified interest or interests.

   The above discussion demonstrates that limitation or restriction of human rights in legally prescribed circumstances, particularly in the common (public) interest, is an accepted practice in international human rights theory. However, consistent with the human-centred theories that underpin human rights, these restrictions reflect concern to protect only human social ethics (human health, safety, order, morals, etc). The extent to which these restrictions might be extended to include ecological limitations consistent with recognition of an ecocentric ethic, as opposed to human social ethics, is discussed below in the specific context of the property right prescribed by the Universal Declaration.

Property as an international human right: Existing restrictions

Article 17 of the Universal Declaration states quite simply that:

1   *Everyone has the right to own property alone as well as in association with others.*

2   *No one shall be arbitrarily deprived of his property.*

Advocates of liberal-capitalist ideology tend to follow in the wake of Locke, arguing that 'property' was one of the most sacred rights of man. Property was seen to be essential to individual freedom, and particularly to dignity, self-respect and happiness; it was the real basis of personal existence and development.

According to Locke's social contract theory, the role of the state then was to protect property from other people or from other nations. In stark contrast, socialist ideology asserted that private property ownership led to the exploitation of the working classes. Productive property was better vested in the state, so that the state could make decisions as to its use and disposal in the collective interest. As it stands, Article 17 is a compromise between these two opposing ideologies; one might say that it represents the lowest common denominator. Read literally, it is only a basic statement of freedom to own property, and not to be deprived of it by capricious action. However, it must be read together with Article 29 of the Universal Declaration, which describes general limitations: in the form of duties to the community (Article 29(1)); respect for the rights and freedoms of others, and the requirements of morality, public order and general welfare in a democratic society (Article 29(2)); and compliance with the purposes and principles of the United Nations (Article 29(3)).

In contrast to Article 17 of the Universal Declaration, statements of property rights under municipal law, and in regional human rights documents, are more qualified. Take, for example, Article 14 of the German Grundgesetz, which contains a clear statement of social obligation in the form of attendant duties:

14(1)   *Property and the right of inheritance shall be guaranteed. Their content and limits shall be determined by the laws.*
14(2)   *Property imposes duties. Its use should also serve the public weal* [or good].

Most of the regional treaties also state a property right in qualified terms, referring to the right of 'use and enjoyment' rather than to ownership. These treaties give public authorities plenty of latitude for intervention in the exercise of property rights, on grounds such as the 'public interest', 'interest of society', 'public need and utility', and the 'general interest'. Taking into account the scope of state intervention granted by language such as this, Sieghart concludes that 'in sum, whatever the "right to property" may be, it is more weakly protected than any other [right] in these treaties' (Sieghart, 1985, p132). Thus many post-war human rights conventions demonstrate that the strict 19th-century liberal rhetoric surrounding 'property' has been substantially eroded in the interests of society as a whole.

Ecological limitations

As seen above, express restrictions and limitations upon the exercise of international human rights is standard practice. At present, such restrictions impose duties and responsibilities on rights holders and give states the power to make appropriate laws in the collective interest. Most importantly, these restrictions are currently limited to protection and advancement of individual or collective human interests. As human interests and welfare are now seen to be so clearly linked to, and dependent upon, the environment, it can be argued that many of these broadly framed limitations would currently permit clear and necessary environmental regulation (which restricts use and enjoyment/ownership of property or imposes duties) to the extent necessary to protect a range of human interests. Thus, state environmental laws, such as planning, building and land-use regulations, can be easily reconciled with property rights. This was the rationale employed by the European Court of Human Rights in the case of *Pine Valley Developments Ltd. and Others v. Ireland*, which recognized that interference with the right to peaceful enjoyment of property, in conformity with planning legislation designed to protect the environment, was clearly legitimate under Article 1 of the First Protocol to the European Convention. As ecological awareness grows, this trend of treating environmental protection as a 'public concern' will continue. In this sense, the ecological blindness of human rights is incrementally reduced.

However, the idea of ecological limitations advanced here goes beyond environmental protection for the sake of human interests. The question then becomes: Could existing restrictions to human rights be expanded to permit regulation for the protection of intrinsic values and/or interpreted to include individual and state duties or responsibilities towards nature? From a technical point of view, ecological limitations could be implemented following the standard formulations for boundaries to rights and freedoms. A number of options exist, including:

- prescribing the right to the use and enjoyment of property, together with a duty not to cause harm to the ecological integrity of the natural environment;
- prescribing the right to the use and enjoyment of property, together with a responsibility to protect and enhance the ecological integrity of the natural environment;
- prescribing the right to the use and enjoyment of property, subject to a specific, or general, limitation in the interests of the general welfare of both nature and humanity;
- reinterpreting or extending phrases such as 'general welfare' (used in Article 29(2) of the Universal Declaration), to include respect for ecological integrity; or
- reinterpreting or extending phrases such as 'duties to the community' (used in Article 29(1) of the Universal Declaration), to include duties to the natural and human communities.

From a theoretical point of view, human rights are not always absolute in the face of the competing needs of human society. The issue of whether human rights can be qualified in the face of the competing needs of the natural community is not so much one of legal theory, but one of moral value or worth. It is therefore suggested that duties and responsibilities towards the natural community could be included in the framework of international human rights when our moral theories have developed sufficiently to expand moral value to the natural community. What evidence is there that this is occurring? The next section briefly considers some of the precedents for recognition of intrinsic values and duties towards nature in international law.

PRECEDENTS

Concepts such as intrinsic values and duties towards nature have only recently emerged in jurisdictions following Western cultural and legal traditions. They have been brought to the fore over the last 60 years by debates within environmental philosophy over new and prevailing environmental ethics and by the influence of writers such as Aldo Leopold, Albert Schweitzer and Thomas Berry. Despite this recent emergence, the recognition of intrinsic values and responsibility for nature are not unknown at the level of international law.[2] However, as yet they are of binding legal significance in only a few instances.

In international law, the 1982 World Charter for Nature (the Charter) was the first international document to introduce ecocentrism. Its preamble expresses some distinctly ecocentric thinking, referring to mankind as part of nature, to civilization as rooted in nature, to every form of life being unique and meriting respect regardless of its worth to man, and to the need for man to be guided by a code of moral action. It further declares that nature shall be respected, that, given humanity's capacity to alter nature and exhaust its resources, humanity must maintain the stability and quality of nature and conserve its natural resources. Essential ecological processes and life-support systems must be maintained in the interests of subsistence as well as for the diversity of living organisms. Practical applications of these concepts are described in the Charter; for example, the discharge of pollutants into natural systems is to be avoided rather than merely regulated. Although the Charter is only declaratory and not legally binding, in the opinion of commentators on international environmental law, Charter principles 'indicate the prevailing concepts and direction of international environmental law' (Kiss and Shelton, 1991, pp46–48). Furthermore, Charter principles have been incorporated into some important international conventions (Kiss and Shelton, 1991, p48).

Between 1982 and 1992, a number of international treaties emerged that referred to the intrinsic value of the environment. In comparison, the UNCED documents are remarkably silent. The one exception is the Convention on Biological Diversity, the preamble of which contains the phrasing 'conscious of the intrinsic value of biological diversity and of the ecological, genetic, social, economic, scientific, educational, cultural, recreational and aesthetic values of biological diversity and its components'. The draft IUCN International Covenant on Environment and Development draws more explicitly from the

Charter and states as a fundamental principle that 'nature as a whole warrants respect; every form of life is unique and is to be safeguarded independent of its value to humanity' (Article 2).

One of the most developed international precedents is to be found in the provisions of the Earth Charter. While not yet a legally binding instrument itself, it is rapidly gaining international recognition, and influencing a growing number of declaratory and binding legal agreements (Corcoran et al, 2005; Taylor, 2006). As an ethical framework for a just, sustainable and peaceful world, the Earth Charter sets out universal values and principles. It considers human rights as vital to the attainment of human wellbeing, and acknowledges the role their exercise can play in achieving environmental objectives and in alleviating poverty (which in turn causes ecological degradation). But it does much more than this: it also recognizes that the exercise of certain rights needs to be restricted (via the exercise of duties and responsibilities) to secure the 'long-term flourishing of Earth's human and ecological communities' (Principle 4b). In short, some rights are strengthened and others limited. Some selected extracts here will be illustrative.

The Earth Charter Preamble includes the sentence, 'We must join together to bring forth a sustainable global society founded on respect for nature, universal human rights, economic justice and a culture of peace.' Principles contributing to this goal, and which *strengthen* substantive rights include:

- 'Ensure that communities at all levels guarantee human rights and fundamental freedoms and provide everyone an opportunity to realize his or her full potential' (Principle 3a).
- 'Adopt patterns of production, consumption and reproduction that safeguard Earth's regenerative capacities, human rights, and community well-being' (Principle 7).
- 'Guarantee the right to potable water, clean air, food security, uncontaminated soil, shelter, and safe sanitation' (Principle 9a).
- 'Affirm gender equality and equity as prerequisites to sustainable development and ensure universal access to education, health care, and economic opportunity' (Principle 11).

Principles that contribute to the goal of a sustainable global society, but which *limit* substantive rights, stem from Principle 1a: 'Recognize that all beings are interdependent and every form of life has value regardless of its worth to human beings'. To achieve respect for intrinsic value we must:

- 'Accept that with the right to own, manage, and use natural resources comes the duty to prevent environmental harm and to protect the rights of people' (Principle 2a).
- 'Affirm that with increased freedom, knowledge and power comes increased responsibility to promote the common good' (Principle 2b).

In summary, the Earth Charter is unique in its efforts to reframe a range of substantive human rights within a context of responsibility for the interdependent community of all life.

CONCLUSION

One of the most notable contributions of GEIG has been the development of the concept of 'ecological integrity' as the basis for a new relationship between humanity and nature. This chapter has considered how ecological integrity could be implemented in law, using the tool of ecological human rights. This work is intended to advance understanding of 'ecological integrity' and its application. It also makes a contribution to the rights vs. responsibilities debate. Rather than introduce new rights, or rely solely on environmental rights, the ecological rights approach takes existing human rights and places their exercise within an ecological context. This ecological context acknowledges human need to use natural resources, but goes further to recognize that humanity is an integral part of ecological systems. Human activity now threatens the ability of these ecological systems to provide the conditions essential to the continuance of life. This requires us to find ways to limit our demands and bring them back within the finite limits of the Earth's biosphere. A sense of moral responsibility towards nature will be an essential component of this endeavour. In recognition of this, ecological human rights give legal effect to moral obligations by expressing them in terms of responsibilities to protect and enhance ecological systems, in acknowledgement of a range of values.

Ecological human rights, as advanced here, do not deny the utility of environmental human rights. However, it is an approach that attempts to ensure that the exercise of human rights, like all legal entitlements that affect ecological systems, respect the finite limits of those systems.[3] Returning to the rights vs. responsibilities debate within GEIG, clearly ecological human rights advocates the use of law to promote and reflect ethical and behavioural change in society. While all legal responses are subject to their inherent limitations, law is *an* important social mechanism for guiding behaviour. This is not to contend that law alone will change consciousness and behaviour. As many great writers remind us, this is the domain of the human spirit. The signs that our collective spirit is rising to embrace the Earth will first be found in our religion and our philosophy.

NOTES

1   Article 46 of the Universal Declaration on the Rights of Indigenous Peoples includes the words 'most compelling requirements of a democratic society'.
2   At the national level, examples include the New Zealand Resource Management Act 1991 (see Taylor, 1998a). Other examples come from efforts to reform the German, Swiss and Austrian Constitutions (see Bosselmann, 1998).

3 The focus of this chapter has been on the international human right to property. An important development, which sits alongside an ecological understanding of this human right, is the development of ecological property rights. For a discussion of this, see Taylor, 1998a, pp384–394.

REFERENCES

Aarhus Convention or Convention on Access to Information, Public Participation in Decision-Making, and Access to Justice in Environmental Matters, available at www.unece.org/env/pp/documents/cep43e.pdf, accessed 2 December 2007

African Charter on Human and Peoples' Rights (1982) 21 *International Legal Materials* 59

Agenda 21 (1992) A/CONF.151/26 (Vols I, II, II)

Birnie, P. and Boyle, A. (2002) *International Law and the Environment*, Oxford University Press, Oxford, UK

Bizkaia Declaration on the Right to the Environment, UN Educational, Social and Cultural Organization, UN Doc. 30C/INF.11 (24 September 1999)

Bosselmann, K. (ed) (1998) *Ökologische Grundrechte*, Nomos, Baden-Baden, Germany

Bosselmann, K. (2001) 'Human rights and the environment: Redefining fundamental principles?', in B. Gleeson and N. Low (eds) *Governance for the Environment*, Palgrave, London

Brown, P. (2001) *The Commonwealth of Life*, Black Rose Books, Montreal, Canada

Convention on Biological Diversity (1992) 31 *International Legal Materials* 818

Corcoran, P. B., Vilela, M. and Roerink, A. (eds) (2005) *Toward a Sustainable World: The Earth Charter in Action*, Kit Publishers, Amsterdam

Draft Declaration of Principles on Human Rights and the Environment, Annex I of Ksentini Report

Earth Charter, available at www.earthcharter.org, accessed 2 December 2007

Giagnocavo, C. and Goldstein, H. (1990) 'Law reform or world re-form', *McGill Law Journal*, vol 35, p346

Gibson, N. (1990) 'The right to a clean environment', *Saskatchewan Law Review*, vol 54

IPCC (2007) Assessment Reports available at www.ipcc.ch, accessed 2 December 2007

IUCN International Covenant on Environment and Development, www.iucn.org/themes/law/pdfdocuments/EPLP31EN_rev2.pdf, accessed 2 December 2007

Kiss, A. and Shelton, D. (1991) *International Environmental Law*, Transnational, New York

Ksentini Report (1994) 'Review of further developments in fields with which the Sub-Commission has been concerned, human rights and the environment: Final report', prepared by Mrs Fatama Zohra Ksentini, Special Rapporteur, UN ESCOR Commission on Human Rights, Sub-Commission on Prevention of Discrimination and Protection of Minorities, UN Doc. E/CN.4/Sub.2/1994/9

Manno, J. (2007) 'Canada–USA–First Nations collaboration for Great Lakes ecosystem restoration and sustainable development', unpublished paper presented to GEIG Conference, Halifax, CA

Mollo, M. et al (2005) 'Environmental human rights report: Human Rights and the Environment', materials for the 61st Session of the United Nations Commission on

Human Rights, Geneva, 14 March–22 April 2005, Earthjustice Legal Defence Fund, Oakland, CA

Nickel, J. (1993) 'The human right to a safe environment: Philosophical perspectives on its scope and justification', *Yale Journal of International Law*, vol 18, p281

Paris Appeal, http://partnerships4planet.ch/en/environmental-rights.php, accessed 2 December 2007

Pimentel, D., Westra, L. and Reed, N. (2000) *Ecological Integrity*, Island Press, Washington, DC

Pine Valley Developments Ltd. and Others v. Ireland, 222Eur.Ct.H.R. (ser.A) 1991, p54

Port Hope Case, E. H. P. v. Canada, No.67/1980, in *Selected Decisions of the Human Rights Commission Under the Optional Protocol* (1990) p20

Protocol of San Salvador or Additional Protocol to the American Convention on Human Rights in the Area of Social and Cultural Rights (1988) O.A.S.T.S. 69, OEA/ser.L.V/II.92, doc.31 rev.3 (1988)

Redgwell, C. (1996) 'Life, the universe and everything: A critique of anthropocentric rights', in A. Boyle and M. Anderson (eds) *Human Rights Approaches to Environmental Protection*, Clarendon Press, Oxford, UK

Rio Declaration on Environment and Development (1992) 31 *International Legal Materials* 874

Rolston, H. (1993) 'Rights and responsibilities on the home planet', *Yale Journal of International Law*, vol 18

Shelton, D. (1991) 'Human rights, environmental rights and the right to environment', *Stanford Journal of International Law*, vol 25

Sieghart, P. (1985) *The Lawful Rights of Mankind: An Introduction to the International Legal Code of Human Rights*, Oxford University Press, Oxford, UK

Smith, J. and Shearman, D. (2006) *Climate Change Litigation*, Presidian Legal Publications, Adelaide, Australia

Soskolne, C. (2007) *Sustaining Life on Earth*, Lexington Books, Lanham, MD

Stockholm Declaration (Declaration of the United Nations Conference on the Human Environment), 16 June 1972, 11 *International Legal Materials* 1416

Taylor, P. (1998a) 'From environmental to ecological human rights: A new dynamic in international law', *The Georgetown International Environmental Law Review*, vol 10, issue 2, pp309–397

Taylor, P. (1998b) *An Ecological Approach to International Law*, Routledge, London

Taylor, P. (2006) 'The business of climate change: What's ethics got to do with it?', *Pacific McGeorge Global Business and Development Law Journal*, vol 20

United Nations Convention on the Rights of the Child (1989) 28 *International Legal Materials* 1448

Universal Declaration on the Rights of Indigenous Peoples, available at www.un.org/esa/socdev/unpfii/en/declaration/html, accessed 2 December 2007

UN MEA (United Nations Millennium Ecosystem Assessment Report) (2005) available at www.millenniumassessment.org, accessed 2 December 2007

Westra, L. (2004) *Ecoviolence and the Law*, Transnational, New York

Westra, L. (2006) *Environmental Justice and the Rights of the Unborn and Future Generations: Law, Environmental Harm and the Right to Health*, Earthscan, London

Westra, L. (2007) *Environmental Justice and the Rights of Indigenous Peoples*, Earthscan, London

World Charter for Nature (1982) 22 *International Legal Materials* 455

7

Eco-epidemiology: On the Need to Measure Health Effects from Global Change

Colin L. Soskolne[1]

While illnesses manifest in various ways, it is epidemiologists who work to unravel the patterns of these illnesses within populations. The expectation, in both communicable and chronic diseases epidemiology, is that relevant measurements of:

- exposure;
- health and wellbeing outcomes;
- factors that increase people's risk of disease; and
- interventions for tackling the problems that impact on human health

will allow us to determine whether population health is improving or not (Beaglehole et al, 1993). However, other branches of epidemiology, like disaster epidemiology and eco-epidemiology, do not easily conform to this model. Since one-third to one-half of the global disease burden (the brunt of which falls on children under the age of five) has been attributed to environmental risk factors (Smith et al, 1999), a new epidemiological approach that addresses the needs of eco-epidemiology is needed. The challenge for the eco-epidemiologist is to find new ways of measuring the effects of environmental degradation on human health in order to maximize the impact of policies designed to maintain or improve the health status of populations.

COMMUNICABLE DISEASES

In communicable (or infectious) diseases epidemiology, the intervention is usually a serial process: sometimes policy in nature; sometimes narrowly focused on immunization campaigns; or sometimes similar to the famous intervention of John Snow in his removal of the Broad Street pump handle believed to result in progressive and rapid declines in the number of cases of cholera in mid-19th century London (Snow, 1855). The communicable diseases epidemiologist deals

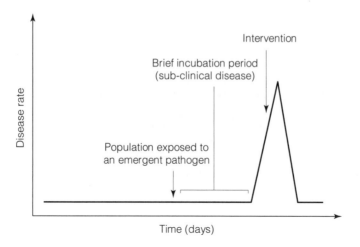

Figure 7.1   *Threshold effect in a hypothetical time trend study*
of a communicable disease

with the rapid action – the sudden increase in disease rates following a brief, but relatively uniform, latent period of sub-clinical disease – seen in a threshold effects model whenever the emergence of a new pathogen could result in an acute disease outbreak. Within the exposed population, one expects a consistent and sudden increase in disease rates as everyone falls ill at about the same time, usually within days of one another, constituting a point source epidemic. Thus, following a Sunday picnic with *Clostridium perfringens*-contaminated food, all the picnickers become ill within twenty-four hours; the negative health impacts distribute as a threshold response (Mausner and Bahn, 1974). In this situation, the threshold effects model associated with acute epidemic outbreaks is usually confined to a narrow geographic region, affecting a smaller population (Figure 7.1).

CHRONIC DISEASES

In the developed world, chronic diseases (or the diseases of affluence) have gained in importance. In chronic diseases epidemiology, exposure risk factors are multiple, occurring over long periods of time (McMichael, 1999). The natural history of chronic disease is one of a slow and progressive decline following some initial physiological response. Despite long latent periods, which are the hallmark of chronic diseases, the negative health impacts of chronic diseases are often measurable early in disease progression, and some form of intervention is often possible. Moreover, latency has a far more varied duration than that of sub-clinical disease following exposure to a pathogen that is communicable. For instance, the presentation and eventual spread of breast cancer in a population would have a variable timeframe; the negative health impacts distribute as

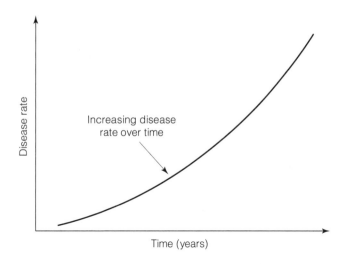

Figure 7.2   *Non-threshold effect in a hypothetical time trend study of a chronic disease*

a curve. There is no threshold effect. Note that not all cancers conform to the chronic diseases model; the exponential growth of some especially aggressive tumours do show threshold effects (Figure 7.2).

ECO-EPIDEMIOLOGY

In communicable diseases, the vector or pathogen is of relatively recent appearance, with a relatively brief incubation period. For the chronic diseases, exposures usually persist over long periods of time and, following the onset of disease, tend to be chronic and of long duration. Despite these differences between communicable and chronic diseases epidemiology, the negative health effects in both are proximate and quantifiable.

The specialty of disaster epidemiology probably comes closest to the issues at the heart of this chapter. Environmental health impacts occur through a multitude of pathways, some of which are understood, but many of which remain, as yet, unknown. In eco-epidemiology, however, the determinants (exposures) are both distal and usually have a longer duration than in disaster epidemiology as we erode the natural environment and degrade ecological systems. This occurs through policies that, directly or indirectly, aid and abet the process of environmental degradation. In eco-epidemiology, the exposures are long-term (chronic) and the effects may be both chronic and acute (in other words have threshold effects).

Population exposure to altered ecosystem states is proceeding unchecked. A variety of means are now available with which we can characterize ecosystem resilience, including biodiversity, the index of biological integrity, the measure of mean functional integrity, ecological footprint analysis and the World Wide Fund for Nature (WWF) Living Planet Index.[2] These indicators are consistently telling us that we are rapidly losing what Ulanowicz calls 'overhead' – the overlapping nutrient/waste pathways between species that provide an evolutionary cushion during times of upheaval (Figure 7.3). Highly evolved systems with many committed pathways for the cycling of nutrients/wastes are therefore increasingly sensitive to any species loss or pathway interruption. After a long period of resilience, a now 'brittle' system may rapidly collapse. Superimposed on this pattern, humanity is rapidly effecting a dramatic change on its surroundings. The 'business as usual' approach being taken towards anthropogenic (human-induced) environmental pollution results in, among other things, global warming.[3] Under current business-as-usual approaches to population growth, consumption and waste, and the inappropriate uses of technology, along which future path in Figure 7.3 is humanity most likely to travel and with what velocity?

Non-threshold and threshold health effects, induced by exposure to degraded ecosystem states, must be understood to occur within populations rather than at the individual level. Non-threshold health effects occur because the population consists of individuals with varied genetic susceptibility to slowly mounting ecosystem collapses. Disease prevalence grows as those who are susceptible join the ranks of the ill. On the other hand, threshold effects occur with ecological

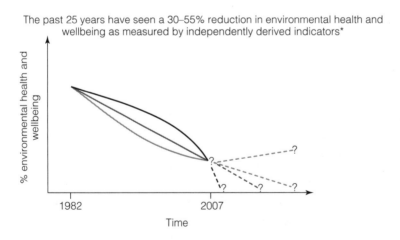

Figure 7.3 *Profound declines in ecological integrity demonstrated by indicators measuring the state of the environment*

Notes: *Index of biological integrity:* James Karr, University of Washington, from his study of streams; *Measure of mean functional integrity:* Orie Loucks, Miami University, from his study of soils and forests; *WWF:* 16 indicators of environmental health, including the Living Planet Index; *Ecological footprint:* William Rees and Mathis Wackernagel

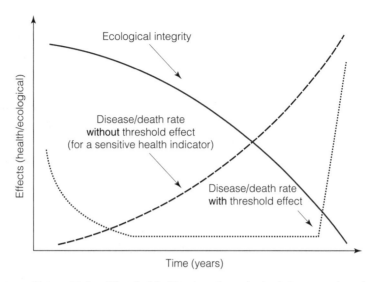

Figure 7.4 *Threshold effect in a hypothetical time trend study, superimposed on an idealized relationship between ecological integrity and a sensitive health indicator*

disasters and with system flips that arise when systems are so stressed that they reach a point beyond which they can no longer provide their customary life-sustaining services.

An ecological steady state, followed by a rapid decline in integrity, results when there is natural buffering against environmental pollutants or other destructive pressures (Figure 7.4). Consider, for instance, the threshold effects of acid rain on lakes and streams carved into limestone beds (calcium carbonate being a natural buffer) as compared to those bodies of water in Vermont and New Hampshire carved into granite formations (with no acid-buffering capacity). In the latter, acidification is a chronic process. In the former, as in a titration experiment, eventually, once a lake's buffering capacity is exhausted, the pH drops rapidly and a large-scale decline of fish populations ensues (Lloyd, 2001). Threshold health effects are far more difficult to predict and, therefore, to prevent, because inadequate notice is provided in anticipation of a system flip.

So what interventions can best be applied through the science of environmental epidemiology or, more specifically, eco-epidemiology?

DENOMINATORS

Traditional non-eco-epidemiological investigation rarely requires us to step outside of the readily available geo-political boundaries that constitute our denominators and facilitate the comparison of disease rates between two defined geographic

A hypothetical prairie eco-region extends beyond political boundaries. The elliptical shape, including sections of the provinces of Alberta and Saskatchewan in Canada, and the states of Montana and North Dakota in the US, represents a hypothetical eco-region.

Figure 7.5   *Eco-region denominators*

areas. How much more meaningful would our comparisons in eco-epidemiology be if, instead of – or in addition to – such denominators, we also had well-defined climate or eco-regions against which to make our comparisons?

Consider two geo-political (or administrative) districts being compared and where both are included, to a substantial extent, in one eco-region. Then, contrasts between rates in the two districts on an environmental determinant of concern would probably be attenuated towards the null hypothesis of 'no difference', making it unlikely to demonstrate any effect, owing to the uniform distribution and homogeneous nature of the exposure of interest.

For making meaningful eco-regional comparisons, or for examining temporal trends based on a putative environmental determinant, epidemiologists must be able to relate health outcomes, not to the traditional base of geo-political boundaries (for example census tracts, provinces, states and/or countries), but, more appropriately, to climate or eco-regions (Figure 7.5). In addition, ecologically determined disease rates would be more meaningfully interpreted if the ecological regions being compared were similar in terms of known confounders of environmentally determined causes of premature morbidity and mortality.

Consider, for example, the migration of mosquitoes across an ecosystem, or the increase in disaster-mediated negative health impacts following flooding along the entirety of a coastline or a floodplain, or a regional drought, where in each case the eco-region is far more expansive than any single geo-political boundary. A concentration of otherwise slight changes in illness or death would, on a regional basis, become statistically significant because the epidemiologist could look, for instance, for an increase in suicide rates in the drought-stricken agricultural region, compared to suicide rates in a non-drought-stricken region. Comparing suicide rates across two administrative districts contained within the single drought-stricken eco-region would probably be attenuated toward the null hypothesis of 'no difference', making it unlikely to demonstrate any effect.

Small-area studies have already proved successful in reducing the camouflage of localized environmental health effects and in improving statistical relationships for studies at industrial point sources (Elliot et al, 1992a and b). The small area health statistics unit (SAHSU), for example, consists of arbitrary circles drawn anywhere in Britain and correlated to postal codes (approximately 14 households) and enumeration districts from the national census. Britain has a well-developed registry of mortality, cancer incidence, childhood leukaemia, non-Hodgkin's lymphoma, live births, still births and congenital malformation data. The SAHSU was applied to the mortality rates from mesothelioma and asbestosis within a 3km radius of the Plymouth naval dockyards, with significant findings (Elliot at al, 1992b). To increase statistical power, the environmental health effects from several similar sites may be combined into a single analysis.

Certain limitations, however, remain: migration of individuals, socio-economic confounders (which may be minimized by comparing environmentally similar but socio-economically dissimilar regions) and the lack of morbidity data (hospital or GP visits) linked to postal codes. Moreover, as eco-epidemiology considers the impacts of climate change, it is obvious that this type of work must be extrapolated to an eco-region scale with the help of geographic information system (GIS) analysis.

Thus an administrative infrastructure is needed so that meaningful eco-epidemiology can be conducted. Ecologists would systematically map the landmass into small, harmonious eco-regions. Reparameterization of eco-regions must be possible, so that the designated eco-region can be responsive to ecological changes at any level (in other words any portion within its boundaries). Then a database could be assembled, linking the ecological data to postal codes and thereby a variety of social and health data. Governments must establish procedures for reporting eco-region-based analysis. If this infrastructure were available, direct comparisons of negative health impacts could be made between similar eco-regions that have undergone different kinds of environmental degradation. Furthermore, time trend studies following populations through ecologically homogeneous changes would become possible.

NUMERATORS

If we are to have any chance of detecting the health effects associated with declines in ecological integrity, appropriately sensitive indicators of health and wellbeing will be needed. Epidemiologists need indicators that are responsive to the shifts in health status that might parallel ecological declines. The HEADLAMP (Health and Environment Analysis for Decision-Making) project, a joint collaboration between the United Nations Environment Programme, the US Environmental Protection Agency and the World Health Organization (WHO), laid out a strong set of guidelines to direct the further development of environmental health indicators (Corvalan et al, 1996). The importance of transparent, well-documented indicator design criteria cannot be overemphasized when research is directed at policy formulation.

Selection of an environmental health indicator appropriate to a research question is essential. Traditional environmental health hazards generally have closely related health effects with obvious environmental health indicators (for example mesothelioma and asbestosis for asbestos exposure) (Selikoff and Hammond, 1979). On the other hand, the stressing of global limits by climate change acts through numerous impact pathways, is making indicator selection more difficult (Corvalan et al, 1999).

The HEADLAMP project proposed a conceptual framework characterizing some of the complexities of environment–health effect interactions: the DPSEEA (driving forces, pressures, state, exposure, effects, actions) analytical framework (Corvalan et al, 1996) (Table 7.1). This approach recognizes the sequential connections moving from upstream determinants through downstream effects to interventions. Indicators from any point in the sequential chain have strengths and weaknesses. Generally, downstream indicators have the advantage of being more clearly linked to specific effects, whereas upstream indicators (higher up the DPSEEA chain) have the advantage of being more easily obtained and provide better early warning signs for environmental and broader ecosystem decay. Actions or interventions, meanwhile, may be targeted at any or all levels in the chain.

Some environmental health indicators have already been developed. One of the most obvious repercussions of global warming is an increased frequency of heatwaves and the accompanying heat-related health effects, ranging from cramps to strokes. The well-documented increase in mortality with increased temperature makes heat-related mortality a good environmental health

Table 7.1   *DPSEEA model for climate change*

Driving forces	Pressures	State	Exposure	Effects	Actions
Global limits: • Energy demand • Food and agriculture needs • Industry • Development	Release of greenhouse gases	Climate change: • Temperature and precipitation change • Increased climate variability • Sea level rise	Population residing in an affected eco-region	• Heat-related morbidity and mortality • Redistribution and re-emergence of vector- and water-borne diseases • Large-scale malnutrition and starvation	• Research • Monitoring • Education • Legislation

Source: Adapted from Corvalan et al (1996)

indicator.[4] This is so, especially in urban centres and among elderly Americans in the presence of unremitting night-time temperatures. However, this is not so among elderly Canadians, suggesting a socio-economic component. Further, an increase in non-melanomatous skin cancers may be used as an environmental health indicator because the relationship has a well-studied exposure–response curve (Lloyd, 1993 and 2001) and because the effects of stratospheric ozone depletion and global warming often are considered together. These two processes are highly interconnected, sharing many of the same mediators of damage: the CFCs which destroy ozone are also greenhouse gases, and UV-irradiated phytoplankton loses its ability to function as an effective carbon sink (Last, 1998). Another environmental health indicator concerns the redistribution of the *Anopheles* mosquito breeding grounds according to new rainfall patterns. The spread of malaria has been the subject of extensive modelling (Martens, 1998, pp27–80). Despite this, other environmental and ecosystem health indicators will be required for different research questions. Regardless, the inherent ambiguity present when examining a population (with genetic variation) within a region (with temporal and geographic variation) is best served by a credible exposure–response relationship for proposed environmental health indicators (in other words a clear indication of a correlation between exposure and illness).

The HEADLAMP project discouraged the use of mortality rates in eco-epidemiology as an insensitive early warning indicator. Nonetheless, traditional measures of health (for example life expectancy, percentage of babies with low birth weight and infant mortality) are the only health effects easily obtainable on a global scale, and are intuitively linkable to effects from environmental pollution. Work by Sieswerda et al confirms the expectations of the HEADLAMP project: traditional measures do not necessarily provide an early warning indication of negative health impacts (Sieswerda et al, 2001). This is likely to be because international trade allows rich nations to insulate and buffer themselves (as measured by the traditional health indicators) from the effects of environmental degradation by virtue of appropriating the resources they need from ecologically intact regions (usually poorer nations) while simultaneously exporting their wastes to such regions. This is not likely to be a formula for a sustainable – or ethical – future: 'business-as-usual' attitudes will need to change.

The decrease in environmental disease with increased economic development is a recurrent theme in eco-epidemiological research. Complementing issues of hazardous waste transport and environmental justice (Soskolne, 2001) is the changing disease burden associated with different types of environmental hazard exposure (Smith et al, 1999). Alongside industrialization is a shift from indoor air pollution associated with cooking to ambient air pollution from industrial development and fossil fuel energy. Temporary, distant, widespread environmental degradation has less negative health effects, especially for respiratory ailments, than the proximate contamination of indoor air pollution;

however, we now observe that these distant environmental states are encroaching upon human populations.

The search for sensitive environmental health indicators has led some researchers to consider aggregate indicators (de Hollander et al, 1999). Aggregate indicators better reflect the full scope of adverse environmental health effects by incorporating measures of morbidity, but they introduce additional uncertainty with the relatively subjective weighting of disease severity. De Hollander et al worked with disability-adjusted life years (DALYs) for a variety of environmental health indicators, giving different weights to different morbidities (for example a weighting of 0.01 each for noise-pollution-induced stresses (severe annoyance and sleep disturbance), 0.08 for asthma, 0.21 for lower respiratory tract infections, 0.43 for lung cancer morbidity and 1.00 for lung cancer mortality). Those adverse environmental health effects with minimal severity and a large population impact are the most susceptible to even slight changes in weighting. However, aggregate indicators do challenge the traditional definitions of scientific investigation and understanding.

New methods in eco-epidemiology will need to transcend the traditional boundaries of the individual disciplines to achieve new models for understanding or explaining complex issues (Rosenfield, 1992). Such factors include sensitive measures of wellbeing and health, together with models of those human behaviours that contribute to climate change and those exposure factors (such as pollution) that are made worse by global warming. A willingness to adopt aggregate health indicators when addressing environmental issues reflects the rising support for transdisciplinary approaches within the scientific community.

GENUINE PROGRESS INDICATOR ACCOUNTS

Alternative measures of health, such as social wellbeing, may be needed now, more than ever before, for epidemiological research. The psychosocial and economic factors which impact human health may be more sensitive to altered environmental states than the standard measures of, say, life expectancy. Despite having long been described as a confounding factor in ecological analysis, socio-economic status and degraded environmental conditions are often likely to aggregate together, as higher-income households have better means (including access to knowledge and a stronger political voice) with which to insulate themselves. The widening gap between 'rich' and 'poor' may provide a sensitive measure of declining social wellbeing (Wilkinson, 1996).

The most appropriate measure of social health is likely to be an aggregate indicator. For instance, genuine progress indicator (GPI) accounts (Anielski and Soskolne, 2002), originally conceived as a replacement for gross domestic product (GDP) as a measure of economic wellbeing, are an amalgamation of economic, social, health and environmental indicators that take not only GDP into consideration, but also some 30–50 other factors, including crime, suicide rates, air pollution, and the value of unpaid household, parenting, care for the elderly and volunteer work. The indicators are compiled into an index according to standard accounting procedures and may be considered separately or as specific arrays. Such flexibility should permit epidemiologists to access reliable and standardized international statistics on social wellbeing. Epidemiologists should both support the refinement of such aggregate indexes, especially the refinement of the weighting of the various individual indicators, and their application in lieu of GDP. Even the dependence on GDP as a measure of economic wellbeing has been reconsidered in economic circles (Sen, 1999).

The advantage of GPI accounts is that they are entirely transparent. All aspects are presented in the balance sheet of the accounts. Thus this approach, which is one of a full-cost accounting, lends itself to the accountability advocated within the HEADLAMP project.

INTERVENTIONS

The prevention goals of the epidemiologist are most effectively met when a quantifiable negative health impact can be linked to a proximal risk or pathogen, and an appropriate intervention can be implemented. Conversely, when the negative health impacts of an altered environmental state are multiple, direct and indirect, proximate and distant, discovering the linkages and formulating various interventions are more challenging. Moreover, where threshold health effects induced through environmental collapse are the concern, the role of epidemiology would at best be limited. However, if epidemiologists could successfully refine their evaluation of denominators and related numerator events, epidemiological inputs might yet contribute to a concerted prevention effort, through rational preventative planning and health policy formulation.

Considering the high risks and great uncertainties associated with modelling environmental degradation, implementation of the precautionary principle (in other words erring on the side of caution) is one possible solution (Tickner et al, 1999; Tickner, 2000). Societal inertia, combined with the resistance of policymakers to a radical systems overhaul without a demonstrated risk, however, invites additional approaches. Integrated assessments, which distil social, environmental and economic patterns into policy development, provide a fertile venue for epidemiological research (Aron et al, 2001).

In anticipation of threshold environmental health effects, adaptations, such as emergency services planning under various possible scenarios, would be crucial in mitigating the negative health impacts of environmental degradation. Evidence suggests that vulnerabilities in social structure are of greater importance than are the physical determinants of an environmental disaster in assessing the magnitude of negative societal impacts from extreme weather or climate events.

For instance, increased destruction by hurricanes in the US, without an associated increase in hurricane frequency or severity, may be attributed to population expansion and construction along vulnerable coastlines (Kunkel et al, 1999). Moreover, in comparison to their counterparts in developing nations, these inhabitants are still shielded by the technological ability to forecast severe storms and broadcast warnings, by the public institutions that enforce building safety requirements and prepare contingency plans, and by emergency medical services. Thus the average of 500 deaths per disaster among industrialized nations balloons to over 3000 deaths per disaster in the developing world (Noji, 1997). For instance, consider flood-mediated mortality. In the US, the vast majority of flood-related deaths are by drowning (especially inside vehicles during a flash flood); whereas in Brazil, the number of drowning deaths are overshadowed by those caused by mudslides in urban areas and subsequent leptospirosis, and in Bangladesh, the number of drowning deaths are superseded by the additional deaths caused by the onslaught of intestinal diseases following the displacement of populations and the disruption and contamination of the water supply (Toole, 1997; Roberts et al, 2001).

Whether the protective importance of social structures will be maintained during widespread environmental collapse is unknown. One wonders whether the social structures themselves could be maintained throughout such a collapse. Nevertheless, adaptation planning will be an important means of intervention.

CONCLUSIONS

Epidemiology's role in assessing health effects associated with progressive losses of, or changes in, nature's services needs to be firmly established (Butler, 2001). For several decades, ecologists, biologists, philosophers and others have been warning us against a trend towards environmental degradation. All forms of degradation, not only climate change impacts, must be considered.

The consequences of ecological collapse have been brought to society's attention. Until the WHO text *Our Planet, Our Health* and Anthony J. McMichael's book *Planetary Overload*, epidemiologists paid scant attention to these warnings (WHO, 1992; McMichael, 1993). But now it behoves the epidemiologist to hear these dire warnings and make efforts to find linkages between altered environmental states and their effects on human health. Being so self-centred a species (in other words anthropocentric), human beings are likely to implement policies only once the effects of environmental degradation are actually shown to have a negative impact on human health and wellbeing. If, through epidemiology, negative health and wellbeing impacts related to ecological declines could be demonstrated, then policy changes that might lessen the stresses on degrading ecosystems would be more likely to be implemented. A sustainable future could thereby be more assured.

NOTES

1   This chapter is adapted from a paper co-authored with Natasha Broemling (Soskolne and Broemling, 2002). I acknowledge Natasha's substantive contribution to the original paper, to which the one significant change for this chapter has been my revision of the section on denominators; relatively minor revisions were also made throughout.
2   See Karr et al, 1986; Karr, 1987; Wackernagel and Rees, 1996; Loh et al, 1998; Loucks, 1999; Ulanowicz, 2000.
3   See McMichael, 1993; Soskolne and Bertollini, 1999; Allen et al, 2000; National Health Assessment Group, 2001 (www.jhsph.edu/nationalassessment-health); IPCC, 2007.
4   See Kilbourne et al, 1982; Kalkstein and Smoyer, 1993); National Health Assessment Group, 2001 (also available at www.jhsph.edu/nationalassessment-health).

REFERENCES

Allen, M. R., Scott, P. A., Mitchell, J. F. B., Schnur, R. and Delworth, T. L. (2000) 'Quantifying the uncertainty in forecasts of anthropogenic climate change', *Nature*, vol 407, pp617–620

Anielski, M. and Soskolne, C. L. (2002) 'Genuine progress indicator (GPI) accounting: Relating ecological integrity human health and wellbeing', in P. Miller and L. Westra (eds) *Just Ecological Integrity: The Ethics of Maintaining Planetary Life*, Rowman and Littlefield, Lanham, MD, pp83–97

Aron, J. L., Ellis, J. H. and Hobbs, B. F. (2001) 'Integrated assessment', in J. L. Aron and J. A. Patz (eds) *Ecosystem Change and Public Health: A Global Perspective*, Johns Hopkins Press, Baltimore, MD, pp116–162

Beaglehole, R., Bonita, R. and Kjellstrom, T. (1993) *Basic Epidemiology*, WHO, Geneva

Butler, C. D. (2001) 'Epidemiology, Australians and global environmental change', *Australasian Epidemiologist*, vol 8, no 1, pp13–16

Corvalan, C., Briggs, D. and Kjellstrom, T. (1996) 'Development of environmental health indicators', in D. Briggs, C. Corvalan and M. Nurminen (eds) *Linkage Methods for Environment and Health Analysis: General Guidelines*, WHO, Geneva, pp19–53

Corvalan, C., Kjellstrom, T. and Smith, K. R. (1999) 'Health, environment and sustainable development: Identifying links and indicators to promote action', *Epidemiology*, vol 10, no 5, pp656–660

de Hollander, A. E. M., Meisse, J. M., Lebret, E. and Kramers, P. G. N. (1999) 'An aggregate public health indicator to represent the impact of multiple environmental exposures', *Epidemiology*, vol 10, no 5, pp606–617

Elliot, P., Cuzick, J. and English, D. (1992a) *Geographical and Environmental Epidemiology: Methods for Small-Area Studies*, Oxford University Press, Oxford, UK

Elliot, P., Westlake, A. J., Hills, M., Kleinschmidt, I., Rodrigues, L., McGale, P., Marshall, K. and Rose, G. (1992b) 'The small area health statistics unit: A national facility for investigating health around point sources of environmental pollution in the United Kingdom', *Journal of Epidemiology and Community Health*, vol 46, no 4, pp345–349

IPCC (Intergovernmental Panel on Climate Change) (1997) 'Fourth Assessment Report', www.ipcc.ch

Kalkstein, L. S. and Smoyer, K. E. (1993) 'The impact of the climate on Canadian mortality: Past relationships and future scenarios', Canadian Climate Centre Report No 93-7, Downsview, Ontario, Canada (unpublished manuscript)

Karr, J. R. (1987) 'Biological monitoring and environmental assessment: A conceptual framework', *Environmental Management*, vol 11, no 2, pp249–256

Karr, J. R., Fausch, K. D., Angermeier, P. L., Yant, P. R. and Schlosser, I. J. (1986) 'Assessment of biological integrity in running water: A method and its rationale', *Bulletin of the Illinois Natural History Survey Division*, Publication 5, Champaign, IL

Kilbourne, E. M., Keewhan, C., Jones, S. and Thacker, S. B. (1982) 'Risk factors for heatstroke: A case-control study', *Journal of the American Medical Association*, vol 247, no 24, pp3332–3336

Kunkel, K. E., Pielke, R. A. Jr and Changnon, S. A. (1999) 'Temporal fluctuations in weather and climate extremes that cause economic and human health impacts: A review', *Bulletin of the American Meteorological Society*, vol 80, no 6, pp1077–1098

Last, J. M. (1998) *Public Health and Human Ecology* (second edition), Appleton and Laing, Stamford, CT

Lloyd, S. A. (1993) 'Health and climate change: Stratospheric ozone depletion', *Lancet*, vol 342, pp1156–1158

Lloyd, S. A. (2001) 'The changing chemistry of the Earth's atmosphere', in J. L. Aron and J. A. Patz (eds) *Ecosystem Change and Public Health: A Global Perspective*, Johns Hopkins Press, Baltimore, MD, pp188–232

Loh, J., Randers, J., MacGillivray, A., Kapos, V., Jenkins, M., Groombridge, B. and Cox, N. (1998) 'Living Planet Report: Overconsumption is driving the rapid decline of the world's natural environments', World Wide Fund for Nature International, Gland, Switzerland

Loucks, O. L. (1999) 'Impoverishment of ecosystem integrity and community health: A tragedy in Appalachia, USA', in C. L. Soskolne and R. Bertollini 'Global ecological integrity and 'sustainable development": Cornerstones of public health – A discussion document', European Centre for Environment and Health, Rome Division, WHO, www.euro.who.int/document/gch/ecorep5.pdf

Martens, P. (1998) *Health and Climate Change: Modelling the Impacts of Global Warming and Ozone Depletion*, Earthscan, London

Mausner, J. S. and Bahn, A. K. (1974) 'Epidemiologic aspects of infectious disease', in *Epidemiology: An Introductory Text*, WB Saunders Company, Philadelphia, PA

McMichael, A. J. (1993) *Planetary Overload: Global Environmental Change and the Health of the Human Species*, Cambridge University Press, Cambridge, UK

McMichael, A. J. (1999) 'Prisoners of the proximate: Loosening the constraints on epidemiology in an age of change', *American Journal of Epidemiology*, vol 149, no 10, pp887–897

National Health Assessment Group (2001) *Climate Change and Human Health: The Potential Consequences of Climate Variability and Change*, Johns Hopkins University Press, Baltimore, MD

Noji, E. K. (1997) 'The nature of disaster: General characteristics and public health effects', in E. K. Noji (ed) *The Public Health Consequences of Disasters*, Oxford University Press, New York, pp3–20

Roberts, L., Confalonieri, U. E. C. and Aron, J. L. (2001) 'Too little, too much: How the quantity of water affects human health', in J. L. Aron and J. A. Patz (eds) *Ecosystem Change and Public Health: A Global Perspective*, Johns Hopkins Press, Baltimore, MD, pp409–429

Rosenfield, P. (1992) 'The potential of trans-disciplinary research for sustaining and extending linkages between health and social sciences', *Social Science and Medicine*, vol 35, no 11, pp1343–1357

Selikoff, I. J. and Hammond, E. C. (eds) (1979) 'Health effects of asbestos exposure', *Annals of the New York Academy of Sciences*, vol 330, New York Academy of Sciences, New York

Sen, A. (1999) *Development as Freedom*, Alfred A. Knopf, Inc., New York

Sieswerda, L. E., Soskolne, C. L., Newman, S. C., Schopflocher, D. and Smoyer, K. E. (2001) 'Towards measuring the impact of ecological disintegrity on human health', *Epidemiology*, vol 12, pp28–32

Smith, R. K., Corvalan, C. F. and Kjellstrom, T. (1999) 'How much global ill health is attributable to environmental factors?', *Epidemiology*, vol 10, no 5, pp573–584

Snow, J. (1855) *On the Mode of Communication of Cholera*, Churchill, London

Soskolne, C. L. (2001) 'International transport of hazardous waste: Legal and illegal trade in the context of professional ethics', *Global Bioethics*, vol 14, no 1, pp39–44

Soskolne, C. L. and Bertollini, R. (1999) 'Global ecological integrity and "sustainable development": Cornerstones of public health – A discussion document', European Centre for Environment and Health, Rome Division, WHO, www.euro. who.int/document/gch/ecorep5.pdf

Soskolne, C. L. and Broemling, N. (2002) 'Eco-epidemiology: On the need to measure health effects from global change', *Global Change and Human Health*, vol 3, no 1, pp58–66, www.springerlink.com/content/v97xv0l42845407u/fulltext.pdf

Tickner, J. A. (2000) 'Precaution in practice: A Framework for implementing the precautionary principle', DSc Thesis, University of Massachusetts, Lowell, MA

Tickner, J. A., Raffensperger, C. and Myers, N. (1999) *The Precautionary Principle in Action: A Handbook*, Science and Environmental Health Network, Windsor, ND, www.biotech-info.net/handbook.pdf

Toole, M. J. (1997) 'Communicable diseases and disease control', in E. K. Noji (ed) *The Public Health Consequences of Disasters*, Oxford University Press, New York, pp79–100

Ulanowicz, R. E. (2000) 'Toward the measurement of ecological integrity', in D. Pimental, L. Westra and R. F. Noss (eds) *Ecological Integrity: Integrating Environment, Conservation and Health*, Island Press, Washington, DC, pp99–113

Wackernagel, M. and Rees, W. (1996) *Our Ecological Footprint: Reducing Human Impact on the Earth*, New Society Publishers, Gabriola Island, British Columbia, Canada

WHO (1992) *Our Planet, Our Health: Report of the WHO Commission on Health and the Environment*, World Health Organization, Geneva

Wilkinson, R. G. (1996) *Unhealthy Societies: The Afflictions of Inequality*, Routledge, London

8

Finding 'Paradise' in a Complex Web: The Inter-relation of Biodiversity, Ecosystems and Human Health

Carijn Beumer, Maud Huynen and Pim Martens

JOHANNES AND THE WEB OF LIFE

A Dutch literature classic tells about a boy named Johannes who finds himself in a class of crickets having a zoological lesson (Van Eeden, 1905). In this lesson the cricket teacher tells his students that all living creatures can be classified into three groups: those who jump, those who fly and those who crawl. The ability of crickets to jump places them in the highest order of beings. Humans are in the lowest order because they can neither jump nor fly.

For ages we humans have been struggling and wondering about the position we are taking in nature. Through the ages, many ideas and conceptualizations have been considered. We have seen Aristotelian hierarchy in the Middle Ages, where everything had its natural place; the 'great chain of being' (Lovelock, 2000), where the hierarchically ordered creatures were linked to each other in a kind of universal harmony; or modern mechanical atomism, a view of a clockwork-like functioning of all separate elements of life. This last view – developed by many great thinkers and scientists such as Copernicus, Galileo, René Descartes, Francis Bacon and Isaac Newton – has evolved as the dominant view in science since the Scientific Revolution in the 16th and 17th centuries (Shapin, 1996). It has had enormous consequences for the way we have utilized nature for the sake of our own wellbeing in the last few centuries (Capra, 1996). Nowadays, due to global developments affecting all people in the world, an urgent need is evolving to reconsider our conceptualization of nature. Environmental degradation, climate change, and the increased risk of the spread and development of infectious diseases are some of the contemporary problems we encounter. Many of them are somehow related to the modern mechanical and reductionist worldview where human (and largely white male) domination, expansion, and the control and exploitation of the natural world play a major role (Nash, 1989; Capra, 1996). But the arising global problems are too complex to be solved with the same linear and reductionist methods. They cannot be understood in isolation. They are interconnected, interdependent, systemic problems (Capra, 1996; Kemp and Martens, 2007). So, in facing our contemporary world and the effects of our modern lifestyles, we are slowly learning that everything is related to everything else in many complex ways. This pushes us towards a revival of the concept of the 'great chain' and the interconnectedness of all beings by a more contemporary concept, befitting our globalizing network society: the 'web of life' (Lovejoy, 1936; Prigogine and Stengers, 1984; Capra, 1996).

The 'web of life' idea mainly stems from systems theory (Laszlo, 1996 and 2006; Capra, 1996; Boogerd and Bruggeman, 2007) and shows the connectivity and the natural equilibrium of all elements, organisms and natural systems of the world. It differs from the 'chain of being' concept in the sense that the model of nature can no longer be seen as structured purely hierarchically. Boundaries between species, subspecies and ecosystems are seen rather as fuzzy than clearly distinguishable. In this chapter, this close interconnection of all living beings will be shown in the context of the relationship between biodiversity, ecosystems and human health.

In relation to this 'network' concept of nature, two important and closely connected insights have trickled down to our consciousness. They both have important implications for how we deal with health problems, especially in governance settings. First, because of the complexity of the relationships in ecosystems, it is hard to measure and quantify biodiversity and its relation to health in time and space (Martens et al, 2003). Therefore we need flexible and adaptive solutions in policy- and decision-making (Kemp and Martens, 2007). The ultimate health-governing strategy does not exist. Nevertheless, many variable views and strategies can be combined to meet actuality and to define flexible paths and visions for future strategies (Swart et al, 2004; Van Asselt et al, 2005). This adaptive quality – ever balancing ecological, economic and social capital for the benefits of present *and* future generations – is one of the main features of 'sustainable development' (Giddings et al, 2002; Swart et al, 2004; Kemp and Martens, 2007).

The second insight is that we can never learn *everything* about the complex systems of nature (Capra, 1996). At this moment we still only know just the tip of the iceberg of all existing species, of their features, their habitats, their lifestyles and their functions. Only approximately 10 per cent of all existing species – the Earth system is estimated to contain between 2 million and 100 million species – are classified and documented (Duraiappah, 2005). There is still a lot to be discovered of what can help us to learn about nature, about ourselves and about our health (Gibbons, 1993). But we are now in the process of learning to accept uncertainty and the fact that the time limits by which our lives are framed will never be sufficient to learn everything to save our planet with the tool of 'knowledge'.

Nevertheless, we are still used to the attitude of seeing ourselves on the outside of nature: the web of life concept has a strong biological connotation.

It is most commonly used to point to the biophysical relationships between animal organisms, micro-organisms, vegetation, ecosystems and habitat. This chapter will extend this traditional view by including humanity in the web. But not simply by putting ourselves into the system as a biological entity: the web system does not consist of living creatures and of natural and built surroundings only, but also of our immaterial social structures, organizations and – more abstract – our institutions and values. In this 'multiple' environment, we play a role as self-conscious actors with the ability to effectively and intently influence evolutionary processes in the web for better and for worst. To be able to safeguard our resources for future generations and to sustain and improve our health and wellbeing, we must become more aware of the intrinsic interwovenness of all natural, social and value systems. This integrative awareness will be of great importance in extending our palette of choices of how to encounter nature. Although all our activities are building on what the natural system delivers us, it is important to keep in mind that nature is more than a pack of services. We have the option to leave her abundance, her genuineness, her integrity intact (Westra, 1998; Miller and Westra, 2002). And even better, seen from our present situation: to heal and to improve what we destroyed before. The web of life concept of nature gives us back the responsibility for our planet (Capra, 1996; Tress in Robinson and Westra, 2002).

BIODIVERSITY, ECOSYSTEMS AND THEIR IMPORTANCE TO HEALTH AND HUMAN WELLBEING

An abundant diversity of species is considered a prerequisite for ecosystems to function well and be considered healthy (Gibbons, 1993; Takacs, 1996). Sometimes, when we linger in romantic mood, intact and proper functioning ecosystems (Costanza et al, 1997; De Groot et al, 2002) in their rich abundance remind us of a paradisiacal state of nature (Takacs, 1996): nature being able to take care of its own needs and being able to sustain and renew itself and its resources and biodiversity (Miller and Westra, 2002). But there we – humans – step in. And, as we know, with us entering the world, paradise was lost. Sustaining the human species as a part of the global ecosystem turns out to be not so easy, not so harmoniously 'natural'. Since the start of our existence we have worked with, on and against nature to be able to sustain our basic needs for living and a quality of life (Nash, 1989). But now we increasingly realize we can't possibly survive by 'fighting' nature (Capra, 1996; Laszlo, 2006).

How important biodiversity and well-functioning ecosystems are for our human wellbeing and health can be researched by investigating the goods and services they supply (Costanza et al, 1997; De Groot et al, 2002; Martens et al, 2003; Huynen et al, 2004). What are these goods and services? Recently, one of the authors was cycling on a path where many nuts had fallen from a tree. After she crushed the nuts with her bike, some birds waiting on the roadside came to pick them up: animal life made easier by human technology. In general, though, a human perspective to ecosystem services is taken, mostly related to our human wellbeing and comfort. Here we also want to focus on the self-sustaining, intrinsic qualities of nature – the ecological integrity – in relation to human health (Pimentel et al, 2000), considering human systems to be part of the ecosystems in the way mentioned above.

Ecosystem services of importance for our health, in the first place, are those which meet our primary needs: water supply by watersheds, reservoirs and aquifers; food supply by the availability of fruits, crops, herbs, nuts, fish, game and livestock; and shelter and clothing (De Groot et al, 2002; Huynen et al, 2004; Duraiappah, 2005).

Services such as air-quality regulation, climate regulation and water-quality regulation are significant both for our human health (guaranteeing our primary needs) and for the state of ecosystems themselves. Healthy ecosystems and animal and plant species are primarily significant because of their pest and disease regulatory services. Second, some animal and plant species have a buffering function by being carriers of specific viruses, bacteria and parasites, containing them in themselves and so preventing them from directly infecting us, though on the other hand, of course, some species are the main vectors infecting people. Third, biodiversity is important in the regulation of natural hazards such as the prevention of floods, landslides or avalanches by reeds, mangroves or forests.

Biodiversity is also directly related to health through the medicinal powers of plants, micro-organisms and animal species or their products. Cone snails, for example, are very promising species for delivering many new pharmaceuticals, such as non-addictive pain-relievers which are much stronger than morphine (Hart, 1997). Because of their enormous species diversity, tropical rainforests are an important source for our pharmaceutical products and for future medicines yet to be discovered (Duraiappah, 2005; Corvalan et al, 2005).

Often neglected in publications and discussions about biodiversity and its relation to human health are the species used for biomedical research and genetic experiments. Laboratory animals, microbes and plants have been used for centuries to understand the human physiology and to learn about the treatment of diseases (Noske, 1988; Chivian, 2002). Human wellbeing and health are often brought forward as the main legitimating factors of biomedical research on living beings (Noske, 1988). There is a problem with this reasoning, considering the integrity of nature, however. Illness and a lack of human wellbeing are often seen as an 'attack' on human integrity, but why would we impair nature's integrity to restore our own when we are part of the same system (Capra, 1996; Pimentel et al, 2000)?

Biodiversity also functions as a 'canary in a coalmine' (Takacs, 1996, p202). Especially the status of certain keystone species (often endangered species) can alarm us when we are in peril. Because of their vulnerable nature, butterflies, for example, are good indicators for the health of an ecosystem. When they suddenly disappear, the natural system is most certainly suffering from an imbalance (Takacs, 1996). Also foetuses and children – called the 'new canaries' by the WHO (WHO, 2004; Westra, 2006) – can be seen as significant indicators of the state of the environment. They are, for example, more vulnerable to diseases, because of their developing immune systems, or to pollution with industrial chemicals, which can impair their physical and cognitive development and can cause lifelong disability (Grandjean and Landrigan, 2006; Grandjean et al, 2007).

Next to these services and goods, the proper functioning of biodiversity and ecosystems has its impact on our social relations, cultural freedoms and values and on the way we organize ourselves in institutions and organizations (Costanza et al, 1997; Chivian, 2002; Martens et al, 2003; Duraiappah, 2005). Through all these strands of the web of life, biodiversity and the world's ecosystems reach to the micro-levels of our physiological cells and of our cognitive and emotional condition (Kaplan, 1995). And the other way around the same inter-relationship can be discerned: our cognition, our ideas and values, and our physical and mental health influence the way we inter-relate with our surroundings and how we engage in co-designing the natural world.

THE IMPACTS OF BIODIVERSITY LOSS ON HUMAN HEALTH AND WELLBEING

Biodiversity has never been stable. Darwin's evolutionary theory has shown the evolution of new species through specialization and isolation of older species. Extinctions have always occurred on Earth, sometimes unnoticed, sometimes massive, like the extinction of 70 per cent of all species – including the dinosaurs – at the end of the Cretaceous Period approximate 65 million years ago. But human domination of the ecosystems has changed the main causes of extinction and has accelerated the speed 100 to 1000 times compared to the natural speed of extinction (Larson, 2001; Martens et al, 2003). The Biodiversity Synthesis of the Millennium Ecosystem Assessment (MEA) (Duraiappah, 2005) coordinated by the United Nations Environmental Programme (UNEP) frames the drivers of direct or indirect changes in ecosystem and biological diversity. The MEA stresses that most changes in biodiversity and in ecosystems are caused by multiple drivers interacting on various scales of time, space and organization. Martens et al (2003) mention the complex interaction of economic, socio-cultural and ecological components in relation to the loss of biodiversity (Martens et al, 2003). Human activity is seen as a significant factor in actual changes in biodiversity and ecosystems (Gibbons, 1993; Takacs, 1996; Duraiappah, 2005).

A main driver of biodiversity loss according to the MEA is change of land use. The conversion of natural habitat to agricultural land and the use of fresh waters and oceanic territory for fisheries have affected all biogeographical realms

(Duraiappah, 2005, p42). Fragmentation of landscapes – through cities, industry or infrastructure – is also a serious threat to biodiversity. Invasive alien species, often brought to new places by people, cause much extinction, especially on islands and in freshwater habitats. Overexploitation and nutrient loading are also mentioned.

Climate change – for the first time in history caused by human activity (IPCC, 2007) – has already had its impact on biodiversity and on ecosystems already under pressure due to other factors. Deserts are emerging, the cryosphere is melting at a rapid speed, small islands are slowly disappearing, rivers are flooding. Droughts and fires are consuming areas in the warmer parts of the world, and storms – such as Katrina in 2005 – seem to get bigger. Small overland tornadoes were even witnessed in The Netherlands last summer. Climate change evokes questions related to our present and future health and wellbeing: Who will be able to survive? Who will be fit to adapt to new climatological conditions? Where do we have to go? Who will become extinct? Not only can climate change lead to major shifts in ecosystems and related health patterns in developing countries, our Western world will also (re-)encounter 'old' infectious diseases. Changing climate patterns around the world can also increase the emergence of new diseases or mutations of older ones, affecting both human and animal species (IPCC, 2007). We can already see such developments in the (re)emergence of, for example, malaria and the West-Nile virus.

Another important driver for human-induced environmental change, degradation and biodiversity loss, in our view, is left out of the MEA. It can be found in the deep-seated lack of human happiness and wellbeing itself, our recurring physical and mental shortcomings, a genuine longing for the better, and an enduring search for something we might call 'paradise'. In our search for this ideal pristine state of healthy and wealthy being in an ideal and peaceful world – employing our modern expansionist thought modes, industrialized technologies and materialistic consumption patterns – we often seem to lose it more and more ...

The Lake Victoria case

A haunting example of this loss of 'paradise' can be seen in the case of Lake Victoria, strikingly shown in Hupert Sauper's documentary *Darwin's Nightmare* (Sauper, 2004). The lake, located in the midst of Tanzania, Kenya and Uganda – known as the birthplace of humankind – is Africa's largest and the world's second largest freshwater lake. The documentary can be criticized for its one-dimensional perspective on the African situation. It oversimplifies Africa as a continent of poverty, corruption, AIDS, other diseases and armed conflict. It does not show the beneficial sides of the economic developments and gives no voice to village people who do have stable, good and wealthy lives. Nevertheless, the problems – which indeed do occur – around Lake Victoria and its fishing industry can stand as a model for the situation we manoeuvre the world and ourselves into. This can best be seen in the context of another important contemporary development: globalization.

In the 1950s and 1960s, British officials introduced Nile perch to the lake to maintain its economic significance for the export market (LVFO, 2003; Kayombo and Jorgensen, 2006). The introduction of the alien predator species turned out to be a disputable blessing for the lake regions. It increased ecological, economic, social and health problems. Smaller algae-eating endemic fish such as the haplochromine cichlids could not cope with the new situation. Increasing nutrient loading, pollution of the lake with industrial waste and chemicals, and deoxygenation by the covering of the lake with algae and water hyacinth put additional pressures on the lake (LVFO, 2003), to the extent that there were uninhabitable oxygen-free 'dead zones' by the 1980s (LVFO, 2003; Sauper, 2004; Kayombo and Jorgensen, 2006).

Sauper shows the social and economic problems of Mwanza village life in relation to the state of the lake. Ecological damage, population growth and increasing mobility all have their effects on human health (Corvalan et al, 2005), and all these changes are complexly interconnected. The consequences of the situation of Lake Victoria for the wellbeing and health of the local people are severe. But not only is human health itself afflicted: all the systems people live in (from the environment around the lake to the local and regional economy, companies, politics and social life) are also becoming more and more 'unhealthy'.

The perch invading the lake are not primarily meant to be sold on the local market. They are caught and processed to fillets by large commercial companies with well-equipped boats. High fish prices on the local markets cause protein malnutrition in many people. The bad economic situation causes many women to work as prostitutes to earn something for a living, spreading AIDS rapidly through the country and leaving many children orphaned. Most of these children don't go to school but live on the streets. Rumours go around that planes flying in to collect the fish for Europe and Asia don't come loaded with commodities for the local markets but carry weapons for the wars in other African countries. This course of events seems to be a one-way ticket to corruption, poverty, and physical, psychological and social misery. And this is before the epidemics and diseases caused by the dumping of waste, sewage and agricultural chemicals into the lake are taken into account. Diarrhoea, cholera and typhoid are common diseases in the area associated with the degradation of the lake and its surroundings (LVFO, 2003; Sauper, 2004).

The example of Lake Victoria clearly demonstrates the inter-relation of biodiversity, ecosystems, and human health and wellbeing. It shows the complexity and the broad contextuality of the health problems initiated by the introduction of a new species to the lake. Local and international governance initiatives have not seemed to be strong enough to manage the multiple problems around the lake. The case illustrates that the loss of biodiversity is more than an extinction of species. It is inter-related with many other occurrences and it can start an avalanche of various serious problems on multiple levels and scales and in many ecological and societal fields.

But these 'exterior' multi-environmental disasters contain one hope for the future: they bring about an important effect which has more to do with the abstract 'interior' life of people, with the value-strands of the web of life. The problems caused by human-induced ecological degradation are affecting our species so much that they are bringing a growing consciousness about the practical and ethical role we play in the web. In this sense ecological problems have a transformative value: they can lead to pro-environmental behaviour as a means of coping (Takacs, 1996, p229; Homburg and Stolberg, 2006).

PATHWAYS TOWARDS PARADISE?

Although globalization and the rise of international markets can cause a lot of trouble for the environment and for many people involved, growing global relationships between countries and people become increasingly important in recognizing these problems and setting agendas to find sustainable solutions. But advocates of more regionalized and nationalized perspectives and managing styles can also be heard. Painting pictures of paths to possible futures through scenario development (Swart et al, 2004; Van Asselt et al, 2005; Van Notten, 2005) is one way of trying to visualize the way we might deal with biodiversity and health issues in the near future.

The scenarios from the MEA (Carpenter et al, 2005) are a good example of picturing paths to future health for the world population and the way we manage biodiversity. It is important to keep in mind, however, that the future of human health cannot be predicted with scenarios. They only show 'possibilities', hypothetical futures. But there are patterns of change, transitions and signs that can be anticipated (Huynen, 2008).

Exploring future wellbeing[1] was one of the initial goals of the MEA. In their own words, the MEA provides 'a first order attempt to assess future health' (Corvalan et al, 2005). The report explicitly acknowledges the multi-causality of human health. The MEA scenarios address plausible future changes in ecosystems, in the supply and demand for ecosystem services, and in the consequent changes in human wellbeing. This scenario study builds on earlier scenarios and modelling efforts. The names given to the MEA scenarios are 'Global Orchestration', 'TechnoGarden', 'Adapting Mosaic' and 'Order from Strength' (Duraiappah, 2005; Corvalan et al, 2005; Huynen, 2008).

The MEA report 'Ecosystems and human wellbeing: Health synthesis' (Corvalan et al, 2005) outlines the possible future changes in health resulting from developments in 'critical drivers and other relevant factors'. All MEA storylines describe health as a more or less integrated outcome of multiple developments. However, the MEA primarily focuses on the health implications of changing ecosystem functioning.

Huynen (2008) argues there are some inconsistencies in the MEA reports, which probably arise from the lack of a clear conceptualization of population health and population health determination. It is mentioned that in three out of four scenarios, global health will broadly improve for both the developed and the developing world (Carpenter et al, 2005). However, it is also stated that 'ecosystems services are indispensable to the wellbeing of people throughout the world' and that 'under the MEA scenarios, an increasing number of people may be unable to replace satisfactorily, or escape from, the effects of depleted ecosystem services' (Corvalan et al, 2005). Also, in the Global Orchestration scenario, for example, there is an increasing risk of emerging infectious disease, ecological shocks, environmental pollution and unhealthy lifestyles. Hence the finding that health improvements are largest in this scenario is primarily based on the assumption that other developments (for example income growth, education, global governance and improved health services) are able to offset all these negative influences. The question is, of course, whether this is realistic or not.

To explore the MEA scenarios and to be able to make a stronger link between developments in health and ecosystems, we have put them in the context of four other possible health futures. These health futures are based on existing views in current literature[2] (Huynen and Martens, 2006; Huynen, 2008) and possible 'early signs' observed within our society. They are not sharply delineated – there is always a continuum. There is also the possibility that economic, political, social or environmental crises will cause the process of transition to stagnate, or even to go into reverse.

An age of emerging infectious diseases

The emergence of new infectious diseases or the re-emergence of 'old' ones will have a significant impact on global health (Newcomb, 2003). Other factors, such as increased travel and trade, microbiological resistance, human behaviour, breakdowns in health systems, and increased pressure on the environment, will cause global health risks. The control of infectious diseases will be hampered by political, financial and technological obstacles. As a result, life expectancy will fall and countries will be caught in a downward spiral of environmental degradation, lower levels of economic activity and income, and bad health (Martens and Huynen, 2003).

An age of medical technology

In this 'age', increased health risks caused by changes in lifestyle and the environment will be offset by increased economic growth, improvements in technology and well-organized health services (Omran, 1983 and 1998; Bobadilla and Possas, 1993). If there is no long-term sustainable economic development, increased environmental pressure and social imbalance may eventually propel poor societies into the 'age of emerging infectious diseases'. On the other hand, if environmental and social resources are eventually balanced with economic growth, sustained health may be achieved in the long run (Martens and Huynen, 2003).

An age of sustained health

Here, economic growth will stay within social and ecological limits. Combating the wide range of risk factors, social participation, social justice and harmony with the environment play an important role in achieving human wellbeing. Health policies will be designed to improve the health status of all populations, rich and poor, in such a way that the health of future generations is not compromised by the depletion of resources needed by future generations. Improved worldwide surveillance and monitoring systems will mean that any disease outbreak is properly dealt with (Martens and Huynen, 2003).

This picture of future health is comparable with Omran's vision of future health described as 'quality of life, equity, development and social justice for all' (Omran, 1998), which takes a holistic view of health in the context of human wellbeing, human rights and nature (Earth Charter, 2000; GEO3, 2002; Martens, 2002; Martens and Huynen, 2003).

An age of chronic diseases

In developing countries, infectious diseases make way for chronic and lifestyle-related diseases. It is possible for current developing countries to skip the 'age of chronic diseases' and shift directly to the 'age of sustained health', 'age of medical technology' or 'age of emerging infectious diseases'.

Linking these possible health futures to the MEA scenarios will show more clearly the interdependence of complex global developments as a context of the relationship between health, ecosystems and biodiversity. But do they show a path to a sustainable world with sustained health?

Future health in Global Orchestration

The Global Orchestration scenario unfolds increasing globalization with a focus on fair liberal economics and social policies. Due to the worldwide communication and governance structures, the institutional capacity to respond to global health threats increases. There are high investments in education, human capital and health services, combined with a global flow of knowledge and technology. Democracy and cooperation result in declining tensions. Nevertheless, some regions lag behind.

The environment has less priority. People rely on economic growth, technology and market mechanisms to react to any mounting ecological problems. There is limited environmental research. Pressures on ecosystems increase and environmental security declines, resulting in a risk of ecological surprises. The reactive approach characterizing this scenario could also spill into health services provision (for example prevention having less priority). Levels of water stress increase over those of today in many developing countries. Despite the increasing pressures on food systems, food availability increases and malnutrition decreases, probably due to reduced poverty, technological developments and the focus on equality. People increasingly demand 'beautiful' surroundings, but long-term and hard-to-address environmental problems start to have an effect on the physical living environment, in particular affecting the poor. The risk of infectious disease emerges due to deteriorating ecosystems, travel and trade. If health risks are unexpected, control proves to be difficult, despite global response structures. The increasing (global) environmental problems possibly affect the economy in the long run (Carpenter et al, 2005; Huynen, 2008).

The MEA reports that health improvements are largest in this scenario. However, there are also multiple unhealthy developments, especially in environmental factors, to anticipate. In this scenario the developed world will probably advance into the 'age of medical technology'. Most of the developing world will see some great health improvements, shifting to the 'age of chronic diseases' and perhaps even into the 'age of medical technology'. Both developed and developing regions face, however, an increasing burden of unhealthy lifestyles, of environmental problems and of a coexisting risk of sliding off into the 'age of emerging infectious diseases' (Huynen, 2008).

Future health in TechnoGarden

In TechnoGarden, globalization is characterized by a reliance on technological solutions and a focus on environmental concerns. Global market expansion is strictly monitored, causing a lower rate of economic growth. Global governance structures and organizations develop a strong set of proactive global (environmental) treaties and large-scale health networks. A global society emerges (although local cultures are at risk). Social issues have less priority. Poverty declines, but the rich–poor gap remains huge as some regions lag behind. The diffusion of information, knowledge and technology is high, with a focus on ecosystem research, (health) education and the development of green technology in both developed and developing regions. Overall, the global environment improves and part of climate change is offset. Provision of ecosystem goods and services is high, but also often pushed to the limits due to reliance on technology. Highly engineered ecosystems result in biodiversity loss and increasing vulnerability. Unexpected secondary effects of technology pose new problems.

Tensions result from existing inequities and conflicts arise in isolated regions, resulting in ecosystem decline (Carpenter et al, 2005; Huynen, 2008).

In TechnoGarden, the developed world will advance into the 'age of medical technology' rapidly. Despite the lower economic growth, large parts of the current developing world will experience some great health improvements and technological innovations. But it is important to note that the envisioned developments in this future are ambiguous. The complexities involved are underestimated and technology is barely ahead of the declining ecosystems. Both developed and developing regions face unhealthy lifestyles and a coexisting risk of emerging infectious diseases. Additionally, the uneven socio-economic development in this scenario causes other parts of the developing world to face a negative spiral of violence, ecosystem degradation, diseases and poverty. So there is a significant risk of major system breakdowns and ecological surprises in this future and a consequent risk of shifting all regions into the 'age of emerging infectious diseases' (Huynen, 2008).

Future health in Adapting Mosaic

In Adapting Mosaic, globalization reverses and makes way for fragmented approaches to trade and sustainability. The current division between developed and developing world changes.[3] Governance is based on learning through local adaptive and flexible management. Proactive policies aim at balancing natural, human and manufactured capital, but there's a diversion of management discourses, resulting in a lack of global (health) policies. Technological developments take place at the local level, but knowledge about successful local experiments is easily shared among regions. Unfortunately, the fragmentation results in inattention to inequalities. There is less economic growth. Poverty reduction through education proves to be fairly successful, however, although some regions lag behind. Ecosystem functions are highly valued and ecosystems are seen as part of local culture and identity, but the limited capacity to address global issues results in large-scale environmental problems (Carpenter et al, 2005; Huynen, 2008).

In this MEA scenario, heterogeneity in health service provision (quality and access) increases. The most successful countries will experience great improvements in both social and human capital and the local environment. They move towards the 'age of sustained health', but this transition remains incomplete due to the neglect of global environmental issues and the existing inequalities. The developing countries that are left behind will probably shift into to the 'age of emerging infectious diseases' rapidly due to, for example, a lack of health services, ecosystem failures and increasingly severe water stress. The developed countries will run a significant risk of shifting into the 'age of infectious diseases' due to the neglected global environmental developments and socio-economic inequities (Huynen, 2008).

Future health in Order from Strength

Order from Strength is characterized by fragmentation and inward-looking national policies, focusing on national security and protectionism. Economic liberalization retreats and trade primarily takes place in regional trading blocks. Fragmentation and narrow interests mask global reality. The rich–poor gap widens and most developing countries are left behind. The Western countries face stagnating economies. There is only limited cross-cultural interaction and there is no sense of a global society. Safety nets for the poor collapse and social exclusion (within and between nations) increases. The inward-looking focus on security results in increasing tensions between countries. Due to high spending on security, there is little investment in human capital. Technological progress is slow and knowledge is not globally shared, as scientific exchange weakens. Increasing disease outbreaks and environmental problems are reactively dealt with, but the underlying problems remain unaddressed. Climate change affects both rich and poor. Ecosystems are pushed to the limits and environmental protection is highly fragmented. Access to ecosystem functions becomes very uneven and developing countries are increasingly exploited. As a result, the poor face ecosystems of poor quality and low functioning levels. The elites/rich increasingly feel more and more pressure from 'outside' as well (Carpenter et al, 2005; Huynen, 2008).

This envisioned future does not look very promising. Due to the localized and reactive approach characterizing this future, developing countries are caught in a negative spiral of poverty, exclusion, lacking (health) services, violence, water and food scarcity, and environmental degradation. These detrimental developments will lead them to the 'age of emerging diseases' very rapidly. The developed countries will be able to offset some of the negative developments by focusing on national (environmental) security, at least for a while. However, technological development is slow and the rich countries will only advance towards the 'age of medical technology' at a very slow pace. Unhealthy lifestyles and environmental pollution will increase chronic diseases, and eventually the rich will progressively experience the negative effects of, for example, global environmental change, water stress, violence and a lack of a global approach to address disease outbreaks. Eventually they will start to shift to the 'age of emerging infectious disease' as well.

IS PARADISE POSSIBLE?

The futures pictured in the MEA scenarios are diverse, but none of them provides a future vision really worth pursuing when contemplating the implications for human health, ecosystems and biodiversity. The 'age of sustained health' is very weakly represented. Only Adapting Mosaic shows some signs of sustainable development. But the balance between social, economic and environmental domains is not equal, due to fragmented governance and local policy strategies. The MEA scenarios miss a view of a sustainable 'globalized' world.

Although it is important to gain insight into less optimistic future scenarios, because they could be seen as realistic developments coming forth from our contemporary situation, we think more emphasis could and should be put on building *desirable* scenarios for future ecological diversity and human health and wellbeing. There are other studies, such as the GEO3 (GEO3, 2002) or the IPCC Special Report on Emissions Scenarios (SRES) (IPCC, 2000), which include an optimistic sustainable outlook among their future scenarios, but lacked the focus on the close relationship between biodiversity and human health. Within these optimistic scenarios,[4] the move towards sustainable health is spurred by a wide-ranging societal change rather than a top–down policy push, which is in line with the stronger sustainability stance described in current literature (e.g. Robinson, 2004 and Williams and Millington, 2004). They also reflect important sustainability principles such as the ones from the Earth Charter Initiative, or the Club of Budapest (Laszlo, 2006). These sustainable scenarios envision a massive movement promoting a global ethic for a sustainable world, based on a 'wide-ranging societal change' (Huynen, 2008), which in the Earth Charter is called 'a change of mind and heart' (Earth Charter, 2000). The ideas reflected here could be useful guidelines to help building a new variety of sustainable scenarios related to human health and biodiversity. The more visions of pathways towards a sustainable world, the better. These could give us a variety of options to cope with our global environmental and health problems in flexible and adaptive manners (Kemp and Martens, 2007; Soskolne, 2007).

While developing these scenarios, it is important to be mindful of the role we play in the web of life: as biological, conscious and intentional beings in an ecological setting, but also as active constituents of our values and of our social, institutional and organizational environment. It is especially these latter threads of the web that need revision to become carriers of a sustainable future. We need to make use of our human drive for improvement – of our quest for paradise – by developing and improving our own levels of (self-)consciousness and our values and concepts of nature (Capra, 1996; Laszlo, 2006). A better understanding of ourselves and what it truly means to be a human being in the world – being dynamically interconnected in the web of life – could result in new and meaningful sustainable strategies for governance in the fields of human rights, peace, biodiversity and health. Eventually, sustainable development is mainly an 'inner' development of us – of human beings. The fabric of the web can only be fixed by the more subtle cords of this conscious evolution of humanity as a species: of our worldviews, our values, our institutions, our organizations, and our own psychological and spiritual wellbeing. We need to change towards a more holistic, whole, holy, healing, healthy way of thinking and acting to become healthy humans on a healthy and abundant planet

(Takacs, 1996, p229; Westra, 1998; Crabbé et al, 2000). All reality has been envisioned once. The question is: Do we have enough time left to make our sustainable world come true?

NOTES

1 The MEA identified the following components of wellbeing: material wellbeing, health, good social relations, security and freedom of choice.
2 See Huynen (2008) and Martens and Huynen (2003) for references.
3 The current developed world becomes divided into two groups. The 'Sustainers' are those countries that retained high levels of social and human capital, while the 'Northern Sleepers' had a high potential for local proactive ecosystem management at the turn of century, but this capability is lost over time. The current developing world can also be divided into two groups: the 'Pumas' started with low capacity for proactive, local ecosystem management, but this capacity grows significantly during the scenario; the 'Trapped' do not manage to raise their social and human capital (Carpenter, 2005).
4 The 'sustainable' scenario in the GEO3 study is named Sustainability First; the 'sustainable' scenario in the SRES study is B1 (Huynen, 2008).

REFERENCES

Bobadilla, J. L. and Possas, C. (1993) 'Health policy issues in three Latin American countries: Implications of the epidemiological transition', in J. N. Gribble and S. H. Preston (eds) *The Epidemiological Transition: Policy and Planning Implications for Developing Countries*, National Academy Press, Washington, DC

Boogerd, F. C. and Bruggeman (eds) (2007) *Systems Biology: Philosophical Foundations*, Elsevier, Amsterdam

Capra, F. (1996) *The Web of Life: A New Scientific Understanding of Living Systems*, Anchor Books, New York

Carpenter, S., Pingali, P., Bennett, E. and Zurek, M. (eds) (2005) *Ecosystems and Human Wellbeing: Scenarios. Findings of the Scenarios Working Group*, Island Press, Washington, DC, www.millenniumassessment.org/en/Scenarios.aspx, accessed 1 October 2007

Chivian, E. (2002) *Biodiversity: Its Importance to Human Health*, Centre for Health and the Global Environment and Harvard Medical School, Cambridge, MA

Corvalan, C., Hales, S. and McMichael, A. J. (eds) (2005) *Millennium Ecosystem Assessment. Ecosystems and Human Wellbeing: Health Synthesis*, World Health Organization, Geneva, www.millenniumassessment.org/documents/document.357.aspx.pdf, accessed 1 October 2007

Costanza, R., D'Arge, R. and de Groot, R. (1997) 'The value of the world's ecosystem services and natural capital', *Nature*, vol 387, pp253–260

Crabbé, P., Westra, L., Holland, A. and Ryczkowski, L. (eds) (2000) *Implementing Ecological Integrity: Restoring Regional and Global Environmental and Human Health*, NATO Scientific Publications, Kluwer Academic Publishers, Dordrecht, The Netherlands

De Groot, R. S., Wilson, M. A. and Boumans, R. M. J. (2002) 'A typology for the classification, description and valuation of ecosystem function, goods and services', *Ecological Economics*, vol 41, no 3, pp393–408

Duraiappah, A. K. (ed) (2005) *Millennium Ecosystem Assessment. Ecosystems and Human Wellbeing: Biodiversity Synthesis*, World Resources Institute, Washington, DC, www.millenniumassessment.org/documents/document.354.aspx.pdf, accessed 1 October 2007

Earth Charter (2000) 'The Earth Charter', available for download from website of Earth Charter Initiative, www.earthcharter.org, accessed 24 January 2006

GEO3 (Global Environmental Outlook) (2002) *Past Present and Future Perspectives*, UNEP/Earthscan, London

Gibbons, W. (1993) *Keeping all the Pieces: Perspectives on Natural History and the Environment*, Smithsonian Institution Press, Washington, DC, and London

Giddings, B., Hopwood, B. and O'Brien, G. (2002) 'Environment, economy and society: Fitting them together into sustainable development', *Sustainable Development*, vol 10, pp187–196

Grandjean, P. and Landrigan, P. J (2006) 'Developmental neurotoxicity of industrial chemicals', *The Lancet*, vol 368, issue 9553, pp2167–2178

Grandjean, P., Bellinger, D., Bergman, Å. et al (2007) 'The Faroes Statement: Human health effects of developmental exposure to chemicals in our environment', *Basic and Clinical Pharmacology and Toxicology*, Nordic Pharmacological Society, www.blackwell-synergy.com/doi/pdf/10.1111/j.1742-7843.2007.00114.x?cookieSet=1, accessed 25 October 2007

Hart, S. (1997) 'Cone snail toxins take off: Potent neurotoxins stop fish in their tracks – And may provide new pain therapies', *Bioscience*, vol 47, no 3, pp131–134

Homburg, A. and Stolberg, A. (2006) 'Explaining pro-environmental behaviour with a cognitive theory of stress', *Journal of Environmental Psychology*, vol 26, pp1–14

Huynen, M. (2008) *Future Health in a Globalizing World*, Universitaire Pers Maastricht, Maastricht

Huynen, M. M. T. E., Martens, P. and de Groot, R. S. (2004) 'Linkages between biodiversity loss and human health: A global indicator analysis', *International Journal of Environmental Health Research*, vol 14, no 1, pp13–30

IPCC (2000) *Special Report Emissions Scenarios: Summary for Policymakers*, Intergovernmental Panel on Climate Change, Geneva

IPCC (2007) *Climate Change 2007: The Physical Science Basis*, Fourth Assessment Report, Cambridge University Press, New York

Kaplan, S. (1995) 'The restorative benefits of nature', *Journal of Environmental Psychology*, vol 15, pp169–182

Kayombo, S. and Jorgensen, S. E. (2006) 'Lake Victoria: Experience and lessons learned brief', International Lake Environment Committee Foundation, Shiga Prefecture, Japan, www.ilec.or.jp/eg/lbmi/reports/27_Lake_Victoria_27February2006.pdf, accessed 16 October 2007

Kemp, R. and Martens, P. (2007) 'Sustainable development: How to manage something that is subjective and never can be achieved?', *Sustainability: Science, Practice and Policy*, vol 3, no 2, pp1–10

Larson, E. J. (2001) *De Proeftuin van de Evolutie: God en de Wetenschap op de Galapagoseilanden* [*Evolution's Workshop: God and Science on the Galapagos Islands*], Olympus, Amsterdam

Laszlo, E. (1996) *The Systems View of the World: A Holistic Vision for Our Time*, Hampton Press Inc., Cresskill, NJ

Laszlo, E. (2006) *Chaos Point: The World at the Crossroads*, Hampton Roads Publishing Company, Charlottesville, VA

Lovejoy, A. O. (1936) *The Great Chain of Being: A Study of the History of an Idea*, Harvard University Press, Cambridge, MA

Lovelock, J. (2000). *Gaia: A New Look at Life on Earth*, Oxford University Press, Oxford, UK

LVFO (Lake Victoria Fisheries Organization) (2003) 'Strategic vision', www.inweh.unu. edu/lvfo/Strategic%20Vision.htm, accessed 17 September 2007

Martens, P. (2002) 'Health transitions in a globalizing world: Towards more disease or sustained health?', *Futures*, vol 37, no 7, pp635–648

Martens, P. and Huynen, M. (2003) 'A future without health? Health dimension in global scenario studies', *Bulletin of the World Health Organization*, vol 81, no 12

Martens, P., Rotmans, J. and de Groot, R. (2003) 'Biodiversity: Luxury or necessity? A scenario approach to explore future biodiversity patterns', *Global Environmental Change*, vol 13, no 2, pp75–81

Miller, P. and Westra, L. (eds) (2002) *Just Ecological Integrity: The Ethics of Maintaining Planetary Life*, Rowman Littlefield, Lanham, MD

Nash, R. F. (1989) *The Rights of Nature: A History of Environmental Ethics*, University of Wisconsin Press, London

Newcomb, J. (2003). *Biology and Borders: SARS and the New Economics of Bio-security*, Bio Economic Research Associates, Cambridge, UK

Noske, B. (1988) *Mens en Dier. Vriend of Vijand?* [*Beyond Boundaries: Humans and Animals*], Van Gennip, Amsterdam

Omran, A. (1983) 'The epidemiological transition: A preliminary update', *Journal of Tropical Pediatrics*, vol 29, pp305–316

Omran, A. (1998) 'The epidemiologic transition theory revisited thirty years later', *World Health Statistics Quarterly*, vol 51, pp99–199

Pimentel, D., Westra, L., and Noss, R. (eds) (2000) *Ecological Integrity: Integrating Environment, Conservation and Health*, Island Press, Washington, DC

Prigogine, I. and Stengers, I. (1984) *Order Out of Chaos: Man's New Dialogue with Nature*, Heinemann, London

Robinson, T. and Westra, L. (eds) (2002) *Thinking about the Environment: Our Debt to the Classical and Medieval Past*, Lexington Books, Lanham, MD

Sauper, H. (2004) *Darwin's Nightmare*, International Film Circuit, New York

Shapin, S. (1996) *The Scientific Revolution*. University of Chicago Press, Chicago, IL

Soskolne, C. L. (ed) (2007) *Sustaining Life on Earth: Environmental and Human Health through Global Governance*, Lexington Books, Lanham, MD

Swart, R. J., Raskin, P. and Robinson, J. (2004) 'The problem of the future: Sustainability science and scenario analysis', *Global Environmental Change*, vol 14, pp137–146

Takacs, D. (1996) *The Idea of Biodiversity: Philosophies of Paradise*, Johns Hopkins University Press, Baltimore, MD

Van Asselt, M. B. A., Rotmans, J. and Rothman, D. S. (eds) (2005) *Scenario Innovation. Experiences from a European Experimental Garden*, Taylor and Francis, Leiden, The Netherlands

Van Eeden, F. (2004, original 1905) *De Kleine Johannes*, Van Schaik Publishers, Pretoria, South Africa

Van Notten, P. (2005) *Writing on the Wall: Scenario Development in Times of Discontinuity*, www.dissertation.com, Boca Raton, FL

Westra, L. (1998) *Living in Integrity: Toward a Global Ethic to Restore a Fragmented Earth*, Rowman Littlefield, Lanham, MD

Westra, L. (2006) *Environmental Justice and the Rights of Unborn and Future Generations: Law, Environmental Harm and the Right to Health*, Earthscan, London

WHO (2004) *The Future for our Children: Fourth Ministerial Conference on Environment and Health*, World Health Organization, Budapest

Williams, C. and Millington, A. (2004) 'The diverse and contested meanings of sustainable development', *The Geographical Journal*, vol 170, pp99–104

PART III

ECOLOGICAL INTEGRITY AND ENVIRONMENTAL JUSTICE

Introduction

Laura Westra

This part is a showcase of our concern with environmental justice. Following upon the connection between ecological integrity and human rights, one can indeed extend the argument to argue for environmental justice. That connection includes two separate but connected aspects: first, the human being's right to a liveable habitat; and second, the human right to health (an extension of the right to life, basic to natural law) and to the right to the normal functionality that each of us can have as we develop.

Chapter 9 discusses what is perhaps the most basic right of all, the right to nourishment, that is the right to an income that will permit all human beings to feed themselves and their families, as well as the right to a liveable habitat. Famines are endemic to several areas in the world, especially in sub-Saharan Africa and in other developing countries. The environmental degradation, the disintegrity that fosters desertification, and the global warming that exacerbates extreme weather episodes like tidal waves and tsunamis further aggravate the extreme poverty that affects, according to Thomas Pogge, over 2.5 billion people today. The conditions of these impoverished people are made worse by the present environmental situation; this is in addition to chronic malnutrition and no access to safe drinking water and other hygienic necessities or to essential medicines, adequate shelter and electricity.

The root causes of these conditions can be found first in the colonial history of many of the worst-affected areas; second in our present beliefs about what is morally permissible; and finally in our present 'global institutional arrangements'. After exposing these conditions of injustice, Pogge asks:

> *What entitles a small, global elite – the citizens of the rich countries* and *the holders of political and economic power in the resource-rich developing countries – to enforce a global property scheme under which we may claim the world's natural resources for ourselves and can distribute these among ourselves on mutually agreeable terms?*

Chapter 10 turns to an examination of the relationship between the rights of some of the most vulnerable of today's poor: the indigenous peoples of the world. Bradford Morse emphasizes the plight of indigenous communities, but also the leading role that these groups may have in indicating the right way for the rest of the world to follow. Traditional communities demonstrate with their lifestyles a respect for the Earth that ensures the protection of ecological integrity. Morse particularly explores the connection between indigenous rights and environmental protection so as to assess the potential for indigenous peoples to compel states to provide greater attention to sustainability through asserting their unique rights.

Chapter 11 returns to another aspect of environmental justice, with a discussion of one among the ecological rights we must have: the right to water. After air, water is the most necessary natural 'service' required for survival. Joseph Dellapenna points out that, under a system of common property (such as the one considered in the previous chapter, that of indigenous peoples), 'each person has lawful access [and] a legal right to water'. But after the 'transition to private and public property', this right is no longer a guaranteed entitlement, but must be entrenched in law.

For instance, in the US, water consumption has skyrocketed for various reasons, well beyond the amounts expected because of population increases, and all the water uncertainties connected with climate change aggravate further the situation.

In order to re-establish a right to water, many 'hard law' instruments can be read as supporting that right; in addition, the UN Committee issued a 'General Comment' (No 15) on the topic, an optional protocol based on many other instruments, from which the right to water may be inferred. Many countries' constitutions already require such a right explicitly, but implementation and enforcement remain doubtful and sporadic. Dellapenna concludes by listing several state obligations that would make such a right a reality, and citing the 'Berlin Rules' of the International Law Association as a summary of the human right to water.

Chapter 12 features the question of climate change itself. From the beginning of our work, as we saw, for instance, in Konrad Ott's chapter, there has been an ongoing debate between contrasting philosophical positions, between bio- and ecocentrism and anthropocentric arguments. Most of the scholars featured in this volume are on the side of ecocentrism. Don Brown, however, views that debate as unnecessary to his main concern: global warming. Whatever the merits on either side of that debate, climate change is one issue that can easily be attacked on traditional moral grounds. Hence the lack of decisive action on the part of today's political and corporate leaders is unequivocally unethical from almost any possible point of view.

This final chapter in Part III presents the perfect introduction to the three chapters of Part Four, where climate change and energy issues are examined.

9

Aligned: Global Justice and Ecology

Thomas Pogge

One important aspect of globalization is the increasingly dense and consequential regime of global rules that govern and shape development everywhere. Covering trade, investment, loans, patents, copyrights, trademarks, labour standards, environmental protection, use of seabed resources and much else, these rules – structuring and enabling, permissive and constraining – have a profound impact on the lives of human beings and on the health of our planet. This impact is catastrophic. Billions of human beings are avoidably mired in severe poverty and avoidably exposed to a variety of diseases that do little or no damage in the more affluent parts of the world. And our planet's natural diversity and beauty – its resources, ecosystems, atmosphere and climate – are avoidably being degraded at an alarming rate.

These three scourges – poverty, disease and environmental degradation – are related not merely through their common causal origin in an especially brutal path of globalization that the governments of the most affluent countries, acting on behalf of their most powerful corporations, have imposed upon the rest of the world. They are related also in that they aggravate one another. Severely impoverished people are especially vulnerable to diseases and to environmental degradation because their bodies and minds suffer the effects of inadequate nutrition, unclean water, insufficient clothing and shelter, poor sanitation, and unhealthy working and living conditions. Severely impoverished people are also least able to protect themselves against such hazards through medical care or relocation, or through legal processes or political mobilization. In these ways ill health and environmental degradation reinforce poverty by sapping the creative energies and earning potential of people and, all too often, even killing them in their prime while decimating their families' income.

Poverty and disease also reinforce environmental problems, because the poor typically cannot afford to take proper account of the long-term environmental impact of their conduct. Poor people cannot afford fuel-efficient and low-pollution cooking, and must take what combustible materials they can find regardless of cost to the environment. To be sure, poor people do far less environmental damage *per person* than is typical among the more affluent. But they do far more environmental damage *per unit of income*. And this suggests that, other things being equal, a more even distribution of income and wealth that would avoid severe poverty is environmentally preferable to the existing extremely uneven distribution. This consideration is complemented by another of even greater long-term significance. Very poor people cannot afford to limit their offspring because they face serious uncertainly about whether any given child will survive and about whether, without surviving children, they could survive beyond their prime. As is very well confirmed empirically (Sen, 1994, pp22–71), severe poverty is causally related to more rapid population growth, which in turn is one main driver of environmental degradation. Eradicating severe poverty is thus a plausible and effective strategy of working for an early levelling-off of the human population, hopefully below the 10 billion mark.

These two kinds of relationship – common causal origin and mutual reinforcement – suggest that those opposed to any one of the three scourges should collaborate intellectually and politically in developing and implementing reform ideas that address all three. In this vein I have proposed adding to the existing monopoly-patent regime (Trade-Related Aspects of Intellectual Property Rights, TRIPS) for incentivizing the development of new medicines a second track, on which pharmaceutical innovators could forgo their claim to market exclusivity on a product in exchange for a stream of reward payments proportional to the product's health impact. By making advanced medicines immediately available at generic prices, by stimulating new research into diseases concentrated among the poor and by encouraging pharmaceutical innovators to foster the actual health impact of their inventions, this reform would substantially reduce both avoidable severe poverty and the global disease burden.[1] I have also developed the idea of a 'global resources dividend' that would put a price on resource depletion and pollution, thereby slowing down these main contributors to environmental degradation while also creating a stream of revenues that could be directed at poverty reduction – at funding the second track for pharmaceutical research and development, for example.[2]

In this brief chapter, my objective is less ambitious. I will merely add to this collection on ecological integrity a brief account of the global poverty problem. Adding this perspective is important for the reasons outlined above. My account will follow in broad outlines the fuller analysis I have given in my book *World Poverty and Human Rights* (Pogge, 2008).

WORLD POVERTY: EXPLANATION AND RESPONSIBILITIES

Despite a high and growing global average income, billions of human beings are still condemned to lifelong severe poverty, with all its attendant evils of low life expectancy, social exclusion, ill health, illiteracy, dependency and effective enslavement. The annual death toll from poverty-related causes is around 18 million, which adds up to some 320 million deaths since the end of the Cold War.[3]

This problem is hardly unsolvable, in spite of its magnitude. The World Bank defines as severely poor households whose annual expenditure per person has less purchasing power than US$786 had in the US in 1993. To count as poor by this '$2-a-day' standard, a US household today would have to get by on less than US$1131 per person per year.[4] In poor countries, which have lower price levels, even a quarter or a fifth of this amount is typically deemed sufficient to escape severe poverty. Nonetheless, of a total of 6.6 billion human beings, over 2.5 billion are estimated to live in severe poverty. Their average shortfall is 41 per cent, and 950 million are said to live on less than half (in other words on annual expenditure per person with less purchasing power than US$393 had in the US in 1993).[5] Though constituting 38 per cent of the world's population, the people the World Bank counts as living in severe poverty consume only 1 per cent of the global product, and would need just 0.7 per cent more to escape poverty so defined.[6] The high-income countries, by contrast, with only 15 per cent of the world's population, have over 79 per cent of the global product.[7] With our average per capita income over 200 times greater than that of the poor at market exchange rates, we could eradicate severe poverty worldwide if we chose to try – in fact, we could have eradicated it decades ago.

Citizens of the rich countries are, however, conditioned to downplay the severity and persistence of world poverty and to think of it as an occasion for minor charitable assistance. Thanks in part to the rationalizations dispensed by our economists, most of us believe that severe poverty is a minor problem or one that is rapidly disappearing or one whose persistence is due exclusively to local causes. It is worthwhile briefly to address these common prejudices.

Though the aggregate income shortfall of the global poor is small, the effects of this shortfall are unimaginably large: 830 million human beings are undernourished, 1.1 billion lack access to safe drinking water and 2.6 billion lack adequate sanitation (UNDP, 2006, pp33 and 174). About 2 billion lack access to essential medicines,[8] 1 billion have no adequate shelter and 2 billion lack electricity (UNDP, 1998, p49). Some 774 million adults are illiterate[9] and over 200 million children between the ages of 5 and 17 do wage work outside their household – often under harsh or cruel conditions: as soldiers, prostitutes or domestic servants, or in agriculture, construction, or textile or carpet production.[10]

Severe poverty is not rapidly disappearing. The number of persons in severe poverty is higher than it was 20 years ago[11] and the reported number of chronically malnourished remains around 800 million in successive United Nations Development Programme (UNDP) Human Development Reports. The persistence of such severe poverty in the face of solid increases in the global average income is due to rapidly rising global inequality. In the high-income Organisation for Economic Co-operation and Development (OECD) countries, household final consumption expenditure per capita (in constant 2000 US dollars) rose by 56.3 per cent over the 1984–2004 globalization period.[12] We can compare this with how the poorer half of humankind fared, in terms of their real (purchasing-power adjusted) consumption expenditure, during this same period. Here are the gains at various percentiles of world population, labelled from the bottom up:

- 48.62% gain at the 50th percentile (median)
- 42.20% gain at the 30th percentile
- 33.72% gain at the 15th percentile
- 31.92% gain at the 7th percentile
- 22.87% gain at the 2nd percentile
- 9.64% gain at the 1st percentile

Source: iresearch.worldbank.org/PovcalNet/jsp/index.jsp

Consumption expenditure is growing faster at the top, more slowly lower down and most slowly at the very bottom.[13]

Severe poverty is also not a purely home-grown phenomenon, caused by factors that are purely domestic to the countries in which it persists. Since this prejudice is the most important and the hardest to dislodge, I will discuss it at greater length. Few realize that severe poverty is an ongoing harm we inflict upon the global poor. If more of us understood the true magnitude of the problem of poverty and our causal involvement in it, we might do what is necessary to eradicate it.

That world poverty is an ongoing harm *we* inflict seems completely incredible to most citizens of the affluent countries. We call it tragic that the basic human rights of so many remain unfulfilled, and are willing to admit that we should do more to help. But it is unthinkable to us that we are actively responsible for this catastrophe. If we were, then we, civilized and sophisticated denizens of the developed countries, would be guilty of the largest crime against humanity ever committed, the death toll of which exceeds, every week, that of the 2004 tsunami and, every three years, that of World War II, the concentration camps and gulags included. What could be more preposterous?

But think about the unthinkable for a moment. Are there steps the affluent countries could take to reduce severe poverty abroad? It seems very likely that there are, given the enormous inequalities in income and wealth already mentioned. The common assumption, however, is that reducing severe poverty abroad at the expense of our own affluence would be generous on our part, not something we owe, and that our failure to do this is thus at most a lack of generosity and does not make us morally responsible for the continued deprivation of the poor.

I deny this popular assumption. I deny that the 1 billion citizens of the affluent countries are morally entitled to their 79 per cent of the global product in the face of 2.5 times as many people mired in severe poverty. Is this denial really so preposterous that one need not consider the arguments in its support? Does not the radical inequality between our affluence and their dire need at least put the burden on us to show why we should be morally entitled to so much while they have so little? In *World Poverty and Human Rights*, I dispute the popular assumption by showing that the usual ways of justifying our great advantage fail. My argument poses three mutually independent challenges.

The first challenge: The actual history

Many believe that the radical inequality we face can be justified by reference to how it evolved, for example through differences in diligence, culture and social institutions, soil, climate, or fortune. I challenge this sort of justification by invoking the common and very violent history through which the present radical inequality accumulated. Much of it was built up in the colonial era, when today's affluent countries ruled today's poor regions of the world: trading their people like cattle, destroying their political institutions and cultures, taking their lands and natural resources, and forcing products and customs upon them. I recount these historical facts specifically for readers who believe that even the most radical inequality is morally justifiable if it evolved in a benign way. Such readers disagree about the conditions a historical process must meet for it to justify such vast inequalities in life chances. But I can bypass these disagreements because the actual historical crimes were so horrendous, diverse and consequential that no historical entitlement conception could credibly support the view that our common history was sufficiently benign to justify today's huge inequality in the starting positions human beings face at birth.

Challenges such as this are often dismissed with the lazy response that we cannot be held responsible for what others did long ago. This response is true but irrelevant. We indeed cannot inherit responsibility for our forefathers' sins. But how then can we plausibly claim the *fruits* of their sins? How can we be entitled to the great head start our countries enjoyed going into the post-colonial period, which has allowed us to dominate and shape the world? And how can we be entitled to the huge advantages over the global poor we consequently enjoy from birth? The historical path from which our exceptional affluence arose greatly weakens our moral claim to it – certainly in the face of those whom the same historical process has delivered into conditions of acute deprivation. They, the global poor, have a much stronger moral claim to that 0.7 per cent of the global product they need to meet their basic needs than we affluent have to take 79 rather than 78.3 per cent for ourselves. Thus, as I have written, 'A morally deeply tarnished history should not be allowed to result in *radical* inequality' (Pogge, 2008, p209).

The second challenge: Fictional histories

Since my first challenge addressed adherents of historical entitlement conceptions of justice, it may leave others unmoved. These others may believe that it is permissible to uphold any economic distribution, no matter how skewed, if merely it *could* have come about on a morally acceptable path. They insist that we are entitled to keep and defend what we possess, even at the cost of millions of deaths each year, unless there is conclusive proof that, without the horrors of the European conquests, severe poverty worldwide would be substantially less today.

Now, *any* distribution, however unequal, *could* be the outcome of a sequence of voluntary bets or gambles. Appeal to such a fictional history would 'justify' anything and would thus be wholly implausible. John Locke does much better, holding that a fictional history can justify the status quo only if the changes in holdings and social rules it involves are ones that all participants could have rationally agreed to. He also holds that in a state of nature persons would be entitled to a proportional share of the world's natural resources. Whoever deprives others of 'enough and as good' – either through unilateral appropriations or through institutional arrangements, such as a radically inegalitarian property regime – harms them in violation of a *negative* duty. For Locke, the justice of any institutional order thus depends on whether the worst-off under it are at least as well off as people would be in a state of nature with a proportional resource share.[14] This baseline is imprecise, to be sure, but it suffices for my second challenge: however one may want to imagine a state of nature among human beings on this planet, one could not realistically conceive it as involving suffering and early deaths on the scale we are witnessing today. Only a thoroughly organized state of civilization can produce such horrendous misery and sustain an enduring poverty death toll of 18 million annually. The existing distribution is then morally unacceptable on Lockean grounds insofar as, I point out, 'the better-off enjoy significant advantages in the use of a single natural resource base from whose benefits the worse-off are largely, and without compensation, excluded' (Pogge, 2008, p208).

The attempt to justify today's coercively upheld radical inequality by appeal to some morally acceptable *fictional* historical process that *might* have led to it thus fails as well. On Locke's permissive account, a small elite may appropriate all of the huge cooperative surplus produced by modern social organization. But this elite must not enlarge its share even further by reducing the poor *below* the state-of-nature baseline to capture *more* than the entire cooperative surplus. The citizens and governments of the affluent states are violating this negative duty when we, in collaboration with the ruling cliques of many poor countries, coercively exclude the global poor from a proportional resource share or any equivalent substitute.

The third challenge: Present global institutional arrangements

A third way of thinking about the justice of a radical inequality involves reflection on the institutional rules that sustain it. Using this approach, one can justify an economic order and the distribution it produces (irrespective of historical considerations) by comparing them to feasible alternative institutional schemes and the distributional profiles they would produce. Many broadly consequentialist and contractualist conceptions of justice exemplify this approach. They differ in how they characterize the relevant affected parties (groups, persons, time slices of lives and so on), in the metric they employ for measuring how well off such parties are (in terms of social primary goods, capabilities, welfare and so forth), and in how they aggregate such information about wellbeing into one overall assessment (for example by averaging, or in some egalitarian, prioritarian or sufficientarian way). These conceptions consequently disagree about how economic institutions should be best shaped under modern conditions. But I can bypass such disagreements insofar as these conceptions agree that an economic order is unjust when it – like the systems of serfdom and forced labour prevailing in feudal Russia or France – foreseeably and avoidably gives rise to massive and severe human rights deficits. My third challenge, addressed to adherents of broadly consequentialist and contractualist conceptions of justice, is that we are preserving our great economic advantages by imposing a global economic order that is unjust in view of the massive and avoidable deprivations it foreseeably reproduces: 'There is a shared institutional order that is shaped by the better-off and imposed on the worse-off', I contend:

> This institutional order is implicated in the reproduction of radical inequality in that there is a feasible institutional alternative under which such severe and extensive poverty would not persist. The radical inequality cannot be traced to extra-social factors (such as genetic handicaps or natural disasters) which, as such, affect different human beings differentially. (Pogge, 2008, p205)

THREE NOTIONS OF HARM

These three challenges converge on the conclusion that the global poor have a compelling moral claim to some of our affluence and that we, by denying them what they are morally entitled to and urgently need, are actively contributing to their deprivations. Still, these challenges are addressed to different audiences and thus appeal to diverse and mutually inconsistent moral conceptions.

They also deploy different notions of harm. In most ordinary contexts, the word 'harm' is understood in a historical sense, either diachronically or subjunctively: people are harmed when they are rendered worse off than they were at some earlier time, or than they would have been had some earlier arrangements continued undisturbed. My first two challenges conceive harm in this ordinary way, and then conceive justice, at least partly, in terms of harm: we are behaving unjustly towards the global poor by imposing on them the lasting effects of historical crimes, or by holding them below any credible state-of-nature baseline. But my third challenge does not conceive justice and injustice in terms of an independently specified notion of harm. Rather, it relates the concepts of *harm* and *justice* in the opposite way, conceiving harm in terms of an independently specified conception of social justice: we are *harming* the global poor if and insofar as we collaborate in imposing an *unjust* global institutional order upon them. And this institutional order is definitely unjust if and insofar as it foreseeably perpetuates large-scale human rights deficits that would be reasonably avoidable through feasible institutional modifications.[15]

The third challenge is empirically more demanding than the other two. It requires me to substantiate three claims. First, global institutional arrangements are causally implicated in the reproduction of massive severe poverty. Second, governments of our affluent countries bear primary responsibility for these global institutional arrangements and can foresee their detrimental effects. And third, many citizens of these affluent countries bear responsibility for the global institutional arrangements their governments have negotiated in their name.

Two main innovations

In defending these three claims, my view on these more empirical matters is as oddly perpendicular to the usual empirical debates, as my diagnosis of our moral relation to the problem of world poverty is to the usual moral debates.

The usual *moral* debates concern the stringency of our moral duties to help the poor abroad. Most of us believe that these duties are rather feeble, meaning that it isn't very wrong of us to give no help at all. Against this popular view, some – for example Peter Singer, Henry Shue and Peter Unger[16] – have argued that our positive duties are quite stringent and quite demanding, and others – such as Liam Murphy (Murphy, 2003) – have defended an intermediate view according to which our positive duties, insofar as they are quite stringent, are not very demanding. Leaving this whole debate to one side, I focus on what it ignores: our moral duties not to harm. We do, of course, have positive duties to rescue people from life-threatening poverty. But it can be misleading to focus on them when more stringent negative duties are also in play: duties not to expose people to life-threatening poverty and duties to shield them from harms for which we would be actively responsible.

The usual *empirical* debates concern how developing countries should design their economic institutions and policies in order to reduce severe poverty within their borders. The received wisdom (often pointing to China these days) is that they should opt for free and open markets with a minimum in taxes and regulations so as to attract investment and to stimulate growth. But some influential economists call for extensive government investment in education, healthcare and infrastructure (as illustrated by the example of the Indian state of Kerala), or for some protectionist measures to 'incubate' fledgling niche industries until they become internationally competitive (as illustrated by the example of South Korea). Leaving these debates to one side, I focus once more on what is typically ignored: the role that the design of the *global* institutional order plays in the persistence of severe poverty.

Thanks to the inattention of our economists, many believe that the existing global institutional order plays no role in the persistence of severe poverty, but rather that national differences are the key factors. Such 'explanatory nationalism' (Pogge, 2008, pp145ff) appears justified by the dramatic performance differentials among developing countries, with poverty rapidly disappearing in some and increasing in others. Cases of the latter kind usually display plenty of incompetence, corruption and oppression by ruling elites, which seem to give us all the explanation we need to understand why severe poverty persists there.

But consider this analogy. Suppose there are great performance differentials among the students in a class, with some improving greatly while many others learn little or nothing. And suppose the latter students do not do their reading and skip many classes. This case surely shows that local, student-specific factors play a role in explaining academic success. But it decidedly *fails* to show that global factors (the quality of teaching, textbooks, classroom and so forth) play no such role. A better teacher might well greatly improve the performance of the class by eliciting stronger student interest in the subject and hence better attendance and preparation.

Once we break free from explanatory nationalism, global factors relevant to the persistence of severe poverty are easy to find. In the World Trade Organization (WTO) negotiations, the affluent countries insisted on continued and asymmetrical protections of their markets through tariffs, quotas, anti-dumping duties, export credits and huge subsidies to domestic producers. Such protectionism provides a compelling illustration of the hypocrisy of the rich states that insist and command that their own exports be received with open markets (Pogge, 2008, pp18–23). And it greatly impairs export opportunities for the very poorest countries and regions. If the rich countries scrapped their protectionist barriers against imports from poor countries, the populations of the latter would benefit greatly: hundreds of millions would escape unemployment, wage levels would rise substantially and incoming export revenues would be higher by hundreds of billions of dollars each year.

The same rich states also insist that their intellectual property rights – ever-expanding in scope and duration – must be vigorously enforced in the poor countries. Music and software, production processes, words, seeds, biological species and medicines – for all these, and more, rents must be paid to the corporations of the rich countries as a condition for (still multiply restricted) access to their markets. Millions would be saved from diseases and death if generic producers could freely manufacture and market life-saving drugs in the poor countries (Pogge, 2008, pp222–227, 230–235).

While charging billions for their intellectual property, the rich countries pay nothing for the externalities they impose through their vastly disproportional contributions to global pollution and resource depletion. The global poor benefit least, if at all, from polluting activities, and also are least able to protect themselves from the impact such pollution has on their health and on their natural environment (such as flooding due to rising sea levels). It is true, of course, that we pay for the vast quantities of natural resources we import. But such payments cannot make up for the price effects of our inordinate consumption, which restrict the consumption possibilities of the global poor as well as the development possibilities of the poorer countries and regions (in comparison to the opportunities our countries could take advantage of at a comparable stage of economic development).

More important, the payments we make for resource imports go to the rulers of the resource-rich countries, with no concern about whether they are democratically elected or at least minimally responsive to the needs of the people they rule. It is on the basis of effective power alone that we recognize any such ruler as entitled to sell us the resources of 'his' country and to borrow, undertake treaty commitments and buy arms in its name. These international resource, borrowing, treaty and arms privileges we extend to such rulers are quite advantageous to them, providing them with the money and arms they need to stay in power – often with great brutality and negligible popular support. These privileges are also quite convenient for us, securing our resource imports from poor countries irrespective of who may rule them and how badly. But these privileges have devastating effects on the global poor by enabling corrupt rulers to oppress them, to exclude them from the benefits of their countries' natural resources, and to saddle them with huge debts and onerous treaty obligations. By substantially augmenting the perks of governmental power, these same privileges also greatly strengthen the incentives to attempt to take power by force, thereby fostering coups, civil wars and interstate wars in the poor countries and regions – especially in Africa, which has many desperately poor but resource-rich countries, whose resource sector constitutes a large part of the gross domestic product.

Reflection on the popular view that severe poverty persists in many poor countries because they govern themselves so poorly shows, then, that such poor governance is evidence not for but against explanatory nationalism. The populations of most of the countries in which severe poverty persists or increases do not 'govern themselves' poorly, but *are* very poorly governed, and much against their will. They are helplessly exposed to such 'government' because the rich states recognize their rulers as entitled to rule on the basis of effective power alone. We pay these rulers for their people's resources, often advancing them large sums against the collateral of future exports, we allow our banks to harbour the funds they embezzle (Baker, 2005), and we eagerly sell them the advanced weaponry on which their continued rule all too often depends. Yes, severe poverty is fuelled by local misrule. But such local misrule is fuelled, in turn, by global rules that we impose and from which we benefit greatly.

Once this causal nexus between our global institutional order and the persistence of severe poverty is understood, the injustice of that order, and of our imposition of it, becomes visible: 'What entitles a small global elite – the citizens of the rich countries *and* the holders of political and economic power in the resource-rich developing countries – to enforce a global property scheme under which we may claim the world's natural resources for ourselves and can distribute these among ourselves on mutually agreeable terms?', I ask. 'How, for instance, can our ever so free and fair agreements with tyrants give us property rights in crude oil, thereby dispossessing the local population and the rest of humankind?' (Pogge, 2008, p148).

NOTES

1 Pogge (2008), Chapter 9. The idea of such a second track for pharmaceutical innovation was first presented in 'Human rights and global health: A research programme', *Metaphilosophy*, vol 36, nos 1–2, January 2005, pp182–209.

2 Pogge (2008), Chapter 8. This global resources dividend was first described in 'An egalitarian law of peoples', *Philosophy and Public Affairs*, vol 23, no 3, Summer 1994, pp195–224, and 'Uma proposta de reforma: Um dividendo global de recursos', translated into Brazilian Portuguese by Álvaro de Vita, in *Lua Nova*, vol 34, 1994, pp135–161. It is much in the spirit of the ecological integrity movement as manifest in, for example, Pimentel et al, 2000.

3 See Annex Table 2 in WHO, 2004; also available at www.who.int/whr/2004.

4 See www.bls.gov/cpi; accessed 15 October 2007.

5 See http://iresearch.worldbank.org/PovcalNet/jsp/index.jsp; accessed 15 October 2007.

6 These figures are based on market exchange rates and take account of the fact that the World Bank inflates incomes in poor countries by factors of three to nine to account for the greater purchasing power of money there. The methodological flaws in the Bank's method are discussed in Pogge, 2004, based on my joint work with Sanjay G. Reddy, 'How *not* to count the poor', forthcoming in Anand and Stiglitz, also available at www.socialanalysis.org.

7 See p289 in World Bank (2006), giving data for 2005.

8 See www.fic.nih.gov/about/plan/exec_summary.htm.

9 See www.uis.unesco.org.

10 Table 1.1 in ILO, 2006; also available at www.ilo.org/public/english/standards/relm/ ilc/ ilc95/pdf/rep-i-b.pdf.

11 See http://iresearch.worldbank.org/PovcalNet/jsp/index.jsp; accessed 15 October 2007.

12 See http://devdata.worldbank.org/dataonline; accessed 15 October 2007.

13 See http://iresearch.worldbank.org/PovcalNet/jsp/index.jsp; accessed 15 October 2007; see also Milanovic (2005), pp108–111.

14 For a fuller reading of Locke's argument, see Pogge (2008), Chapter 5.

15 One might say that the existing global order is not unjust if the only feasible institutional modifications that could substantially reduce the offensive deprivations would be extremely costly in terms of culture, say, or the natural environment. I pre-empt such objections by inserting the word 'reasonably'. Broadly consequentialist and contractualist conceptions of justice agree that an institutional order that foreseeably gives rise to massive severe deprivations is unjust if there are feasible institutional

modifications that foreseeably would greatly reduce these deprivations without adding other harms of comparable magnitude.

16 Singer (1972, pp229–243); Shue (1996); Unger (1996).

REFERENCES

Anand, S. and Stiglitz, J. (eds) (forthcoming) *Measuring Global Poverty*, Oxford University Press, Oxford, UK

Baker, R. (2005) *Capitalism's Achilles Heel*, John Wiley and Sons, Hoboken, NJ

ILO (International Labour Office) (2006) *The End of Child Labour: Within Reach*, International Labour Office, Geneva

Milanovic, B. (2005) *Worlds Apart: Measuring International and Global Inequality*, Princeton University Press, Princeton, NJ

Murphy, L. B. (2003) *Moral Demands in Nonideal Theory*, Oxford University Press, New York

Pimentel, D., Westra, L. and Noss, R. F. (eds) (2000) *Ecological Integrity: Integrating Environment, Conservation, and Health*, Island Press, Washington, DC

Pogge, T. (2004) 'The first UN Millennium Development Goal: A cause for celebration?', *Journal of Human Development*, vol 5, no 3, pp381–85

Pogge, T. (2008) *World Poverty and Human Rights: Cosmopolitan Responsibilities and Reforms* (second edition), Polity Press, Cambridge, UK

Sen, A. (1994) 'Population: Delusion and reality', *New York Review of Books*, 22 September

Shue, H. (1996) *Basic Rights: Subsistence, Affluence and US Foreign Policy*, Princeton University Press, Princeton, NJ

Singer, P. (1972) 'Famine, affluence and morality', *Philosophy and Public Affairs*, vol 1, no 3

UNDP (United Nations Development Programme) (1998) *Human Development Report 1998*, Oxford University Press, New York, also available at http://hdr.undp.org/reports/global/1998/en/

UNDP (2006) *Human Development Report 2006*, Palgrave Macmillan, Basingstoke, UK

Unger, P. (1996) *Living High and Letting Die*, Oxford University Press, New York

WHO (2004) *World Health Report 2004*, World Health Organization, Geneva

World Bank (2006) *World Development Report 2007*, Oxford University Press, New York

10

Indigenous Rights as a Mechanism to Promote Environmental Sustainability

Bradford Morse

The very food we eat is being threatened by outside forces we have no control over ... The animals we eat are contaminated by PCB, DDT, heavy metals and radionuclides, and these are entering our bodies. These contaminants are in the blood of pregnant women. So that's what we have to grapple with: how do we minimize the impact of these things that originate a long way away. (McKiver, 2004, p164)

INTRODUCTION

Environmental degradation is arguably the greatest threat to human security around the world. The magnitude of the environmental damage that has already occurred in many regions of the world, especially when coupled with the massive risks of climate change, suggests that our very survival as a species is potentially in danger.

Not surprisingly, those people who are particularly dependent on the land for their food supply are most aware of and affected by environmental changes. For those who pursue a significant portion of their diet through hunting, fishing, trapping and gathering, the maintenance of the Earth in its natural state is vital. Put another way, having a right to hunt and fish recognized by the state or by the international community is illusory and even meaningless if there is nothing in fact to harvest or what can be harvested is unsafe to consume. The migration of persistent organic pollutants, such as pesticides, from thousands of miles away taints the food chain in the Arctic, on which the Inuit depend for survival, with surprisingly dangerous intergenerational consequences. As David Boyd indicates, 'Levels of persistent organic pollutants are five to ten times higher in the breast milk of Inuit women than in women from southern Canada' (Boyd, 2003, p67).

The imbalance among countries, with wealthy nations producing most of the emissions and developing ones bearing much of the burdens, becomes particularly acute for indigenous communities that are living primarily 'off the land'. They face the brunt of climate change exposure as well as other forms of environmental degradation. The people of the Arctic are perhaps the most endangered, not only as individuals, but as peoples. The effects of climate change are having a particularly profound impact in the Arctic region, where melting sea ice and snow is making surface travel dangerous, traditional environmental knowledge (TEK) unreliable, hunting harder or impossible, igloo-building snow scarcer, erosion and landslides more common, permafrost unstable, and weather patterns more erratic.[1] In light of the major effects already emerging from climate change, their culture and very identity are under severe threat.[2] Continuing dependence upon the land and waters as a source of a significant part of local diet, as well as the primary means to convey TEK and cultural values to subsequent generations, has profound and unequal effects upon many indigenous societies in comparison to others.

In the same manner, coastal and island indigenous communities are exposed to multiple threats: to health, to life, but also to their cultural integrity and identity. They may in the near future be forced to leave their lands as environmental refugees due to sea levels rising or to withdraw from unsafe conditions, such as sea ice losing its stability (Watt-Cloutier, 2007b).

This chapter will seek to identify how asserting the recognized unique rights of indigenous peoples through international and domestic law forums can provide a foundation for environmental sustainability to be accepted as a paramount principle. Such an outcome is vital to the survival of indigenous societies, and may well be essential for all of humanity.

THE IMPORTANCE OF THE LAND TO INDIGENOUS PEOPLES

Indigenous peoples are almost invariably tied inextricably to the lands and waters of their traditional territories for sustenance, cultural identity and spiritual belief systems. Indigenous communities are not merely users of land, as they carry explicit obligations that can be characterized as cultural and religious imperatives to protect their historic natural space as its physical custodians or stewards to protect spiritual beings. Many indigenous societies believe that all things – both animate and inanimate – are alive, such that a rock is as much a living being as a bird or human. All aspects of our universe have a spirit identity and are, therefore, sacred.

The Supreme Court of Canada, in a recent unanimous judgement, recognized the importance of this connection between people and territory in these terms:

1   *To the west of the mainland of British Columbia lie the Queen Charlotte Islands, the traditional homeland of the Haida people. Haida Gwaii, as the inhabitants call it, consists of two large islands and a number of smaller islands. For more than 100 years, the Haida people have claimed title to all the lands of the Haida Gwaii and the waters surrounding it. That title is still in the claims process and has not yet been legally recognized.*

2   *The islands of Haida Gwaii are heavily forested. Spruce, hemlock and cedar abound. The most important of these is the cedar which, since time immemorial, has played a central role in the economy and culture of the Haida people. It is from cedar that they made their ocean-going canoes, their clothing, their utensils and the totem poles that guarded their lodges. The cedar forest remains central to their life and their conception of themselves.*[3]

The Court realized that there was a fundamental conflict between the Provincial Government and the Haida Nation. The former favoured logging (through licensing large blocks of land to a multinational forestry company), with no regard for the concerns of the Haida people until their interest in the islands was successfully proven in the Canadian courts. From the Haida perspective, a future victory in a judicial arena after years of litigation would come far too late, as much of the forest would be gone. In addition, they wished to preserve the old growth red cedar forest as being irreplaceable and spiritually very significant, an importance known to the Crown since at least 1846.[4]

Recognizing the essential link between land and indigenous peoples, and thereby the importance of strong protection of the environment in order to sustain their traditional way of life, has occurred at the global level for many decades. The 1987 UN World Commission on Environment and Development report *Our Common Future*, most commonly known as the Brundtland Report, supported traditional land and resource rights in very strong terms. Similarly, the Inter-American Commission on Human Rights has stated that the 'protection for indigenous populations constitutes a sacred commitment of the states'.

RATIONALES FOR INDIGENOUS RIGHTS TO A SAFE ENVIRONMENT

The right of indigenous peoples to a vibrant, safe and sustainable environment has generally been asserted as being grounded upon two models: the 'cultural integrity' model, which is based on the theory that the indigenous right to a safe environment is essential to the right to cultural protection, and the 'self-determination' model, which asserts that indigenous peoples have the right to control the development of their own land (Metcalf, 2003/4, pp101–140). More recently, a third rationale that combines elements of each has been advocated in Laura Westra's most recent book as an 'ecological integrity' model (Westra, 2007).

Indigenous peoples have become recognized over the past few decades as being more significant actors in international law.[5] In recent years, the need to include the interests of indigenous peoples in the development of environmental law and environmental protection has been somewhat grudgingly accepted by states. The unique interests of indigenous peoples to the right to preserve the environmental integrity of what remains of their traditional territory has been affirmed in legally binding instruments such as International Labour Organization (ILO) Convention No 169 Concerning Indigenous and Tribal Peoples in Independent Countries[6] and the Convention on Biological Diversity.[7] Despite these advances, however, the domestic law of many countries does not adequately protect indigenous peoples' right to a healthy environment.

The cultural integrity model is based on human rights principles of environmental quality that transcend state sovereignty.[8] According to Metcalf, this theory has generally been limited to giving indigenous peoples procedural rights, rather than a substantive right to environmental protection, through classifying the right as a special circumstance where indigenous rights and environmental rights intersect.[9]

The environment is widely accepted as being an essential component to indigenous cultures in the cultural integrity model. Sustaining the environment is necessary for indigenous cultures to survive, let alone flourish, because indigenous peoples' cultural beliefs dictate that they must live in harmony with nature. The following is an example of how the need to protect the environment's quality has been recognized globally as an essential component of indigenous culture:

> *Indigenous communities are the repositories of vast accumulations of traditional knowledge and experience that links humanity with its ancient origins. Their disappearance is a loss for the larger society, which could learn a great deal from their traditional skills in sustainably managing very complex ecological systems .... The starting point for a just and humane policy for such groups is the recognition and protection of their traditional rights to land and the other resources that sustain their way of life.*[10]

The intersection between indigenous culture and the environment is also expressed in Principle 22 of the Rio Declaration on the Environment and Development:

> *Indigenous people and their communities and other local communities have a vital role in environmental management and development because of their knowledge and traditional practices. States should recognize and duly support their identity, culture and interests and enable their effective participation in the achievement of sustainable development.*[11]

Chapter 26 of Agenda 21 demands that governments must cooperate with indigenous people to protect the inherent 'inter-relationship between the natural environment and its sustainable development and the cultural, social, economic and physical wellbeing of indigenous peoples'.[12] ILO Convention No 169 similarly recognizes indigenous rights to the environment in order to protect their culture by stating the parties' recognition of the 'distinctive contributions of indigenous and tribal peoples to the cultural diversity and social and ecological harmony of humankind'.[13]

The UN Charter guarantees that member countries must ensure that the interests of all peoples (thereby including indigenous peoples) within their territories are paramount and held in a sacred trust, 'with due respect for the culture of the peoples concerned, their political, economic, social and educational advancement, their just treatment, and their protection against abuses'.[14]

ILO Convention No 169 makes particular references to the importance of the environment to indigenous cultures in Articles 13 and 23:

> *PART II. LAND*
> *Article 13*
>
> 1 *In applying the provisions of this Part of the Convention governments shall respect the special importance for the cultures and spiritual values of the peoples concerned of their relationship with the lands or territories, or both as applicable, which they occupy or otherwise use, and in particular the collective aspects of this relationship.*
>
> *PART IV. VOCATIONAL TRAINING, HANDICRAFTS AND RURAL INDUSTRIES*
> *Article 23*
>
> 1 *Handicrafts, rural and community-based industries, and subsistence economy and traditional activities of the peoples concerned, such as hunting, fishing, trapping and gathering, shall be recognized as important factors in the maintenance of their cultures and in their economic self-reliance and development. Governments shall, with the participation of these people and whenever appropriate, ensure that these activities are strengthened and promoted.*

Article 30 of the Convention on the Rights of the Child states that a child has the critical right to learn aspects of his or her culture. The right to an environment that can support traditional cultural practices that are central to indigenous cultures, such as hunting and fishing, would be a necessary precondition to this right:

> *In those States in which ethnic, religious or linguistic minorities or persons of indigenous origin exist, a child belonging to such a minority*

or who is indigenous shall not be denied the right, in community with other members of his or her group, to enjoy his or her own culture, to profess and practise his or her own religion, or to use his or her own language.[15]

The Convention on Biological Diversity also effectively makes reference to the necessity of the right to a sustainable environment for indigenous peoples:

Article 10. Sustainable Use of Components of Biological Diversity

Each Contracting Party shall, as far as possible and as appropriate:

(c) Protect and encourage customary use of biological resources in accordance with traditional cultural practices that are compatible with conservation or sustainable use requirements.[16]

The Declaration on the Establishment of the Arctic Council (Ottawa, Canada, 1996) also acknowledges the interconnectedness of indigenous peoples with the lands, sea ice and waters of the Arctic in these terms:

- *Affirming our commitment to the well-being of the inhabitants of the Arctic, including special recognition of the special relationship and unique contributions to the Arctic of indigenous people and their communities;*
- *Affirming our commitment to sustainable development in the Arctic region, including economic and social development, improved health conditions and cultural well-being;*
- *Affirming concurrently our commitment to the protection of the Arctic environment, including the health of Arctic ecosystems, maintenance of biodiversity in the Arctic region and conservation and sustainable use of natural resources;*
- *Recognizing the traditional knowledge of the indigenous people of the Arctic and their communities and taking note of its importance and that of Arctic science and research to the collective understanding of the circumpolar Arctic.* (Arctic Council, 1996)

The proposed American Declaration on the Rights of Indigenous Peoples[17] has yet to come close to a consensus draft among the state party members of the Organization of American States (OAS) and with representatives of indigenous peoples. The latest draft[18] has square-bracketed the text regarding a right to cultural identity and its connection to indigenous heritage in Article XII; however, agreement was reached at the 26 January 2007 session on Subsection 3:

> *Indigenous people have the right to the recognition and respect for all*
> *their ways of life, world views, spirituality, uses and customs, norms*
> *and traditions, forms of social, economic and political organization,*
> *forms of transmission of knowledge, institutions, practices, beliefs,*
> *values, dress, and languages, recognizing their inter-relationship as*
> *elaborated in this Declaration.*

Recognition of traditional knowledge and 'the right to preserve, use, develop, revitalize and transmit to future generations' was agreed to on 24 January 2007 as forming part of Article XIII. On the other hand, the right to medicinal usage and protection of flora and fauna in Article XVII has not achieved consensus.

The self-determination model is grounded on the theory that indigenous peoples have a right to manage the environment as an aspect of their right to autonomy over their traditional territory and its development.[19] This model can clearly have a more fundamental impact on international environmental law, as it creates the potential for enforceable, substantive rights that limit state sovereignty.[20]

The Vienna Declaration and Programme of Action[21] indirectly supports in Article 20 the theory that indigenous peoples have environmental rights through their entitlement to 'economic, social and cultural well-being and their enjoyment of the fruits of sustainable development' based on their 'inherent dignity and the unique contribution' they have made to the world as well as their fundamental freedoms.

In addition, the United Nations Declaration on the Rights of Indigenous Peoples[22] expressly supports the theory that indigenous peoples have environmental rights based on their right to self-determination. Article 3 states that 'Indigenous peoples have the right of self-determination. By virtue of that right they freely determine their political status and freely pursue their economic, social and cultural development.' It further implicitly supports this intersection with the environment in Article 4:

> *Indigenous peoples, in exercising their right to self-determination, have*
> *the right to autonomy or self-government in matters relating to their*
> *internal and local affairs, as well as ways and means for financing*
> *these autonomous functions.*

Article 29 gives clear recognition of indigenous rights in the context of the environment, as well as placing express obligations on states to aid in this regard, when it states:

> *1   Indigenous peoples have the right to the conservation and*
> *protection of the environment and the productive capacity of their*
> *lands or territories and resources. States shall establish and*

implement assistance programmes for indigenous peoples for such conservation and protection, without discrimination.

One of the most fundamental provisions in the draft American Declaration on the Rights of Indigenous Peoples focuses in Article XX upon principles of self-determination in a broad list of spheres of human activity that includes jurisdiction over the right to the environment. There is, once again, however, no consensus among the parties on this subject. The same is true concerning the seven-section-long Article XVIII, which describes in detail a potential right of indigenous peoples to protection of a healthy environment. This latter right is effectively suggested to be connected to principles of self-government as it could include 'the right to conserve, restore, recover, manage, use and protect the environment, and to the sustainable management of their lands' (XVIII(2)). The article also proposes to include an explicit right to 'participate fully and effectively in the formulation, planning, organization and implementation of measures, programs, laws, policies, and any other public [or private] activity that could affect the environment, for the conservation, use and management of their [the] lands, [territories] [and resources]' (XVIII(4)). Inclusion of a detailed provision (Article XXIV) on property rights in relation to traditional lands and resources coupled with harvesting rights and the environment in which these elements exist as part of a wide-ranging articulation of 'social, economic and property rights' in Section 5 is still very much under debate.

INTERNATIONAL LAW INSTRUMENTS AND INDIGENOUS ENVIRONMENTAL RIGHTS

As mentioned previously, international human rights law has been evolving in recent decades in a manner that reflects greater recognition of the individual and collective rights of indigenous peoples. A similar but more recent development has been occurring in reference to international environmental law. The intersection of these two fields can provide a solid foundation upon which indigenous peoples can assert both rights in their traditional lands and resources and the authority to protect those territories from environmental degradation.

The International Covenant on Economic, Social and Cultural Rights of 1966 recognizes the right to food and health, while the International Covenant on Civil and Political Rights (ICCPR) expressly emphasizes the importance of cultural continuity among minority populations free from discrimination. The ICCPR can have far greater significance than most United Nations treaties as it has a mechanism in which redress can be sought. The UN Human Rights Committee has received complaints from a number of indigenous applicants under the Optional Protocol over the past three decades. It has declared that the protection of cultural continuity for minorities under Article 27 of the ICCPR includes indigenous peoples (see, for example, *Lovelace v. Canada*[23]). On the other hand, the Committee has no mandate to receive complaints from indigenous peoples as distinct groups as it can only address petitions from individuals (*Ominayak v. Canada*).

In this latter decision, the Committee found that the Canadian Government had failed adequately to address the Band's need for a stable land base in combination with the granting of large-scale resource development concessions so as to 'threaten the way of life and culture of the Lubicon Lake Band, and constitute a violation of article 27 so long as they continue'.[24] The Committee has also declared that domestic legislation which controls membership in a manner that disentitles residency rights for some members is contrary to the Convention (*Lovelace v. Canada*).

The results were less satisfying for the Sami in *Länsman et al v. Finland*, in which they were unsuccessful in blocking a stone quarry operation that threatened local reindeer herding. The Committee concluded that adequate consultation had occurred by Finland with the Sami that led to measures being taken to address their environmental concerns so as to minimize the negative impact on reindeer herding. The Committee interpreted Article 27 to mean that actions with a limited impact on the way of life of persons belonging to a minority were acceptable, whereas those initiatives that constituted an effective denial of the right to culture were not acceptable and would violate the treaty.

ILO Convention No 169 Concerning Indigenous and Tribal Peoples in Independent Countries contains an express obligation on states regarding environmental protection by stating in Article 4.1 that 'Special measures shall be adopted as appropriate for safeguarding the persons, institutions, property, labour, cultures and environment of the peoples concerned.' Article 4.2 goes on to declare that 'Such special measures shall not be contrary to the freely-expressed wishes of the peoples concerned.' The Convention further provides that indigenous peoples have the right to control their own development as well as development on their lands (Article 7.1). Not only are governments directed to carry out environmental impact assessments with indigenous participation (Article 7.3), but they are also compelled to 'take measures, in co-operation with the peoples concerned, to protect and preserve the environment of the territories they inhabit' (Article 7.4). The Convention also recognizes the 'rights of ownership and possession of the peoples concerned over the lands which they traditionally occupy' (Article 15.1) and that 'the natural resources pertaining to their lands shall be specially safeguarded. These rights include the right of these peoples to participate in the use, management and conservation of these resources' (Article 16.1).

Unfortunately, Convention No 169 explicitly declares in Article 38 that it is only binding upon those nations that register their ratification. As of writing, there are still only 19 countries that have done so, with Spain being the last one (on 15 February 2007). The Convention also contains no mechanism for redress of alleged violations or even a regular reporting requirement with a monitoring system. It can be argued, however, that it now reflects customary international law so as to be enforceable through other domestic or international forums.

The UN Declaration on the Rights of Indigenous Peoples is structured in a similar fashion to Convention No 169 in that it contains no reporting, monitoring or dispute-resolution components. Instead, it relies upon all states to respect its terms and implement the rights confirmed within domestic systems by 'appropriate measures, including legislative measures, to achieve the ends of this Declaration' (Article 38) and to create 'just and fair procedures for the resolution of conflicts and disputes with States or other parties, as well as effective remedies for all infringements of their individual and collective rights' (Article 40). It must be remembered, however, that this Declaration was passed overwhelmingly (143 to 4) by the General Assembly, so it can be taken as reflecting global acceptance that these standards are more than mere aspirational goals. The previously quoted Article 4 on self-determination and Article 29 recognizing the right to environmental protection set a new benchmark by which state action can be assessed.

The OAS human rights system has been far more proactive in its efforts to respect indigenous rights. Having the robust mechanisms of the Inter-American Commission on Human Rights (IACHR) and the Inter-American Court of Human Rights creates real opportunities for indigenous peoples to provoke action through litigation. The IACHR has interpreted the American Declaration of the Rights and Duties of Man (American Declaration) the Inter-American Charter of Social Guarantees, both adopted in 1948, and the American Convention on Human Rights (American Convention), adopted in 1978, as confirming human rights for all peoples of the Americas, with particular application to the more than 40 million who identify themselves as indigenous peoples, from more than 400 indigenous groups. The Inter-American Democratic Charter (Democratic Charter), officially adopted on 21 March 2002, refers to 'the promotion and protection of human rights of indigenous peoples and migrants' (Article 9) and to the environment (Article 15). These international instruments can have significant value for indigenous peoples, even through their general recognition of the right to life, liberty and personal security (Article 1 of the American Declaration) and the right to property (Articles 21 and 23 of the American Convention).

The Commission and the Court have both been very receptive to petitions from indigenous individuals and communities. The Yanomami of Brazil were successful in one of the earliest invocations of the jurisdiction of the IACHR by an indigenous nation. The Commission concluded that the construction of a road through their Amazon homelands violated their rights to life and the preservation of health and wellbeing due to its negative environmental and social effects.[25]

The best-known case to date is the *Awas Tingni* case, which was the first one ever heard by the Inter-American Court where the central issue was indigenous collective rights, specifically pertaining to traditional lands and natural resources. At the IACHR, the Commission found that the Nicaraguan Government had failed to take steps necessary to protect the land rights of the Mayagna Indigenous

Community of Awas Tingni and therefore recommended appropriate remedial action. When Nicaragua refused to demarcate Awas Tingni and other indigenous traditional lands, the IACHR brought the case before the Inter-American Court of Human Rights. In February 2002, it was reported that Nicaragua had begun implementing the court ruling, which ordered them to pay the Awas Tingni community US$50,000 in damages and US$30,000 in legal expenses and to demarcate and title property claimed by the Awas Tingni and other tribes by paying the legal expenses. However, in January 2003, the Indigenous Community filed suit in the Nicaragua Appeals Court in view of the failure of the State to carry out the implementation of the decision.[26] In 2003, Nicaragua's legislature adopted a comprehensive law to ensure the demarcation and titling of the land and the President assigned his personal adviser to ensure the implementation of the decision occurred smoothly. This will mean that the Mayagna Indigenous Community of Awas Tingni was successful in stopping logging licences from being granted on their land so as to protect religious sites and the habitat relied on to support traditional subsistence practices.[27]

This duty of states to defend indigenous lands was first established in 1970 in the case of the Guahibo in Columbia and has since been considered in *Enxet v. Paraguay*, where on 25 March 1998, the first 'friendly settlement agreement' was achieved under the Inter-American system to restore legitimate property rights to an indigenous community.[28]

There have been other notable petitions to the IACHR regarding natural resources that were all found to be admissible. In 1998, the Toledo Maya Cultural Council filed a petition protesting against the Belize Government's grants of logging and oil concessions to sections of the rainforest. In 1999 Mary and Carrie Dann filed a petition against the US, claiming the infringement of ancestral lands and development from gold mining and other environmentally destructive activities. Finally, the Carrier Sekani Tribal Council of British Columbia filed a petition against the Government of Canada in May 2000 to prevent the Province of British Columbia from reallocating timber rights to large corporate logging companies.

In the IACHR's decision on the merits of the case of *Maya Community of Toledo District v. Belize*, the petitioners claimed that the State had granted logging and oil concessions on Mayan lands without meaningful consultations with the Mayan people and in a manner that caused substantial environmental harm and threatened long-term and irreversible damage to the natural environment upon which the Maya depend.[29] This case is unique in the sense that Belize has not ratified or signed the American Convention on Human Rights and thus the Inter-American human rights bodies are only able to use the American Declaration as a tool to enforce compliance with human rights. However, the IACHR in this case emphasized that 'developments in the corpus of international human rights law relevant to interpreting and applying the American Declaration may be drawn from the provisions of other prevailing international and regional human rights instruments', before setting out an analysis on the international human rights of indigenous peoples (at Paragraph 87). In their analysis, the IACHR again emphasized that to properly recognize indigenous human rights inherently requires an understanding that the rights and freedoms of those peoples are often exercised and enjoyed in a collective manner and that the right to property has been recognized as one of the rights having such a collective aspect. The Commission ultimately concluded that the concessions were made on land historically occupied by Mayan peoples and that, as a result of such concessions, environmental damage was occasioned in a way that has negatively affected the members of these indigenous communities. The Commission recognized the importance and necessity of economic development in the Americas, but also noted that:

> ... development activities must be accompanied by appropriate and effective measures to ensure that they do not proceed at the expense of the fundamental rights of persons who may be particularly and negatively affected, including indigenous communities and the environment upon which they depend for their physical, cultural and spiritual wellbeing. (Paragraph 87)

The Commission subsequently found that the right to property, among other rights, was violated by the State of Belize and that negotiations were required to delimit, demarcate and award title to Mayan communities for their ancestral lands, as well as to repair environmental damage sustained by concessionary activities. The Mayan groups continue to fight for the legal recognition of these rights in ongoing litigation in domestic courts.

In *Aloeboetoe v. Suriname* in 1993, the Court recognized the lawfulness of reparations based on indigenous customary law, including polygamy, thereby confirming the rights of the family.[30] The rights of the family are considered under Article 17 of the American Convention, which recognizes the family as the natural and fundamental unit of society and that it is entitled to protection by society and the state. This was particularly significant in *Aloeboetoe v. Suriname*, where they took into account the matriarchal family structure of the Maroons, for whom polygamy is common and property is communal along matriarchal lines. Compensation was given to the indigenous groups, whose representatives would distribute it among their members.

A landmark decision by the Inter-American Court of Human Rights was issued in March 2006 and can be considered a comprehensive authority that canvasses indigenous land rights in a variety of situations. In *Sawhoyamaxa Indigenous Community v. Paraguay*,[31] the Court found violations to articles 4.1, 8, 21 and 25 of the American Convention. The Sawhoyamaxa indigenous group had been living on the sides of highways for over eight years after being denied access to nearby ancestral lands since the land's title had been legally transferred into private hands pursuant to state law. The main issue before the Court in this case was to determine how to balance the rights of the Sawhoyamaxa indigenous community with those of the legal titleholders under the state regime. Paraguay recognized its obligation to restore land rights to the Sawhoyamaxa, but claimed that they were barred from doing so since the claimed land had been registered in private hands for many years and proof of historical Sawhoyamaxa links rested exclusively on one anthropological report.

In assessing the community's claims of various human rights violations under the American Convention, the Court reviewed Inter-American jurisprudence on indigenous land possession, separating the case law into three categories. The *Maygna (Sumo) Awas Tingni Community* case provided the authority that simple possession of the land can suffice for indigenous communities lacking state-recognized title to the land, in order to obtain legal recognition of that property and registration. The case of *Moiwana Community* determined that an indigenous group can be deemed to be the legitimate owners of their traditional lands even where they are not in possession of the land if they can demonstrate that they left the land as a result of acts of violence perpetrated against them. The final category was illustrated by the case of *Yakwe Axa Indigenous Community*, in which the Court held that members of an indigenous community can submit claims for traditional lands and the Court may order the State to transfer those lands on a case-by-case basis as a measure of reparation. The conclusions of this jurisprudence were fourfold:

1 traditional possession of the land by indigenous people has the equivalent effect of state-granted freehold title;
2 traditional possession entitles indigenous peoples to demand official recognition and registration of their property title;
3 members of indigenous groups who have unwillingly left their traditional lands, or lost possession thereof, still maintain their property rights even though they lack legal title, unless the lands have been lawfully transferred to third parties in good faith; and
4 where members of indigenous groups have unwillingly lost possession of lands subsequently lawfully transferred to innocent third parties, then they are entitled either to restitution or to obtain other lands of equal size and quality.

The Court then went on to hold that Articles 1(1) and 2 of the American Convention oblige the State to provide for appropriate procedures in its national legal system to process the land claim proceedings of indigenous peoples with an interest in their ancestral lands. As a result, the Court held that the land claim administrative proceedings had been ineffective and failed to grant to the Community the real possibility to regain access to their traditional lands. Subsequently, the Court determined that Article 8 (the right to judicial protection) and Article 24 (the right to a fair hearing) had been unlawfully violated.

Arguably, the most important provision in respect of indigenous land claims is found under Article 21 of the Convention, in the form of the right to property. The Court held that:

> ... the close ties the members of indigenous communities have with their traditional lands and the natural resources associated with their culture thereof, as well as the incorporeal elements deriving therefrom, must be secured under article 21 of the American Convention. The culture of the members of indigenous communities reflects a particular way of life, of being, seeing and acting in the world, the starting point of which is their close relation with their traditional lands and natural resources, not only because they are their main means of survival, but also because they form part of their worldview, of their religiousness and consequently of their cultural identity. (Paragraph 118)

The Court emphasized that indigenous communities may have a collective understanding of concepts of property and possession that do not conform with classic individualized concepts of property. This difference in perspective, however, should not diminish the right to equal protection under Article 21. The Court further determined that Paraguay had violated the community's right to life under Article 4. The Court reiterated that there is a general obligation within the Convention for a state to carry out special duties respecting the particular needs of vulnerable groups.

The Court determined that a number of actions should be carried out as reparations. The traditional lands of the community were ordered to be returned within three years; however, the Court left it to Paraguay to decide whether they would be returned by way of purchase, expropriation or the selection of alternative lands. An additional US$1 million was ordered to be paid into a community fund to construct and implement educational, agricultural and health projects and provide housing, sanitary infrastructure and potable water, to be completed within two years from the date of the handover of the lands. The projects are to be determined by a committee of three representatives, selected to represent the state, the community and a third jointly selected. The case of *Sawhoyamaxa Indigenous Community* has outlined that the state's duty to ensure equal property rights under the American Convention cannot be undermined by state-sanctioned title held in private hands. While the state still has a duty to provide suitable land to indigenous groups who have lost possession of their ancestral lands, it is unclear what practical effect the assignment of 'alternative lands' may have on indigenous communities.

The legal principles on indigenous land rights outlined in the case of *Sawhoyamaxa Indigenous Community* may prove helpful for cases currently being litigated in the Inter-American system. The IACHR upheld the admissibility of the petition in *Aboriginal Community of Lhaka Honhat v. Argentina*[32] on

21 October 2006. The petition centres on the state's failure, in contravention of the national and provincial constitutions, to legally recognize the indigenous peoples' communal possession and ownership of the lands they have traditionally occupied as well as the group's right to manage the land's natural resources. The main issue of contention has focused not on the possession of the lands, but on the fact that non-Aboriginal groups have carried out activities on the land that have resulted in detrimental effects that have interfered with the indigenous group's ability to live self-sufficiently from the land. To date, the IACHR has not yet ruled on the merits of the case.

THE INUIT PETITION AS AN EXAMPLE OF TAKING ACTION UNDER INTERNATIONAL LAW INSTRUMENTS

As is evident from the foregoing review of some of the key decisions within the UN and OAS human rights systems, the focal point for indigenous peoples has been on trying to secure ownership or control over traditional territories. Often the triggering event that causes the community to take the unprecedented step of litigating their rights assertions is the arrival of major forestry, mining or petroleum interests with the imprimatur of the national government's land law system. In other words, land rights arguments are being used in part to block or minimize environmental damage from resource development projects going forward, through seeking confirmation of territorial rights to traditional lands. These cases will also occasionally seek recognition of indigenous authority to manage their lands to enforce conservation priorities.

A petition filed with the IACHR on 7 December 2005 by 63 Inuit individuals provides an excellent example of a different approach that is directly concentrating upon achieving a positive environmental outcome, the reduction of greenhouse gas (GHG) emissions by the US through international law. The 163-page petition was spearheaded by Sheila Watt-Cloutier, then the elected Chair of the Inuit Circumpolar Conference (ICC), and included supporting testimony from other Inuit from Alaska and northern Canada, although this is not formally a claim filed by the ICC. The petition relies upon the evidence of traditional knowledge of hunters and elders as well as the 2004 Arctic Climate Impact Assessment to substantiate levels of existing and anticipated future destruction of the Arctic environment caused by global warming, which would terminate the culture and hunting-based economy of the Inuit. The petition itself emanates from the combined work of the Center for International Environmental Law (CIEL), Earthjustice and the ICC.

The Inuit petitioners ground their legal arguments primarily in the protection of individual rights under the American Declaration. They rely upon the right to life, liberty and the security of the person under Article 1 to argue that the effects of global warming are already depriving the Inuit of these rights. Severe alterations in weather patterns are rendering travel in the Arctic far more dangerous and have resulted in deaths of Inuit hunters falling through sea ice. The risk from fatal disease has heightened due to the migration of species previously unknown in the Americas. The argument relies upon the aforementioned Yanomami case as well as the Commission's 'Report on the situation of human rights in Ecuador' of 1997, in which it concluded that environmental degradation that 'may cause serious physical illness, impairment and suffering' of the local indigenous people is 'inconsistent with the right to be respected as a human being' and so violates Article 1.

The complainants also assert that the right to own and enjoy property under Article XXIII of the American Declaration (and the similar provision in the American Convention) is unduly interfered with by the damage produced by GHGs, even to the extent that lands are eroding and sea ice disappearing. Reliance is placed upon the Awas Tingni decision of the Court in asserting that the destruction of their property rights is contrary to international law. They further argue that the American Declaration's recognition of the right to the preservation of one's health is being violated by the impact of global warming through its introduction of new diseases, reduction in traditional food sources and deteriorating air quality. Finally, the petitioners assert that the right to benefit from the enjoyment of one's culture is being infringed by environmental degradation through increasing emissions of GHGs.

The petition was initially rejected by the Commission without prejudice on 16 November 2006; however, it reversed its position the following February and invited submissions from the petitioners. Sheila Watt-Cloutier, and legal counsel from the two non-governmental organizations in support, made strong arguments on 1 March 2007 and the Commission's decision is still pending.

Challenging the US before the IACHR for its insufficient action on climate change is, needless to say, a controversial move. Some could argue that those Canadian Inuit applicants should focus their petition on Canada, as it has an even worse record on reducing GHG emissions despite having signed the Kyoto Protocol. Others may suggest that the petition should have been formally brought by Inuit communities and/or associations, rather than individuals, with the emphasis placed upon the infringement of collective rights instead of individual ones. Nevertheless, litigating against the most powerful state in the Western Hemisphere clearly attracts far greater media attention. The American refusal to endorse the Kyoto Protocol, particularly in the days leading up to its expiration, makes the US a more attractive target, with a positive decision by the Commission hopefully resulting in increased pressure on the US to favour the Protocol's replacement by a stronger international treaty.

Linking international human rights law directly to the impact of global or large-scale environmental deterioration in the context of formal legal proceedings is a significant milestone that must be applauded. It clearly demonstrates how indigenous peoples, even when not placing heavy reliance upon their unique legal rights specifically as indigenous peoples, can be in the vanguard of pressing for a new, realistic approach to embracing sustainability as *the* operating principle for governmental policy.

DOMESTIC INDIGENOUS RIGHTS AND THE ENVIRONMENT

It is important to realize that indigenous peoples in many countries also have collective rights as the original owners and sovereign governments of their lands. A number of nations have sought to reflect this reality through their domestic legislation, jurisprudence and policies to varying degrees. A comprehensive review of this huge body of law and policy in the context of environmental protection is not possible within this short chapter. Therefore, only a few highlights can be noted.

Australian legislation and courts have both recognized traditional, or customary, title of the Aboriginal and Torres Strait Islander people to their lands, waters and seabed since the High Court's decision in the Mabo case in 1992. Further, land rights legislation in the Northern Territory goes back to 1976, and several states followed with their own statutory forms of recognition before the Commonwealth Parliament passed the Native Title Act in 1993. As a result of these statutory initiatives, approximately 15 per cent of the land mass of Australia is confirmed as being set aside for traditional owners. It must be noted, however, that these lands are primarily in the desert regions in the centre of the continent, rather than interwoven through the whole country, so many Aboriginal people still have no land base. Furthermore, their effective decision-making regarding natural resource development on these lands is extremely limited and they possess virtually no local governmental control or legislative authority over its management.

The position in New Zealand is somewhat more positive as the Treaty of Waitangi of 1840 between Maori leaders and the British Crown establishes a partnership arrangement in which Maori ownership of lands, resources and its treasures, as well as chiefly authority (or governance), are confirmed. Despite the terms of the Treaty, however, the Maori have lost most of their original land base and no longer possess their effective traditional governance system as national legislation over time has superimposed majority wishes upon them. Negotiations of new treaty settlements have dominated much of Maori–Government efforts during the past 15 years, to redress historic injustices and improper land seizures. The bicultural Waitangi Tribunal has worked tirelessly for many years to hear both Maori claims of historic treaty violations as well as to apply the Treaty to modern issues such as radio and television airwaves, deep sea commercial fishing, intellectual property, and pollution. The Tribunal has held hearings and reported on several environmental disputes over the past 20 years, such as the Te Atiawa attack on sewage effluent being discharged into the ocean and damaging reefs, seabeds and fish, and has consistently held that such governmental actions violate the Treaty's commitments and should be stopped. The government has accepted such recommendations on occasion and Parliament does require the principles of the Treaty to be considered (and thereby compels attention to Maori concerns) in decisions taken by local governments under the Resource Management Act and by the Department of Conservation in dealing with Crown lands and before allocating any future state interests in Crown property. Local Maori also have real control concerning land use and environmental management of those lands remaining under Maori trusts or with individual beneficiaries of previously allotted lands as landowners. Nevertheless, Maori *iwi* (or tribes) possess exceedingly little direct authority of a governmental nature over resource management and environmental protection to date.

Indian Nations in the US have had some significant success through litigation in preserving treaty harvesting rights in the Northwest and Midwestern parts of the country. In *US v. Washington*,[33] the court declared that tribal fishing rights included the right to have the fish protected from environmental degradation. As the court reasoned in logical terms, 'The most fundamental prerequisite to exercising the right to take fish is the existence of fish to be taken.' The judge went on to say that:

> ... it is equally beyond doubt that the existence of an environmentally acceptable habitat is essential to the survival of the fish, without which the expressly reserved right to take fish would be meaningless and valueless. Thus, it is necessary to recognize an implied environmental right in order to fulfil the purpose of the fishing clause.

Therefore he ordered the state to 'refrain from degrading the fish habitat to an extent that would deprive the tribes of their moderate living needs'. The American courts have long recognized a tribal right to sufficient water quantity to meet their own needs (*Winters v. United States*, 207 U.S. 564 (1908)). Treaty rights to hunting and fishing have also been viewed as including a right to conservation of water sufficient to support the ongoing survival of the resources on which those activities depend.[34]

The continued presence of sovereign Indian Nations in the US with tribal governments that retain significant legislative and executive jurisdiction under the 'domestic dependant nation' theory of the US Supreme Court since 1832 means that tribes are able to enact their own environmental protection laws that regulate reservation lands. The power that many tribes possess as recognized governments with important landholdings also generates a willingness by many state governments to enter into compacts with tribes to co-manage certain shared natural resources and develop complementary environmental management regimes.

The struggle by indigenous peoples in Canada to regain significant governance jurisdiction is of more recent vintage than that of its neighbour; however, many communities, particularly in northern regions, are landowners of significant portions of their traditional territories. Over the past 33 years, modern comprehensive land claim settlements have resulted in 7 per cent of Canada now being in exclusive First Nation, Inuit and Métis hands. These indigenous peoples control land and resource use through their governments.

Environmental assessment mechanisms are also increasingly part of treaty settlements. For example, the Nisga'a Final Agreement confirms the right of the Nisga'a Lisims Government to create its own environmental assessment process; however, the minimum environmental protection standards must meet or exceed relevant federal and provincial laws or else the latter will prevail if there is a conflict.

Co-management of shared waterways, wildlife and fish has also become a common element of these new treaties, usually in relation to remaining Crown lands. For example, the Nunavut Impact Review Board, which contains representatives of the Federal and Nunavut Territorial governments as well as the Inuit settlement beneficiaries, determines whether major projects will be approved as meeting all environmental concerns. The federal Mackenzie Valley Resource Management Act creates a local joint environment assessment board that assesses development proposals in this region, and it prevails over the Canadian Environmental Assessment Act.

Even where public governments exist in Canada's three northern territories and northern parts of Labrador and Quebec, the presence of dominant or significant minority indigenous populations has meant that these governments are also highly responsive to indigenous concerns regarding the preservation of the environment upon which so much of their life depends. Overwhelming Inuit voter dominance in some of these areas ensures that virtually all of the government ministers and legislators are themselves Inuit, so emphasis upon using the powers of those governments legislatively and administratively to protect the environment are at the forefront. As the opening quote of this chapter indicates, however, many of the environmental threats stem from climate change and industrial activities far removed from the territorial scope of these governments.

Aboriginal and/or treaty rights to hunt and fish are widespread in Canada for indigenous peoples. These rights have been regularly recognized by Canadian courts, particularly since their constitutional entrenchment in 1982. These harvesting rights also encompass incidental rights that are reasonably necessary to give the main rights meaning. Incidental rights have been held by Canadian courts to include the right to possess firearms, to transport firearms, to possess fishing equipment and boats, to construct hunting and trapping cabins in provincial parks, to conduct ceremonies, to build fires in conservation areas, and to convey traditional knowledge to the next generation. There are, however, precious few examples where these ancillary rights have been used as the foundation to argue that a right to gather flora and fauna must entail the presence of the substances themselves and in a condition in which they can be safely consumed. The legal basis to make such arguments remains available.

More recently, the Canadian judiciary has embraced a theory that the federal and provincial governments owe an enforceable legal duty to consult with First Nations, Inuit and Métis people whenever contemplating any action that might impact upon Aboriginal or treaty rights. This obligation can arise when a government is considering issuing a forestry, aquaculture, mining or petroleum licence, or if contemplating approving industrial, residential or commercial projects that could impact upon the environment. The duty must reflect the obligation on the Crown to act honourably in all its dealings with Aboriginal peoples. The effect of this duty is that any asserted Aboriginal or treaty right, whether previously proven to exist or not yet judicially considered, must be taken into account by the government prior to taking action that could infringe those rights. The stronger the right that may be affected and the more severe the potential impact, the more the duty will move beyond an obligation to consult into a duty to negotiate how indigenous concerns can be accommodated and may evolve into a necessity to obtain Aboriginal consent.

Conclusions

Indigenous peoples are not merely the 'canaries' that will be the first to suffer from environmental degradation. They possess the capacity to generate a form of 'reverse environmental imperialism', as they clearly can be:

- teachers regarding sustainable living;
- the lead activists for social change;
- the rights holders whose unique legal rights, if respected, can force states towards true environmental protection; and
- the governors of their traditional lands in a sustainable manner so as to provide viable alternative visions of the future.

I am not suggesting that using the legal tools available should be *the*, or even a primary, solution. It can, however, be a very useful strategy to prod reluctant governments to move forward more vigorously in protecting the environment and taking action where serious deterioration has occurred or is threatened. Utilizing domestic and international law arguments is sometimes the only effective, peaceful way to compel action in this domain. Hopefully the discussion of the opportunities available under emerging international law standards and through domestic law in a few selected national examples provides some encouragement that legal support for change is possible.

Is it not appropriate that indigenous peoples can once again be more than repositories of TEK, but leaders in the struggle to protect and rehabilitate the environment of our shared planet? Just as so many of their ancestors did in aiding newcomers to survive in unfamiliar terrains, there is an opportunity for indigenous peoples to once again be teachers and leaders in reawakening an awareness of the fragility of our environment. Asserting indigenous rights can be one vehicle in the movement for the transformative change that is so desperately needed.

ACKNOWLEDGEMENTS

I would like to thank Holly Levalliant and Kendra Lakusta, both law students at the University of Ottawa, for their invaluable research assistance, as well as Joe Williams, Chair of the Waitangi Tribunal and Chief Judge of the Maori Land Court, for providing such an ideal environment in which this chapter could be written in Wellington, Aotearoa.

NOTES

1 Watt-Cloutier, 2007b; see also 'Global warming and human rights', www.earthjustice. org/library/references/Background-for-IAHRC.pdf.

2 McMichael et al, 2003, 2004; Patz et al, 2005, pp310–317.

3 *Haida Nation v. British Columbia (Minister of Forests)*, [2004] 3 S.C.R. 511.

4 *Haida Nation v. British Columbia (Minister of Forests)*, *ibid.*, at para 65.

5 For example, indigenous peoples participated quite directly in the creation of the UN Draft Declaration on the Rights of Indigenous Peoples through the UN Working Group on Indigenous Populations, the Sub-Commission on Prevention of Discrimination and Protection of Minorities, and the Human Rights Commission and its Working Group on the Draft Declaration. They also actively engaged in lobbying for approval of the Declaration by the Human Rights Council and its ultimate passage by the General Assembly on 13 September 2007.

6 International Labour Organization Convention No 169 Concerning Indigenous and Tribal Peoples in Independent Countries, reprinted in 28 I.L.M. 1382 (1989) [ILO 169]. The previous ILO Convention No 107 of 1957 on Indigenous and Tribal Populations was ratified by 27 nations of which 8 have subsequently ratified Convention 169. For a detailed review see Rodríguez-Piñero (2005). For a comprehensive review of international law and indigenous rights see Anaya (2004), Xanthaki (2007) or Morse (2006).

7 Convention on Biological Diversity, 5 June 1992, 1760 U.N.T.S. 79, Can. T.S. 1993 No. 24, 31 I.L.M. 818 [CBD].

8 Metcalf, C, 'Indigenous rights and the environment: Evolving international law,' (2003-2004) 35 Ottawa L. Rev. 101–140 at 105.

9 Metcalf, *ibid.*, at 105–106.

10 Brundtland, 1987, pp114–115.

11 Rio Declaration on the Environment and Development, United Nations Conference on Environment and Development, Annex, Resolution 1, UN Doc. A/Conf.151/26/ Rev.1(vol 1) (1993) at 3, 31 I.L.M 876 [Rio Declaration cited to UN Doc.A/Conf. 151/26/Rev.1 (vol 1)]; Agenda 21, United Nations Conference on Environment and Development, Annex, Resolution 1, UN Doc. A/conf.151/26/ Rev.1(vol 1) (1993) at 7.

12 Agenda 21, United Nations Conference on Environment and Development, Annex, Resolution 1, UN Doc. A/conf.151/26/Rev.1(vol 1) (1993) at 385 art. 26.1.

13 International Labour Organization: Convention (No 169) Concerning Indigenous and Tribal Peoples in Independent Countries, reprinted in 28 I.L.M. 1382 (1989).

14 Charter of the United Nations, signed 26 June 1945, came into force 24 Oct 1945; see www.un.org/aboutun/charter/, Chapter XI, Article 73(a).

15 Convention on the Rights of the Child, Canada, signed 28 May 1990, ratified with reservations 13 Dec 1991, available online at www.unhchr.ch/html/menu3/b/k2crc.htm.

16 CBD, *supra* note 7.

17 Proposed American Declaration on the Rights of Indigenous Peoples, approved by the Inter-American Commission on Human Rights (Organization of American States) on 26 February 1997, at its 1333rd session, 95th regular session, Doc. OEA/Ser/LV/II.90, Doc. 9, rev. 2 (1997).

18 Outcome of the Tenth Meeting of the Working Group to Prepare the Draft American Declaration on the Rights of Indigenous Peoples mandated by the Committee on Juridical and political Affairs, April 2007, www.oas.org/OASpage/Indigenas/documentos/XreunionE01.doc.

19 Metcalf, *supra* note 8, at 106.

20 Metcalf, *ibid*, at 106.

21 Vienna Declaration and Programme of Action, United Nations, World Conference on Human Rights, Vienna, 25 June 1993, UN Doc. A/CONF. 157/23 (1993), available online at www2.ohchr.org/english/law/vienna.htm.

22 Article 31 in a former draft of the United Nations Declaration on the Rights of Indigenous Peoples drew the linkage more explicitly when it stated in Article 31 that 'Indigenous peoples, as a specific form of exercising their right to self-determination, have the right to autonomy or self-government in matters relating to their internal and local affairs, including culture, religion, education, information, media, health, housing, employment, social welfare, economic activities, land and resources management, environment, and entry by non-members, as well as ways and means for financing these autonomous functions.'

23 HRC Comm. No. 24/1977, *Lovelace v. Canada*, views of 30 July 1981, A/36/40, Annex XVIII, par. 13.1.

24 *Chief Bernard Ominayak and the Lubicon Lake Band v. Canada*, Communication No. 167/1984, UN Doc. CCPR/C/38/D/167/1984 (1990), http://www1.umn.edu/humanrts/undocs/session38/167-1984.html.

25 *Yanomami Community v. Brazil*, Inter-Am, Comm. H.R. No. 7615, *Annual Report of the Inter-American Commission on Human Rights* 1984-85, OEA/Ser. L./V/II.66/doc. 10 rev. 1.

26 Indian Law Resource Center, 'Indigenous Nicaraguans sue the President', www.marrder.com/htw/2003jan/central.htm.

27 *Mayagna (Sumo) Awas Tinga Community v. Nicaragua Case* (2001), Inter-Am. Ct. H.R. (Ser. C) No 79, available online at http://humanrights.law.monash.edu.au/iachr/AwasTingnicase.html.

28 *Yakye Axa indigenous community of the Enxet-Lengua people v. Paraguay*, Case 12.313, Report No. 2/02, Inter-Am. C.H.R., Doc. 5 rev. 1 at 387 (2002); www1.umn.edu/humanrts/cases/2-02.html.

29 *Maya indigenous community of the Toledo District v. Belize*, Case 12.053, Report No. 40/04, Inter-Am. C.H.R., OEA/Ser.L/V/II.122 Doc. 5 rev. 1 at 727 (2004); www1.umn.edu/humanrts/cases/40-04.html.

30 *Aloeboetoe et al v. Suriname*, Inter-Am. Ct. H.R. 66, OAS/ser.L./V./III.29, doc. 4 (1993); www1.umn.edu/humanrts/iachr/e!11fndo.pdf.

31 *Sawhoyamaxa Indigenous Community of the Enxet People v. Paraguay*, Case 0322/2001, Report No. 12/03, Inter-Am. C.H.R., OEA/Ser.L/V/II.118 Doc. 70 rev. 2 at 378 (2003); www1.umn.edu/humanrts/cases/12-03.html.

32 IACHR, Report No 78/06, Aboriginal Community of Lhaka Honhat, Argentina, Petition 12.094, Admissibility, 21 October 2006, available online at www.cidh.oas.org/annualrep/2006eng/ARGENTINA.12094eng.htm.

33 *US v. Washington*, 506 F. Supp. 187, 11 Envtl. L. Rep. 20016 (W. D. Wash. 1980).

34 *US v. Adair et al*, 723 F2d 1394 (9th Cir. 1983).

REFERENCES

Arctic Council (1996) 'Declaration on the Establishment of the Arctic Council (Ottawa, Canada, 1996)', joint statement made by the Governments of Canada, Denmark, Finland, Iceland, Norway, the Russian Federation, Sweden and the United States of America (known as the Arctic Council), signed 19 September, full text available at www.dfait-maeci.gc.ca/circumpolar/ottdec-en.asp

Anaya, S. J. (2004) *Indigenous Peoples in International Law*, 2nd edition, Oxford University Press, Oxford

Boyd, D. (2003) *Unnatural Law: Rethinking Canadian Environmental Law and Policy*, UBC Press, Vancouver, Canada

Brundtland, G. (1987) *Our Common Future: World Commission on Environment and Development*, Oxford University Press, Oxford, UK

McKiver, J. (2004) 'Environmental protection, indigenous rights and the Arctic Council: Rock, paper, scissors on the ice?', in L. Watters (ed) (2004) *Indigenous Peoples, the Environment and Law*, Carolina Academic Press, Durham, NC

McMichael, A. J., Campbell-Lendrum, D. H., Corvalan, C. F., Ebi, K. L., Githeko, A., Scheraga, J. D. and Woodward, A. (eds) (2003) *Climate Change and Human Health: Risks and Responses*, World Health Organization, Geneva

McMichael, A., Campbell-Lendrum, D., Kovats, S., Edwards, S., Wilkinson, P., Wilson, T., Nicholls, R., Hales, S., Tanser, F., Le Sueur, D., Schlesinger, M. and Andronova, N. (2004) 'Global climate change', in M. Ezzati, A. D. Lopez, A. Rodgers and C.J.L. Murray (eds) *Comparative Quantification of Health Risks: Global and Regional Burden of Disease due to Selected Major Risk Factors*, World Health Organization, Geneva

Metcalf, C. (2003/4) 'Indigenous rights and the environment: Evolving international law', *Ottawa Law Review*, vol 35, pp101–140

Morse, B. W. (2006) 'The Rights of Indigenous and Minority Peoples' in *La Convergence des Systèmes Juridiques au 21e Siècle [Convergence of Legal Systems in the 21st Century]*, Bruylant, Bruxelles

Patz, J. A., Campbell-Lendrum, D., Holloway, T. and Foley, J. A. (2005) 'Impacts of regional climate change on human health', *Nature*, vol 438, no 17, pp310–317

Rodríguez-Piñero, L. (2005) *Indigenous Peoples, Postcolonialism, and International Law: The ILO Regime (1919–1989)*, Oxford University Press, Oxford

Watt-Cloutier, S. (2007a) 'Testimony before the Inter-American Human Rights Commission, Washington, DC', www.ciel.org/Publications/IACHR_WC_Mar07.pdf

Watt-Cloutier, S. (2007b) 'Global warming and human rights', www.earthjustice.org/library/references/Background-for-IAHRC.pdf

Westra, L. (2007) *Environmental Justice and the Rights of Indigenous Peoples*, Earthscan, London

Xanthaki, A. (2007) *Indigenous Rights and United Nations Standards*, Cambridge University Press, Cambridge, UK

11

A Human Right to Water: An Ethical Position or a Realizable Goal?

Joseph W. Dellapenna

INTRODUCTION

While more than three-quarters of the Earth's surface is covered by water, only a tiny fraction is fresh water suitable for use by humans and by most of the plants and animals on which human survival depends (Gleick et al, 2006). While it is one of the most essential resources for human survival, the quantity of fresh water on the planet essentially is fixed or declining. Human activity easily pollutes water, rendering it unfit for human use, while desalination remains an expensive alternative, probably too expensive for use on a mass scale (California Coastal Commission, 2003; Uche, 2003; Symposium, 2006). Moreover, fresh water all too often is available at the wrong time, in the wrong place, or in the wrong amounts: seasonal rains or snows often have run off or been consumed before the end of the growing season, while rain or snow usually falls most heavily on mountains, where the rugged terrain discourages agriculture, rather than on the easily farmed plains. Floods can be followed by drought. All of this has created the felt necessity to manage and control the development and use of water through elaborate engineering schemes and highly centralized political arrangements (Wittfogel, 1957; Teclaff, 1967; Downing and Gibson, 1975).

Today, the demand for usable water is growing exponentially, not only because of growing human populations, but even more because of changing patterns of use (Dellapenna, 1997). For example, while the population of the US doubled between 1950 and 1980, the per capita consumption of water (mostly indirectly through the consumption of goods and services that use water) rose by 600 per cent (Ashworth, 1982; Powledge, 1982). The resulting 1200 per cent increase in total water use during this period thus was driven far more by changing patterns of use than by population growth. While the use of water has become somewhat more efficient in the US since 1980, because of the costs imposed on water consumption in order to meet water quality regulations, the decline in total water consumption in the US in the last two decades has been very small compared to the massive increases in the preceding three.

Although the precise patterns of change vary somewhat from country to country, the overall pattern is similar as populations grow and as living standards rise. The result is considerable stress on existing legal regimes as they attempt to respond to increasing and changing demands for water without unduly destabilizing existing expectations expressed in investments in water-using facilities (Brans et al, 1997; Postel, 1999). These problems are exacerbated as water management systems struggle to adapt to the altered precipitation and flow patterns deriving from global climate change (Dellapenna, 1999). To the extent that global climate change reduces the supply of water in particular basins, competition between important (and not so important) new or enlarged uses and existing uses can only intensify. If global climate change leads to an increase of water supplies in particular basins, it would at least temporarily ease stress on the water regimes in those areas, but this would possibly create a need for new legal responses to flooding or other problems.

A great deal of recent legal activity and scholarship has focused on the resulting problems of revising water law to cope with these problems. Initially this work centred on allocating water among states and strengthening the ability of governments to manage the water resources within their jurisdiction (UN, 1997; Dellapenna, 2007). Rather less was said and done regarding the rights of individuals to use water, and most of what work was done on the rights of individuals took the form of advocacy of greater reliance on markets or market-like mechanisms for the allocation and management of water (Anderson and Snyder, 1997; Merrett, 1997; Easter et al, 1998; Griffin, 2006). Others have raised serious questions about the wisdom of relying on markets as a water management tool (Dellapenna, 2000).

An important feature of the current debates about markets has been the claim advanced in the past 15 years, in part at least as a reaction against the pressure to introduce markets as the primary water management tool, that there is a human right to water (McCaffrey, 1992; Gleick, 1999; Schorn, 2000). This has proven to be a highly controversial claim, with few governments accepting the existence of such a human right. In this chapter, I discuss the legal basis for such a right, its meaning and what would be required to realize it. In so doing, I raise the question of whether the claimed human right to water is merely an ethical position or a realizable goal.

WHY DOES RECOGNIZING A HUMAN RIGHT TO WATER MATTER?

What difference does it make if the global society recognizes a human right to water? The bare statement of such a right does not fill anyone's cup. The basic answer is that by recognizing a human right, the global community places a legal floor under those claiming a need for access to water. While numerous international meetings – including the Third World Water Forum in Kyoto and the World Summit on Sustainable Development in Johannesburg (World Water Council, 2003; UN, 2003) – call for major investment in providing water to the people who presently either have inadequate supplies or unsafe supplies, very little has actually been done. A human right, in contrast with simple promises to provide resources, means something that every person is entitled to simply because that person is human. A human right is a universal moral and legal right that cannot be denied any person without a grave affront to justice (Cranston, 1973; Thorme, 1991). More specifically, by recognizing the human right to water, the community recognizes a legal claim to adequate legal arrangements and levels of investment to ensure access to secure, sanitary supplies of water (Gleick, 1999; Bluemel, 2004).

We live in a world in which an estimated 1.2 billion people do not have access to safe drinking water and 2.4 billion people lack proper sanitation (WHO/UNICEF, 2002). In such a world, strengthening the possibility of adequate investment in water management is no small achievement. While recognizing water as a human right would not solve the resource problem, such recognition would provide more effective protection for those in desperate need of safe water and proper sanitation (Brundtland, 2002). Such recognition grounds the obligation to provide access to water in law and maintains attention on the present, all too often deplorable state of water management. Yet in order for such recognition actually to impact on the situation of those most in need, one must translate the general proposition into specific obligations on states to realize, progressively but with reasonable dispatch, the steps necessary to provide access to safe and sanitary water, including the equitable resolution of conflicts among states over shared waters and the setting of priorities for water policy.

THE LEGAL BASIS FOR RECOGNIZING A HUMAN RIGHT TO WATER

Historically, in many parts of the world, water has been treated as a form of common property shared among all with legal access to the resource. In response to the stresses created by the growing shortages of suitable water around the world, however, in many parts of the world water has been transformed into either private property or public property (International Conference on Water, 1992, Principle 4; Dellapenna, 1999). Under a system of common property, each person with lawful access – often all or nearly all persons in need of water – have a legal right to the water they need based upon their common ownership of the water. After a transition to private or public property, most persons no longer have a direct legal claim on water resources. Such transitions then underlie the growing recourse to the notion of a human right to water (Calaguas, 1999, p12; Bluemel, 2004, pp963–967).

Thus far, no treaty or other binding legal document expressly recognizes a human right to water, though arguably such a right is inferable from a number of human rights treaties and other legal documents. The legal argument in favour of a human right to water took a big step forward on 26 November 2002, when the UN Economic and Social Council Committee on Economic, Social, and Cultural Rights adopted 'General Comment 15' to the International Covenant on Economic, Social, and Cultural Rights (ECOSOC, 2002). General Comment 15 expressly recognizes the existence of a human right to water based upon several articles of the International Covenant.

The status of general comments by the UN Committee is controversial, however. The Committee itself is empowered under an optional protocol to the International Covenant to receive reports from participating states and to comment specifically on those reports (International Covenant, 1966, Articles 16–22). There is no explicit authority for the UN Committee to adopt general comments that are not related to a specific country report, but the Committee not only adopts general comments, it also treats them virtually as if they were amendments to the Covenant – even though the Covenant can only be amended through an elaborate process that requires ratification by national governments around the world. Regardless of its precise legal status, though, General Comment 15 is the first formal recognition of a human right to water in the international legal arena.

The UN Committee based its conclusion in General Comment 15 on inferences drawn from Articles 11(1) and 12(1) of the International Covenant. Article 11(1) recognizes the human right to an adequate standard of living, including food, clothing, and housing. Clearly, water is essential to providing food and to manufacturing the other elements of an adequate standard of living (Bluemel, 2004, pp971–972). Article 12(1) recognizes a human right to the highest attainable standard of health. Water is more essential to human health than anything other than air. Deprive us of air and we die in minutes. Deprive us of water and we die in days. Deprive us of food and we can go on for weeks or months, depending on our physical condition at the beginning of the fast – and on whether we have adequate supplies of water. And, as a Turkish businessman once commented, 'countless millions of people have lived without love, but none without water' (Nachmani, 1994). Furthermore, water is essential for a thriving ecosystem, without which human health cannot be maintained.

The UN Committee might have drawn further inferential support for its conclusion from Article 15(1) of the International Covenant, which guarantees a human right to participate in cultural life. Water remains central to numerous cultural practices all over the globe. Consider the Christian baptism, Jewish ritual bathing, the Muslim washing before prayers or the Hindu goal of bathing in the Ganges, to mention only a few. Even when water is only used symbolically, it remains a central feature of cultural life.

Numerous other international instruments similarly provide a strong basis for inferring a human right to water; several of them come close to a direct recognition of a general human right to water (Bluemel, 2004, pp970–971). The Convention on the Elimination of All Forms of Discrimination against Women, in Article 14(2)(h), provides that women are to 'enjoy adequate living conditions, particularly in relation to ... water supply'. The Convention on the Rights of the Child, in Article 24(2)(c), requires States to combat disease and malnutrition 'through the provision of adequate nutritious food and clean drinking water'. Several other provisions of the Convention on the Rights of the Child are also relevant (Convention on the Rights of the Child, 1989, Articles 20, 26, 29 and 46). Finally the Conventions on the Laws of War, particularly Additional Protocol I to the Geneva Conventions, provides support for a human right to water. Article 54 of Protocol I provides for the protection of objects indispensable for the survival of the civilian population, specifically including drinking water installations and irrigation works, along with foodstuffs, crops, and livestock, as among the objects that are not to be attacked, destroyed, removed, or rendered useless if the purpose is to deny their availability to the civilian population. Article 54 leaves open such destruction or removal if for legitimate military purposes. Article 55 further provides, however, that combatants are not to use methods that cause long-term or severe damage to the natural environment – without allowance for military necessity. Other provisions of Additional Protocol 1 or of the laws of war generally can be cited in support of a human right to water.

Finally, one can point to evidence of a human right to water in the constitutions of many states. Article 39 of the constitution of the Republic of South Africa alone expressly recognizes a human right to water (Bluemel, 2004, pp977–980), but more than 60 states, from many different legal traditions and in different stages of development, recognize a right to a clean and healthy environment. Among such constitutional provisions are those of are Argentina [Art. 124(2)], Belarus [Art. 46], Chile [Ch. III, Art. 19(8)], Ethiopia [Art. 44(1)], Hungary [Ch. I, § 18], the Republic of Korea [Ch. II, Art. 35], Nicaragua [Tit. IV, Ch. III, Art. 60], Peru [Ch. II, Art. 123], the Philippines [Art. II, § 15], Portugal [Pt. I, § III, Ch. II, Art. 66(1)], and Turkey [Ch. VIII(A), Art. 56] (Bluemel, 2004, pp980–985).

The foregoing are all 'hard law', in other words clearly binding on states that have ratified the constitutions, covenants and conventions. Arguably some or all of these instruments have risen to the level of customary international law binding on all states (Wolfke, 1993). Given their importance, they generally represent what international lawyers call *jus cogens* – cogent rules that bind even states that have persistently objected to the law in question. The conclusion that these instruments and the inferred human right to water is in fact a binding rule of customary international law from which states are not free to derogate is strengthened by the many instruments of 'soft law' that also – and often more directly – support the conclusion that there is a human right to water. These include that preamble to the Mar del Plata Declaration (UN, 1977), the Dublin Statement on Water and Sustainable Development (International Conference on Water, 1992, Principle 3), an entire chapter of Agenda 21 adopted at the Rio Conference in 1992 (UN, 1992, Chapter 18), and the Programme of Action of the UN International Conference on Population and Development (International Conference on Population and Development, 1994, Principle 2). Today the conclusion seems irrefutable that there is in fact a human right to water (International Law Association, 2004).

OPERATIONALIZING A HUMAN RIGHT TO WATER

It is all very well to recognize a human right to water in theory, but if it never progresses beyond theory towards being actually realized in people's lives, what is the point? For example, while the Republic of South Africa expressly recognized a right to water in its constitution adopted in 1994, millions of poor people in that country simply do not have real access to water or are having their access to water reduced as the country seeks to 'marketize' its water utilities (Thompson, 2003; Bluemel, 2004, pp977–980). The question to be confronted, then, is how to move a human right to water, once it is recognized, from the status of an ethical proposition to the status of a realizable goal. Space does not allow full elucidation of the steps necessary to realize the right to water. Here I only sketch the several normative requirements for realizing the right and outline the obligations that states must undertake if they are to realize those normative requirements – normative requirements are simple to state, but difficult to implement.

The first point to be made is that any attempt to realize the human right to water must depend upon its progressive realization. That is, one cannot expect that upon recognition of the right to water, the next day the state will make adequate supplies of water available to everyone. Instead, the state must take steps that will, over time, make water available in adequate amounts and of sufficient quality to ensure that basic needs are satisfied (Gleick, 1996). In other words, states must ensure that all persons have access to the water needed to realize other goods – human survival and thriving, with all that those goals imply. This will require the state to make water physically accessible to all over time, without imposing or tolerating economic barriers to access. It also requires that states provide access to the necessary information so that individuals can realize not only access to water, but also an ability to evaluate accurately their own needs and the quality and amounts of water necessary to fulfil those needs. Finally, all of this must be done without discrimination on the basis of race, gender, age, disability, whether the water user lives in an urban or rural setting, or whether the water user is nomadic or settled.

Translating these lofty normative requirements into specific policies and programmes will not be easy, but they can be realized by a programme built around three sets of policies:

1   The state must respect the right to water.
2   The state must protect the right to water.
3   The state must take steps to fulfil the right to water.

To respect the right to water, the state must take no step that interferes with a person's access to adequate water, and it must take no step (for example during war) that deprives a population of the water indispensable to its survival. To protect the right to water, the state must prevent third parties from interfering with a person's right to water and it must regulate water providers to ensure fair and equal access to all. Finally, to fulfil the right to water, the state must facilitate the right to water through legal recognition and enforcement, it must provide education regarding hygienic and sustainable water use, and it must progressively make water available to persons or groups that are unable, for reasons beyond their control, to realize the right themselves with the means at their disposal.

The foregoing obligations will require a state to take steps to ensure, over time, a minimum essential amount of water for each person in the society. States themselves are not to be obligated to provide every person with all of the water they want, but only that amount of water truly necessary to meet vital human needs, and then only when the individuals are not able to provide for those needs themselves (Gleick, 1996; UN, 1997, Article 10). The state will have to undertake to ensure physical access to sufficient and safe water on a regular basis without undue difficulties. That in turn requires provision of a sufficient number of outlets for water, so that there is no exorbitant wait for water and that water is found at a reasonable distance from households, and ensuring physical security while accessing water. Ensuring access to water on a non-discriminatory basis requires that states undertake to ensure the equitable distribution of water throughout society, to prevent, treat and control diseases linked to water, including by providing adequate sanitation, and to adopt and implement a national plan of action. The plan of action must be subject to periodic review through a participatory and transparent process that provides benchmarks for progress in fulfilling the right to water, along with monitoring of the realization of the right to water. All of this in turn requires states or national communities to find equitable solutions for the sharing of transboundary resources (UN, 1997).

The International Law Association has a long history of crafting summaries of international law, particularly international water law, in terms that successfully crystallize the content and effect of hitherto vague or contentious customary rules of law (Bourne, 1996; McCaffrey, 2001, pp321–322). The

Berlin Rules on Water Resources, its recent synthesis of the international customary law applicable to water resources (International Law Association, 2004), summarized the right to water in these terms:

Article 17
The Right of Access to Water

1   *Every individual has a right of access to sufficient, safe, acceptable, physically accessible and affordable water to meet that individual's vital human needs.*
2   *States shall ensure the implementation of the right of access to water on a non-discriminatory basis.*
3   *States shall progressively realize the right of access to water by:*
      a   Refraining from interfering directly or indirectly with the enjoyment of the right;
      b   Preventing third parties from interfering with the enjoyment of the right;
      c   Taking measures to facilitate individuals access to water, such as defining and enforcing appropriate legal rights of access to and use of water; and
      d   Providing water or the means for obtaining water when individuals are unable, through reasons beyond their control, to access water through their own efforts.
4   *States shall monitor and review periodically, through a participatory and transparent process, the realization of the right of access to water.*

This is probably as reasonable a summary of the human right to water as it exists today.

CONCLUSION

The human right to water is gradually gaining acceptance in the international community. Two benchmarks in the process were the approval of General Comment 15 by the UN Economic and Social Council Committee on Economic, Social, and Cultural Rights in 2002, which expressly recognized a human right to water as implicit in the International Covenant on Economic, Social and Cultural Rights, and the approval of the Berlin Rules on Water Resources by the International Law Association in 2004, which expressly recognized a right of access to water as part of customary international law and provides a summary of the legal principles that are necessary to realize such a right. The challenge to the world community now, acting for the most part at the national level, is to operationalize these legal principles in such a manner as to ensure that all persons actually have access to the water they need to survive and to thrive. That will take time and resources, but recognition of a human right to water will provide a legal obligation to make the necessary commitment, and hence an impetus for governments to fulfil that obligation.

REFERENCES

Anderson, T. L. and Snyder P. (1997) *Water Markets: Priming the Invisible Pump*, Cato Institute, Washington, DC

Ashworth, W. (1982) *Nor Any Drop to Drink*, Summit Books, New York

Bluemel, E. B. (2004) 'Comment: The implications of formulating a human right to water', *Ecology Law Quarterly*, vol 31, pp957–1006

Bourne, C. B. (1996) 'The International Law Association's contribution to international water resources law', *Natural Resources Journal*, vol 36, pp155–216

Brans, E. H. P., de Haan E. J., Nolkaemper, A. and Rinzema, J. (eds) (1997) *The Scarcity of Water: Emerging Legal and Policy Responses*, Kluwer Law International, London

Brundtland, G. H. (2002) 'Press release: Water for health enshrined as a human right', 27 November 2002, available at www.who.int/mediacentre/releases/pr91/en/print.html

Calaguas, B. U. (1999) *The Right to Water, Sanitation and Hygiene and the Human Rights-Based Approach to Development*, IRC International Water and Sanitation Centre, Delft, the Netherlands

California Coastal Commission (2003) 'Seawater desalination in California', available at www.coastal.ca.gov/desalrpt/dtitle.html

Convention on the Elimination of All Forms of Discrimination against Women, opened for signature 18 December 1979, entered into force 3 September 1981, General Assembly Resolution 34/180, 34 UN GAOR Supp. 46, UN Doc. A/34/46, at 193 (1979), UN Treaty Series vol. 1249, p13

Convention on the Rights of the Child, opened for signature 20 November 1989, entered into force 2 September 1990, General Assembly Resolution 44/25, UN Doc. A/RES/44/25 (1989), UN Treaty Series vol. 1577, p3

Cranston, M. (1973) *What Are Human Rights?*, Taplinger Publishing Co, New York

Cummings, R. G. and Nercissiantz, V. (1992) 'The use of water pricing as a means for enhancing water use efficiency in irrigation: Case studies in Mexico and the United States', *Natural Resources Journal*, vol 32, pp731–755

Dellapenna, J. W. (1997) 'Population and water in the Middle East: The challenge and opportunity for law', *International Journal of Environment and Pollution*, vol 7, pp72–111

Dellapenna, J. W. (1999) 'Adapting the law of water management to global climate change', *Journal of the American Water Resources Association*, vol 35, pp1301–1326

Dellapenna, J. W. (2000) 'The importance of getting names right: The myth of markets for water', *William and Mary Environmental Law and Policy Review*, vol 25, pp317–377

Dellapenna, J. W. (2007) 'Riparianism', in Robert E. Beck (ed) *Waters and Water Rights* (Volume 1, Chapters 6–9), LexisNexis, New York

Downing, T. E. and Gibson, M. (eds) (1975) *Irrigation's Impact on Society*, Arizona University Press (Anthropological Papers, No 25), Tucson, AZ

Easter, K. W., Rosengrant, M. W. and Dinar, A. (eds) (1998) *Markets for Water: Potential and Performance*, Kluwer Academic Publishers, Boston, MA

Economic and Social Council (2002) Resolution 2002/6, adopted 29 November 2002, available at www.unhchr.ch/tbs/doc.nsf/0/a5458d1d1bbd713fc1256cc400389e94

ECOSOC (United Nations Economic and Social Council, Committee on Economic Social and Cultural Rights) General Comment 15, approved 26 November 2002, E/C.12/2002/11 ('ECOSOC, 2002'), available at www.umn.edu/humanrts/gencomm/escgencom15.htm

Gleick, P. H. (1996) 'Basic water requirements for human activities: Meeting basic needs', *Water International*, vol 21, pp83–92

Gleick, P. H. (1999) 'The human right to water', *Water Policy*, vol 1, pp487–503

Gleick, P. H. et al (2006) *The World's Water: The Biennial Report on Freshwater Resources*, Island Press, Washington, DC

Griffin, R. C. (2006) *Water Resources Economics: The Analysis of Scarcity, Policies and Projects*, MIT Press, Cambridge, MA

International Conference on Population and Development (1994) Final Report, UN Dept. of Economic and Social Information and Policy Analysis, 18 October, UN Doc. A/CONF.171/13, available at www.undp.org/popin/icpd/conference/offeng/poa.html

International Conference on Water and the Environment (1992) 'The Dublin Statement and report of the conference', approved 31 January 1992

International Covenant on Economic, Social and Cultural Rights, opened for signature 16 December 1966, entered into force 3 January 1976, General Assembly Resolution 2200A(XXI), UN Doc. A/6316 (1966), UN Treaty Series vol. 993, p3

International Law Association (2004) 'Berlin Rules on Water Resources', in *Report of the Seventy-First Conference, Berlin, 2004*, International Law Association, London

McCaffrey, S. C. (1992) 'A human right to water: Domestic and international implications', *Georgetown International Environmental Law Journal*, vol 5, pp1–24

McCaffrey, S. C. (2001) *The Law of International Watercourses: Non-Navigational Uses*, Oxford University Press, Oxford, UK

Merrett, S. (1997) *Introduction to the Economics of Water Resources: An International Perspective*, UCL Press, London

Nachmani, A. (1994) 'The politics of water in the Middle East: The current situation, imaginary and practical solutions', in Ali İhsan Bagis (ed) *Water as an Element of Cooperation and Development in the Middle East*, Haceteppe University, Ankara, pp301–319

Powledge, F. (1982) *Water: The Nature, Uses and Future of Our Most Precious and Abused Resource*, Farrar, Straus, Giroux, New York

Postel, S. (1999) *Pillar of Sand: Can the Irrigation Miracle Last?*, W.W. Norton & Co., New York

Protocol I Additional to the Geneva Conventions of 12 August 1949 and Relating to the Protection of Victims of International Armed Conflicts, adopted 8 June 1977, entered into force, 7 December 1979, available at www.unhchr.ch/html/menu3/b/93.htm

Schorn, T. J. (2000) 'Drinkable water and breathable air: A liveable environment as a human right', *Great Plains Natural Resources Journal*, vol 4, pp121–142

Symposium (2006) 'Desalination in California: Should ocean water be utilized to produce freshwater?', *Hastings Law Journal*, vol 57, pp1343–1366

Teclaff, L. A. (1967) *The River Basin in History and Law*, W. S. Hein, Buffalo, NY

Thompson, G. (2003) 'Water tap often shut to South Africa poor', *New York Times*, 29 May, pA1

Thorme, M. (1991), 'Establishing environment as a human right', *Denver Journal of International Law and Policy*, vol 19, pp301–342

Uche, J. (2003) 'Costes energeticos', in J. Albiac (ed) *Alegaciones al Proyecto de Transferencias Autorizadas por la Ley del Plan Hidrologico Nacional y Estudio de Impacto Ambiental*, 20 Centro de Investigación y de Tecnología Agroalimentaria de Aragón, Working Paper No 03/3, Madrid

UN (1977) 'Report of United Nations Water Conference, Mar del Plata, 14–25 March 1977', UN Doc. E.CONF.70/29, UN Pub. 77.II.A.12

UN (1992) Agenda 21: Programme of Action for Sustainable Development, approved 13 June 1992, UN Doc. A/CONF.151/26/Rev. 1, vol I, Annex II, available at www.un.org/esa/sustdev/documents/agenda21/english/agenda21toc.htm

UN (1997) Convention on the Law of Non-Navigational Uses of International Watercourses, approved 21 May, UN Doc. No. A/51/869, available at www.un.org/law/ilc/texts/nnavfra.htm

UN (2003) 'Report of the World Summit on Sustainable Development, Plan of Implementation', approved 4 September 2002, p5, UN Doc. A/199/20, available at www.ods-dds-ny.un.org/doc/UNDOC/GEN/N02/636/93/PDF/N0263693.pdf?OpenElement

WHO/UNICEF (2002) 'Global water supply and sanitation assessment 2002 report', available at www.who.int/water_health/Globalassessment/GlobalTOC.htm

Wittfogel, K. A. (1957) *Oriental Despotism: A Comparative Study of Total Power*, Yale University Press, New Haven, CT

Wolfke, K. (1993) *Custom in Present International Law* (2nd revised edition), Martinus Nijhoff Publishers, Dordrecht, The Netherlands

World Water Council (2003) 'Press Release: 3rd World Water Forum concludes: 100 new commitments made', Third World Water Forum, Kyoto, Japan, 23 March 2003, available at www.worldwatercouncil.org/download/PR_finalday_23.03.03.pdf

12

The Case for Understanding Inadequate National Responses to Climate Change as Human Rights Violations

Donald A. Brown

INTRODUCTION: THE SIGNIFICANCE OF HUMAN RIGHTS FOR CLIMATE CHANGE

Human rights are often thought of as such things as the right to a fair trial or the right to not have one's property confiscated by government without due process of law. Environmental problems are rarely understood to create human rights violations, although recently there has been increasing interest in legal environmental literature on human rights issues. Many of the members of the Global Ecological Integrity Group (GEIG) have worked on those topics, from the standpoint of human 'ecological rights' in general (see, for example, Taylor, this volume), to the right to water (Dellapenna, this volume), to the right to health in relation to climate change (McMichael, 2000; Westra, 2007), as well as Westra viewing violations of the right to a safe environment as criminal in nature (Westra, 2004). Without doubt, the destruction of global ecological integrity, which has been a major focus of GEIG, is a fundamental threat to human dignity, which, as we shall see, is the foundational concern of human rights theory. Yet much of the environmental literature that raises rights questions has been devoted to whether non-human animals and plants have rights, rather than expressly developing the bases for seeing harmful environmental behaviour as triggering human rights violations.

This chapter examines what sense can be made of the claim that failure of nations to reduce their greenhouse gas (GHG) emissions can be understood as a violation of the human rights of others.

If climate change policies are understood to raise human rights issues, the consequences for policymaking are huge. This is so because if governments' approach to climate change can create human rights violations:

- Nations will not be able to look at national interest alone in creating climate change policies.

- Economic arguments such as cost to national economies used as justification for not reducing GHG emissions will not be viable.
- Nations will be viewed as having immediate mandatory duties to reduce their GHG emissions to their fair share of safe global emissions.

The significance of understanding climate change policies as raising human rights issues can be particularly seen by looking at the economic justifications that some have used for not reducing GHG emissions. A few nations have justified national climate policy on cost to their national economy alone (Brown et al, 2006). But because those who violate others' human rights may not justify their continuing behaviour in terms of the costs to those causing the harm, these justifications must cease if inadequate climate change policies are seen as human rights violations.

There is also a large economics literature that analyses climate change policy options to see which approaches maximize total global human welfare. Examples of this literature include numerous cost–benefit analyses of climate change policies, including those relied upon by the Intergovernmental Panel on Climate Change (IPCC, 2001). Because these analyses look at aggregate cost and benefits without regard to the fact that the harms may be experienced by one group of people in such a way that their basic human dignity is threatened, many governments around the world that rely on these standard economic analyses would need to cease doing so to guide national policy once it is determined that human rights have been violated.

Along this line, the recent Stern Report issued by the chief economist for the UK found, not withstanding the results of any cost–benefit analysis of climate change policies, that if rights theories are applied to climate change, there could be a moral, if not legal, responsibility to reduce the threat of climate change, which would have particular impact on those groups or nations whose past consumption has caused climate change (Stern, 2006, p42). Therefore, according to Stern, if climate change policies are viewed as creating human rights violations, it could be argued that all coutnries have the right only to emit very small amounts of greenhouse gases, and that no one has the right to emit beyond that level without incurring the duty to compensate (Stern, 2006, p42).

Without doubt, if climate change policies trigger human rights issues, then the international conversation about solutions to human-induced climate change taking place in the climate change negotiations under the United Nations Framework Convention on Climate Change (UNFCCC) will need to change.

One significant example of this is the acceptability of various proposals that have been made for the post-Kyoto, second commitment period international climate change regimes that began at the 13th Conference of the Parties under the United Nations Framework Convention on Climate Change in December 2007. An understanding that climate change creates human rights issues could seriously affect the acceptability of these proposals, because many of the post-Kyoto proposals have not acknowledged mandatory duties of nations to reduce their GHG emissions to their fair share of safe global emissions.

As we shall see, climate change both threatens and is already harming human health, lives and natural resources necessary to sustain lives. These are the most basic protection goals of human rights theory and law. Without doubt, climate change protection strategies are needed to safeguard not only human dignity but human life itself.

The chapter begins by examining what human rights are and where they came from. Following this is a description of international and regional human rights regimes. Next the chapter looks at the factual basis for classifying climate change-causing behaviour as triggering human rights violations. It then looks at a number of traditional criticisms of human rights claims to see how they may be relevant to climate change. This discussion is followed by examining differences between moral arguments for human rights and legal human rights claims. The chapter concludes with a discussion of what nations must do to avoid human rights violations.

WHAT ARE HUMAN RIGHTS?

Human rights are understood to be the 'rights that one has simply because one is a human being' (Donnelly, 2003, p10). They are often understood to be the basic moral guarantees that people have because they are human. Because all people are understood to have human rights, these rights are viewed to apply to all people equally. That is, human rights are understood to attach to individuals regardless of country and culture.

Where do human rights come from? Many assert that the basis for recognition of human rights is respect for the dignity of all humans. For instance, the Universal Declaration of Human Rights (UDHR) declares that 'recognition of the inherent dignity and of the equal and inalienable rights of all members of the human family is the foundation of freedom, justice and peace in the world' (UN, 1948, Preamble). To say that persons have human rights therefore is understood to assert that there are certain minimum conditions below which people cannot live in dignity. Therefore to violate someone's human rights is to treat that person as though he or she were not human. For this reason, to advocate human rights is to demand that the human dignity of all people be respected (Human Rights Resource Center, 2006). Therefore those advocating for human rights protections from human-induced climate change are implicitly arguing that global warming will undermine the ability of some humans to achieve basic human dignity.

According to Henry Shue, a human right provides two things: a rational basis for justification that actual enjoyment of the substance of the right may be enjoyed by the right holder; and that the right be socially guaranteed (Shue, 1980, p13).

In other words, to have a right is to be in a position to make demands on others about one's entitlement to enjoy the right. As Shue asserts, if a person has a right, the right can be insisted on without embarrassment (Shue, 1980, p15). To have a right also entitles the right holder to expect that those who can do so guarantee that the right can be enjoyed by the right holder. For this reason, if a person has a right to be protected from climate change caused by others, than they may expect that those who can act to prevent harm caused by climate change will take protective action.

Although many derive human rights from the idea of the minimum conditions necessary to achieve human dignity, human rights have also been derived from a variety of moral theories, including natural law, utility theory, deontological theories of morality, ideas about what institutions need to do to produce virtuous citizens, and contract theories (Donnelly, 2003, p41).

Some base human rights on an 'interests theory' that holds that all people should recognize human rights because such rights are justifiable on the grounds of their instrumental value in creating the necessary conditions for human wellbeing. In other words, if human rights are recognized and enforced, human wellbeing will be enhanced for all, and therefore their existence should be accepted on the grounds of human interests.

Of course, not all societies have recognized the existence of human rights. In fact many societies have expressly treated outsiders as falling outside of the orbit in which rights are recognized and expressly rejected some substantive rights claims. Even the most superficial knowledge of human history in respect to slavery, torture and genocide demonstrates that universal human rights have not been recognized by most of humanity throughout human history. In fact, some of the world's most respected sacred texts include passages that condone slavery and cruelty to non-believers (Donnelly, 2003, p74). To this day, women and homosexuals in many parts of the words still struggle for the most basic respect.

Given this history, one might ask how claims can be made about the universality of human rights claims. But supporters of human rights also often point to the gradual evolution of human rights throughout history as a second basis for the existence of human rights. If recognition of human rights has gradually evolved, it supports the claim that additional minimum conditions for assuring minimum human dignity are discoverable and that the scope of recognized protections under rights theory may be expanded. As we shall see, since climate change is already killing people, destroying the natural resources upon which humans depend to survive and damaging human health, a strong argument can be made that it should be categorized as a human rights problem.

The world's great religious traditions of Christianity, Buddhism, Islam, Hinduism, Judaism, Confucianism, Taoism and others described moral codes of conduct, often based on divine law, that are in many respects consistent with some aspects of modern human rights codes (Ishay, 2004, pp5–41). These religious codes prescribe duties and obligations of people to others, if not universally, at least to some believers. It can be said, therefore, that in the world's religions the precursors of human rights can be found (Ishay, 2004, p5). Although, in some cases, these codes are more about obligations of believers than rights of individuals, they are often consistent with human rights theories that are now accepted in most parts of the world (Donnelly, 2003, p73). However, at the same time, many of these religions expressly authorized unequal treatment for slaves, homosexuals and non-believers (Ishay, 2004, p7).

Although legal systems such as the Code of Hammurabi, which set out certain duties of people to others, have existed for many millennia, respect for universal human rights not dependent upon divine law has been gaining momentum only in the last several hundred years (Ishay, 2004). Although a history of the evolution of human rights is somewhat contentious in terms of which historical developments have been most responsible for the gradual recognition of human rights, some more important highlights of this history of the expansion of human rights can be identified. These are discussed in the following paragraphs.

Some see one of the earliest secular acknowledgements of universal human rights in the Magna Carta, issued by King John in England in 1215, which contained recognition of certain rights of citizens to be free of certain types of government interference (Human Rights Web, 2006). However, most European governments refused to acknowledge rights to freedoms of religion and speech for hundreds of years after that.

Major advances in the secular recognition of universal human rights can be seen in:

- philosophical arguments about 'natural rights' that were advanced in the 18th and 19th centuries;
- the inclusion of 'inalienable rights to life, liberty and pursuit of happiness' by Thomas Jefferson in the American Declaration of Independence; and
- the publishing of the Declaration of the Rights of Man and the Citizen after the French Revolution in 1789 (Ishay, 2004).

These advances in human rights acceptance were influenced by the writings of Grotius, John Locke, Hobbes, Jean-Jacques Rousseau and the Baron de Montesquieu, among others (Ishay, 2004).

Yet even for John Locke, the protection of rights, liberty and estates did not exist for women, savages, servants or labourers (Donnelly, 2003, p60), and the greatest expansion of human rights only emerged out of the political struggles of minorities in the last several hundred years (Donnelly, 2003, p67). Some argue that this recognition of human rights would not have been possible until economic systems evolved out of feudalism into pre-capitalist systems, which created the new class of the bourgeoisie, which had sufficient economic power to fight for rights recognition from the aristocracy (Ishay, 2004).

Natural law theories in the 18th and 19th centuries were also very influential in generating eventual acceptance of human rights. Natural rights were based upon the 'natural' moral order and often derived from religious precepts found in sacred texts that have existed for centuries but whose existence as rights were only expressly recognized in the last several hundred years. Human rights theories are now less frequently tied to natural rights, because many human rights theorists don't believe that the existence of human rights depends upon the existence of natural law.

Although there is considerable controversy about the influence of non-Western cultures in the development of human rights acceptance, in the last two centuries, writings of a number of individuals have been particularly influential in the emergence of the widespread acceptance of the existence of human rights at least in Western countries. These writings have included Thomas Paines's *The Rights of Man*, Henry David Thereau's *On Civil Disobedience* and John Stewart Mill's *Essay on Liberty* (Human Rights Web, 2006). These writers in turn influenced many others who fought for recognition of human rights, including Mahatma Gandhi and Martin Luther King.

Written in 1792, Mary Wollstonecraft's *A Vindication of the Rights of Woman* is one of the most influential writings on women's rights and a work that inspired the earliest feminists in Britain and America, who gained momentum in the 19th century in achieving rights to vote for women. Women in many nations of the world have seen considerable expansion of the recognition of their rights in the last hundred years, although women's rights are still not acknowledged in other parts of the world.

Perhaps the most important milestones in human history in the development of widespread acceptance of human rights as universal cross-cultural norms took place shortly after World War II in reaction to the Holocaust and the growing brutality of war. Two important post-World War II milestones include the adoption of the United Nations Charter and the adoption of the United Nations Universal Declaration of Human Rights (UDHR) in 1948 by the General Assembly of United Nations (UN, 1945 and 1948). As we shall see in later sections of this chapter, these documents have led to a blossoming of international, regional and national human rights regimes.

Based upon this historical evolution, some rights, for example the right to life and security, are acknowledged to have widespread support, while other rights are recognized in fewer places in the world.

It is therefore clear that human rights advocates find support for the existence of human rights in different traditions. For this reason, it is not necessary to agree upon the moral basis for deriving human rights to have agreement that certain human rights exist. Along this line, it is often said that there is an overlapping consensus among various moral theories that supports at least some human rights claims (Donnelly, 2003, p40). The 'overlapping consensus' justification for human rights is based on the assertion that most contemporary societies believe that individuals should be treated with respect, even though the grounds for demanding this respect come from different sources (Donnelly, 2003, p510). If human-induced climate change can be shown to prevent individuals from living their life with deep respect, then there is probably sufficient agreement among cultures to find widespread support for applying human rights recognition to the victims of climate change.

There are several lessons to be learned from this historical analysis of the development of human rights for climate change. The first is that recognition of specific human rights evolved over time as various minorities fought to be protected from powerful majorities or elites (Ishay, 2004). For this reason, the failure of governments to give legal recognition for human rights protection from climate change does not ultimately undermine arguments for new human rights recognition, because new rights may be recognized when it is established that basic human dignity is under threat because of the actions of others. In addition, because, as we will see, some human rights are often viewed to be more basic than others, and because some rights have been premised on others that are not widely contested, new human rights claims are on particularly sound ground if it can be demonstrated that they provide protection from fundamental threats to human dignity equally as destructive as those threats for which human rights protections have been widely acknowledged. Furthermore, as we shall see when we look at specific rights regimes, legal recognition of human rights by legislative action is not a condition for their ultimate acknowledgement. In fact, rights are understood to be pre-legal in that they exist as moral commands that courts have discovered in some cases even in the absence of constitutional protection. This was the basis, for instance, in the prosecution of the Nazis after World War II and NATO action in Kosovo (Doyle and Gardiner, 2003).

HUMAN RIGHTS REGIMES

Thus far we have examined how human rights have gained recognition over time. As we shall see, one can claim that there is an ethical duty to acknowledge human rights obligations, even if there is no legal regime that recognizes and enforces those rights. Yet many legal human rights regimes have evolved around the world. These legal human rights regimes are comprised of both global and regional regimes that have varying power, scope of interest, implementation and enforcement potential, and ability to be accessed by citizens. Any nation may join a global human rights regime, while only those nations within the relevant geographic region may join a regional regime.

It is usually agreed that the UDHR is the foundational document in modern international human rights law (UN, 1948). The UDHR is a non-binding, 'soft-law' agreement among nations that over time has been complemented by a series of legally binding international treaties while retaining the status of customary international law.

The two most important global human rights treaties in addition to the UDHR are often stated to be the International Covenant on Civil and Political Rights (ICCPR) and the International Covenant on Economic, Social and Cultural Rights (ICESCR).

The UDHR identifies the following rights that are relevant to climate change causing behaviour or climate change policy formation:

- life, liberty and security of person (Article 1);
- the right to an effective remedy by national tribunals for violations of fundamental or constitutionals rights (Article 8);
- full equality to a fair and public hearing by an independent and impartial tribunal, in the determination of his rights and obligations (Article 10);
- freedom from arbitrary interference with privacy, family, home or correspondence (Article 12);
- freedom from being arbitrarily deprived of property (Article 17);
- the right to a standard of living adequate for the health and wellbeing of himself and his family, including food, clothing, housing, and medical care and necessary social services, and the right to security in the event of unemployment, sickness, disability, widowhood, old age or other lack of livelihood in circumstances beyond his control (Article 25); and
- rights to a social and international order in which the rights and freedoms can be fully recognized (Article 28) (UN, 1948).

The ICESCR identifies the following rights that are relevant to climate change causing behaviour or climate change policy formation:

- *The States Parties to the present Covenant recognize the right of everyone to an adequate standard of living for himself and his family, including adequate food, clothing and housing, and to the continuous improvement of living conditions. The States Parties will take appropriate steps to ensure the realization of this right, recognizing to this effect the essential importance of international co-operation based on free consent;* (Article 11)
- *The States Parties to the present Covenant, recognizing the fundamental right of everyone to be free from hunger, shall take, individually and through international cooperation, the measures, including specific programmes, which are needed:*
  (a) To improve methods of production, conservation and distribution of food by making full use of technical and scientific knowledge, by disseminating knowledge of the principles of nutrition, and by developing or reforming agrarian systems in such a way as to achieve the most efficient development and utilization of natural resources; and

> *(b)   Taking into account the problems of both food-importing and food-exporting countries, to ensure an equitable distribution of world food supplies in relation to need;* (Article 11)
> • *The right of everyone to the enjoyment of the highest attainable standard of physical and mental health ... The steps to be taken by the States Parties to the present Covenant to achieve the full realization of this right shall include those necessary for ... prevention, treatment and control of epidemic, endemic, and occupational and other diseases.* (Article 12(2)(c)) (UN, 1966a)

The ICCPR identifies the following rights that are relevant to climate change causing behaviour or climate change policy formation:

• an inherent right to life, which shall be protected by law (Article 5); and
• a right to be protected from arbitrary and unlawful interference with his privacy, family and home (Article 15) (UN, 1966b).

The UDHR, ICESCR and ICCPR are often considered to be the foundational documents that comprise an international bill of rights. Yet not all nations have adopted all three. Although the UDHR has been accepted by most nations of the world, the ICESCR and ICCPR have been less widely adopted. To date, these two treaties have been ratified by about 75 per cent of the world's countries (Stanford, 2007). The UDHR is a 'soft-law' document which has normative, but not legal, force in the international system. The ICESCR and ICCPR, on the other hand, were the first of many treaties that have been enacted to give the protections identified in the UDHR the force of law.

A country ratifying a UN human rights treaty agrees to respect and implement within domestic law the rights the treaty covers. It also agrees to accept and respond to international scrutiny and criticism of its compliance. It does not necessarily agree, however, to make the human rights norm directly enforceable in domestic courts (Stanford, 2007). That usually requires implementing legislation.

Treaty enforcement is often accomplished within the UN with the creation of a body to monitor states' performance and to which member states are required to submit periodic reports on compliance (Stanford, 2007). For instance, the ICCPR is implemented through the Human Rights Committee (HRC), which was created to promote compliance with its provisions (Stanford, 2007). The HRC frequently expresses its views as to whether a particular practice is a human rights violation, but it is not authorized to issue legally binding decisions (Stanford, 2007). Other treaties and bodies exist within the UN system with varying enforcement and implementation powers and duties to implement human rights goals (Stanford, 2007). For the most part, these enforcement powers are weak and improvements in human rights compliance are best achieved through holding offending nations guilty in the court of international opinion rather than law.

In addition, several regional human rights regimes have been enacted that promote human rights in particular parts of the world. These regions include Europe, the Americas and Africa, which all have their own declarations and conventions for enforcement of human rights on a regional basis (Stanford, 2007).

Thus far no one has successfully brought a human rights claim for climate change damages, although the Inuit Indians filed such a claim change with the Inter-American Commission on Human Rights (Black, 2005). Before a successful human rights claim can be brought to an existing legal forum, several legal hurdles would need to be overcome that have little to do with whether a nation has committed a human rights violation. These hurdles include jurisdictional, issues, questions of proof and the authority of the relevant forum. For this reason, the failure to successfully bring legally recognized human rights claims may have little to do with whether the offending behaviour has created a violation of the protected right but more with the limitation of the existing legal regime. As we shall see, there is an important difference between the moral force of a human rights claim and the legal enforceability of such claim.

CLIMATE CHANGE AND HUMAN RIGHTS

A very strong case can be made that human-induced climate change triggers human rights violations because of the destructive nature of climate change damages. If human rights are to be understood to be recognition of those norms that are necessary to protect human dignity, inadequate climate change policies must be understood to trigger human rights violations, because climate change will not only make human dignity impossible for tens of millions of people around the world, including countless members of future generations, but directly threatens life itself and resources to sustain life. That is, inadequate climate change policies qualify as human rights violations because of the enormity of harm to life, health, food and property and the inviolability of the right to enjoy the places where people live. These harms are already being experienced by tens of thousands in the world, will be experienced in the future by millions of people from GHG emissions that have already been emitted (but not yet felt due to lags in the climate system), and will increase dramatically in the future unless GHG emissions are dramatically reduced from existing global emissions levels. The harms include deaths from disease, droughts, floods and heat, storm-related damage, damage from rising oceans, heat impacts on agriculture, loss of animals that people are dependent upon for subsistence purposes, social disputes caused by diminishing resources, sickness from a variety of diseases, the inability to rely upon traditional sources of food, the inability to use property that people depend upon to conduct their lives, including houses or sleds in cold places, the destruction of water supplies, and the inability to live in places where communities have lived to sustain life. The very existence of some small island nations is threatened by climate change.

A recent article in the respected scientific journal *Nature* concluded that the human-induced warming that the world is now experiencing is already causing 150,000 deaths and 5 million incidents of disease each year from additional malaria and diarrhoea, mostly in the poorest nations. Death and disease incidents are likely to soar as warming increases (Patz, 2005). Facts such as this demonstrate that climate change is already compromising rights to life, liberty and personal security, and inadequate government climate change policies will assure that these harms will multiply.

It is very unlikely that atmospheric levels of CO_2 equivalent can be stabilized much below 450 parts per million (ppm) during this century (Stevens, 1997). This virtually guarantees significant additional warming and associated harms to some people and places around the world (Baer and Athanasiou, 2005).

Human-induced climate change is now discernable and is already adversely affecting some humans, plants, animals and ecosystems around the world. However, as some parts of the world are warming faster than others, climate change damages are more discernable in some parts of the world (IPCC, 2001). For instance, destruction of homes from melting permafrost in polar regions is now visible, and increases in vector-borne disease are most discernable in tropical and semi-tropical areas.

The developed nations are mostly responsible for the build-up of GHGs in the atmosphere to present levels, although total emissions and per capita emission levels vary greatly among nations and the percentage of GHGs from developing nations is increasing (Argawal and Nairin, 1991; Estrada-Oyuela, 2002; Müller, 2002; Munasinghe, 2002; Muylaert and Pinguelli-Rosa, 2002; Pinguelli-Rosa and Munasinghe, 2002; Paavola, 2005). In addition, those most vulnerable to climate change damages are often the least responsible for GHG emissions. (IPCC, 2001; Estrada-Oyuela, 2002)

Climate change threatens the very existence of numerous communities around the world through no fault of their own. For instance, climate change is likely to cause agricultural decline around the world in places dependent upon local agricultural production, with resultant displacement of people from their native region. In many parts of the world it will no longer be possible to depend upon water availability that societies have used for centuries or temperatures that sustain agricultural activity.

Studies have shown that if uncontrolled emissions cause a 2°C temperature rise by 2050, something which is more probable than not, an additional 25 million people will be threatened by coastal flooding, 180 to 250 million people will suffer from vector-borne disease, and 200 to 300 million people will be threatened by water shortages. For these reasons, climate change damages will make survival tenuous, let alone human dignity.

The type of damages to life and security from human-induced climate change are much more destructive to human interests than many harms that are prevented by existing human rights protections. In fact, climate change damages are likely to exceed in sheer destructive power human behaviours which are viewed to be most heinous, including crimes against humanity and war crimes, matters about which there is little contention in international law that basic rights are violated.

CRITICISMS OF HUMAN RIGHTS THEORIES

Human rights claims are often challenged on several bases, including on grounds of cultural relativism, cultural imperialism, the unjustified extension of rights claims to contested matters, and difficulties in implementing rights regimes because of ambiguities as to who has duties to ensure the rights. This chapter next examines some of these challenges to human rights claims to determine their potential relevance to climate change.

Relativism

A common challenge to human rights comes from those that assert that these rights cannot be universal because values are relative to the communities and cultures of the world. Therefore, there is no basis for finding that these rights are universal.

As we have seen, for most of human history, universal human rights were not only not accepted by most of the world's civilizations but expressly contradicted by the ethos of dominant culture. Although recognition of human rights has been increasing in most Western countries for the last few hundred years, there are many non-Western countries that have no such traditions even today. If this is the case, surely the claim about the universality of human rights has little force outside the Western cultures where they have been widely accepted.

To counter arguments that human rights are not universal based upon the undeniable fact that they have not been recognized in human history, proponents of universal human rights often point to the evolution of their acceptance around the world. That is, the fact that not all historical periods and cultures accepted human rights is of less significance than the gradual expanding recognition of human rights leading to the current widespread respect for human rights theories in most parts of the world. Moreover, the fact that ideas first appeared in one part of the world does not necessarily lead to the conclusion that they should not be accepted in other parts of the world. Even if one concludes, in the face of some controversy, that human rights are an invention of liberal Western cultures, this does not mean that they should be rejected on the basis of where they originated.

This leads to the conclusion that the cultural norms that existed in the past can't limit new moral claims. That is, according to a well-accepted ethical maxim often referred to as the 'is/ought dichotomy', what 'is' cannot logically compel what 'ought' to be. More specifically, the fact that some cultures did not accept human rights does not settle the question of whether current governments and peoples should be bound by human rights obligations. For instance, although some societies condoned human sacrifices, this fact does not necessarily undermine the assertion that humans have a right to life and that human sacrifices should be outlawed just as torture and slavery have now been in most parts of the world. The proponents of human rights see, in the growth in the acceptance of human rights, support for the conclusion that human rights represent a cross-cultural consensus on what morality requires to assure minimum human dignity. As we have seen above, there is an 'overlapping consensus' among moral theories that the most basic human rights exist.

The relativism argument sometimes used to challenge the universality of human rights has less force in the case of climate change than in regard to most other matters which are the subject of the rights claims. This is so because climate change threatens the very life and ability of people to subsist – matters of the highest importance to all cultures. That is, because the very life and survival of people are at stake from human-induced climate change, claims that climate change triggers human rights violations cannot seriously be challenged on the basis of cultural relativism.

Cultural imperialism

Another criticism of human rights claims very similar to the charge of relativism is the assertion that those who argue in support of human rights claims are guilty of cultural imperialism. Those who often make this charge claim that the concept of human rights should not be applied to all cultures because human rights are the product of Western values that are not accepted elsewhere. Without doubt, those writers who are usually most identified with human rights theories, such as John Locke or John Stuart Mill are Western. In addition, it has been Western countries that most widely initially adopted legal human rights regimes in the last 100 years. Yet, as we have seen, the cultural imperialism argument is not completely accurate in that human rights ideas can be seen in many world cultures and religions and, like with the argument based upon relativism, the fact that certain cultures did not recognize human rights does not defeat arguments that they should do so. If this were the case, then there would never be any basis for condemning the behaviour of another culture for such things as slavery, genocide or forced labour.

In the case of climate change, the cultural imperialism argument is clearly without justification compared to potential other human rights claims, because a claim to the right to be protected from climate change will be asserted by the culture asserting the right to maintain cultural practices, not by cultures who are being asked to adopt new cultural norms. In other words, it would be the absence of the right to be protected from climate change damages that might correctly trigger imperialism charges not the right to be protected from climate change harms.

Extension of rights to contested matters

Probably the most serious challenges to new human rights claims arise when new claims are based upon formerly unrecognized rights. In such matters, those opposing the claim often assert that the right does not exist. For instance, when some asserted that physically handicapped people had rights to have public money spent to assure adequate access to buildings, opponents denied that such rights existed. Some social and economic rights enumerated in the UN conventions on social and economic rights are hotly contested and as a result some governments deny that they are bound by these provisions. Although some human rights, such as the right to life and liberty, have widespread acceptance, other rights are more contentious. In fact human rights claims are often made about some things for which there is very little agreement that rights exist. For instance, some assert that all people have a right to a free education, including graduate school, a matter about which there is significant disagreement.

For these reasons, tests for the existence of certain human rights are sometimes said to be the degree of acceptance that these rights have in the international community. Along this line, it is sometimes said that it is the community that creates certain rights by their express recognition.

Yet, because climate change threatens the most basic and well-accepted rights, namely the rights to life and security, while violating many other widely recognized rights, the argument that climate change is extending rights claims into contested matters does not make sense.

Rights to physical security (and thus protection from murder, mayhem, rape or assault) are considered basic rights (Shue, 1980, p20). Other well-accepted rights depend upon these basic rights. For instance, in order to enjoy the right of free speech and assembly, it is necessary to be protected from physical assault. Very few people in the world challenge the idea that people have a right to basic security (Shue, 1980, p21). Because climate change threatens not only physical security but life itself, climate change interferes with the most basic human rights.

As we have also seen from the above analysis of the three widely internationally recognized international human rights documents, the UDHR, ICCPR and ICSECR, rights have also been expressly recognized to a home, a family, a minimum standard of living adequate for wellbeing, security from sickness, freedom from hunger, and prevention of diseases. Surely human-induced climate change interferes with these basic rights. And so it can be said that climate changing-causing behaviour causes interference with enjoyment of rights that have been very widely recognized around the world. Furthermore, individuals have been promised under the UDHR a social and international order in which their rights and freedoms can be fully recognized (Article 28) (UN, 1948).

Difficulties in assigning duties

Some have made arguments against the existence of rights because of unanswered questions about who has the duty to uphold human rights. For some human rights issues, it is sometimes more difficult to identify who is the duty holder than it is to support the existence of the rights. Yet anyone who speaks of rights asserts that certain institutions or individuals have obligations to protect the marginalized where they have the ability to do so. As we have seen, the essence of a human right is the duty imposed upon others to assure that right holder can enjoy that right. National governments by limiting domestic emissions have the ability to assure that GHGs being emitted from their countries do not interfere.

Moreover, under the UNFCCC, nations of the world have already agreed that they are duty holders (UN, 1992). That is, nations have expressly agreed 'to reduce their emissions to prevent dangerous interference with the climate system' (UN, 1992, Article 2). For this reason, governments cannot deny that they have obligations to prevent harm to others from climate change.

DIFFERENCES BETWEEN LEGAL AND MORAL CLAIMS TO HUMAN RIGHTS

Although many human rights have been codified in international and national law, it is not necessary for human rights to have legal protection for one to assert that they exist. Human rights can be understood to be either morally compelled as a shared norm of acceptable behaviour recognized by a relevant community or as a justified moral norm supported by strong reasons (Stanford, 2007).

The aspiration of many interested in human rights is often that that all human rights eventually receive legal recognition, yet legal recognition is not necessary to ground assertions that human rights exist. All societies have moral norms that can exist independently of law and can be enforced by non-legal means, such as taboos and other social sanctions. As we have seen, many of the world's religions recognize rights and obligations that are precursors to those human rights that now have widespread international legal support. A strong moral argument for the existence of human rights can be made for those rights that have widespread support across cultures. Using this line of reasoning, since most cultures have prohibitions against killing others, it can be said that a human right to life exists and that those who interfere with rights to life violate well-established moral norms.

In addition, the existence of human rights is often asserted based upon strong moral arguments. As we have seen, the moral justification of human rights can be found in a variety of moral theories. For this reason, the doctrine of human rights aims to provide a fundamentally legitimate moral basis for regulating the contemporary geo-political order even in the absences of legal recognition. Using moral arguments alone, it can be claimed that there is a human right against torture, because under all moral systems, torture is usually condemned, at least in non-emergency situations.

As we have seen, since human rights are understood to apply to all human beings everywhere, regardless of whether they have received legal recognition, legal recognition is not a precondition for asserting the existence of human rights. In countries where legal rights have not received legal recognition, supporters of human rights insist that the rights remain valid as compelled by minimum conditions of basic morality.

For these reasons, human rights cannot be reduced to legal rights. For instance, the opponents of apartheid argued that the system violated basic human rights despite the fact that it had legal support in South Africa.

CONCLUSIONS

From the above it is clear that a strong claim can be made that those nations who refuse to reduce their emissions to their fair share of safe global emissions violate the human rights of others. Although it is true that what constitutes any nation's fair share is also a moral question worthy of additional moral discussion, no nation may argue that self-interest is justification for national climate change policy or that it need not act to reduce threats to human lives of others when emissions are beyond ethically determined allocations.

Climate change is a classic problem of distributive justice. Distributive justice is concerned with allocating burdens and responsibilities among people. Distributive justice requires that difference in allocations among parties be based upon ethically relevant criteria, not on self-interest. Although justice does not require that all nations reduce their emissions by the same amounts, if a nation wants to be treated differently from others it must identify reasons for being treated differently that pass ethical scrutiny. Ethically relevant criteria for national climate change policies might include differences in population, responsibility for causing the existing problem, ability to pay for new technologies and a few other considerations. Yet this list of ethically supportable criteria is limited. Although nations might reasonably differ on what justice requires of them or about what constitutes their fair share of global emissions, negotiations should be limited to resolving differences among ethically supportable options. If nations agreed to limit negotiating positions to those that satisfy principles of justice, the international negotiations would be vastly reduced in complexity while providing reasonable grounds for supportable compromise among ethically supportable options. But nations must now approach international negotiations with justice as a guide. If they fail to do this, a strong case can be made that they are causing human rights violations.

In addition, as we have seen, those who have rights to live and to security may demand that those who can guarantee these rights take actions to do so. For this reason, all nations must take immediate action to reduce their emissions to their fair share of global emissions to protect all human life, security and other things protected by rights theories.

References

Agarwal, A. and Narain S. (1991) *Global Warming in an Unequal World: A Case of Environmental Colonialism*, Centre for Science and Environment, New Delhi

Baer, P. and Athanasiou, T. (2005) 'Honesty about dangerous climate change', EcoEquity, www.ecoequity.org/ceo/ceo_8_2.htm, accessed 30 September 2007

Black, R. (2005) 'Inuit sue US over climate policy', BBC News, http://news.bbc.co.uk/1/hi/sci/ tech/4511556.stm, accessed 30 November 2007

Brown, D., Tuana, N., Averill, M., Baer, P., Born, R., Brandão, C., Cabral, M., Frodeman, R., Hogenhuis, C., Heyd, T., Lemons, J., McKinstry, R., Lutes, M., Meulller, B., Miguez, D., Munasinghe, M., Muylaert de Araujo, M. S., Nobre, C., Ott, K., Paavola, J., Pires de Campos, C., Pinguelli-Rosa, L., Rosales, J., Rose, A., Wells, E. and Westra, L. (2006) 'White paper on the ethical dimensions of climate change', The Collaborative Programme on the Ethical Dimensions of Climate Change, Rock Ethics Institute, Penn State University, http://rockethics.psu.edu/climate/whitepaper-intro.htm, accessed 30 November 2007

Donnelly, J. (2003) *Universal Human Rights, In Theory and Practice* (second edition), Cornell University Press, Ithaca, NY, and London.

Doyle, M. and Gardner, A. M. (2003) 'Introduction: Human rights and international order', in J-M. Coicaud, M. W. Doyle and A. M. Gardner (eds) *The Globalization of Human Rights*, United Nations University, Tokyo

Estrada-Oyuela, R. A. (2002) 'Equity and climate change', in L. Pinguelli-Rosa and M. Munasinghe (eds) *Ethics, Equity and International Negotiations on Climate Change*, Edward Elgar, Cheltenham, UK, pp36–46

Human Rights Resource Center (2006) 'Human rights here and now', University of Minnesota, www1.umn.edu/humanrts/edumat/hreduseries/hereandnow/Default.htm, accessed 3 October 2007

Human Rights Web (2006) 'A short history of the human rights movement: Early political, religious and philosophical sources', www.hrweb.org/history.html, accessed 1 October 2007

IPCC (Intergovernmental Panel on Climate Change) (2001) This multi-volume work was published as (i) *Climate Change 2001: Synthesis Report*; (ii) *Climate Change 2001: The Scientific Basis*; (iii) *Climate Change 2001: Impacts, Adaptation and Vulnerability*; (iv) *Climate Change 2001: Mitigation*; see www.ipcc.ch/pub/reports.htm, accessed 1 October 2007

Ishay, M. R. (2004) *The History of Human Rights: From Ancient Times to the Globalization Era*, University of California Press, Berkley and Los Angeles, CA, and London

McMichael, A. (2000) 'Global environmental change in the coming century: How sustainable are recent health gains?', in D. Pimentel, L. Westra and R. Noss (eds)

Ecological Integrity: Integrating Environmental, Conservation and Health, Island Press, Washington, DC, pp245–260

Müller, B. (2002) *Equity in Climate Change: The Great Divide*, Oxford Institute for Energy Studies, Oxford, UK

Munasinghe, M. (2002) 'Analysing ethics, equity and climate change in the sustainomics trans-disciplinary framework', in L. Pinguelli-Rosa and M. Munasinghe (eds) *Ethics, Equity and International Negotiations on Climate Change*, Edward Elgar, Northampton, MA

Muylaert, M.-S. and Pinguelli-Rosa, L. (2002) 'Ethics, equity and the convention on climate change', in L. Pinguelli-Rosa and M. Munasinghe (eds) *Ethics, Equity and International Negotiations on Climate Change*, Edward Elgar, Northampton, MA

Paavola, J. (2005) 'Seeking justice: International environmental governance and climate change, *Globalizations*, vol 2, pp309–322

Patz, J. (2005) 'Impact of regional climate change on human health', *Nature*, vol 384, pp310–317

Pinguelli-Rosa, L. and Munasinghe, M. (2002) *Ethics, Equity and International Negotiations on Climate Change*, Edward Elgar, Cheltenham, UK

Shue, H. (1980) *Basic Rights, Subsistence, Affluence, US Foreign Policy*, Princeton University Press, Princeton, NJ

Stanford University (2007) 'Stanford encyclopaedia of philosophy', http://plato.stanford.edu/entries/rights-human/#regional, accessed 30 November 2007

Stern, N. (2006) 'Stern review on the economics of climate change', HM Treasury, www.hm-treasury.gov.uk/independent_reviews/stern_review_economics_climate_change/sternreview_index.cfm, accessed 13 September 2007

Stevens, W. (1997), 'Experts doubt greenhouse gases can be curbed', *New York Times*, 3 November

UN (1945) The United Nations Charter, www.un.org/aboutun/charter, accessed 24 March 2008

UN (1948) Universal Declaration of Human Rights (UDHR), UN Doc. A/RES/21, www.hrweb.org/legal/udhr.html, accessed 30 November 2007

UN (1966a) International Covenant on Economic, Social and Cultural Rights, www.unhchr.ch/html/menu3/b/a_cescr.htm, accessed 30 November 2007

UN (1966b) International Covenant on Civil and Political Rights, www1.umn.edu/humanrts/instree/b3ccpr.htm, accessed 21 November 2007

UN (1992) United Nations Framework Convention on Climate Change Nations, UN Document, A:AC237/18, available at http://unfccc.int/resource/docs/convkp/conveng.pdf, accessed 25 March 2008

Westra, L. (2004) *Ecoviolence and the Law*, Transnational Publishers, Inc., Ardsley, NY

Westra, L. (2007) *Environmental Justice and the Rights of Indigenous Peoples*, Earthscan, London

Wollstonecraft, M. (1792) *Vindication of the Rights of Woman*, reprint (1972) by Dover Publications, Mineola, NY

PART IV

ECOLOGICAL INTEGRITY,
CLIMATE CHANGE
AND ENERGY

Introduction

Helmut Burkhardt and Richard Westra

In Chapter 13, Goodland and Counsell present a scathing critique of the World Bank Group's energy and climate change policy. A chronology of mistakes is given, among them a 130 per cent increase in financial support for the traditional power sector against a 1.4 per cent increase for renewables in the same 13-year period.

The urgency of immediate action is forcefully established. Among the energy solutions recommended are an accelerated transition to renewable energy, instant ban of all fossil fuel subsidies, a carbon tax and full-cost pricing of all energy productions, and application of the principle of contraction and convergence towards global energy justice. A comprehensive list of issues related to the transition to renewable energy is given, with a focus on the World Bank Group's livestock and forestry policies.

In Chapter 14, we find David Pimentel presenting a definitive statement on the nonsense of ethanol production replacing gasoline. From the perspectives of physical science, ecological integrity and food ethics it appears that Pimentel is making the case for something that should be obvious. Unfortunately, the US and other governments around the globe are still promoting agrofuels with billions; therefore, his arguments are relevant and deserve to be distributed widely.

Some agrofuel proponents now agree that ethanol from corn is neither economical nor environmentally sustainable and therefore set their sights on the emerging technology of the production of cellulosic alcohol. However, this is not much better with respect to environmental impact. All agrofuels are detrimental to ecological integrity. By contrast, conservation, wind energy, technical conversion of solar energy and geothermal energy can reduce humankind's ecological footprint sufficiently to be accommodated by this planet at present world population levels; those are the feasible alternatives to fossil fuels (Burkhardt, 2007).

In Chapter 15, Peter Miller is concerned with the split between economy and ecology. Most economists and politicians argue on purely economic grounds, which leads to messages that are ecologically untenable, such as the ubiquitous 'economic growth is good' philosophy. Miller's call for full-cost accounting including externalities is timely. The use of the genuine progress indicator (GPI) makes good sense; it must replace the gross domestic product (GDP), particularly in measuring the impact of environmentally destructive energy technologies. Specific examples from Manitoba, Canada are given for illustration.

One of Miller's basic and relevant messages is that government regulation is needed for a quick transition to a carbon-free economy. The US and Canadian policy of voluntary compliance fails because it creates an economic advantage for the ecologically irresponsible corporation. Courageous governance is needed to stop ecologically inappropriate subsidies, and to create mandatory compliance with environmental standards through regulations and legislation for all. Instruments for implementing changes are given with social justice in mind. In addition to education, social marketing, fee structures, government incentives and taxation are discussed.

Supplementing the recommendations of the three chapters in this part, an action framework for preventing ecological disaster through climate change and inappropriate energy technology was developed recently by an Interdisciplinary Roundtable on Climate Change and Energy Strategies (Science for Peace, 2007). The roundtable was attended by some 30 prominent scientists, politicians, corporate executives and activists; they called their summary conclusion the 'Wasan Action Framework', referring to Wasan Island, where the meeting took place, and where up to 140 years ago Aboriginals went for spiritual renewal and meditation. Here is the one-page declaration of the roundtable:

> The first clear warnings of danger due to emissions of greenhouse gases due to human activity emerged 25 years ago. Prudence would have called for precautionary action at that time to slow down the growth in emissions of greenhouse gases. Since then, the scientific understanding of the impact of human activity on global warming has been overwhelmingly confirmed; key predictions based on that understanding have started to come true. Evidence has emerged that the potential impacts of global warming will be much worse than predicted even five years ago.
>
> Individuals, corporations and all levels of government around the world have a duty to act as global citizens on the basis of the danger posed to life on Earth and to the wellbeing of the human race as whole.
>
> 1   We declare that human induced climate change and energy security, in particular peaking of the world oil supply, are crucial issues requiring immediate action.
> 2   We declare agreement with the IPCC Working Group 1 on the physical basis of climate change that: 'Most of the observed increase in global average temperatures since the mid-20th century is very likely due to the observed increase in anthropogenic greenhouse gas concentrations.' (IPCC, 2007)
> 3   We identify as the root causes of this crisis:
>   a)   the large per capita overconsumption and waste of natural resources in the industrialized countries;
>   b)   the growth paradigm (economic growth for its own sake);

c)   the large and growing human population;

d)   the very large dependence on fossil fuel-based energy;

e)   the resistance by vested interests to necessary change in energy technology;

f)   the lack of appropriate political leadership; and

g)   the lack of global governance to protect the global commons.

4   A global solution framework – We must begin immediately to:

a)   curb overconsumption and give priority to efficiency, conservation and the avoidance of waste;

b)   promote lower birthrates by empowerment of women through educational, economic and social measures, including access to birth control information and services;

c)   focus globally and locally on developing low-impact renewable energy infrastructure and technologies (e.g. biomass, geothermal, hydro, ocean energy, solar, wind) to its full potential, so as to avoid large scale biofuel usage and nuclear energy;

d)   reduce carbon emissions by creating a just and universal framework through the implementation of appropriate incentives, government regulation, legislation and taxation; and

e)   preserve forests, especially tropical rainforests.

5   Implementation of solutions – We urge that:

a)   all levels of government as well as the UN and international organizations can and should embrace the Wasan Action Framework; and

b)   media, corporations, the educational system from kindergarten to university, and all civil society should collaborate on implementing this Wasan Action Framework.

REFERENCES

Burkhardt, H. (2007) 'Physical limits to large-scale global biomass generation for replacing fossil fuels', *Physics in Canada*, vol 63, no 3

IPCC (2007) 'Summary for policymakers', in S. Solomon, D. Qin, M. Manning, Z. Chen, M. Marquis, K. B. Averyt, M. Tignor and H. L. Miller (eds) *Climate Change 2007: The Physical Science Basis. Contribution of Working Group I to the Fourth Assessment Report of the Intergovernmental Panel on Climate Change*, Cambridge University Press, Cambridge, UK, and New York

Science for Peace (2007) 'Climate change and energy strategies: The Wasan Action Framework', declaration and recommendations of the Interdisciplinary Roundtable on Climate Change and Energy Strategies, 13–15 September, Wasan Island, Muskoka Lakes, Ontario, Canada, sponsored by Science for Peace, the David Suzuki Foundation and the Breuninger Foundation

13

How the World Bank could Lead the World in Alleviating Climate Change

Robert Goodland and Simon Counsell

CLIMATE CHANGE

Forty-six nations and 2.6 billion people are now at risk of being overwhelmed by armed conflict and war related to climate change. A further 56 countries face political destabilization, affecting another 1.2 billion individuals (Smith and Vivekananda, 2007). Climate change is today's biggest threat to international security and will intensify North–South tensions (Campbell et al, 2007). Climate change from greenhouse gas (GHG) emissions is a global externality that is almost irreversible, as GHGs reside in the atmosphere for centuries. Humans would be much better off reducing GHG emissions substantially rather than suffering the consequences of failing to meet this challenge (Arrow, 2007; Stern, 2007). The world cannot continue to emit increasing amounts of GHGs without eventually provoking unacceptable climate changes; many climate professionals claim we already have exceeded prudent levels of emissions.

The world has to end growth in GHG emissions within seven years (by 2015) and reduce emissions by about 80 per cent by 2050 (IPCC, 2007). The World Bank should take this emergency even more seriously, because at least two-thirds of energy demand over the next 25 years will come from developing countries. The World Bank Group violates its own policies on sustainability, the precautionary principle, the goal of reducing poverty for the bottom billion, standard good economics and the integrity principle (Miller and Westra, 2002; Soskolne, 2007; Westra, 2007 and 2008), because so far the Bank has not taken this massive threat seriously.

A brief history of climate change in the World Bank

The Nobelist Svante Arrhenius (1859–1927) warned the world about climate change from 1896 on. While science adviser to the World Bank in the late 1980s, his nephew, Erik Arrhenius, repeatedly urged the Bank to heed the risk of climate change while time remained for an orderly transition. A decade later Goodland and El Serafy (1998), among many others, continued such warnings. Most recently, former Bank Vice-President Sir Nicholas Stern (2007), Herman Daly (2007a and b) and Nobelist Kenneth Arrow (2007) have ratcheted up such warnings. Now the world has almost run out of time; the adjustment to a low-carbon economy will be wrenching, and some climate change impacts appear inevitable.

Between 1992 and 2005, the World Bank Group (WBG) committed more than US$28 billion to fossil fuel projects, 17 times more than its financing for renewable energy and energy efficiency. Last year the World Bank (WB) increased energy lending from US$2.8 billion to US$4.4 billion. Oil and gas received a massive 93 per cent increase in funding, while power sector funding increased by 130 per cent. In comparison, finance for new renewables increased by 1.4 per cent (all data from Meinhardt, 2007). Oil, gas and power commitments account for 77 per cent of the total energy finance; renewables account for 5 per cent (Meinhardt, 2007).

The most ominous signal of lack of attention to climate change is the October 2007 International Development Association (IDA) report 'Making climate change work for development' (World Bank, 2007a). This report clearly shows near-total omission of the urgent transition to renewable energy, price signals and other mechanisms for reducing GHG emissions and the paramount need to phase down coal (and oil) and close the worst coal plants. To state that the International Finance Corporation (IFC) may finance 'three geothermals, three wind energy plants, and biomass energy in Nicaragua and Haiti' in the future is incommensurate with the problem.

BOX 13.1 CHRONOLOGY ON GHG EMISSIONS

1992	WB's new Forest Policy: moratorium on financing any logging in natural forests.
2000	'Fuel for thought', WB's Energy Policy: weak on reducing GHG emissions, weak on renewable energy.
2000–2003	WBG's independent Extractive Industry Review recommended halting finance for coal immediately and oil by 2008.
2001	WB's Livestock Strategy: Phase-out of large-scale, grain-fed livestock production; violated by IFC.
2002	WB's new Forest Policy adopted, rescinding its 1992 ban on tropical forest logging and encouraging industrial logging in the vast forests of the former communist countries.
2002	WBG resumed lending to coal projects.
2002	IFC's first AMaggi (The AMaggi Corporation is a contraction of the owner's name Andre Maggi) soy loan in the Amazon forest region.
2004	IFC's US$30m AMaggi second soy loan in the Amazon forest region.
2005	G8 Summit, Gleneagles, Scotland (July) tasked WB to calculate an investment framework for clean energy. The WB's framework (2006)

	includes coal and atomic energy; weak on renewable energy and zero targets for GHG emissions.
2005	IFC's Compliance Adviser and Ombudsman (CAO) investigation found AMaggi soy projects in the Amazon forest region violated policies.
2006	WB's Nutrition Strategy emphasizes grain-based diets and is silent on the use of animal products.
2006	World Bank Inspection Panel condemns Bank activities in Cambodia, where encouragement of industrial logging has led to serious environmental damage.
2007	Brazilian Government closes down the biggest exporter of soy, Cargill's US$20m soy port in Santarém, for environmental violations (March).
2007	IFC's US$90m Bertin Amazon forest region cattle-ranching project approved.
2007	IDB prepares US$250m loan for Bertin Amazon Cattle Ranching, Project No. BR-L-1115.
2007	IFC reported to be preparing further Amazon forest region cattle-ranching projects in Acre, Brazil.
2007	World Bank establishes Forest Carbon Partnership Facility.
2007	World Bank conducts five-year evaluation of its 2002 Forest Strategy but fails to publish the results.
2007	World Bank Inspection Panel condemns Bank interventions in Democratic Republic of Congo for financing industrial logging and ignoring rights of forest-dependent people.
2007	Thirteenth UN Climate Change Conference of the Parties, Bali, 3–14 December: launch of negotiations for a new pact to succeed the Kyoto Protocol, to be sealed in 2009 in Copenhagen.
2007	IFC supports Tata Power Company Limited setting up a 4000MW supercritical coal-based power plant in Kutch, Gujarat, India; goal of 100,000MW of coal-fired power by 2012.
2008	Thirty-fourth G8 Summit, Japan (July).
2008	IFC plans to support Bertin's US$12m cattle slaughterhouse, leather treatment plant and biodiesel mill using animal fat as raw material in Diamantino, Mato Grosso.

Faulty GHG accounting

The World Bank's policy is to address only the direct on-site GHG emissions of each project, rather than the more meaningful aggregate emissions of the coal, oil, gas and other sectors it finances. Such faulty accounting cannot supply decision-makers with reliable estimates of the World Bank's climate footprint. Commercial banks and development agencies follow faulty World Bank accounting methods (Vallette et al, 2004).

The Bank developed an investment framework to guide the G8's GHG reduction priorities. Specifically, in April 2006 it published *Clean Energy and*

Development: Towards an Investment Framework. However, the framework's proposals are neither clean nor climate-friendly, and the large-scale energy development schemes and technologies it encourages (including nuclear power and carbon capture and storage) are expensive and dangerous. The framework also fails to grapple with its own schizophrenia in financing climate change through fossil fuel investments. Furthermore, the framework gives reason for grave concern, as an earlier draft suggests that atmospheric concentrations of GHG in the range of 450–1000 parts per million (ppm) are acceptable. A later draft removed all reference to atmospheric targets (Wysham and Makhijani, 2008).

The framework specifically downplays the potential role of renewable energy: 'This report does not equate clean energy only with small-scale modern renewable energy technologies, but with a complete suite of clean and efficient production, supply and end-use technologies' (World Bank, 2006b). Instead of calling for a rapid transition to renewable energy, the framework recommends reliance mainly on fossil fuel thermal power plants. Fossil fuel power plants can indeed be made more efficient (through coal gasification, combined cycle or supercritical boilers). But all investments in coal permanently lock in coal mining and burning at least for another 50 to 75 years (the normal life of a coal power plant) at a time when GHG emissions have to be reduced by 80 per cent within 10 years. The framework's reliance on burning coal and then capturing and storing the GHG thus produced depends on expensive and untested technologies.

The energy industry calculates that several thousand billion tonnes of coal remain in the ground – 150 years' worth at current extraction rates. It is therefore clear that most of the remaining coal has to stay in the ground if we are to avoid climate catastrophe. Three-quarters of coal reserves are in five nations: the US, Russia, China, India and Australia. Thus the fate of human civilization probably hinges on the coal decisions of six nations (Canada should be added to the list of critical nations because of the scale of its Athabasca tar sands and boreal peat deposits) and on preventing extensive forest fires in three others (Brazil, Indonesia and Congo). Those who place their hopes in bolt-on adjustments to the fossil fuel status quo, notably 'clean coal', carbon capture and storage technology, face the problem that mass mobilization of such technology is more than a decade off.

Solutions in the energy sector

Any solution must acknowledge the urgency of the massive changes needed to stabilize climate below risky levels. Nature's long-predicted deadline is now less than ten years away. The solution is to consume much less individually and in all sectors of the economy by focusing on efficiency and eliminating all wastage through pricing and conservation, while accelerating the transition to renewable energy, especially small-scale systems for the rural poor. A full 25 per cent of the world's poor lack access to basic electricity supply.

Only eight years remain before the UN's target date, during which time GHG emissions must start to decline if we are to have a realistic chance of limiting eventual global warming to 2°C above pre-industrial levels (as the EU, among many others, demands). Therefore a major element in any solution is a mandatory international GHG treaty to reduce the atmospheric concentration of GHG below 450 ppm within eight years. This translates into major reductions of GHG emissions of around 80 per cent for industrial nations. The world must reduce annual carbon emissions from today's 8 billion tonnes down to about 2 billion tonnes to balance the assimilation capacity of the world's carbon sinks (such as oceans, forests and other biomass).

Lighting accounts for 20 per cent of global energy use. Over the past decades voluntary switching from 5 per cent efficient incandescent light bulbs to 15 per cent efficient fluorescents has not worked; incandescents must be banned outright. More efficient, and with much longer lives than compact fluorescents, LEDs (light-emitting diodes) are already available. The even newer Ceravision lamp has no electrodes, is 50 per cent efficient and does not wear out. Commendably, the IFC is contemplating the introduction of LEDs throughout Africa. The lesson is that pricing, codes and policies are all needed to accelerate uptake of efficient technologies.

The polluters, the historical emitters of GHGs, must pay developing countries to leave coal and oil in the ground, leave their forests intact and plant trees. In 2007 the Bank proposed a new fund (the Forest Carbon Partnership Facility, FCPF) that might in principle serve to do that. At the time of writing, however, the details had still not been worked out, and Bank staff have so far refused to rule out that industrial logging in tropical forests will be eligible for FCPF funds. The International GHG Treaty should ban all subsidies to fossil fuels immediately and insist on full-cost pricing for all energy production. The US$250 billion in subsidies currently allocated to fossil fuels and nuclear energy should be switched to renewable energy. Proceeds from a carbon tax will probably have to be earmarked for the transition to renewables.

The monumental error of relying on efficiency first

The WBG is massively financing coal, oil and gas, with efficiency as the top goal. The other element of the Bank's priorities is carbon trading. Over-reliance on efficiency and carbon trading is a monumental error. Neither efficiency nor carbon trading reduces the causes of climate change or the amount of GHGs emitted. On the contrary, efficiency and trading may intensify climate change by encouraging more carbon to be burned (albeit more efficiently) and by postponing the overdue transition to renewable energy by letting carbon emitters trade away their emissions instead of reducing them. The term 'carbon trading' conflates 'cap–give away quotas–trade' with 'cap–auction–trade'. In both cases the cap is to the good, but giving away the rights to historical polluters means blessing the existing theft of the commons and letting scarcity rents go to private corporations rather than capturing them for public revenue. Trading at the national level, and maybe at a regulated international level, may be useful. Carbon emitters have to pay a higher price more commensurate with their pollution, and trading opens up a source of funds to transfer to the poor. But a global carbon tax might do all this better. The Bank's policy of efficiency first does not lead to sustainability second. Sustainability is an official policy that the Bank keeps overlooking (Daly, 2007a and b).

It is a monumental error to think that energy efficiency leads to a sustainable aggregate level of energy consumption. Efficient vehicles tend to increase driving; efficient light bulbs are less likely to be switched off; efficiently burned coal fosters increased use of coal. Efficiency increase is like a price decrease; there is a substitution effect and an income effect. The first stimulates consumption of the resource whose efficiency increased (i.e. coal); the second stimulates consumption of other resources. Whether the substitution increase is less, equal to or more than the decreased use of the resource in question resulting from greater efficiency depends on elasticity of demand. The Bank has forgotten Jevons's paradox (Polimeni et al, 2008). The Bank can correct its error by prioritizing 'sustainability first' as the direct policy variable (through carbon caps or carbon tax); then it will arrive at 'efficiency second' as an adaptation to more expensive carbon fuels. A policy of sustainability first, leading to efficiency second, should be the first design principle for energy and climate policy (Daly, 2007b).

Ecological tax reform is a big part of the solution: a stiff severance tax on carbon levied at the wellhead and mine mouth, accompanied by equalizing tariffs on carbon-intensive imports and rebating the revenues by abolishing regressive taxes on low incomes. Such a policy would reduce carbon use, spur the development of less-carbon-intensive technologies and redistribute income progressively. Higher input price (on fossil fuels or carbon content) induces efficiency at all subsequent stages of the production process, and limiting depletion ultimately limits pollution (Daly, 2007b).

The transition to renewable energy

The transition to renewable energy should be accelerated as urgently as possible. Although most (such as geothermal) is site-specific, the potential is limitless. For example, wind energy in the Dakotas could supply adequate electricity to the whole US. The entire world demand for electricity could be met from 254×254km of Sahara Desert. Desert nations should be financially encouraged to export solar electricity and eventually hydrogen from water. Offshore wind, wave, current and tidal power could become the backbone of the UK's electricity (CAT, 2007).

Fossil fuels

Coal: The WBG should finance no new coal mines, no new coal-fired thermal plants and no exploration for any fossil fuels. There is increasing support for banning all new coal-fired power plants that do not have provisions for CO_2 capture and sequestration. Since wind-generated electricity is already economic relative to coal with sequestration, there is no reason to allow the building of new power plants that would emit large amounts of CO_2 for decades (Makhijani, 2007). Care must be taken to ensure that all former coal industry employees are retrained for sustainable jobs or fully compensated. Boosting efficiency by retrofitting existing coal power plants should be accelerated, as should phase-out of the dirtiest coal plants.

Clean coal: No reliance should be placed on 'clean coal' because it does not yet exist. It could become available after 2020, too late for the climate crisis.

Carbon sequestration: There is scope for carbon sequestration (CS) by reducing deforestation, planting trees and managing land on a global scale.

Oil: It seems likely that the world cannot afford to burn its remaining oil. The era of cheap oil is already over; exploration for new deposits should be discouraged. Canadian tar sands should be left in place and revegetated.

Natural gas: As the transition to renewables will be wrenching, natural gas will have a role as a bridging fuel.

Nuclear energy

Nuclear energy is not a panacea. Full environmental and social costing, including the risk of terrorism and accidents and the diversion of radioactive materials to weaponry, must be mandated. The industry must pay for permanent storage of nuclear wastes. All waste storage and insurance against accidents must be the responsibility of the nuclear industry from now on. All subsidies to the nuclear industry must cease and preferably be reallocated to renewable forms of energy.

Hydroprojects

Reservoirs are the largest single source of anthropogenic methane emissions, contributing around a quarter of these emissions, or more than 4 per cent of global GHG emissions. The Bank invested more than US$800 million in nine hydropower projects in 2007, vastly exceeding its investments in renewable energy and efficiency projects (IRN, 2007). The solution is simple: the Bank should follow the recommendations of the World Commission on Dams (2000), which were impugned by the Bank. In particular, hydroelectric projects likely to emit substantial amounts of GHGs should be banned. Carbon emissions from any dam should be subject to the proposed global carbon tax.

Caveat on cap-and-trade schemes

The forestry and carbon sink projects proposed for inclusion in the Bank's Clean Development Mechanism are a way for industrialized countries, responsible for 75 per cent of GHG emissions, to obtain access to cheap ways of buying emission rights without committing themselves to reducing their emissions. At least they have to pay more to emit, and what they pay goes to a country that has not used its quota. But GHG emission reductions must become the over-riding priority and are achieved by a low cap, not by trading. Almost all such reductions must come from the polluters, namely the industrial nations.

BOX 13.2 SECTOR SOLUTIONS TO REDUCE CLIMATE RISKS

Transportation: Pedestrianism (including moving walkways) and non-motorized transport (such as bicycles) must become the priority. Transportation will become almost entirely electricity-driven.

Buildings: Changes include insulation, solar windows, new lighting technology, efficiency standards for appliances, and rooftop and parking-lot solar systems.

Industry: The most energy-intensive industries should be phased down. Combined heat and power systems will become commonplace.

Urban and Municipal Authorities: Telecommuting should become the norm; working from home would reduce congestion and transport costs. Urban design should prioritize pedestrianism and facilitate bicycles.

Agricultural: Innovations include efficient solar and wind irrigation pumps, solar and wind-powered desalination, rainwater harvesting, water conservation and the lowest-impact irrigation. Agrofuels from whatever food source (corn, maize, grains and sugarcane alcohols, soy and palm oils) will be marginal at best (Smolker et al, 2007). Livestock constitute the least efficient form of producing human food and consume more water than any other product. For these reasons, CAT (2007) and many scientists conclude that meat and dairy production should decline by 60 per cent or more within 20 years.

LIVESTOCK

The agriculture sector is generally agreed to account for one-quarter of GHG emissions, of which deforestation and livestock are the main elements. However, the UN Food and Agricultural Organization (FAO) (Steinfeld et al 2006) projects a doubling of livestock numbers in the next few decades. This increase could more than double the present proportion of GHG emissions attributable to agriculture, particularly if other sectors' contributions decrease over the same period.

Commendably, the World Bank published a Livestock Strategy, *Livestock Development: Implications for Rural Poverty, the Environment and Global Food Security*, in 2001, stating that the Bank would 'avoid funding large-scale commercial, grain-fed feedlot systems and industrial milk, pork and poultry production except to improve the public good areas of environment and food safety'. Since then the International Bank for Reconstruction and Development (IBRD) and the International Development Association (IDA) branches of the Bank Group have not funded a single large-scale livestock project. Notable by omission and discussed later is the IFC.

The World Bank's nutrition strategy supports a reduction in the consumption of livestock products. For example:

> *A recent review of the EU Common Agricultural Policy noted that its support for the cattle sector produced excess dairy products and aided consumption of saturated fats. As a result, diet-related disease, particularly cardiovascular disease, claims more than seven million years of life annually and obesity-related costs are seven per cent of the EU healthcare budget. In Poland, the withdrawal of large consumer subsidies (especially for foods of animal origin) and subsequent substitution of unsaturated for saturated fats and an increased consumption of fresh fruits and vegetables are believed to have decreased the incidence of ischaemic heart disease and mortality from circulatory diseases since 1991.* (World Bank, 2006a)

Similarly, in the 1980s World Bank staff documented studies in 65 counties in China showing that the height of adults is strongly associated with the intake of plant-based foods rather than livestock products. Relying largely on plant-based foods, China reduced infant mortality by about 80 per cent, while childhood growth rates were increasing as rapidly as those observed in Japan during the 1950s to 1980s (Piazza, 1986).

In the Bank's report, Hu and Willett (1998), of the Harvard School of Public Health, concluded that when investments in animal products are being considered in development, 'The use of plant source of protein and fat, such as soy products, nuts and vegetable oils, may provide even greater health benefits and should therefore be considered.' This report provided a detailed review of relevant epidemiological literature and concluded, 'Higher red meat consumption probably increases risk of coronary heart disease, colon cancer and prostate cancer, and possibly breast cancer.'

In contrast, the IFC has not publicly disclosed any strategy document for the livestock sector. It has stated that it need not abide by the World Bank's Livestock Strategy. It even disputes that the World Bank has a livestock strategy, although the Bank's public website states, 'In 2001, the World Bank released a strategy for the livestock sector.'

Following publication of the Bank's Livestock Strategy, new estimates were published on the proportion of global GHG emissions attributable to livestock. One journal estimated that 23 per cent of global carbon emissions derive merely from keeping livestock alive (Calverd, 2005). The FAO (Steinfeld et al 2006) provided a lower but still startlingly high estimate of 18 per cent of GHGs attributable to the raising, processing and transportation of livestock and their products. A Sierra Club report (2006) estimated that the proportion of GHGs attributable to livestock may be 40 per cent or higher. The livestock sector is responsible for the following proportions of global anthropogenic GHG emissions: 37 per cent of methane (CH_4), 65 per cent of nitrous oxide (N_2O) and 9 per cent of carbon dioxide (CO_2).

Since the Bank's Livestock Strategy (2001), the IFC has invested US$732 million to promote 22 livestock production projects totaling US$2.219 billion. Most of the IFC's project write-ups omit any mention of GHG emissions. The total amount of financing put into these projects dwarfs and undermines the IBRD/IDA's comparatively modest financing to reduce deforestation and GHG emissions. Almost all of the IFC's projects involve precisely the type of livestock system that the World Bank's Livestock Strategy seeks to avoid: large integrated producers rather than small mixed farmers. These projects conflict with and undermine other key elements of the Livestock Strategy, notably in the area of environmental management. For example, the IFC's financing for expansion of cattle production in the Amazon forest region is leading to decreased biodiversity in the region, while the Bank's Livestock Strategy seeks to conserve it.

Many other sources besides the Bank's 2001 Livestock Strategy recognize the problems analysed in that document. Many findings in the Bank's Livestock Strategy were published earlier (in 1999) in a Livestock Sector Environmental Assessment compiled at the Bank, which describes the major, critical environmental problems that can be attributed to large-scale livestock projects (Goodland, 1999).

Despite this, the publicly disclosed 'Summaries of project information' for the IFC's investments in livestock projects claim that these projects will lower the price of livestock products for consumers and thereby improve the nutritional status of local populations. In their statements and activities the International Livestock Research Institute, Consultative Group on International Agricultural Research, International Food Policy Research Institute, Food and Agriculture Organization and IFC generally promote more meat in human diets, claiming it is good for health in the face of impeccable evidence to the contrary (FAO et al, 1997; Steinfeld et al, 2006).

The FAO claim that an increasing proportion of animal products in the diet mix is inevitable, and that the chances of reducing this, as proposed by 'environmentalists such as Goodland', is nil:

Arguably, the environmental problems associated with livestock production would best be resolved by reducing consumption of their products, as many environmentalists (see, for example, Goodland, 1996) suggest. We believe that chances for lowering the overall demand are close to nil and that the billions of poor people have a right to improve their diet. We acknowledge that consumption of meat and other livestock products is, in some countries and social classes, excessive, causing medical problems such as cardiovascular diseases and high blood pressure. (FAO, World Bank and USDA, 1997; see also Goodland, 1997, 1998a, b, 2000; Goodland and Pimentel, 2000)

Solutions

Better results for the food industry have clearly been seen when financial resources have been provided, both to producers to provide and market healthy products and to public health groups to conduct public-awareness campaigns. Therefore this is what International Livestock Research Institute (ILRI), Consultative Group on International Agricultural Research (CGIAR), International Food Policy Research Institute (IFPRI), FAO, IFC and World Bank should be supporting.

Scarce agricultural development resources are more economically allocated to promoting increased accessibility by the poor to healthy foods, because such foods provide lower risks and impacts for the environment and public health, are more efficient in resource use, and are more equitable to poor farmers. Since most meat and dairy products are now available in soy-based versions, this alternative would not require lowering nutritional standards; on the contrary, it would improve them.

FOREST POLICY

More than 35 million acres of tropical forests are destroyed annually (particularly in developing countries), releasing more than 1.5 billion metric tonnes of CO_2, methane, and NOx into the atmosphere every year. Climate change is intensifying drought and the risk of forest fires. In some years, like the 1997/1998 El Niño year when fires released some 2 billion tonnes of carbon from peat swamps alone in Indonesia, emissions are more than twice that.

The World Bank reports that deforestation accounts for about 20 per cent of global carbon emissions, mainly from fires set to clear land. In 2007 the Bank established a US$250 million Forest Carbon Partnership Facility (FCPF), which aims to establish pilot activities to enable tropical countries to prepare for the inclusion of 'avoided deforestation' in a post-Kyoto agreement in 2012.

The Bank's BioCarbon Fund finances projects that sequester or conserve greenhouse gases in forest, agro and other ecosystems. The BioCarbon Fund aims to 'test and demonstrate how land use, land-use change and forestry activities can generate high-quality emission reductions with environmental and livelihood benefits that can be measured, monitored and certified and stand the test of time'. BioCarbon Fund projects have to fulfil criteria to ensure that the fund meets its own targets in the areas of climate and environment, poverty alleviation, project management and learning, and portfolio balance. Each BioCarbon Fund project is expected to deliver between 400,000 and 800,000 tonnes of CO_2 equivalents (CO_2e) over a period of 10 to 15 years. In return, a typical project will receive about US$2 million to 3 million in payments (US$3–4 per tonne CO_2e) (Bosquet, 2000, 2006). It is still too soon to judge the extent to which this can reduce atmospheric GHG concentrations, however.

The US$80 million Amazon Region Protected Areas Project expands Brazil's protected areas system in the Amazon region. This is undermined by the IFC's Bertin cattle-ranching projects. The issue of the IFC undercutting other Bank policy calls for more explanation as they are theoretically governed by the same board. Similar IBRD projects finance forest conservation in Mexico (US$45 million), Costa Rica (US$32 million) and Peru (US$23 million). Such initiatives need to be monitored, revised and ramped up.

The Bank's Independent Evaluation Group (World Bank, 2007a) calculates that the middle-income countries (MICs) account for 60 per cent of the world's total forest area, which is being destroyed fast, especially in Brazil, Indonesia, Mexico and the Philippines. Although high-income countries remain the largest emitters of carbon dioxide, three-quarters of MICs, including China, have increased their total emissions since 1995. China has recently become the world's largest emitter of GHGs, although it lags far behind on both per capita and historical emissions.

Bank finance for logging forests has long been controversial in view of the damage caused to forest dwellers, indigenous peoples, biodiversity and watershed management, combined with widespread corruption and lack of benefits for the forest-owning nations and the rural poor (Haworth et al, 1999; Lele et al, 2000; Counsell, 2002; Carrere and Colchester, 2005; WRM, 2005; Global Witness, 2006; Counsell et al, 2007; *The Economist*, 2007; Goodland, 2007). The only non-controversial period followed the ban on logging by the Bank's 1992 Forest Policy, which was rescinded in 2002. This retrogression fuelled renewed controversies and damage (Minnemeyer, 2002; Counsell, 2005; WRM, 2005; Greenpeace, 2007a; REM, 2007; World Bank Inspection Panel, 2007d).

In 2007 the Bank's former Chief Economist and Vice-President, Sir Nicholas Stern, urged the Bank to desist from financing deforestation, as the biggest and most immediate contribution it could make to reducing GHG emissions. However, the Bank has a long track record of funding industrialization of natural forest areas in the tropics and, more recently, in the former communist countries. Although the Bank has long argued that the development of timber industries can be a way to both stimulate economic growth and 'sustainably manage' forest resources, the evidence that the Bank has achieved either is extremely sparse.

The case of the Congo Basin

Throughout the 1990s and 2000s, the Bank has invested hundreds of millions of dollars in the forest sectors of Cameroon, Gabon, Congo-Brazzaville, Central African Republic and the Democratic Republic of Congo. Following a pattern established early on in Cameroon, the Bank's interventions typically supported reform of the forestry laws, geographic zoning and strengthening of forestry institutions (DRC, 2002; World Bank 2002a and b, 2003 and 2004; DRC/FAO, 2003). In practice, Bank finance prioritized extensive industrial timber exploitation instead of community control of forest resources.

Forests across virtually the entire region have for several thousand years been inhabited by both hunter-gatherer 'Pygmies' and agricultural Bantu communities, which have subtle and complex traditional tenure-rights regimes and sustain themselves with forest resources. However, the Bank-backed 'modernized' forestry laws in countries such as Cameroon and Gabon laid the basis for the consolidation and extension of the system of large-scale logging concessions. Through national zoning plans these concessions were superimposed over large areas of the forest, often setting the scene for endemic, low-level conflict with forest-dependent communities.

The timber industries encouraged by the Bank have proven to be systemically ungovernable (REM, 2007). The region's forest sectors are now typically characterized by high levels of corruption, resource mismanagement, predation, serious environmental damage, social conflict and rural 'de-development'. Forest-dependent communities have found their subsistence economies shattered as logging companies have eliminated vital resources, while poorly paid logging workers have exterminated local game supplies through intensive hunting. Adding to local social costs, logging camps have acted as a magnet for sex workers and drug traffickers, thus establishing centres for the spread of AIDS. Logging also favours the reproduction of malaria-bearing *Anopheles* mosquitoes, bringing further misery and death to rural communities with no means to acquire medicines (Counsell et al, 2007).

In 2002 the Bank became engaged in the forest sector of the Democratic Republic of Congo (DRC), whose forests cover an area of 1.3 million square kilometres, more than twice the size of France. According to World Bank estimates, some 40 million people (70 per cent of the national population) reside in, or to some extent depend on, the country's forests (World Bank, 2002a).

In August 2002 a new forest code was adopted by the (unelected) interim government of the DRC (DRC, 2002), broadly modelled on the forest law the Bank developed for Cameroon in 1994, including state ownership over all areas of forest. Certain categories of forest are broadly defined for exploitation, community use and conservation. The Bank supported the drafting of the code and made its adoption a condition for the release of a US$15 million forest sector tranche of a structural credit in May 2002 (World Bank, 2002b).

In January 2003 a Bank-financed FAO project zoned the DRC's entire forest into areas for logging, conservation and other uses (DRC/FAO, 2003). The Bank pressed the government to cancel a number of existing logging contracts and revoke 6 million hectares of logging concessions illegally allocated to a Portuguese company. The government adopted a moratorium on issuing new logging concessions in April 2002. The Bank also urged that the level of forestry taxes increase substantially to generate greater revenues for the Congolese Treasury. However, the logging industry has resisted these changes, and forestry taxes remain very low, at US$0.25 per hectare. Government officials illegally issued some 15 million to 20 million hectares of concessions in contravention of the moratorium.

The World Bank has been closely involved in discussions with the DRC Government about a massive expansion of the country's timber industry. Bank documents refer to a possible 60- to 100-fold increase of timber production to around 6 million to 10 million cubic metres of timber per year and to the 'creation of a favourable climate for industrial logging'. According to the Bank, an area of some 60 million hectares (somewhat larger than the size of France) is considered as 'production forests' (World Bank, 2002a).

To lay the geographical basis for forestry in the DRC, the Bank included a US$4 million forestry component in its 'Emergency Economic and Social Reunification Support Project', which it approved in September 2003. The Bank would support the preparation of a forest zoning plan, which would 'organize rural areas into three broad categories according to their primary objectives (rural development, sustainable production, environmental protection)'. Although the Bank stated that such zoning is 'critical to secure land rights and transparent access to forest resources for *all* stakeholders' (emphasis added), its likely intention was belied by the second forestry element of the project: to 'lay the ground for implementation of the new law's forest concession system'. In fact, of only two performance indicators the Bank was aiming to achieve for the forestry component of this project, one is the 'number of new [industrial logging] concessions attributed in a transparent manner'.

Between 250,000 and 600,000 hunter-gatherer Pygmy people live in Congo's forest. Concerned about the potential impact of Bank investment on the forest resources and traditional rights of forest peoples, and having failed to gain any reassurances from the Bank through informal channels, a Congolese group (including some indigenous Pygmy people themselves and others who work with Pygmy communities) made a formal complaint to the World Bank Inspection Panel. The panel then made two inspection visits to the DRC, in February 2006 and February 2007, and presented their report to Bank management in August 2007.

The Inspection Panel report strongly reaffirms critiques of the Bank that the Rainforest Foundation and many groups in the DRC have been making since 2003. The report (World Bank Inspection Panel, 2007) states:

- Industrial logging in the DRC has profound social and environmental impacts, and in its current state it may well exacerbate poverty, not alleviate it.
- The DRC Government at present lacks the basic capacity to manage the logging of its forests, and Bank interventions have not paid sufficient attention to this fact.
- The Bank failed to comply with its own policies on Indigenous Peoples (Operational Directive 4.20), Cultural Property (Operational Policy 11.03), Environmental Assessment (Operational Policy 4.01) and Natural Habitats (Operational Policy 4.04) and has shown serious inadequacy in complying with its overarching objective of Poverty Reduction (Operational Directive 4.15).
- The Bank effectively misled the Congolese Government at the start of its engagement in the forest sector by vastly overestimating the export revenue from logging concessions, thus encouraging the government to look to industrial timber exploitation as a source of revenue.
- The Bank made some basic errors in the development of the projects. Project documents did not identify the existence of Pygmy peoples in the areas affected by the project and made no provision to identify or include them in project planning. (According to the Panel, as many as 600,000 Pygmy people may live in the DRC.)
- The Bank downgraded projects to lower levels of potential environmental risk, thus reducing the level of environmental assessment required, and then failed to carry out environmental and social impact assessments before the projects started.
- The Bank did not produce an Indigenous Peoples' Development Plan as required under Operational Policy 4.20.
- The Bank has made some improvements in its approaches in the past two years but initiated most of these only after the initial Request for Inspection was submitted to the Panel.
- The Bank demonstrated weak management, for example when it apparently failed to 'make timely follow-up efforts at a sufficiently high level to ensure necessary action in response to its findings'.

At the time of writing, Bank management was still preparing its response to the panel's report.

Through its pro-logging policies in the DRC, the Bank risks contributing to global climate change. The DRC's forests are estimated to contain up to 200 tonnes of carbon per hectare and the country to contain 8 per cent of all forest carbon worldwide.

Bank-financed industrial logging is almost invariably followed by further forest degradation and clearance, usually for agricultural crops. This process has been found to be closely correlated to distance from roads (Chomitz et al, 2007). In the Congo Basin as a whole, a study of satellite images by the World Resources Institute has shown that by 2001 only one-third of forests were considered to be low-access – that is, more than two kilometres from a road and in a block of at least 1000 square kilometres (Minnemeyer, 2002). Most of these remaining areas are in the DRC, precisely in the areas now coming under pressure as a result of Bank-encouraged expansion of the timber industry. The eventual conversion of all of the Congo Basin forests to farmland would cause a contribution to the atmosphere of several tens of gigatonnes of carbon; according to one estimate, the clearance of just the DRC's forests would cause the release of around 34 gigatonnes of carbon, or roughly four times present total global annual anthropogenic emissions (Greenpeace, 2007a).

Cambodia

In 2006 the Bank came under heavy criticism from the Inspection Panel for its interventions in the forest sector in Cambodia. Local communities had lodged a complaint with the panel in 2005, after it became clear the Bank's five-year Forest Concession Management and Control Pilot Project had exacerbated an already dire situation. The panel found that the Bank had broken internal safeguards, violated its own policies, ignored local communities and failed to reduce poverty. The panel reported that the Bank had ignored evidence of the negative impact more industrial, concession-based logging would have on the livelihoods of forest-dependent groups, notably resin tappers. It had similarly failed to recognize that some of the areas put forward for industrial logging were also forests of high ecological value; had failed to ensure adequate detection of cultural and spiritual property in the forests; and had failed to ensure adequate supervision of the project (Global Witness, 2006).

Peru

In Peru, through its Forest Alliance with the World Wide Fund for Nature, in 2002–2003 the Bank supported the repackaging of numerous short-term logging contracts and illegal logging operations into new concessions covering around 4 million hectares of lowland rainforest. At the time, local environmentalists expressed fears that this would simply provide a legal cover for operators to launder the products of what were expected to be continued illegal operations, including in indigenous territories. By 2007 it had become clear that this was precisely what was happening. Some satellite data indicate that forests are being protected, but on-the-ground observers say the logging companies are inflating the amount of mahogany they are allowed to cut legally to conceal illegal felling outside their concessions (*The Economist*, 2007).

Bank-financed logging is a result of the Bank's 2002 Forest Strategy. At the time of its adoption, the Bank promised that the policy would be reviewed, 'mid-term', in 2007. A confidential independent evaluation of the strategy's implementation is critical of the Bank's forestry work, finding that its re-engagement in the forest sector 'has not met expectations' (World Bank, 2007b).

The IFC financing deforestation

More than 2.5 million acres of Indonesian rainforests are cleared for oil palm plantations, and 3.5 million acres of Amazonian rainforest are cleared every year, primarily for enormous soy fields and cattle ranching (Bickel and Dros, 2003; Jaccoud et al, 2003; Dros, 2004; Kaimowitz et al, 2004; Lilley, 2004; Caruso, 2005; Chomitz et al, 2007). The IFC finances oil palm and soy cultivation and cattle ranching in tropical rainforest regions and shrimp cultivation in mangrove forests. For the IFC, destruction of tropical rainforest in general is insufficient reason for the complete Environmental Assessment Category A. For example, the IFC's US$80 million financing of Indonesia's Wilmar Oil Palm Project (Number 25532) in 2006 is the weakest EA Category C. The IFC justifies this as follows: 'It is anticipated that this project will have minimal or no direct, adverse social or environmental impacts.' But the IFC omits emissions of greenhouse gas, risks to indigenous peoples and loss of biodiversity (Greenpeace, 2007b).

Solutions

Outright conversion or fragmentation of natural forests for any purpose, such as oil palm plantations, cattle ranching, soy, logging, agrofuels and mangrove shrimp ponds should cease immediately. Conservation of forests, prevention of forest burning, remote-sensing detection of logging and fires, and enforcement of laws should be emphasized. The Bank should encourage timber plantations and tree plantations on suitable non-forested lands. This policy would follow Sir Nicholas Stern's 2007 advice to the Bank. In addition, the G8/World Bank BioCarbon Fund should increase by orders of magnitude from today's few million dollars to several billion dollars within a very few years, especially in the Congo and Central Africa, Indonesia, Malaysia, Papua New Guinea, Cambodia, Laos and the Amazon forest nations. The FCPF should not directly or indirectly fund any activities connected to industrial forestry in any natural or semi-natural forests.

CONCLUSION

The anti-poor bank

The Bank's financing of GHG emissions through deforestation, fossil fuels and livestock not only increases climate change risks, it shows an anti-poor bias. Climate change means an increase in droughts and floods, more seasonal peaks in river flows, and riskier tropical storms; all translate into damage to agriculture and hikes in food, fuel and water prices (Cline, 2007). Diverting food to produce agrofuels further strains already tight supplies of arable land and water all over the world, thereby raising food prices even further when global food reserves are at their lowest in 25 years. Rice prices rose 20 per cent, maize 50 per cent and wheat 100 per cent over the past 12 months. Even when the price of food was low, 850 million people went hungry because they could not afford it. With every increment in the price of flour or grain, several million more are pushed below the 'bread line'. The IEG found that poverty stagnated or is actually worsening in Bank-assisted countries studied over the past decade (World Bank, 2006a). Financing GHG emissions jeopardizes the Millennium Development Goals of reducing poverty among the 2.7 billion people living on less than US$2 a day. In other words, the costs of climate change are distributed regressively, so the benefits of avoidance will be distributed progressively.

The Bank's GHG financing is anti-poor for six reasons:

1   Poor people are the most vulnerable to climate change: droughts, floods, severe weather and disease affect them first and worst.
2   Poor people have to spend a bigger proportion of their incomes on food and hence are more vulnerable to food price spikes.
3   The poor lack access to energy, without which it impossible to escape poverty.
4   Many poor people depend on forests for their food, fuel, building materials and medicines.
5   Most of the poor do not eat their livestock: livestock products are produced mostly for export and the rich.
6   Although developing countries need to boost their energy use by about five times to develop, the World Bank Group's fossil fuel finances mainly export to help industrial nations, so they do not help the poorest.

Towards solutions

The World Bank Group should assess the risks and opportunities presented by climate change in ways proportionate to its projected impacts; the World Bank Group's fiduciary duty is to its shareholders, and its responsibilities to civil society, especially the poor. The following ten recommendations are offered to help the Bank alleviate climate risks. These ten roughly ranked recommendations strongly support and are generally consistent with those offered by six major recent international studies (CAT, 2007; GLCA, 2007; InterAcademy Council, 2007; Makhijani, 2007; Practical Action, 2007; IEA, 2007). The IEA concludes, 'Vigorous, immediate and collective policy action by all governments is essential to move the world onto a more sustainable energy path.'

Ten key recommendations

1 *Prioritize poverty reduction*: Keep meeting the Millennium Development Goals as the WBG's top priority to reduce poverty and assist the poor to become more resilient in the face of climate impacts. Ramp up direct funding for poverty reduction, job creation, nutrition, education and health. Move away from indirect and inefficient trickle-down economics.

2 *Renewable energy*: Switch from current massive financing of fossil fuels rapidly towards renewable energy (solar, wind, wave, tidal, micro-hydro) with conservation and energy efficiency and especially decentralized systems for the poor. Eliminate all subsidies for fossil fuels and nuclear energy. Assist developing countries to plan for and implement a prompt and orderly transition to renewable energy and GHG reduction.

3 *Get the price right*: Promote all nations' adoption of clear price signals, such as a global carbon tax to be used as each nation sees fit.

4 *Contraction and convergence*: Espouse and promote contraction and convergence to reduce GHG emissions while persuading all borrowing nations to adopt that principle. Support a physical limit (hard cap) that declines to zero before the threshold 2°C rise in temperature occurs.

5 *Comply with livestock rules*: Instruct the IFC to follow all WBG policies and strategies, especially the Livestock Strategy (no more financing for industrial livestock production) and the Nutrition Strategy, which does not recommend meat consumption.

6 *Forest conservation*: Switch from current financing of industrial logging and forest destruction to support strengthening of tenure rights of forest-based communities, community-based forest management, and more conservation, reforestation and afforestation.

7 *Adaptation to climate change*: Assist developing countries to adapt to climate change, starting with vulnerability assessments of small island nation states such as the Maldives and deltaic countries such as Bangladesh.

8 *International agreements*: Vigorously support the process for the comprehensive post-Kyoto international agreement under the auspices of the UNFCCC; announce support at Bali in December 2007; present a draft to the Conference of Parties in 2008.

9 *Stringent standards*: Adopt and revise stringent end-use standards commensurate with evolving science for vehicles, lighting, building codes, electric motors and appliances.

10 *GHG sources and sinks*: Promote accounting and monitoring of GHG emissions and implement agreements on deforestation and livestock. Monitor changes in carbon-sink capacities, including oceanic (marine acidification) as well as terrestrial.

Do the Bank and IFC still have time to play a key role in supporting sustainability and integrity? Can the Bank switch from intensifying climate risks to reducing them in time to prevent severe damage to the 'bottom billion'? The answers depend on a big 'if': only if it musters the political will quickly and acts decisively. The WBG is starting far behind even neutrality on climate change. It rejected the prudent advice of the 2000 World Commission on Dams, as well as the 2003 Extractive Industry Review, so it is not easy to be optimistic. The Bank's previous President, Paul Wolfowitz, did not manage to promote environmental sustainability (Goodland, 2005). The new President, Robert Zoellick, has not announced many improvements in environment or climate change policy in his first and active 100 days. On the contrary, some of his actions seem to threaten the environment and intensify climate change. It would have been appropriate to announce a bold emergency climate-change plan with specific targets and schedules, as outlined in this chapter, at the UN Climate Change Conference in Bali in December 2007, to be fully fledged and implemented starting in 2008. Although President Zoellick was reported to have had several differences with civil society and forest dwellers, he did not unveil any major plan to reduce climate impacts, especially on the poor.

The world's governments, which are the shareholders of the World Bank Group, should demand accountability, transparency and consensual development. Citizens of every country should urge their legislators to demand that their governments take shareholder responsibility for the Bank to end its procrastination on climate change.

ACKNOWLEDGEMENTS

We offer sincere thanks for the contributions to this chapter from Herman Daly, especially his paper (Daly, 2007b) on the monumental blunder of pursuing efficiency in coal-powered electricity generation before sustainability. Aubrey Meyer kindly helped us with 'contraction and convergence'.

REFERENCES

Arrow, K. J. (2007) 'Global climate change: A challenge to policy', *Economists Voice*, June, www.bepress.com/ev

Bickel, U. and Dros, J. M. (2003) 'The impacts of soybean cultivation on Brazilian ecosystems: Three case studies', WWF Forest Conversion Initiative

Bosquet, B. (2000) 'Environmental tax reform: Does it work? A survey of the empirical evidence', *Ecological Economics*, vol 34, pp19–32

Bosquet, B. (2006) 'The BioCarbon Fund: Using the global market to restore ecosystems: New opportunity for public-private partnerships', The World Bank, Washington, DC, http://info.worldbank.org/etools/docs/library/235314/Benoit.BioCF%20Extr%20 Indust%2006-19-6.ppt

Calverd, A. (2005) 'A radical approach to Kyoto', *Physics World*, July, p56

Campbell, K., Gulledge, J., McNeill, J., Podesta, J., Ogden, P., Fuerth, L., Woolsey, R. J., Lennon, A., Smith, J., Weitz, R. and Mix, D. (2007) 'The age of consequences: The foreign policy and national security. Implications of global climate change', Center for Strategic and International Studies (CSIS) and Center for a New American Security (CNAS), Washington, DC, www.csis.org/media/csis/pubs/071105_ageof consequences.pdf

Carrere, R. and Colchester, M. (2005) 'The World Bank and forests: A tissue of lies and deception', in *Broken Promises: How World Bank Group Policies and Practice Failed to Protect Forests and Forest Peoples' Rights*, World Rainforest Movement, Montevideo, Uruguay, pp4–5

Caruso, E. (2005) 'Roads of deforestation in Brazil: How soya and cattle are destroying the Amazon with the help of the IFC', in *Broken Promises: How World Bank Group Policies and Practice Failed to Protect Forests and Forest Peoples' Rights*: World Rainforest Movement, Montevideo, Uruguay

CAT (Centre for Alternative Technology) (2007) *Zero Carbon Britain*, Centre for Alternative Technology, Machynlleth, UK, www.cat.org.uk

Chomitz, K. M., Buys, P., De Luca, G., Thomas, T. S. and Wertz-Kanounnikoff, S. (2007) 'At loggerheads? Agricultural expansion, poverty reduction and environment in the tropical forests', World Bank Report 36789, World Bank, Washington, DC

Cline, W. R. (2007) 'Global warming and agriculture: End of century estimates by country', Center for Global Development, Peterson Institute for International Economics, Washington, DC

Counsell, S. (2002) *Trading in Credibility: The Myth and Reality of the Forest Stewardship Council*, Rainforest Foundation, London

Counsell, S. (2005) 'Democratic Republic of Congo: After the war, the fight for the forest', in *Broken Promises: How World Bank Group Policies and Practice Failed to Protect Forests and Forest Peoples' Rights*, World Rainforest Movement, Montevideo, Uruguay, pp11–19

Counsell, S., Long, C. and Wilson, S. (eds) (2007) *Concessions to Poverty; The Environmental, Social and Economic Impacts of Industrial Logging Concessions in Africa's Rainforests*, Rainforest Foundation UK and Forests Monitor, Cambridge, UK

Daly, H. E. (2007a) *Ecological Economics and Sustainable Development*, Edward Elgar, Cheltenham, UK

Daly, H. E. (2007b) 'Climate policy: From "know how" to "do now"', Paper presented at the AMS special conference on climate change, American Meteorological Society, Washington, DC

DRC (2002) 'Loi No 011/2002, Code Forestière', Government of the Democratic Republic of Congo, Kinshasa

DRC/FAO (2003) *Rapport Synthèse du Projet Appui a la relance du Secteur Forestier*, TCP DRC 2905, Government of the Democratic Republic of Congo/FAO, Kinshasa

Dros, J. M. (2004) *Managing the Soy Boom: Two Scenarios of Soy Production Expansion in South America*, AIDEnvironment, Amsterdam

The Economist (2007) 'Trade, timber and tribes', www.economist.com/world/la/display story.cfm?story_id=9910163

FAO, World Bank and USDA (1997) 'Balancing livestock, the environment and human needs', Keynote Address by H. Steinfeld (FAO), C. de Haan (World Bank) and

H. Blackburn (USDA), 10 March–24 May, www.virtualcentre.org/en/ele/econf_97/lxesumk.htm

GLCA (Global Leadership for Climate Action) (2007) 'Framework for a post-2012 agreement on climate change', United Nations Foundation, Washington, DC, www.global climateaction.com

Global Witness (2006) 'World Bank Inspection Panel finds Slam Bank Forestry Project in Cambodia', press release, 15 June, Global Witness, available at www.globalwitness.org/media_library_detail.php/446/en/world_bank_inspection_panel_finds_slam_bank, accessed 9 April 2008

Goodland, R. (1996) 'Environmental sustainability and eating better: The case against grain-fed meat', mimeo, Arlington, VA

Goodland, R. (1997) 'Environmental sustainability in agriculture: Diet matters', *Ecological Economics*, vol 23, pp189–200

Goodland, R. (1998a) 'The case against consumption of grain-fed meat', in D. Crocker and T. Linden (eds) *The Ethics of Consumption*, Rowman and Littlefield, Lanham, MD, pp95–115

Goodland, R. (1998b) 'Environmental sustainability in agriculture: The bioethical and religious arguments against carnivory', in J. Lemons, L. Westra and R. Goodland (eds) *Ecological Sustainability*, Kluwer, Dordrecht, The Netherlands, pp235–265

Goodland, R. (1999) 'Livestock sector environmental assessment', in M. Hardtlein et al (eds) *Nachhaltigeit in der Landwirtschaft*, E. Schmidt, Berlin, pp239–261

Goodland, R. (2000) 'The case against financing dairy projects in developing countries', www.notmilk.com/wbstance.html, accessed 9 April 2008

Goodland, R. (2005) 'A Green welcome for Paul Wolfowitz upon assuming the Presidency of the World Bank Group on 1 June 2005: "How the World Bank should cut poverty and help make the world environmentally sustainable"', unpublished public letter

Goodland, R. (2007) 'The institutionalized use of force in economic development', in C. L. Soskolne (ed) *Sustaining Life on Earth: Environmental and Human Health through Global Governance*, Lexington Books (Rowman and Littlefield), Lanham, MD, pp339–354

Goodland, R. and El Serafy, S. (1998) 'The urgent need to internalize carbon dioxide emission costs', *Ecological Economics*, vol 27, pp79–90

Goodland, R. and Pimentel, D. (2000) 'Environmental sustainability and integrity in natural resource systems', in D. Pimentel, L. Westra and R. Noss (eds) *Ecological Integrity: Integrating Environment, Conservation and Health*, Island Press, Washington, DC, pp121–138

Greenpeace (2007a) *Carving up the Congo*, Greenpeace International, Amsterdam

Greenpeace (2007b) *How the Oil Palm Industry is Cooking the Climate*, Greenpeace International, Amsterdam

Haworth, J., Counsell, S. and Friends of the Earth (1999) *Life After Logging*, Friends of the Earth, London

Hu, F. B. and Willett, W. C. (1998) 'The relationship between consumption of animal products (beef, pork, poultry, eggs, fish and dairy products) and risk of chronic diseases: A critical review', Report for the World Bank, Harvard School of Public Health, Boston, MA

IEA (2007) *Annual World Energy Outlook*, IEA, Paris

InterAcademy Council (2007) 'Lighting the way: Toward a sustainable energy future', IAC, Amsterdam, www.interacademycouncil.net/?id=9481

IPCC (2007) 'Summary for Policymakers' of the Synthesis Report of the *Fourth Assessment Report*, Intergovernmental Panel on Climate Change, available at www.ipcc. ch/pdf/assessment-report/ar4/syr/ar4_syr_spm.pdf, accessed 9 April 2008

IRN (2007) *The World Bank's Big Dam Legacy*, International Rivers Network, Berkeley, CA

Jaccoud, D' A., Stephan, P., Lemos de Sá, R. and Richardson, S. (2003) 'Sustainability assessment of export-led growth in soy production in Brazil', WWF, www.bothends.org/strategic/soy25.pdf

Kaimowitz, D., Mertens, B., Wunder, S. and Pacheco, P. (2004) *Hamburger Connection Fuels Amazon Destruction*, CIFOR, Bogor, Indonesia

Lele, U., Viana, V., Veríssimo, A., Vosti, S., Perkins, K. and Husain, S. A. (2000) *Brazil: Forests in the Balance: Challenges of Conservation with Development*, Operations Evaluation Department, World Bank, Washington, DC

Lilley, S. (2004) 'Paving the Amazon with soy: World Bank bows to audit of Maggi loan', CorpWatch, www.corpwatch.org/print_article.php?&id=11756

Makhijani, A. (2007) *Carbon-Free and Nuclear-Free: A Roadmap for US Energy Policy*, RDR Books, Berkeley, CA, www.ieer.org/sdafiles/15-1.pdf

Meinhardt, H. (2007) 'World Bank Group fossil fuel and extractive industry financing spreadsheet: FY05-06', www.bicusa.org/en/Article.3395.aspx

Miller, P. and Westra, L. (2002) *Just Ecological Integrity: The Ethics of Maintaining Planetary Life*, Studies in social, political and legal philosophy, Rowman and Littlefield, Lanham, MD

Minnemeyer, S. (2002) *An Analysis of Access into Central Africa's Rainforests*, Global Forest Watch, World Resources Institute, Washington, DC

Piazza, A. (1986) *Food Consumption and Nutritional Status in the People's Republic of China*, Westview Press, Boulder, CO

Polimeni, J., Mayumi, K., Giampetro, M. and Alcott, B. (2008) *The Jevons Paradox and the Myth of Resource Efficiency Improvements*, Earthscan, London

Practical Action (2007) 'Energy to reduce poverty: The urgency for G8 action on climate justice: Stop climate injustice', Intermediate Technology Development Group, Rugby, UK, http://practicalaction.org/docs/advocacy/energy-to-reduce-poverty_g8.pdf

REM (Resource Extraction Monitoring) (2007) 'Progress in tackling illegal logging in Cameroon, 2006–2007: Annual report of the Independent Observer', REM, Cambridge, UK

Sierra Club (2006) 'A report to board members of the World Bank and IFC', Sierra Club, available for download at www.wellfedworld.org/worldbank.htm

Smith, D. and Vivekananda, J. (2007) *A Climate of Conflict: The Links between Climate Change, Peace and War*, International Alert, London

Smolker, R., Tokar, B., Petermann, A. and Hernandez, E. (2007) 'The real cost of agrofuels: Food, forest and the climate', GlobalForestCoalition.org

Soskolne, C. L. (ed) (2007) *Sustaining Life on Earth: Environmental and Human Health through Global Governance*, Lexington Books, Lanham, MD

Steinfeld, H., Gerber, P., Wassenaar, T., Castel, V., Rosales, M. and Haan, C. (2006) *Livestock's Long Shadow: Environmental Issues and Options*, Food and Agriculture Organization of the United Nations, Rome

Stern, N. (2007) *The Economics of Climate Change*, the Stern Review on the economics of climate change for the UK Treasury, TSO, Norwich, UK

Sturm, R. and Wells, K. (2005) *The Health Risks of Obesity: Worse than Smoking, Problem Drinking or Poverty*, Rand Corporation, Santa Monica, CA

Vallette, J., Wysham, D. and Martínez, N. (2004) 'A wrong turn from Rio: The World Bank's road to climate catastrophe', www.seen.org

Westra, L. (2007) *Environmental Justice and the Rights of Indigenous Peoples*, Earthscan, London

Westra, L. (2008) *Environmental Justice and the Rights of Unborn and Future Generations: Law, Environmental Harm and the Right to Health*, Earthscan, London

World Bank (2001) *Livestock Development: Implications for Rural Poverty, the Environment and Global Food Security*, World Bank, Washington, DC

World Bank (2002a) *World Bank, Democratic Republic of Congo, Mission de Suivi Sectoriel, 17–27 April*, internal memo about a mission undertaken during those dates, World Bank, Washington, DC

World Bank (2002b) 'Report and recommendation of the President of the IDA to the Executive Directors on a proposed credit of SDR360.4 million to DRC for an Economic Recovery Credit', World Bank, Washington, DC, 17 May

World Bank (2003) 'Technical annex for a proposed grant in the amount of SDR117 million (US$164 million equivalent) and a proposed credit in the amount of SDR35.7 million) (US$50 million equivalent) to the Democratic Republic of Congo for an emergency economic and social reunification support project', World Bank, Washington, DC, 14 August

World Bank (2004) 'Sustaining forests: A development strategy', World Bank, Washington, DC

World Bank (2006a) 'Repositioning nutrition as central to development: A Strategy for large-scale action', produced by a team led by Meera Shekar, with Richard Heaver and Yi-Kyoung Lee, World Bank, Washington, DC

World Bank (2006b) 'Clean energy and development: Toward an investment framework', document DC2006-0002, World Bank, Washington, DC

World Bank (2007a) 'IDA and climate change: Making climate action work for development', Sustainable Development Network, World Bank, Washington, DC, 11 October

World Bank (2007b) 'A desk evaluation of the implementation of the World Bank's 2002 Forest Sector Strategy', information note, Independent Evaluation Group, World Bank, Washington, DC, 26 July

World Bank (2007c) 'Development results in middle-income countries: An evaluation of the World Bank's support', Independent Evaluation Group, World Bank, Washington, DC

World Bank Inspection Panel (2007) 'Inspection Report, Democratic Republic of Congo: Transitional Support for Economic Recovery Grant (TSERO), IDA Grant No H 1920-DRC) and Emergency Economic and Social Reunification Project (EESRSP) (Credit No 3824-DRC and Grant No H 064-DRC)', World Bank Inspection Panel, Washington, DC, 31 August

World Commission on Dams (2000) *Dams and Development: A New Framework for Decision-Making*, Earthscan, London

WRM (World Rainforest Movement) (2005) *Broken Promises: How World Bank Group Policies and Practice Failed to Protect Forests and Forest Peoples' Rights*: World Rainforest Movement, Montevideo, Uruguay

Wysham, D. and Makhijani, S. (2008) 'World Bank climate profiteering', *Foreign Policy in Focus*, 31 March

14

The Ecological and Energy Integrity of Corn Ethanol Production

David Pimentel

The supply of 'conventional' oil is projected to peak before 2010 and its decline thereafter cannot be compensated fully by other liquid fuels (Youngquist and Duncan, 2003). Then, during the next 40 years, the oil supply will slowly decline until there is little available. The US has a critical need to develop liquid fuel replacements for oil in the near future. Yet so far the response to this crisis by agricultural and energy industry researchers and government officials has often been misleading and ineffectual.

The search for alternative liquid fuels has focused on the heavily subsidized use of corn (maize) biomass. However, the environmental impacts of corn ethanol are enormous. They include severe soil erosion, heavy use of nitrogen fertilizer and pesticides, and a significant contribution to global warming. In addition, each gallon of ethanol requires 1700 gallons of water (mostly to grow the corn) and produces 6 to 12 gallons of noxious organic effluent. The present enthusiasm for developing plant-based fuels could threaten both our environment and our future food security.

Corn and all other kinds of biomass convert solar energy into plant material but require suitable soil, land area, nutrients and fresh water for growth. Then, in the conversion of the biomass into liquid fuel, water, micro-organisms and more energy are required. Andrew Ferguson (2004) makes that astute observation that the proportion of the sun's energy that is converted into useful ethanol, even using very positive energy data, only amounts to 1 part per 1000, or 0.1 per cent of the solar energy.

In the analysis in this chapter, the most recent scientific data for corn production and for fermentation/distillation are used. All current fossil energy inputs used both in corn production and for fermentation/distillation were included to determine the entire energy cost of ethanol production. Additional costs to consumers include federal and state subsidies that total US$6 billion a year (Koplow, 2006), plus costs associated with environmental pollution and/or degradation that occur during the entire production system. Economic and human food supply issues are also discussed.

ENERGY INPUTS IN CORN PRODUCTION

The conversion of corn and other food/feed crops into ethanol by fermentation is a well-known and established technology. The ethanol yield from a large production plant is about a litre of ethanol from 2.69kg of corn grain (Pimentel and Patzek, 2005).

The production of corn in the US requires significant energy and dollar investment for the 14 necessary inputs, including labour, farm machinery, fertilizers, irrigation, pesticides and electricity (Table 14.1). To produce an average corn yield of 8781kg/ha (140 bushels per acre) of corn using up-to-date production technologies requires the expenditure of about 7.5 million kcal of energy inputs (mostly oil and natural gas), as listed in Table 14.1. This is the equivalent of about 854 litres of oil equivalents expended per hectare of corn. The production costs total about US$892/ha for the 8781kg/ha yield, or approximately 10¢/kg (US$2.58/bushel) of corn produced. At present corn grain is selling for more than US$4.00 per bushel (USCB, 2007).

Table 14.1   *Energy inputs and costs of corn production per hectare in the US*

Inputs	Quantity	kcal × 1000	Cost (US$)
Labour	11.4hrs	462	148.2
Machinery	18kg	333	68
Diesel	88L	1003	34.76
Gasoline	40L	405	20.8
Nitrogen	155kg	2480	85.25
Phosphorus	79kg	328	48.98
Potassium	84kg	274	26.04
Lime	1120kg	315	19.8
Seeds	21kg	520	74.81
Irrigation	8.1cm	320	123
Herbicides	6.2kg	620	124
Insecticides	2.8kg	280	56
Electricity	13.2kWh	34	0.92
Transport	204kg	169	61.2
TOTAL		7543	891.76
Corn yield 8,781kg/ha		31,612	
kcal input:output = 1:4.19			

Source: Pimentel et al (2007)

Full irrigation (when there is insufficient or no rainfall) requires about 100cm of water per growing season. Because only about 15 per cent of US corn production is currently irrigated (USDA, 1997), only 8.1cm per hectare of irrigation was included for the growing season. On average, irrigation water is pumped from a depth of 100m (USDA, 1997). On this basis, the average energy input associated with irrigation is 320,000kcal per hectare (Table 14.1).

ENERGY INPUTS IN FERMENTATION/DISTILLATION

The average costs in terms of energy and money for a large (245 to 285 million litres/year), modern ethanol plant are listed in Table 14.2. In the fermentation/distillation process, the corn is finely ground and approximately 15 litres of water are added per 2.69kg (15 gallons of water per 22 pounds) of ground corn. After fermentation, to obtain a litre of 95 per cent pure ethanol from the 8 per cent ethanol and 92 per cent water mixture, the litre of ethanol must be extracted from the approximately 13 litres of the ethanol/water mixture. Although ethanol boils at about 78°C, and water boils at 100°C, the ethanol is not extracted from

Table 14.2 *Inputs per 1000 litres of 99.5 per cent ethanol produced from corn[a]*

Inputs	Quantity	kcal × 1000	Cost (US$)
Corn grain	2690kg[b]	2314[b]	273.62
Corn transport	2690kg[b]	322[c]	21.4
Water	15,000L	90	21.16
Stainless steel	3kg	165	10.6
Steel	4kg	92	10.6
Cement	8kg	384	10.6
Steam	2,546,000kcal	2546	21.16
Electricity	392kWh	1011	27.44
95% ethanol to 99.5%	9kcal/L	9	0.6
Sewage effluent	20kg BOD	69	6
Distribution	331kcal/L	331	20
TOTAL		7333	423.18

Source: Pimentel et al (2007)

Notes: (a) Output: 1 litre of ethanol = 5130kcal

(b) Data from Table 14.1

(c) Calculated for 144km round trip

the water in just one distillation, which obtains 95 per cent pure ethanol (Maiorella, 1985; Wereko-Brobby and Hagan, 1996; S. Lamberson, personal communication, Cornell University, 2000). To be mixed with gasoline, the 95 per cent ethanol must be further processed and more water removed, requiring additional fossil energy inputs to achieve 99.5 per cent pure ethanol (Table 14.2). Thus a total of about 13 litres of wastewater must be removed per litre of ethanol produced, and this relatively large amount of sewage effluent has to be disposed of at an energy, economic and environmental cost.

To produce a litre of 99.5 per cent ethanol uses 43 per cent more fossil energy than the energy produced as ethanol and costs 42¢ per litre (US$1.59 per gallon) (Table 14.2). The corn feedstock requires more than 33 per cent of the total energy input. In this analysis the total cost, including the energy inputs for the fermentation/distillation process and the apportioned energy costs of the stainless steel tanks and other industrial materials, is US$423.18 per 1000 litres of ethanol produced (Table 14.2).

Net energy yield

The largest energy inputs in corn ethanol production are for producing the corn feedstock, plus the steam energy and electricity used in the fermentation/distillation process. The total energy input to produce a litre of ethanol is 7333kcal (Table 14.2). However, a litre of ethanol has an energy value of only 5130kcal. A net energy loss of 2203kcal per litre of ethanol produced means that 43 per cent more energy (from fossil fuels) is expended than is produced as ethanol. However, this energy deficit might be reduced if ethanol producers were able to provide the low-pressure steam required for distillation from cogeneration power facilities or from solar thermal inputs.

Economic costs

Current ethanol production technology uses more fossil fuel and costs substantially more to produce than its energy value on the market. Clearly, without the more than US$6 billion a year in federal and state government subsidies, US ethanol production would be reduced or cease, confirming the basic fact that ethanol production is uneconomical (National Center for Policy Analysis, 2002; Koplow, 2006).

Federal and state subsidies for ethanol production total about US$6 billion/year to produce 19 billion litres (5 billion gallons) of ethanol (Koplow, 2006). Thus the subsidies per gallon of ethanol total US$1.20. In other words the subsidies per gallon of ethanol produced are 60 times greater than the subsidies per gallon of gasoline.

Unfortunately, the costs to the American consumer are greater than the US$6 billion per year expended to subsidize corn ethanol, because diverting the required corn feedstock from livestock increases corn prices for livestock producers and increases the costs of other related foods. Meat, milk, eggs and other foods will cost consumers 10 to 20 per cent more during 2007.

Proportion of total liquid fuel for vehicle use

Currently, about 19 billion litres of ethanol (5 billion gallons) are being produced in the US each year (Urbanchuk, 2007). The total of vehicle liquid fuel used in the US in 2003 was about 1200 billion litres (Pimentel et al, 2004a; USCB, 2004/5). Therefore the amount of ethanol (having an energy equivalent of 13 billion litres of gasoline fuel) represents only about 1 per cent of total vehicle liquid fuel used in the US.

By-products

The energy and dollar costs of producing ethanol can be offset partially by by-products like the dried distiller's grains (DDG) made from dry-milling of corn. From about 10kg of corn feedstock, about 3.3kg of DDG with 27 per cent protein content can be harvested (Stanton, 1999). This DDG is suitable for feeding cattle, which are ruminants, but has only limited value for feeding pigs and chickens. In practice, this DDG is generally used as a substitute for soybean feed, which contains 49 per cent protein (Stanton, 1999). However, soybean production for livestock feed is more energy-efficient than corn production because little or no nitrogen fertilizer is needed for the production of this legume (Pimentel et al, 2002). In practice, 2.1kg of soybean protein provides the equivalent nutrient value of 3.3kg of DDG. Thus the credit fossil energy per litre of ethanol produced is about 445kcal (Pimentel et al, 2002). Factoring this credit for a non-fuel source into the production of ethanol reduces the negative energy balance for ethanol production from 43 per cent to 28 per cent (Table 14.2). The high energy credits for DDG given in some researchers' calculations are unrealistic, because the production of livestock feed from ethanol is uneconomical given the high costs of fossil energy, plus the costs of soil depletion to the farmer (Patzek, 2004).

In short, the resulting overall energy output/input comparison remains negative even with the credits for the DDG by-product.

Cropland use

When considering the advisability of producing sufficient ethanol for automobiles, the availability of cropland required to grow sufficient corn to fuel each automobile is critical. For the sake of argument we use Shapouri's optimistic suggestion that all natural gas and electricity inputs be ignored and only gasoline and diesel fuel inputs be assessed (Shapouri et al, 2002 and 2004). Based on Shapouri's input/output data, 2929 litres of ethanol are produced per corn hectare. When equated to gasoline, this ethanol has the same energy as 1890 litres of gasoline. An average US automobile travels more than 10,000 miles and uses about 1890 litres of gasoline per year (USCB, 2007). To replace this gasoline usage with ethanol, about 1ha of corn would have to be grown. Consider that at present, 0.5ha of US cropland is used to feed each American a diverse and nutritious diet (USCB, 2007). Therefore, even using Shapouri's optimistic energy accounting data, to fuel one automobile with ethanol, as a substitute for the use of gasoline, two times more cropland would be required for corn production and ethanol production than now is required to feed one American.

Worldwide, for ethanol to replace gasoline, about 2.4 billion hectares of cropland planted to corn would be required. This is 60 per cent more cropland than exists in the world (A. R. B. Ferguson, personal communication, Optimum Population Trust, 6 November 2005).

ENVIRONMENTAL IMPACTS

Some of the economic and energy contributions of the by-products are negated by the widespread environmental pollution problems associated with ethanol production. First, US corn production causes more soil erosion that any other US crop (Pimentel et al, 1995; NAS, 2003). In addition, corn production uses more herbicides and insecticides and nitrogen fertilizer than any other crop produced in the US, and these chemicals invade ground and surface water, thereby causing more water pollution than any other crop (NAS, 2003).

As mentioned, the production of a litre of ethanol requires 1700 litres of fresh water for corn production and for the fermentation/distillation processing of ethanol (Pimentel et al, 2004b). In some western irrigated corn acreage, like some regions of Arizona, groundwater is being pumped 10 times faster than the natural recharge of the aquifers (Pimentel et al, 2004b).

All these factors confirm that the environmental and agricultural system in which US corn is being produced is experiencing major degradation. Further, it substantiates the conclusion that the US corn production system, and indeed the entire ethanol production system, is not environmentally sustainable now or for the future, unless major changes are made in the cultivation of this major food/feed crop. Because corn is raw material for ethanol production, it cannot be considered a renewable energy source.

Furthermore, pollution problems associated with the production of ethanol at the chemical plant sites are emerging. The EPA (2002) has already issued warnings to ethanol plants to reduce their air pollution emissions or be shut down. Another pollution problem concerns the large amounts of wastewater produced by each ethanol plant. As noted above, for each litre of ethanol produced using corn, about 13 litres of wastewater are produced. This polluting wastewater has a biological oxygen demand (BOD) of 18,000 to 37,000mg/litre, depending of the type of plant (Kuby et al, 1984). The cost of processing this sewage in terms of energy (4kWh/kg of BOD) was included in the cost of producing ethanol in Table 14.2.

Reports confirm that ethanol use contributes to air pollution problems when burned in automobiles (Youngquist, 1997; Hodge, 2002, 2003 and 2005; Niven, 2005; Jacobson, 2007). The use of the fossil fuels and ethanol releases significant quantities of pollutants to the atmosphere. Furthermore, carbon dioxide emissions released from burning these fuels contribute to global warming and are a serious concern (Schneider et al, 2002). When all the air pollutants associated with the entire ethanol production system are considered, the evidence confirms that ethanol production contributes to the already serious US air pollution problem (Youngquist, 1997; Pimentel and Patzek, 2005). Investments to control these air pollution problems in the ethanol production plant are possible but will add to the significant production costs of ethanol.

FOOD SECURITY

At present, world agricultural land supplies more than 99.7 per cent of all world food (in terms of calories), while aquatic ecosystems supply less than 0.3 per cent (FAOSTAT, 2004). Worldwide, during the last decade, per capita available cropland decreased by 20 per cent and irrigation land by 12 per cent (Brown, 1997). Furthermore, per capita grain production has been decreasing, in part due to increases in the world population (Worldwatch Institute, 2001). Worldwide, diverse cereal grains, including corn, make up 80 per cent of the food of the human food supply (Pimentel and Pimentel, 2008).

The current food shortages throughout the world call attention to the importance of continuing US exports of corn and other grains for human food. During the past 10 years, US corn and other grain exports have nearly tripled, increasing US export trade by about US$3 billion per year (USCB, 2007). Of course, this is now changing with 20 per cent of US corn going into ethanol production. And the percentage is projected to increase to 30 per cent this year.

The expanding world population, now numbering 6.5 billion, further complicates and stresses the food security problem now and for the future (PRB, 2006). Almost a quarter of a million people are added each day to the world population, and each of these human beings requires adequate food. Today, the malnourished people in the world number about 3.7 billion (WHO, 2000). This is the largest number and proportion of malnourished people ever reported in history. Malnourished people are highly susceptible to various serious diseases, and this is reflected in the rapid rise in the number of people in the world infected with diseases such as tuberculosis, malaria and AIDS, as reported by the World Health Organization (Kim, 2002; Pimentel et al, 2006).

FOOD VERSUS FUEL

Using corn, a basic human food resource, for ethanol production raises ethical and moral issues (Wald, 2006). Expanding ethanol production entails diverting valuable cropland from the production of corn needed to nourish people. Furthermore, there are energetic and environmental aspects, as well as moral and ethical issues, which deserve serious consideration. With oil and natural gas shortages now facing the US, ethanol production is forcing it to import more oil and natural gas to produce ethanol and other biofuels (Pimentel and Patzek, 2005).

Furthermore, increasing oil and natural gas imports drives up the price of oil and gas; this is especially critical for the poor in developing countries of the world. The impact is documented by the fact that worldwide per capita fertilizer use has been declining for the last decade (Worldwatch Institute, 2001).

CONCLUSION

The prime focus of ethanol production from corn is to replace the imported oil used in American vehicles, without expending more fossil energy in ethanol production than is produced as ethanol energy. Using food crops, such as corn grain, to produce ethanol raises major ethical concerns. More than 3.7 billion humans in the world are currently malnourished, so the need for grains and other foods is critical. Growing crops to provide fuel squanders resources; better options to reduce our dependence on oil are available. Energy conservation and development of renewable energy sources, such as solar cells and solar-based methanol synthesis, should be given priority.

In a thorough and up-to-date evaluation of all the fossil energy costs of ethanol production from corn, every step in the production and conversion process must be included. In this study, 14 energy inputs in average US corn production are included. Then, in the fermentation/distillation operation, nine more identified fossil fuel inputs are included. Some energy and economic credits are given for the by-products, including dried distiller's grains (DDG).

Based on all the fossil energy inputs, a total of 1.43kcal of fossil energy is expended to produce 1kcal of ethanol. When the energy value of the DDG, based on the feed value of the DDG as compared to soybean meal, is considered, the energy cost of ethanol production is reduced slightly to 1.28kcal fossil energy inputs per 1kcal of ethanol produced.

Several pro-ethanol investigators have overlooked various energy inputs in US corn production, including farm labour, farm machinery, processing machinery, use of hybrid corn and irrigation. In other studies, unrealistically low energy costs were attributed to such inputs as nitrogen fertilizer, insecticides and herbicides. Controversy continues concerning the energy and economic credits that should be assigned to the by-products.

The US Department of Energy reports that 19 billion litres of ethanol was produced in 2006. This represents only 1 per cent of total petroleum use in the US. These yields are based on using about 20 per cent of total US corn production and 20 per cent of corn land. Because the production of ethanol requires large inputs of both oil and natural gas in production, the US is importing both oil and natural gas to produce ethanol.

Furthermore, the US Government is spending about US$6 billion annually to subsidize ethanol production, a subsidy of US$1.20 per gallon of ethanol produced. This subsidy, plus the cost of producing the ethanol, is calculated to be US$2.80 per gallon. The cost of producing a gallon of gasoline is US$0.53 (US$0.55 with subsidy).

The environmental costs associated with producing ethanol are significant but have been ignored by most investigators in terms of energy and economics. The negative environmental impacts on cropland and fresh water, along with air pollution and public health impacts, have yet to be carefully assessed. These environmental costs in terms of energy and economics should be calculated and included in future ethanol analyses. Our environment and future food security are threatened if we do not change course away from plant-based fuels.

ACKNOWLEDGEMENTS

We wish to express our sincere gratitude to the Cornell Association of Professors Emeriti for the partial support of our research through the Albert Podell Grant Program.

REFERENCES

Brown, L. R. (1997) *The Agricultural Link: How Environmental Deterioration Could Disrupt Economic Progress*, Worldwatch Institute, Washington, DC

EPA (Environmental Protection Agency) (2002) 'More pollution than they said: Ethanol plants said releasing toxins', *New York Times*, 3 May

FAOSTAT (2004) 'Statistical database', Food and Agriculture Organization of the United Nations, Rome

Farrell, A. E., Plevin, R. J., Turner, B. T., Jones, A. D., O'Hare, M. O. and Kammen, D. M. (2006) 'Ethanol can contribute to energy and environmental goals', *Science*, vol 311, pp506–508

Ferguson, A. R. B. (2003) 'Implications of the USDA 2002 update on ethanol from corn', *The Optimum Population Trust* (Manchester, UK), vol 3, no 1, pp11–15

Ferguson, A. R. B. (2004) 'Further implications concerning ethanol from corn', draft manuscript for the Optimum Population Trust, Manchester, UK

Hodge, C. (2002) 'Ethanol use in US gasoline should be banned, not expanded', *Oil and Gas Journal*, 9 September, pp20–30

Hodge, C. (2003) 'More evidence mounts for banning, not expanding, use of ethanol in gasoline', *Oil and Gas Journal*, 6 October, pp20–25

Hodge, C. (2005) 'Government and fuels: Increased air pollution with the consumption of ethanol in gasoline', www.arb.ca.gov/fuels/gasoline/meeting/2005/0502052ndopi, accessed 10 October 2005

Jacobson, M. Z. (2007) 'Effects of ethanol (E85) versus gasoline vehicles on cancer and mortality in the United States', *Environmental Science and Technology*, in press, www.stanford.edu/group/efmh/jacobson/E85PaperEST0207.pdf, accessed 10 October 2007

Kim, Y. (2002) 'World exotic diseases', in D. Pimentel (ed) *Biological Invasions: Economic and Environmental Costs of Alien Plant, Animal and Microbe Species*, CRC Press, Boca Raton, FL, pp331–354

Koplow, D. (2006) 'Biofuels – At what cost? Government support for ethanol and biodiesel in the United States', The Global Subsidies Initiative (GSI) of the International Institute for Sustainable Development (IISD), www.globalsubsidies.org/IMG/pdf/biofuels_subsidies_us.pdf, accessed 10 October 2007

Kuby, W. R., Markoja, R. and Nackford, S. (1984) 'Testing and evaluation of on-farm alcohol production facilities', research done for Office of Research and Development, US Environmental Protection Agency, Cincinnati, OH by Industrial Environmental Research Laboratory, Acurex Corporation

Maiorella, B. (1985) 'Ethanol', in H. W. Blanch, S. Drew and D. I. C. Wang (eds) *Comprehensive Biotechnology* (volume 3), Pergamon Press, New York

NAS (2003) 'Frontiers in agricultural research: Food, health, environment and communities', National Academy of Sciences, Washington, DC, http://dels.nas.edu/rpt_briefs/frontiers_in_ag_final%20for%20print.pdf, accessed 5 November 2004

National Center for Policy Analysis (2002) 'Ethanol subsidies', Idea House, National Center for Policy Analysis, www.ncpa.org/pd/ag/ag6.html, accessed 9 September 2002

Niven, R. (2005) 'UNSW academic criticizes decision on ethanol in petrol', www.unsw.edu./news/pad/articles/2005/sep/Ethanol.html, accessed 9 October 2005

Patzek, T. (2004) 'Thermodynamics of the corn-ethanol biofuel cycle', *Critical Reviews in Plant Sciences*, vol 23, no 6, pp519–567

Pimentel, D. (2003) 'Ethanol fuels: Energy balance, economics and environmental impacts are negative', *Natural Resources Research*, vol 12, no 2, pp127–134

Pimentel, D. and Pimentel, M. (2008) *Food, Energy and Society* (third edition), CRC, Boca Raton, FL

Pimentel, D. and Patzek, T. (2005) 'Ethanol production using corn, switchgrass and wood; Biodiesel production using soybean and sunflower', *Natural Resources Research*, vol 14, no 1, pp65–76

Pimentel, D., Harvey, C., Resosudarmo, P., Sinclair, K., Kurz, D., McNair, M., Crist, S., Sphritz, L., Fitton, L., Saffouri, R. and Blair, R. (1995) 'Environmental and economic costs of soil erosion and conservation benefits', *Science*, vol 276, pp1117–1123

Pimentel, D., Doughty, R., Carothers, C., Lamberson, S., Bora, N. and Lee, K. (2002) 'Energy inputs in crop production: Comparison of developed and developing countries', in R. Lal, D. Hansen, N. Uphoff and S. Slack (eds) *Food Security and Environmental Quality in the Developing World*, CRC Press, Boca Raton, FL, pp129–151

Pimentel, D., Pleasant, A., Barron, J., Gaudioso, J., Pollock, N., Chae, E., Kim, Y., Lassiter, A., Schiavoni, C., Jackson, A., Lee, M. and Eaton, A. (2004a) 'US energy conservation and efficiency: Benefits and costs', *Environment Development and Sustainability*, no 6, pp279–305

Pimentel, D., Berger, B., Filberto, D., Newton, M., Wolfe, B., Karabinakis, E., Clark, S., Poon, E., Abbett, E. and Nandagopal, S. (2004b) 'Water resources: Current and future issues', *BioScience*, vol 54, no 10, pp909–918

Pimentel, D., Cooperstein, S., Randell, H., Filiberto, D., Sorrentino, S., Kaye, B., Nicklin, C., Yagi, J., Brian, J., O'Hern, J., Habas, A. and Weinstein, C. (2006) 'Ecology of increasing diseases: Population growth and environmental degradation', *Human Ecology*, www.springerlink.com/content/b7r4322153106513/fulltext.pdf, accessed 5 October 2007

Pimentel, D., Patzek, T. and Cecil, G. (2007) 'Ethanol production: Energy, economic and environmental losses', *Reviews of Environmental Contamination and Toxicology*, no 189, pp25–41

PRB (2006) 'World population data sheet', Population Reference Bureau, Washington, DC

Schneider, S. H., Rosencranz, A. and Niles, J. O. (2002) *Climate Change Policy Change*, Island Press, Washington, DC

Shapouri, H., Duffield, J. A. and Wang, M. (2002) 'The energy balance of corn ethanol: An update', Agricultural Economic Report No 813, Office of Energy Policy and New Uses, USDA

Shapouri, H., Duffield, J., McAloon, A. and Wang, M. (2004) 'The 2001 net energy balance of corn-ethanol', US Department of Agriculture, Washington, DC

Stanton, T. L. (1999) 'Feed composition for cattle and sheep', Report No 1.615, Colorado State University, Fort Collins, CO

Transportation Research Board (2006) 'Integrating sustainability into the transportation planning process', www.trp.org/publications.conf/CP37.pdf., accessed 16 February 2006

Urbanchuk, J. M. (2007) 'Contribution of the ethanol industry to the economy of the United States', report prepared for the Renewable Fuels Association, www.ethanolrfa.org/objects/documents/2006_ethanol_economic_contribution.pdf, accessed 5 October 2007

USCB (2004/5) 'Statistical abstract of the United States, 2004–2005', US Census Bureau, US Government Printing Office, Washington, DC

USCB (2007) 'Statistical abstract of the United States, 2007', US Census Bureau, US Government Printing Office, Washington, DC

USDA (1997) 'Farm and ranch irrigation survey', Special Studies, Part 1, 1997 Census of Agriculture (volume 3)

Wald, M. I. (2006). 'Corn farmers smile as ethanol prices rise, but experts on food supplies worry', *New York Times*, January 16

Wereko-Brobby, C. and Hagan, E. B. (1996) *Biomass Conversion and Technology*, John Wiley and Sons, Chichester, UK

WHO (2000) 'Nutrition for health and development: A global agenda for combating malnutrition', World Health Organization, www.who.int/nut/documents/nhd_mip_2000.pdf, accessed 3 November 2004

Worldwatch Institute (2001) *Vital Signs*, W. W. Norton and Company, New York

Youngquist, W. (1997) *GeoDestinies: The Inevitable Control of Earth Resources over Nations and Individuals*, National Book Company, Portland, OR

Youngquist, W. and Duncan, R. C. (2003) 'North American natural gas: Data show supply problems', *Natural Resources Research*, vol 12, no 4, pp229–240

15

Global Integrity and Utility Regulation: Constructing a Sustainable Economy

Peter Miller[1]

INTRODUCTION

The Global Ecological Integrity Project is a decades-long interdisciplinary collaboration to elucidate and draw the implications of the vague, but powerful, concept of ecological integrity. From the beginning, a guiding hope of the project has been that it might make a real difference in arresting the steady deterioration of the ecosphere while promoting human wellbeing, first by clarifying the integrity concept, which, like health, combines descriptive and valuational attributes, and then by drawing the ethical, social and practical implications to create more just, sustainable and Earth-friendly ways of life.

Among the earlier findings of the integrity project was this observation:

> *Modern economies have a generic flaw: they fail to take into account, in an integrated way, the facts of human ecology. The Cartesian cultural split between people and nature is expressed in ecological sciences that study every creature except humans, and economic analysis that ignores the total dependence of human economies upon ecological processes.* (Miller and Westra, 2002, pxix)

An adequate response to this deficiency will promote a different understanding of human/nature relationships, and an expanded earth ethic that gives weight to global and intergenerational equity and justice among humans and values the multiple forms of life. The Earth Charter, negotiated globally over the course of a decade, is an inspiring expression of such an ethic (see Chapter 3).

Other requirements for an adequate social response are: revised indicators, measurements and reporting of human and ecological wellbeing (and 'illbeing') to inform us of the consequences of our activities; action-guiding prescriptions consistent with the understanding and values above; and social policies and measures that support appropriate responses to the prescriptions (Miller and Westra, 2002, pxx).

All of these elements are necessary and none is sufficient by itself to effect the changes we seek. In particular, however sophisticated our understanding of the workings of the world and human society and however refined and inspiring our global ethic, until we challenge the behaviours and institutions that govern our affairs and propose alternatives, we will not succeed in reconciling human existence with ecological integrity. We must complete the entire arc from general principles to the measurable behavioural reform of individuals, institutions and societies.

This chapter examines resources of ecological economics to guide reform in the energy sector. We move from an ecological understanding of the economy and principles of sustainability and justice to a reformed energy regime based on full-cost accounting, restructured incentives and energy justice. While Manitoba provides the context, the need to act locally is universal and the analysis is readily adaptable to other contexts. The chapter provides practical answers to the question 'What is required and what social levers are available to reconcile human existence with ecological integrity?'.

AN ECOLOGICAL UNDERSTANDING OF THE ECONOMY

The global ecosphere is an evolving complex system of systems. Human economies are dependent subsystems of the ecosphere, which increasingly degrade the whole. Ecological economics seeks to reform the principles of economics to recognize this dependence and the resulting requirements for long-term human welfare.

The human economy functions within a materially finite planet energized by a continuous stream of solar radiation. An ecological view of the economy pays attention to the material and energy flows in and out of the economy and their sources and fates in the ecosphere. It also attends to the complex goods and services and life-support functions of the ecosphere and harms from disease, disaster, depletion and drought. Through environmental assessments and life-cycle analysis, it examines impacts of the economy on the planet and resultant changes in benefits and harms.

In an evolutionary context, the ecosphere is a system of legacies. Physical and biological processes created the atmosphere, hydrological systems, distribution and concentration of material resources, landscapes, and diverse living systems of which we are a part. These comprise life-support, intrinsic, inherent and utilitarian natural values in our world. In economic terms, nature's legacies are natural capital endowments, which are subject to depreciation.

Goodland and Daly (1995) define environmental sustainability with two rules for waste outputs and resource inputs:

1   *Output rule:*
     Waste emissions from a project or action being considered should be kept within the assimilative capacity of the local [and global, we

might add] environment without unacceptable degradation of its future waste absorptive capacity or other important services.

2   *Input rule:*

a   Renewables: *Harvest rates of renewable resource inputs should be within the regenerative capacities of the natural system that generates them; and*

b   Non-renewables: *Depletion rates of non-renewable resource inputs should be set below the rate at which renewable substitutes are developed by human invention and investment. A portion of the proceeds from liquidating non-renewables should be allocated to research in pursuit of sustainable substitutes.*

Current levels of exploitation far exceed the Earth's carrying capacity (see Chapter 17).

Because economic transactions have impacts on third parties and the ecosphere, evaluating transactions should take into account *externalities* to the transacting parties. Two important standards for economic enterprises are *eco-efficiency* and *sustainability*. Eco-efficiency prescribes that ecological harm and resource depletion be minimized in providing a given level of human benefit. Sustainability prescribes that our use of Earth's resources and ecosystems shall not impair their capacity to provide comparable levels of benefits to future generations. *Environmental assessments, life-cycle analysis* and *full-cost accounting frameworks* are tools to evaluate the eco-efficiency and sustainability of human enterprises and products. They are employed against a background of values and principles, which it is the task of ethics to critique, justify, clarify and advance.

AN EXPANDED EARTH ETHIC:
PRINCIPLES OF SUSTAINABILITY AND JUSTICE

Ethical advocacy operates on a number of fronts. One enterprise is to formulate and promulgate an Earth ethic that broadens and deepens the scope of ethical concern to encompass global residents, future generations and the non-human inhabitants with which we share the planet. The Earth Charter movement is one such initiative.

More 'practical' or 'applied' ethics appeals to acknowledged principles and seeks to alter laws, policies, practices and decisions to better reflect an Earth ethic. In this chapter, we use examples from interventions before Manitoba's Public Utilities Board (PUB) by Resource Conservation Manitoba (RCM) and Time to Respect Earth's Ecosystems (TREE). These environmental non-governmental organizations (ENGOs) promote the application of principles of sustainability and social justice in the strategic planning, economic analysis, rates, fees, and conservation and efficiency programming of Manitoba Hydro and its subsidiary Centra Gas.

Manitoba is fortunate to have a Sustainable Development Act (SDA), which enshrines principles of sustainability (SDA, 1997, Schedules A and B). The SDA is an invaluable anchor for our interventions. The Act's Principles and Guidelines of Sustainable Development include:

- Principle 2, **Stewardship**, which speaks of intergenerational equity;
- Principle 5, **Conservation and Enhancement**: 'Manitobans should (a) maintain the ecological processes, biological diversity and life-support systems of the environment' and '(c) make wise and efficient use of renewable and non-renewable resources';
- Principle 7, **Global Responsibility**: 'Manitobans should think globally when acting locally, recognizing that there is economic, ecological and social interdependence among provinces and nations and working cooperatively, within Canada and internationally, to integrate economic, environmental, human health and social factors in decision-making while developing comprehensive and equitable solutions to problems'; and
- Guideline 1, **Efficient Use of Resources**, which means '(a) encouraging and facilitating development and application of systems for proper resource pricing, demand management and resource allocation together with incentives to encourage efficient use of resources and (b) employing full-cost accounting to provide better information for decision-makers'.

Guideline 1 embodies key prescriptions of ecological economics.

For rate hearings, the dominant concept of equity, *cost responsibility*, prescribes that the revenues from each class (and subclass) of customers should cover the costs for which they are responsible.[2] Over time, equitably distributing costs means future generations should not be burdened with the present generation's costs. RCM/TREE add, as a principle of social justice, that a limited amount of energy is a basic need and a just society addresses the basic needs of its members. Satisfactory energy policy and pricing must provide for the energy needs of the least well off while also promoting sustainability.

CONFRONTING PERVERSE ENERGY PRICING: WHAT'S WRONG WITH SUBSIDIES?

Recognizing that energy is a basic need of individuals and industry, governments have a strong incentive to control the cost of energy through regulatory regimes and subsidies. Although most jurisdictions have some subsidies, such as the failure to include environmental costs, Manitoba is the winner of the subsidy sweepstakes. Manitoba Hydro (www.hydro.mb.ca) boasts the lowest rates in North America, a policy supported by the provincial government and achieved by a combination of relatively low embedded costs from depreciated lower-cost dams built decades ago, subsidization of domestic rates by export earnings, absence of dividends to the owner (Manitoba's government) and reduced taxes as a Crown corporation. Large industrial users are the chief beneficiaries. In 2002, after 11 years of no increases (i.e. real decreases at the rate of inflation), the PUB awarded large industrial users a further 2 per cent rate reduction, thanks to soaring export earnings. Thus Manitoba's electrical rates are a classic example of a perverse subsidy, in which an increase in the value of electricity on the open market leads directly, through the subsidy from exports, to a decrease in the price charged in the domestic market.

Centra Gas, a subsidiary of Manitoba Hydro, passes through to customers the market prices the utility must pay for Alberta natural gas plus additional volume-based transmission and distribution charges to deliver the gas. Extraction, processing, supply and burning of natural gas have a variety of environmental impacts, including GHG emissions, for which customers do not pay. In addition, non-renewable natural gas in the ground becomes depleted as it is consumed. Gas customers are thus 'subsidized' by not having to pay for their external environmental impacts and the depreciation of natural capital, creating environmental and resource deficits imposed on the future. In addition, like its parent corporation, Centra pays no dividends to its provincial owner and no federal or provincial income taxes or federal Large Corporations Tax. By not paying their share of the costs of government, Crown corporations are subsidized by other taxpayers who must pick up the tax burden the Crowns fail to assume. Energy in Manitoba is thus not on a level playing field with other goods and services.

Keeping energy costs in check has been a widely popular policy of the Manitoba government. Why, then, should anyone object to the various subsidies to achieve that objective? The short answer is that it undermines conservation, costs money, harms the economy, is inequitable and harms the environment:

- Energy is wasted because the payback to customers for investments in energy conservation is lower when rates are subsidized and thus the economic incentive to conserve, relative to other investments, is less.
- Wasted energy has economic consequences: (a) Manitobans spend energy dollars on a wasted resource, (b) they export extra dollars from Manitoba to Alberta for wasted gas, and (c) higher-than-needed domestic electricity consumption reduces power available for export at higher rates and reduces the inflow of dollars to Manitoba.
- There are lost opportunities for economic development and job creation from conservation and efficiency investments.
- Less efficient homes and businesses are vulnerable to alarming or crippling rate shocks at times when energy prices spike. The impact of price variability is much less for efficient users and widespread conservation moderates prices as demand declines.

- Low prices attract energy-intensive industry, but massive load growth can decrease Manitoba's wealth by (a) using up more of the power supply otherwise available for profitable export and (b) capturing a larger share of the export subsidy, leaving less for other purposes (or users).
- There is a loss to the government treasury. Economist Michael Benarroch reckoned that, when Alberta became debt-free a few years ago, Manitoba could also have retired its debt had Manitoba Hydro sold power at the same rates as Saskatchewan and invested the extra income in debt retirement (Bennaroch and Grant, 1994).
- Subsidies to electrical rates are distributed in proportion to consumption. Those who consume more get more subsidy (or, less politely, the biggest pig gets the most slop). This is an inequitable distribution of wealth earned by a Crown corporation belonging to all citizens.
- If the energy Crown corporations paid their share of provincial revenues, other taxes that put a drag on job creation could be reduced (for example the payroll tax).
- Wasted natural gas, besides economic costs, has direct environmental impacts, including higher GHG emissions; higher upstream air, land and water impacts; the depletion of an accessible non-renewable resource; increased pressures on extraction in more environmentally sensitive areas of the Arctic and offshore; and accelerated reliance on liquid natural gas, which produces more GHGs from longer shipping and transmission lines and increased energy requirements for refrigeration and regasification.
- Wasted electricity, besides its economic costs, has environmental costs from accelerating construction of new dams and transmission and reducing displacement of coal-generated electricity in Ontario and the US.

RCM and TREE have sought to measure some of these losses and costs in their interventions.

MEASURING WHAT COUNTS

James Karr observes that:

> *Humans depend on an astounding variety of indicators to assess their situation. We monitor and evaluate trends in biological (body temperature, cholesterol, death rates), economic (income, expenditures, stock market profit, inflation rate), and social (numerous crime statistics, adult literacy) terms. ... In all dimensions of life, we use scores of indicators to guide individual and collective decision-making.* (Karr, 2002)

The challenge is to identify and develop reliable indicators of what counts, lest we be led astray in what we seek and are blinded to the consequences of our actions. We need appropriate indicators of human wellbeing, ecological integrity and health, the impact and extent of our utilization of nature's resources, and benefits derived from nature. Examples of such indicators are the genuine progress indicator (GPI), the index of biological integrity (IBI), ecological footprint analysis, and cataloguing, quantifying and monetizing nature's goods and services. Each of these global indicators incorporates and synthesizes a vast number of more particular measurements (Karr, 2002).

The task of developing and validating a full array of measurements and indicators to assess ecosystem condition, human wellbeing and their interplay is daunting. But progress is possible by focusing on a few relevant to the decisions at hand, as we do in the next section. While some reported results are specific to Manitoba, others are more general and most can be adapted to utilities in other locations. The lessons are far-reaching.

EXTERNALITIES AND FULL-COST ACCOUNTING FOR THE CONSUMPTION OF ENERGY

Standard accounting considers monetary gains, losses and the financial status of an enterprise and its components and actions. Full-cost accounting broadens the scope to consider benefits and costs for all affected parties and the environment using multiple values in order to assess a 'triple bottom line'. Lying between standard enterprise accounting and global full-cost accounting are various intermediate assessments that consider an enterprise plus its clients or customers, or an enterprise plus the jurisdiction in which it resides (for example benefits and costs to Manitoba).

RCM and TREE have relied on a number of sources for their analysis of externalities. The Pembina Institute for Sustainable Development has developed a full-cost accounting method called life-cycle value assessment (LCVA), which assesses the environmental and economic performance of a product or process throughout its complete life-cycle (www.lcva.ca). For a Centra Gas intervention, we asked Pembina to produce an abridged LCVA for the provision and consumption of natural gas in Manitoba. Our strategy is to initiate full-cost accounting as a regulatory standard. Debates about methods and values and their continued refinement would then become internal to the process and before the minds of the parties when rates are set and policies are made.

Pembina tabulated an array of life-cycle environmental impacts to land, water and air from the discovery, extraction and processing (in Alberta) and transmission and consumption (in Manitoba) of natural gas. They selected from this array GHG emissions, land change impacts and gas depletion for a partial physical and monetary quantification of externalities.

GHG emission impact costs

Emissions pricing occurs in different ways. One way is to estimate the incremental costs of technologies to reduce emissions. A second is to forecast costs of traded carbon offsets on emerging carbon exchanges. A third method (employed by Pembina) is to estimate incremental damages from anthropogenic climate change and then distribute that cost to emission sources. Because fossil fuel users don't actually pay compensation for the incremental harms attributable to their emissions, these costs, though real and paid by those who suffer harm, are externalities.

Pembina's analysis of GHG emissions uses findings from the European ExternE model as interpreted by Venema and Barg (2003). This bottom–up approach follows the pathway from source emissions via quality changes of air, soil and water to physical impacts and then estimates the monetary benefits and costs associated with those physical impacts.

GHG emissions from the activities of discovering, extracting, processing, delivering and consuming natural gas can reasonably be estimated from monitoring the component activities and infrastructure for the provision and consumption of gas. Based on data from these components, Pembina calculates that a gigajoule (GJ) of gas delivered to and consumed in Manitoba generates 0.065 tonnes of GHGs (CO_2e).

Estimating changes in climate and physical impacts resulting from these emissions is much more difficult and uncertain. Pembina adopts the conservative C$22/tonne CO_2e global damage estimate from the Venema and Barg (2003) study, which translates to C$1.45 per GJ of natural gas burned in Manitoba. (They also provided, for comparison, lower estimates of C$15 and C$10/tonne or C$0.99 and C$0.66/GJ respectively.)

Land impact costs

The discovery, extraction, collection and processing of natural gas produces a variety of land impacts from clearing land for seismic surveys, access roads, and well site and production infrastructure. Pembina calculates that supplying a GJ of gas directly impacts 7.729×10^{-6}ha of land for 30 years.

This quantity can be translated into monetary costs. Recognizing that land impacts can affect ecological services, biodiversity, recreation, and aesthetic and other values, Pembina selected, for illustration only, the more readily monetized forgone timber value (estimated to be C$40,410/ha or C$0.31/GJ).

Depreciation of the natural gas resource

Finally, Pembina provided estimates of natural gas depreciation ranging from C$0.39 to C$1.18/GJ for depletion of this non-renewable resource, based on data from the Canadian System of Environmental and Resource Accounts (CSERA) maintained by Statistics Canada (Statistics Canada, 1997).

Avoided costs and forgone economic benefits (opportunity costs)

The incremental consumption of energy not only adds to emissions load, depletes the resource legacy and otherwise impacts the planet, it also drives the need to build additional infrastructure for energy transmission and distribution, electrical generation, and gas exploration, extraction, collection, refining and pumping. Typically the internal costs of additional plant are higher than depreciated current plant, as construction costs escalate and more difficult and expensive sites are exploited. External costs are likely to be greater too as energy supply lines extend and more remote and fragile parts of the planet are exploited. In 2005, California adopted its 'Methodology and Forecast of Long-Term Avoided Cost(s) for the Evaluation of California Energy Efficiency Programs', which documents the derivation and uses in conservation planning of some of these additional costs (Orans et al, 2004).

Additionally, conservation brings economic benefits, including an economic stimulus from retrofits and other efficiency investments and from reinvestment in Manitoba of money otherwise exported to Alberta for gas (Bailie et al, 2002). Another benefit, based on the price elasticity of gas, is the potential to reduce the cost of gas throughout North America from aggregated conservation efforts that lower demand (Elliott et al, 2003). Failure to conserve loses such benefits.

Externalities and forgone benefits from the consumption of hydroelectricity

A basic difference between the gas and electricity utilities in Manitoba is that the former simply distributes imported natural gas purchased primarily in Alberta, whereas the latter generates its own power for distribution and export. This means that if conservation successfully reduces gas consumption, the gas utility must raise its distribution rates to recover the same revenue to finance the pipes that distribute the gas. For Manitoba Hydro, though, successful conservation that reduces electricity consumption at subsidized prices in Manitoba frees up additional power to export at higher average market rates. Thus the electric utility has an internal economic incentive to succeed in conservation that the gas utility lacks. For this reason, the electric division has been more receptive to our proposals. Indeed a recent rate application proposes for the first time inverted electricity rates for residential customers and large industrial customers that exceed their historical load.

Another difference between gas and electricity consumption in Manitoba is that while the former produces quantifiable greenhouse gas emissions, the latter, using electricity generated 95 per cent from hydroelectric turbines, would appear to produce negligible emissions. In that case one might conclude that, whatever the economic rationale for conservation, there is little environmental rationale. Indeed many Manitobans incorrectly conclude that they are helping mitigate climate change if they switch water and space heating from gas to electricity.

What makes these inferences false is the fact that Manitoba is linked to Ontario, Saskatchewan and the Midwestern states by the electrical grid. As a consequence, power not consumed in Manitoba is exported to places where power comes largely from coal and natural gas generation. Not only is that export profitable, it also displaces fossil fuel-generated power and attendant emissions. So increasing hydroelectric power consumption in Manitoba adds to the production of global GHGs by reducing displacement through exports. Counter-intuitively to most Manitobans (including our politicians), when Manitobans switch from gas to hydroelectric heating, they *increase* global GHGs, because gas burned in a 90 per cent efficient gas furnace in Manitoba produces twice the usable energy of a 45 per cent efficient combined-cycle gas turbine generator. Minnesota will burn at least twice the gas and produce twice the emissions saved in Manitoba to generate additional electricity to replace the power lost from Manitoba. And, of course, that net increase in gas consumption accelerates gas depletion and other environmental impacts. So, although eventually natural gas will have to be replaced by renewable energy sources, our message for the present has been 'conservation *yes*; conversion from gas to electricity for heating, if supplied from the grid, *no*'.

In 2006, RCM and TREE's economist Jim Lazar proposed four scenarios to investigate what might happen if electricity were fully costed and priced:

1   Current embedded (operating and financing) costs with the export subsidy removed would cause a 28 per cent increase in domestic rates.
2   If a CO_2e cost of C\$20/tonne is added to (1), domestic rates would rise by 60 per cent; this would value the opportunity cost of otherwise displacing fossil generation in the US.
3   If Manitobans were charged export market rates for bulk electricity, their rates would rise by 95 per cent.
4   If a CO_2e cost of C\$20/tonne is added to (3), domestic rates would rise by 129 per cent.

Furthermore, under each of these scenarios, a rise in rates would lead to a contraction in domestic demand as wasted energy was squeezed out and the economy made more efficient. This in turn would free up more power for export, thus increasing Manitoba's export earnings and reducing global GHG emissions. In scenario 4, for example, domestic consumption would be expected to decline by a third (assuming a conservative elasticity factor of –0.25). At average prevailing export prices, that power could be sold for C\$388 million of new income for Manitoba.

Of course, despite reduced consumption, domestic customers would also pay a lot more in scenario 4, but that extra revenue could be returned to Manitobans through conservation measures, tax reductions and social services, so there would be no loss of collective wealth on that score. The burden on high energy consumers who could or would not reduce their load would increase, though, while the greatest conservers would be the net beneficiaries. These are precisely the economic incentives required to foster conservation. And, by the principle of cost responsibility, the most equitable pricing system for power is to charge customers the full market and external costs of their energy consumption.

The C$388 million of new export earnings, moreover, would be a net gain to the Manitoba economy. And since the additional export of hydroelectricity from Manitoba would displace fossil fuel generation, global GHG emissions (and resultant damage) would be reduced, creating an estimated C$102 million additional societal value. Thus scenario 4 creates a total annual societal net benefit of C$490 million.

Even if one believes the fourth price scenario is politically untenable and an excessive shock to customers and the economy in the short term, the full-cost accounting exercise provides useful information for decision-makers regarding lost revenue and lost mitigation opportunities through pricing choices.

SOCIAL MEASURES TO PROMOTE SUSTAINABILITY, ECO-EFFICIENCY AND JUSTICE

So far we have examined contributions of ecological economics to an expanded understanding of the human economy and new methods and metrics for reckoning externalities and full-cost accounting. We have also identified relevant principles and prescriptions derived from an Earth ethic to guide energy use. But understanding, principles and measurements are not enough. We need behavioural change. What are the social measures available to promote more sustainable and eco-efficient activities by people and enterprises?

Education and social marketing

Education and social marketing attempt to raise awareness and understanding of the wider consequences of our choices and present alternatives. They can also enhance political support for sustainable policy initiatives – necessary in a democratic society. But without other measures, these initiatives must rely on voluntary compliance to redirect behaviour from harmful practices to more sustainable choices. While that might work with some conscientious souls, it leaves untouched the majority who will not pass attractive opportunities by, whatever the wider social and ecological consequences.

Law and regulation

Garret Hardin recognized that an educated conscience is only one motivation among others and insufficient by itself to create ecologically benign pro-social behaviour by everyone all of the time. One need only look at our addiction to travel by road and air, contributing more than our fair share of emissions to an already overburdened atmosphere, to realize how discrepant actual behaviour is from ecological understanding and values. Indeed the situation is more complex than a battle between conscience and temptation, since travel may be driven by the noblest of reasons – to help in a family emergency or confer on the meaning and implications of global ecological integrity! Unaided conscience cannot forestall the tragedy of the commons. Hardin's solution was 'mutual coercion, mutually agreed upon'. Law and regulation must supplement education and awareness by restricting or prohibiting the most harmful behaviours.

Restructuring economic incentives

Finally, governments and other social institutions can influence behaviour through positive and negative incentives created through economic instruments in their control. Incentives encourage more flexible responses to exceed minimum standards set by regulations by rewarding continuous improvement and penalizing backsliding. For governments, green budgeting, fiscal policy and taxation are economic instruments to influence behaviour by affecting the economic climate within which choices are made. Canada's National Round Table on the Environment and the Economy (NRTEE) calls such measures 'Ecological Fiscal Reform' (EFR), defined simply as 'a strategy that redirects a government's taxation and expenditure programmes to create an integrated set of incentives to support the shift to sustainable development' (NRTEE, 2005). NRTEE previously observed:

> *The federal government [of Canada] has made sustainable development an overarching policy objective, but has only employed to a very limited degree its single most powerful policy instrument – fiscal policy.*

The same can be said for Manitoba. Manitoba's current government, in a province blessed with an abundance of hydroelectric power, has made climate change mitigation a signature policy, but sadly resists the fiscal reform necessary to embed sustainable development principles in the economy. The PUB provides an alternative evidentiary, deliberative and quasi-judicial process better suited to hear reasoned debate than the sausage machine of politics. But whatever venue is available for their advancement, the following policies are responsive to the principles of ecological integrity, sustainability and social justice.

Power smart pricing and policies for energy

What are the elements of an energy regime that is sustainable and just? Most of the components can be gleaned from a search for best practices, subject to further development. Seattle City Light (www.seattle.gov/light/), for example, has exemplary rate structures and energy justice programmes and has gone part way towards full-cost accounting.

Full-cost accounting

- Adopt framework principles of ecological integrity, sustainability and social justice.
- Scope out the array of benefits and harms associated with alternative forms of energy development, production and use.
- Devise measurements and indicators for identified benefits and harms. Quantify and monetize these, where possible, but retain qualitative assessments of those that not quantified. California's avoided cost methodology and the work of the Pembina Institute on life-cycle value analysis and the genuine progress indicator provide examples of this type of analysis.
- Require a full-cost accounting (FCA) analysis that synthesizes the above indicators for energy proposals and portfolios. Employ FCA in evaluating alternative energy and conservation portfolios, energy rate proposals and other energy policies.
- Ensure that FCA assesses not only present and near-term benefits and harms, but also long-term energy impacts and transformations required to address climate change and other major sustainability issues.

Fiscal regimes for energy utilities

- Eliminate rate subsidies that depress energy commodity prices. If subsidies are employed, direct them to making the energy system more sustainable and just.
- In particular, energy utilities and their customers should pay the full costs of running a sustainable enterprise, a fair share of taxes and, in the case of Crown utilities, dividends to the owners. Crown-owned generating utilities like Manitoba Hydro that make a profit from export sales should consider that profit a social dividend for public purposes, not a commodity price subsidy.

Rates and fees

- Energy rates should be high enough to raise revenues adequate not only to cover current operating and financing costs, but also to reduce the utility's debt burden on future customers, provide adequate investments for energy efficiency and renewable alternatives, implement energy justice programmes to address the basic energy needs of the poor, and pay fair taxes and social dividends.

- Energy should be sold with an inverted rate structure to capture equitable shared social benefits in a lower first block, with subsequent blocks high enough to capture the full costs of increasing demand, including internal, environmental and social costs, as identified by FCA. An inverted rate structure provides a stronger incentive to conserve, because the pay-off is greater for savings in the higher tail-block, and is more equitable, because those who don't conserve pay closer to the full costs they impose on the planet and society. See, for example, Seattle City Light, which charges 3.76¢/kWh for the first block and 7.93¢/kWh for additional power.
- To encourage higher efficiency standards in new home construction, institute energy hook-up 'feebates', which charge less efficient buildings a higher fee for hook-ups and lower fees or rebates for increasingly efficient buildings. Ideally building codes will progressively improve to catch up with the evolving higher standards.

Energy conservation, renewable energy and low-income programmes

- Invest to achieve all cost-effective conservation, including externalities and marginal costs in the calculation of avoided costs. Promote innovation in design, construction, retrofitting and programme delivery to improve efficiency and cost-effectiveness and advance progress towards net-zero-energy homes.
- Invest to develop, and make more cost-effective, alternative renewable forms of energy.
- Develop comprehensive programmes to ensure energy justice that meets the basic energy needs of low-income citizens. Such programmes include:
  - inverted rates, to ensure a limited amount of low-cost energy for all citizens;
  - special low-income conservation programmes that provide energy retrofits and education without up-front payments;
  - emergency funds to ensure energy supply when money runs out;
  - special rates, such as Seattle City Light's low-income rates; and
  - links to social service agencies.

CONCLUSION

RCM and TREE have met with partial success in their interventions. The PUB and utilities now acknowledge that they are responsible under Manitoba's

Sustainable Development Act and have just begun to discuss externalities and full-cost accounting. Utility conservation programmes have ramped up greatly in the last few years and a new 'hard-to-reach' programme for low-income customers is about to be rolled out. Finally, Manitoba Hydro recently filed a rate application that proposes inverted rates for residential customers and for energy-intensive industrial customers with new loads. On the other hand, export earnings still subsidize Manitoba's rates and the utilities have so far resisted special rates for low-income customers, preferring instead to try to keep rates as low as possible across-the-board. Because progress is incremental, not big and bold, persistence is required.

In Canada and the US we have waited too long for national governments to act on climate change. There is growing momentum among cities, provinces, states and some businesses, but it is often cast in terms of mid- to long-term goals and demonstration projects. Wanting are effective social measures to redirect economies towards sustainability. Ecological economics offers important insights and tools to lever this change, and energy policy is central to that endeavour. The trick is to find effective points of entry into the public policy process. One such, illustrated in this chapter, is to intervene in regulatory reviews of energy utilities. But the principles and policies identified here can be used in other policy forums as well. If a local organization is willing to intervene, there are national and international resources available to develop the case. Many good ideas and precedents exist on the US West Coast and in other jurisdictions. And there is a growing body of the literature and expertise in energy eco-economics needed to construct a more sustainable economy bringing closer the reconciliation of human existence with ecological integrity.

NOTES

1 This chapter draws on research by RCM/TREE consultants Jim Lazar (consulting economist), Steven Weiss (Northwest Energy Coalition), and Matt McCullough and Amy Taylor (The Pembina Institute for Sustainable Development).

2 Cost responsibility is determined on the basis of a cost of service study (COSS), which is a major component of the utility's filing for the proceedings. Typically, much of the debate revolves around the questions 'Have unnecessary costs been incurred?', 'Have the costs been appropriately assigned?' and 'Are the information and methods employed in the COSS correct?'. Interventions by residential, commercial and industrial consumer groups all aim at trying to reduce the share of the costs borne by their constituents by cost-shifting to other parties or reducing current internal costs overall. In the absence of sustainability and social justice advocates, this dynamic has the tendency to defer and externalize costs, thereby threatening to impose greater costs on the environment and future users of the system and failing to address the energy needs of the poor.

REFERENCES

Bailie, A., Bernow, S., Dougherty, W., Runkle, B. and Goldberg, M. (2002) 'The bottom line on Kyoto: Economic benefits of Canadian action', The Tellus Institute, www.davidsuzuki.org/files/kyotoreport.pdf, accessed 26 November 2007

Bennaroch, M. and Grant, H. (1994) 'Is there a debt crisis in Manitoba?', www.fcpp. org/main/publication_detail.php?PubID=792, accessed 26 November 2007

Elliott, R. N., Shipley, A. M., Nadel, S. and Brown, E. (2003) 'Natural gas price effects of energy efficiency and renewable energy practices and policies', Report No EO32, American Council for an Energy-Efficient Economy, www.aceee.org/energy/ e032execsum.pdf, accessed 26 November 2007

Goodland, R. and Daly, H. (1995) 'Universal environmental sustainability and the principle of integrity', in L. Westra and J. Lemons (eds) *Perspectives on Ecological Integrity*, Kluwer, Dordrecht, The Netherlands

Karr, J. (2002) 'Understanding the consequences of human actions: Indicators from GNP to IBI', in P. Miller and L. Westra (eds) *Just Ecological Integrity: The Ethics of Maintaining Planetary Life*, Rowman and Littlefield, Lanham, MD

Miller, P. and Westra, L. (eds) (2002) *Just Ecological Integrity: The Ethics of Maintaining Planetary Life*, Rowman and Littlefield, Lanham, MD

NRTEE (National Round Table on the Environment and the Economy) (2005) 'Economic instruments for long-term reductions in energy-based carbon emissions', www.nrtee-trnee.ca/eng/publications/energy-based-carbon-emissions/full-report/Section1-Energy-Based-Carbon-Emissions-eng.html#1_2, accessed 26 November 2007

Orans, R., Woo, C. K., Horii, B., Price, S., Olson, A., Baskette, C. and Swisheer, J. (2004) 'Methodology and forecast of long-term avoided cost(s) for the evaluation of California energy efficiency programs', Energy and Environmental Economics, Inc., San Francisco, CA, www.ethree.com/cpuc_avoidedcosts.html, accessed 27 November 2007

SDA (Sustainable Development Act) (1997) web2.gov.mb.ca/laws/statutes/ccsm/s270e.php, accessed 26 November 2007

Statistics Canada (1997) *Econnections: Linking the Environment and the Economy: Concepts, Sources and Methods of the Canadian System of Environmental and Resource Accounts*, Government of Canada, Ottawa

Venema, H. D. and Barg, S. (2003) *The Full Costs of Thermal Power Production in Eastern Canada*, International Institute for Sustainable Development, Winnipeg, Canada, www.iisd.org/pdf/2003/energy_fca_canada.pdf, accessed 26 November 2007

PART V

FUTURE POLICY PATHS
FOR ECOLOGICAL INTEGRITY

Introduction

Laura Westra

The final part of this volume truly demonstrates the depth and breadth of 15 years of interdisciplinary research by the scholars of GEIG. We met, yearly, not to demonstrate the superiority of one argument or one line of research over another, but simply to learn from one another, and to better understand how one's work fits with that of others in different disciplines. The common ground remained the quest for respect for ecological and biological integrity.

Today 'the environment', or more specifically climate change, or at least the frequency of 'natural' disasters, is on everyone's mind, and well represented in all media, political campaigns and policy debates. The issues are so obvious and pressing that they can no longer be ignored. Fifteen years ago we were – at best – tolerated at the fringe of our respective disciplines, as we could only maintain our professional credibility through more 'mainstream' research and publications; today, our concerns are becoming increasingly 'mainstream', although the required radical changes we have been proposing are, unfortunately, far from implementation. In this final part, we hear again the call for radical change, and for its urgent implementation, from some of the diverse voices within our group.

The first one comes from a man who is one of the most respected and loved members of GEIG and one of the founders of the Earth Charter, the theologian ethicist Ron Engel. He argues that what can give us hope in these dark times, and is at the core of our commitment to the salvation of creation, is the 'conviction that the most fundamental relationship we enjoy with one another and the rest of nature is covenantal in character', a conviction traditionally expressed in terms of the 'covenant of life', the 'covenant of being', the 'cosmic covenant', or the 'covenant of creation' – all ways of pointing to the primordial covenant whose life-giving and sustaining laws we are called to accept as our own and upon which all the special covenants of human history ultimately must rest and take their bearings. Engel proposes that the great negations of this covenant in the world-shaking events of the early 20th century led many far-sighted scientists, theologians, statesmen and poets, such as Aldo Leopold and Loren Eiseley, to recover its ancient prophetic roots and launch the international covenantal movements for universal human rights and respect and care for nature in which we now participate.

Our future hope, Engel argues, cannot lie in our efforts alone, but in a renewed covenant with the ultimate creativity of nature itself, as we 'join human responsibility and endeavour with nature's inherent capacities for regeneration and survival'.

In Chapter 17, William Rees brings us back to science, hence to the urgency of the radical message that can be found in the final part of this volume. The message he conveys is radical indeed: 'beyond a certain point, the continuous growth of the human enterprise must inevitably destroy the substance and functional integrity of the very ecosystems that sustain it'. Rees's purpose, he writes, is to show the other side of the coin, to explain in no uncertain terms what is missing from the common perspective on economic and technological 'progress'.

If, as Rees demonstrates, all economic activity is 'more consumption than production', that is if all economic growth has the essential effect of reducing our ecological capital, then, clearly, even in simple economic terms, bankruptcy is the final result. GEIG's committed plea to respect and protect integrity is thus fundamentally incompatible with the gospel of 'growth' that our hubris provides to our society today.

In the next chapter, Richard Westra acknowledges that GEIG is 'seeking to synchronize human activity with eco-sustainability', and that, as well as articulating that final goal, the group's work is focused on the steps required in order to achieve that goal. Neoclassical economics and the institutional framework of a capitalist society have failed dismally at their self-avowed task of operating for the betterment of mankind. Any system of institutions and any theoretical framework that ignores the basic scientific realities in which all human activity is grounded is bound to fail.

Richard Westra proposes replacing the present system with an 'eco-sustainable, economically viable, tri-sector Utopian society', which may, or may not, be viewed as a form of socialism.

In the final chapter, Klaus Bosselmann proposes once gain the need for a solid ethical foundation for novel forms of governance for eco-integrity. First and foremost must be the acceptance of our individual and collective responsibility to the community of life. Only then might it be possible to ensure that responsibility might also be incorporated in legal theory and institutionalized in the legal system. Key areas for this attempt concern the concepts of justice and human rights.

16

What Covenant Sustains Us?

J. Ronald Engel

The woods are lovely, dark and deep.
But I have promises to keep,
And miles to go before I sleep,
And miles to go before I sleep.
(Robert Frost, 1923)

HOPE

We live in grief for the desecration and loss of life, human and more-than-human. As I write these lines on 25 October 2007, the United Nations Environment Programme (UNEP) issues an all-too-familiar claim: 'The human population is living far beyond its means and inflicting damage to the environment that could pass points of no return.' Twenty years after the Brundtland Commission's seminal report, it concludes: 'There are no major issues raised in *Our Common Future* for which the foreseeable trends are favourable' (UNEP, 2007).

International economist Nicholas Stern is even more pointed. The crisis of climate change, he concludes in his 2006 review of the issue for the British Government, could create 'risks of major disruption to economic and social activity on a scale similar to those associated with the two world wars and the economic depression of the first half of the twentieth century' (Stern, 2007, p640).

Hope is on everyone's minds in the opening years of the 21st century. We need to believe that 'another world is possible' if we are to work for a reconciliation of human existence and ecological integrity. But where do we find it?

At the age of 90, asked what gives him hope, Barry Commoner replied, 'I'm an eternal optimist, and I think eventually people will come around' (Vinciguerra, 2007). That is not enough for most of us, and we may doubt if it was enough to sustain Commoner's lifelong dedication to 'closing the circle' of humanity, nature and technology. Commoner, a biophysicist, was one of the most outspoken scientists among the public intellectuals of the post-World War II epoch, pioneering the path taken by many members of the Global Ecological Integrity Group (GEIG). He was also a strong advocate of human rights, social justice and peace and a determined witness to the potential of deliberative citizen democracy – and he knew the meaning of defeat.

Vaclav Havel, who has experienced more than his share of defeat, severs the link between hope and optimism: 'Hope is definitely not the same thing as optimism. It is not the conviction that something will turn out well, but the certainty that something makes sense, regardless of how it turns out (Havel, 1996, p181).

Some believe matters are so desperate that we should avoid thinking in terms of hope at all. Derrick Jensen (2006) argues in his book *Endgame*:

> *We're losing badly, on every front. Those in power are hell-bent on destroying the planet, and most people don't care. ... Frankly, I don't have much hope. But I think that's a good thing. [There is] false hope, that suddenly somehow the system may inexplicably change ... and there is hope as a longing for a future condition over which you have no agency; it means you are essentially powerless.*

So what sustains Jensen in these dark times? 'I'm in love', he writes, 'with salmon, with trees outside my window, with slender salamanders crawling through the duff. And if you love, you act to defend your beloved' (Jensen, 2006, p325).

If hope means a belief that the system is suddenly going to change, or a longing for a future condition over which we have no agency, we must agree with Jensen – hope is of little use, and may, in fact, be damaging. We can also agree that we must fight for what we love. But it is precisely because people like Jensen love this planet that the rest of us find hope, and because not enough people are like him that we despair.

Each year for 15 years, GEIG has met because its members have hope and because they need to find again the hope they once had. Keeping hope alive is a daily struggle and we look to one another for help. What gives the members of our group hope?

I offer this meditation as one response to that question, and perhaps to repay some of the debt I owe to those who have helped me keep my hope alive over the years. What I have to share is inevitably shaped by my individual circumstances, yet it has been through the sharing of our different personal and disciplinary perspectives that the members of GEIG have found a larger common ground than any of us could ever have found alone, and the hope to go on.

THE RELIGIOUS QUESTION

The question of hope at the level we are discussing it – our hope for the reconciliation of human existence and ecological integrity, universal human rights and biospheric flourishing, in a word for the 'salvation' of the Earth – is a religious question. Indeed, it is *the* religious question.

The religious perspective differs from all other perspectives in that it asks the most comprehensive of all questions: 'What is our relationship, as creatures, to what ultimately creates, sustains and heals our being?' And after asking this question of questions, it bears down hard, with particular urgency, on the soteriological question: 'What can give our lives meaning in the face of suffering and evil and lead us to the greatest good which humans can attain in their co-evolution with the rest of life on this planet?' It asks these questions with explicit recognition of the full majesty and tragedy of the human condition. All creatures, human and other, are endowed with unique powers of generation, resilience and beauty. Humans are creatures endowed with remarkable powers of self-consciousness, cultural creativity and devotion, and yet we also undergo both (1) the suffering of our inevitable perishing, and the perishing of every person, organism, place and thing that we love, including the knowledge that our lives are unfinished projects, that we die too soon, and (2) the suffering that is unnecessary, which we know as 'evil', the violence that we as the most violent of species wreak upon the planet, one another and innocent newborns (whose placental blood contains no less than 28 toxic chemicals). Our difficulty in facing and accepting the first suffering is undoubtedly a major factor in the second, since so much of the blood-letting of human history has come from the fear of death and the vain effort to escape it by amassing power over others.

When we speak of hope we are asking whether we have reason to believe that the creative powers with which we are endowed are a match for the suffering we endure and the evil we commit – whether what is ultimately creating and sustaining is also redeeming; whether 'salvation' is possible.

The anguish we feel when we try to answer this question is one reason for the growing interest in religion and ecology. Scholars are attending to what different religious traditions believe about creation and evolution. They are uncovering the resources each offers for nurturing respect and care for life. This is a welcome development. But if we stop short and restrict the religious question to self-ascribed 'religious' institutions and traditions, we risk blunting our grasp of just how serious our predicament is – how the question of salvation runs through all our institutions right into the centre of our collective life. We have failed our common creation. Therefore it is not only as members of this or that particular religion, but as citizens, members of communities and nations and a global civil society, that we are faced with the question of finding trustworthy grounds for hope.

RELIGIOUS NATURALISM

Most of us in GEIG hope for something at once quite modest and quite extraordinary. The 'greatest good which humans can attain in their co-evolution with the rest of life on this planet' is not deliverance from suffering or final victory over evil, as some religious traditions claim, but a planet graced by a civilization that takes whatever actions natural and historical circumstances allow to sustain the integrity of the evolutionary process and the dignity of its creatures – the impossible possibility of humankind actively seeking, in the midst of inevitable suffering and evil, a 'sustainable and just world'. Heaven on Earth!

We may call this the answer of religious naturalism, which may, or may not, entail a belief in God as an entity or power prior to, or transcendent of, the natural order. Dietrich Bonhoeffer's 'this-worldly Christianity' is as much a testament to religious naturalism as the evolutionary humanism of scientists such as Julian Huxley, as is evident in one of his 1943 letters from a Berlin prison to his fiancée:

> When Jeremiah said, in his people's hour of direst need, that 'houses and fields shall again be bought in this land' [Jer. 32:15], it was a token of confidence in the future. That requires faith, and may God grant it to us daily. I don't mean the faith that flees the world, but the faith that endures in the world and loves and remains true to that world in spite of all the hardships it brings us. Our marriage must be a 'yes' to God's Earth. It must strengthen our resolve to do and accomplish something on Earth. I fear that Christians who venture to stand on Earth on only one leg will stand in heaven on only one leg too.
> (Bonhoeffer and von Wedemeyer, 1995, p64)

The religious naturalist accepts our tragic predicament as somehow inherent in the life process and proceeds to come to terms with this fact, not through circumvention, but through such participation in the creative effort to sustain and create value as the human situation, in all its mingled pathos and beauty, affords.

Knowing as we do that life will be ever so quickly and inevitably snatched from us, knowing as we do that at this very moment it is being so thoughtlessly and cruelly snatched from so many millions of others, human and other than human, we praise and bend our labours to the preservation and renewal of life and in this praise and bending find what is ultimately sacred, true and good in existence.

Such hope relinquishes any expectation that the human species is the end of evolution, or that its destiny is to humanize the planet or colonize the universe. But it does recognize that we are creatures blessed with capacities for creative self-consciousness, love and action; that we can discover meanings that transcend our grief, and learn ways to contain the evil our species visits on the world so that the abundance of earthly existence is made more secure and widely shared.

THE COVENANT OF LIFE

What enables persons to live this kind of life, to attain this kind of salvation, to be blessed with such hope? What led Chico Mendes and Ken Saro-Wiwa to sacrifice their lives for ecological integrity and social justice in the Brazilian rainforest and on the Niger Delta?

Each of us will have a different way of speaking about what we all must acknowledge is a vast mystery. My own view is that this kind of commitment results from the conviction that the most fundamental relationship we enjoy with one another and the rest of nature is covenantal in character. Each of these persons, and countless others, gave their lives for the communities and places to which they felt covenantally bound.

This is a metaphysical as well as an empirical claim. It involves an intuition that the inclusive wholes in which we participate are ultimately covenantal in character, which is to say that the cosmos, the Earth and the places we inhabit are integrated with an integrity not of a machine, or an organism, but of a community composed of semi-autonomous beings, each of value to itself, to the others and to the whole, and bound by mutual loyalties to the fulfilment of every member and the relationships that join them. The covenantal worldview reconciles human existence and ecological integrity in one unified moral and natural order whose realization is both the precondition and the outcome of the unique vitality of each unique individual and life-form. This intuition is traditionally expressed in terms of the 'covenant of life', the 'covenant of being', the 'cosmic covenant' or the 'covenant of creation' – all ways of pointing to the primordial covenant whose life-giving and sustaining laws we are called to accept as our own and upon which all the special covenants of human history ultimately must rest and take their bearings (Engel, 2007a).

There are other metaphors for the relational whole in which all creatures live, die and have their being, and for bridging 'is' and 'ought', nature and human morality; each, like 'covenant', with its special insights and limitations: 'oikos', 'cosmopolis', 'natural law', 'higher law', 'orchestral causality or Earth symphony', 'commonwealth', 'Dharma', the 'Tao', the 'order of being', 'web of life', 'tree of life', 'Gaia', 'Indra's net', 'circle of life', 'economy of nature'. Members of GEIG have drawn directly or indirectly on a number of these images, especially the tradition of natural law (Westra, 1994, pp92–97).

At this moment of Earth's history, the metaphysical-moral vision of covenant is an especially illuminating and rich metaphor for both describing the biosphere and prescribing our relationship to it and to one another. By its doctrine of internal relations, whereby 'relations are not extraneous to an agent; they are, in important ways, constitutive, albeit not wholly determinative, of an agent's being and character', it provides a way to bridge our obligations to preserve and restore the integrity of ecosystems and our obligations to defend human rights and achieve justice in our relations to other persons and society at large (Sturm, 2000, p2). It is congruent with current evolutionary science, as it characterizes nature not as a static reality, but as a matter of multiple competing self-organizing processes and histories. Covenants are regenerative, open to critical reform in light of new evidence and reasoned argument; in this way they maintain morally justified continuity, purpose, memory and hope in an ever-changing, ever-perishing, ever-new world. Most important, as the examples of Mendes and Saro-Wiwa suggest, a covenant tests to the utmost the commitment of *Homo sapiens* to the wellbeing of the planet. Covenants, like declarations, are built on arguments and judgements regarding what is truly just, right and good; but in contrast to mere statements of 'moral consensus', they commit persons and organizations to be accountable to one another for enacting these values in individual and public life. The idea of covenant is a powerful heuristic tool for understanding why, of the thousands of charters and agreements, some succeed and others fail. Charters and declarations of moral principle do not of themselves change the world; only the covenants that bear them do.

History is nothing so much as a clash and contest of covenants. We consent to, or dissent from, the covenants into which we are born; we keep, break, betray and reform covenants; we give our loyalty to the demonic covenants of superiority, exclusivity and exceptionalism that wreak such havoc in the world, or we try to make new covenants for the sake of more sustainable and just futures. The struggle for human salvation is a struggle for covenants that are truly universal, enduring and life-giving – covenants of gratitude, humility, care, respect, truthfulness, dialogue, steadfastness and loving kindness. These are the terms on which humans can be contributing members of the covenant of life.

I first recognized the significance of the covenant of life for my own sense of moral vocation at a conference in 1990 leading up to the Earth Summit. I was on a panel of religious leaders, and asked how we were personally responding to the environmental crisis, I found myself spontaneously blurting out:

> *Once one begins to locate oneself directly in response to the fate of this Earth, one finds oneself making new covenants. At the deepest level, I have been making new covenants.*
>
> *This means I have become increasingly aware internally of the thousands of human beings who have lived on this Earth and who have loved this Earth and who never thought that it might come to an end or of the destructive consequences that now are so evident to us. I have tried to make a covenant with those people, with that past, with their hopes, and with the future generations they laboured so hard to bring forth. ...*
>
> *This finally involves one's relationship to life itself. And so a term that has become very important to me personally is keeping faith with life.*
> (Rockefeller and Elder, 1992, p177)

If we follow the implications of this line of thought, we are led to the conclusion that our best hope for reconciling human existence and ecological integrity lies in the peoples of the world undergoing a transformation of consciousness that is religious in quality and committing themselves to the all-embracing covenant of life, incorporating it into the more special and explicit covenants of their personal and social lives.

If my fellow members of GEIG frequently assume the 'prophetic' voice in their speaking and writing, it is because they believe everything finally hangs on human adherence to the moral demands of the covenant of life. If we keep the covenant, we and the Earth may prosper. If we violate the covenant, we and the Earth are certain to suffer. It is incumbent upon us to come to the aid of those who are excluded from the covenant and denied its rights and benefits and to condemn the faithlessness of those who waste the Earth's resources and violate its limits. We must bear witness to the enduring beauty and promise of life in the midst of suffering and evil, and find ways to enable others to see and embrace the true source of their salvation.

THE COVENANTAL HISTORY IN WHICH WE STAND

I have long had the conviction that this great metaphoric leap of the human imagination, that the world is a covenantal reality, sustained by covenant-making, covenant-sustaining, covenant-fulfilling powers, which some dare call 'God' and others simply 'creative evolution', found new cogency in the middle of the 20th century when the full impact of the carnage of two world wars and countless other atrocities visited on humans and nature penetrated our global consciousness.

John Elder employs the term 'covenant of loss' to describe the deep bond that forms between persons sensitive to the brokenness of humans and nature, and he finds its most notable modern English-language expressions in the writings of environmental poets and writers such as William Wordsworth, George Perkins Marsh and Robinson Jeffers. 'By looking steadfastly into and through loss', Elder observes, persons become aware of the enduring covenants of life – aware, in the words of George Perkins Marsh, of the reality that 'all nature is linked together by invisible bonds and every organic creature, however low, however feeble, however dependent is necessary to the well-being of some other among the myriad forms of life with which the Creator has peopled the Earth' (Elder, 2006, pp39, 44); or, in the poetry of Robinson Jeffers:

> *Integrity is wholeness,*
> *the greatest beauty is*
> *Organic wholeness, the wholeness of life and things, the divine beauty*
> *of the universe. Love that, not man*
> *Apart from that, or else you will share man's pitiful confusions,*
> *or drown in despair when his days darken.*
> (Jeffers, 1938)

Out of the sympathy that arises from our grief at the losses of history comes an ever-deeper appreciation for the community of humans and nature and renewed determination to recover, restore and realize its promise. As Elder (1998, p20) writes, 'love grows with the growing recognition of perpetual brokenness'.

Although successive empires and waves of colonial expansion devastated humans and natural communities throughout the world prior to the 20th century, most people's experience of loss was local. When war became literally worldwide, the line between the inevitable dissolution of life and the tragedy which humans wilfully visit on life blurred into one fearful possibility – the extinction of life and civilization as such – and loss became, for the first time in history, a global experience. Robert Oppenheimer made this famously clear when, in response to the explosion of the first atomic bomb, he thought of a line from the Bhagavad-Gita: 'Now, I am become Death, the destroyer of worlds.'

People the world over, whether they named it such or not, experienced the devastation of the early 20th century as a new revelation of God's Word, speaking through the Earth itself, calling humanity to repentance and covenantal responsibility for creational survival and planetary citizenship. As Chicago theologian Bernard Meland wrote in his 1947 book *Seeds of Redemption*:

> *Something radically redemptive must occur within five years or less, changing in decisive ways, if not the hearts of men, at least their ways and organized efforts. No one is really realistic who has not faced the possibility of the utter end of this human venture as history has known it. ... Modern man needs to be pressed back to the most elemental events in his life again and again by way of recovering some measure of cosmic expanse in his living and, more particularly, to retain a vivid sense of his own creatureliness and his dependence upon that which daily sustains him'. [We need to make an] act of repentance [that] reaches the depth of a full confession in our culture – so deep that it will cause us to cast out the pride we feel in being so powerful a nation; so great that we will be obsessed with aversion to bigness, competitive gain, possessiveness; so great that we will feel moral indignation at acquisitiveness ... so great that the elemental reverence for life, to use Schweitzer's phrase, will well up in our being to repudiate all acts, decisions and organizations that seek to prostitute life for what is less than life.* (Meland, 1947, pvii)

We need to see our work today for global ecological integrity, universal human rights, democracy and peace as a continuation of the great international covenant-making process set in motion by the events that occurred between the beginning of the First World War in 1914 through the years immediately following the end of the Second World War in 1945. The references we sometimes hear to the 'great turning', or the new 'axial' or 'global' age, most accurately apply not to the beginning of the 21st century, but to the founding of the League of Nations (1919) and the United Nations (1945) and the subsequent efforts of dedicated individuals to create a system of international law and a network of international civil society organizations, with all their associated declarations and charters of global covenantal commitment.

It is instructive to note, in this regard, that the idea of a 'World Convention for the Protection of Nature', or a 'World Charter inspired by the Universal Declaration of Human Rights', which bore fruit in 1982 with the adoption by the United Nations General Assembly of a World Charter for Nature, and the subsequent launch in 2000 of the Earth Charter, the unofficial 'manifesto' of the Global Ecological Integrity Group, was originally proposed by Julian Huxley at the IUPN-UNESCO Conference on the Protection of Nature, held in parallel with the United Nations Scientific Conference on the Conservation and Utilization of Natural Resources (UNSCCUR), a meeting of 4000 scientists and natural resource experts brought together by the United Nations' Economic and Social Council (ECOSOC) at Lake Success, New York, in 1949. IUPN was the acronym for the International Union for the Preservation of Nature, founded in 1948, the forerunner of the International Union for the Conservation of Nature and Natural Resources (IUCN). The protection and sustainable use of nature, human rights, democracy and peace were integrated concerns from the earliest years of the United Nations and the World Conservation Union (Holdgate, 1999).

Of course, there were anticipations of these ideals and movements well before our present era. The First Peoples of the world, the Hebrew prophets, Confucius, the Buddha, Plato and Jesus all staked out audacious claims for a community generous enough to include not only kin and neighbours but Earth as a whole, if not the cosmos itself. The great tradition of natural law and rights that inspired the 18th-century revolutions, Emmanuel Kant's 'Perpetual Peace', the revolutions of 1848, the rise of Darwinian evolutionary science documenting the unity of life, the International Hague Conventions of 1899 and 1907, these and innumerable other events brought the peoples of the world closer to embracing a deliberate commitment to our planetary integrity. And, in spite of devastating betrayals and setbacks, there have been progressive turns since – the 1972 Stockholm Conference and the 1992 Rio Summit, for example – and evidence of a growing global civil society well ahead of most political and economic leaders and determined 'to remake the world' (Hawken, 2007).

But the cradle of concern for our present epoch, when large numbers of people realized that our sense of loss was not only for this place or this society, but for all places and all societies, and that ecological integrity and world community were not only goals to be achieved but the sustaining and saving reality of our existence, occurred in the course of these mid-20th-century years when the world witnessed an unprecedented scale of suffering and loss. Here was the beginning of the global era in which we still live, the history for which we are specifically and concretely responsible, the covenantal struggles to which we are bound.

AMERICAN PROPHETS

If we are going to realize the covenantal promise of reconciling human existence and ecological integrity, we will need to understand the cultural and symbolic systems of each of our respective societies and discover their unique sources of global concern and commitment. We must reclaim these core motivational foundations if we are to renew and expand the international covenants that are currently being so severely tested (Engel, 2007b). We each must take responsibility for the covenants of our own societies.

Americans collectively still account for one-quarter of greenhouse gas emissions, American military and economic power impacts the world to such a degree that peoples throughout the world may justly claim a right to cast a ballot on 4 November 2008, and few events have been more damaging to the founding covenantal commitments of the post-war years than the withdrawal of the US from international treaties and cooperation. It is therefore incumbent on those of us who are American citizens to take responsibility for our nation's betrayals and bring to the centre of public consciousness the examples and ideals of those Americans who embraced the global covenant of loss, recovery and restoration and provided an alternative narrative for our society. Such persons, of course, never acted merely as Americans; they acted in concert with covenanted partners of other nations and participated in international cultural and political movements from which they drew inspiration and to which they contributed.

The same can and should be said of exemplary world citizens within every nation across the planet.

Two Americans who lived through the life-crushing years of the first half of the 20th century, and who were 'pressed back to the most elemental events' in human and natural existence, recovering 'some measure of cosmic expanse' and 'a vivid sense of [their] creatureliness and ... dependence upon that which daily [sustained them]', were Aldo Leopold (1887–1948), a forester and wildlife ecologist and Loren Eiseley (1907–1977), an anthropologist. Leopold's 'land ethic', set forth in *A Sand County Almanac* (1949), was the beginning of the focus on integrity by GEIG (Westra, 1994). For many of us growing up in the US in the post-war years, Eiseley's collections of poetic essays, beginning with *The Immense Journey* (1957), led us to see the religious questions posed by humanity's destructive impact on Earth's evolution.

Leopold and Eiseley were members of a remarkable group of public intellectuals, scientists and naturalists who brought a concern for the fate of the biosphere into the larger public conversation. They and others who shared their concern for reconciling human existence with ecological integrity would readily qualify as religious naturalists. Among their number were Rachel Carson, who, as an aquatic biologist at the US Fish and Wildlife Service, became concerned for the impact of DDT on food chains as early as 1945 and whose eloquent writings – *Under the Sea-Wind* (1952), *The Edge of the Sea* (1955) and *Silent Spring*

(1962) – brought issues of chemical and other environmental contamination into the mainstream of American culture; Barry Commoner, who as a Navy lieutenant helped pass the Atomic Energy Act of 1946 that mandated civilian control of nuclear research and development, and who then went on to advocate a holistic non-reductionistic approach to the unity of the ecosphere and the primacy of the 'natural living organism'; Lewis Mumford, a polymath whose *oeuvre*, ranging across philosophy, theology, history, social science, natural science, politics, urban planning and the arts, was motivated by the question he famously pressed in *Values for Survival* (1946) – 'What must modern man do to be saved in face of the reality of radical evil?' – and the answer he consistently gave – only by embracing an organic 'doctrine of the whole' can humanity and the Earth be freed from the oppression of the mega-machine of industrial capitalism, militarism and nationalism; Fairfield Osborn, whose book *Our Plundered Planet* (1947) first loudly sounded the alarm for the 'silent worldwide war' humanity was waging on itself and the planet, who helped introduce the new science of ecology to the UNSCCUR Conference at Lake Success in 1949 and who co-founded the International Union for the Preservation of Nature; Donald Culross Peattie; Paul Sears; William Vogt; the list goes on. And always in the background were Franklin and Eleanor Roosevelt, without whose steadfast support for the United Nations, universal human rights and conservation of natural resources, the post-war American response may never have got off the ground.

WISCONSIN JEREMIAH

Leopold was a unique member of this community, because he deliberately chose, like the prophet Jeremiah of old, to symbolically enact the covenant of loss, recovery and restoration in the most direct personal and physical terms available to him, and then to explain to the world in tight Anglo-Saxon scriptural prose (preferring, for example, the language of 'land' to 'ecosystem'), the universal significance of what he did.

In 1935, in the deep of winter, Leopold purchased an abandoned farm in Sauk County, Wisconsin. The spent fields were poor, sandy and mostly barren, the farmhouse had burned down, and only a chicken coop, later to be rehabilitated as camping quarters for the Leopold family and dubbed the 'shack,' remained standing. Over the following 13 years, until his premature death in 1948, this was the site for Leopold's hands-on labours to redeem the Earth:

> *on this sand farm in Wisconsin, first worn out and then abandoned by our bigger-and-better society, we try to rebuild, with shovel and axe, what we are losing elsewhere ... and still find our meat from God.*
> (Leopold, 1949, pix)

Do we not find a deep resonance here with Bonhoeffer's letter written during the same Earth-shaking years?

> *When Jeremiah said, in his people's hour of direst need, that 'houses and fields shall again be bought in this land' [Jer. 32:15], it was a token of confidence in the future.* (Bonhoeffer and von Wedemeyer, 1995, p64)

Leopold poured his life's driving ambition, what he described at one point as 'the oldest task in human history to live on a piece of land without spoiling it', into this place and project. Early in his career as a forester he had confronted the devastating reality of soil erosion and ecological degradation on range lands in the American southwest, and when he moved to Wisconsin in 1924 he brought all his knowledge and questions regarding its causes and cures with him. He also brought first-hand experience of healthy land from wild areas that retained their ecological integrity, areas like the Gila Forest in New Mexico and the Sierra Madre in Mexico, and these served as a standard for his goals of land preservation and conservation.

All of this, but especially the joy he found in the wild beauty that endured in the Wisconsin landscape in spite of its brokenness, found expression in *A Sand County Almanac*. In the conclusion of the book, the 'Upshot', Leopold shared his thoughts on the moral lessons of his experience, his famous proposal for a land ethic that made ecological integrity a first principle of environmental ethics: 'A thing is right when it tends to preserve the integrity, stability and beauty of the biotic community. It is wrong when it tends otherwise.' (Leopold, 1949, p224).

By 'land' and 'biotic community' Leopold meant soil, water, plants, animals and people collectively; by 'stability' he meant the capacity of the land to cycle nutrients efficiently and continuously because its biotic pyramid was intact and its food circuits were open; by 'integrity' he meant that the land possessed all the parts, structural relationships and capacities needed to perpetually regenerate itself and successfully evolve under changing conditions; and by 'beauty' he meant the 'pleasing appearance to the eye, ear and soul' of land that possesses stability and integrity (Newton, 2006, p347).

Leopold took a critical attitude to all the classic literature, including scripture, and *A Sand County Almanac* includes a strong scientific and ethical critique of what he considered a biblically inspired narrative of 'Abrahamic land conquest'. At a deeper level, however, it is not difficult to see in his interpretation of the 'biotic community' and the 'land ethic' a modern science-based interpretation of the biblical understanding of an aboriginal covenant between God, people and the Earth, and to surmise that he personally identified with the vocation of the Hebrew prophets in their effort to call the people back to obedience to the eternal moral law written in nature. In 1920, Leopold published an essay, 'The forestry of the Prophets', in which he described Ezekiel's 'doctrine of conservation': 'Seemeth it a small thing unto you to have fed upon the good pasture, but yet must tread down with your feet the residue of your pasture? And to have drunk of the clear waters, but yet must foul the residue with your feet?' He noted how Ezekiel had knowledge of 'forest types and the ecological relation of species' (his first mention of the word 'ecology', still a new science emerging from its infancy), clearly implying that ecology was a way of understanding as old as Ezekiel (Meine, 1988, p184).

The 'place' and 'plot' of *A Sand County Almanac* embrace the struggle for ecological integrity and land health not only at the shack, or in Wisconsin's Sauk County, or even in North America, but in the world at large. From the first page of the foreword, when Leopold claims the right to nature is as inalienable a right as the right to free speech, through his references to Roosevelt's four freedoms and the imagery of responsible land citizenship in the body of the text, to his concluding reflections on the land ethic in the context of human social evolution, it is clear that he has his eye on the interconnections of the local and the global and the challenges of building a democratic world community. In 1946, he and other leaders of the Wilderness Society set a new agenda for the society that included 'Cooperation in World Government'. That same year Leopold drafted a conservation programme for a political party organizing under John Dewey and A. Philip Randolph, and served as chairman of a new Committee on Foreign Relations within the Wildlife Society. In his first draft resolution to the committee members, he stated that 'this Committee wishes to assert flatly its belief that provincialism is as dangerous in the wildlife field as in any other' (quoted in Meine, 1988, p480).

STAR THROWERS

Loren Eiseley, like Aldo Leopold, was a sharp critic of America's growing military, industrial and consumer culture, and he saw little to celebrate in the vaunted 'space age'. As he wrote (1970, pix):

> Stars and the great island galaxies in which they cluster are more numerous than the blades of grass upon a plain. To speak of man as 'mastering' such a cosmos is about the equivalent of installing a grasshopper as Secretary General of the United Nations. ... In breaching the limits of the earthly atmosphere, we have become aware of how closely our fate is bound to that of the Earth – what compelled us into space will inevitably drive us homeward.

Eiseley also turned to his personal experience for parables of how human beings might constructively respond to the religious question posed by their power to affirm or deny their responsibilities as covenantal partners in the immense journey of evolution.

One of the most memorable of his parables was the story of his experience with the 'star thrower' on a shell-littered beach in Costabel, Mexico. Before dawn, before they can return to the water, commercial shellers collect starfish that the surf has cast up. Awakened in the night and seeing the collectors' flashlights, Eiseley gets up and walks out upon the beach, whereupon he sees 'a gigantic rainbow' and at its foot 'a human figure standing'. As he comes closer, he recognizes that the man is scooping up starfish and flinging them beyond the line of breaking surf – saving them from the fate of the collectors' baskets.

The next morning just before dawn Eiseley rises again, this time 'with a solitary mission':

> On a point of land, as though projecting into a domain beyond us, I found the star thrower. In the sweet rain-swept morning, that great many-hued rainbow still lurked and wavered tentatively beyond him. Silently I sought and picked up a still-living star, spinning it far out into the waves.
>
> Only then I allowed myself to think. He is not alone any longer.
>
> Somewhere far off, across bottomless abysses, I felt as though another world was flung more joyfully. I could have thrown in a frenzy of joy, but I set my shoulders and cast, as the thrower in the rainbow cast, slowly, deliberately and well. The task was not to be assumed lightly, for it was men as well as starfish that we sought to save.
>
> I picked up a star whose tube feet ventured timidly among my fingers while, like a true star, it cried soundlessly for life. I saw it with an unaccustomed clarity and cast far out. With it, I flung myself as forfeit, for the first time, into some unknown dimension of existence. From Darwin's tangled bank of unceasing struggle ... had arisen, incomprehensibly, the thrower who loved not only man, but life.
> (Eiseley, 1978, pp184–185)

THE COVENANT THAT SUSTAINS US

We will not be saved by powers beyond us, by the grace that arrives unasked, unbidden, without our aid; nor will we be saved by own powers, by our heroic efforts to preserve and restore the integral wholeness of life on Earth.

We can only be saved by the covenants that bind us to the reality and laws of the creative processes of life; that join human responsibility and endeavour with nature's inherent capacities for regeneration and survival; that close the circle and enable the grace and glory of life to find ever-new revelations of beauty and integrity.

We have made covenants with one another across the centuries; and we have made covenants with God, the ultimate source of existence; but we Westerners, at least, have rarely made covenants with nature itself, with the living flesh of our bodies, with generations past and generations to come, with all those who have laboured to sustain Earth's evolution and build a world community, with the great encompassing circles of life.

This is the threshold we are now seeking to cross; this, and the enduring covenant of life itself, can give us hope.

REFERENCES

Bonhoeffer, D. and von Wedemeyer, M. (1995) *Love Letters from Cell 92*, R. von Bismark and U. Kabitz (eds), Abingdon Press, Nashville, TN

Carson, R. (1952) *Under the Sea-Wind*, Oxford University Press, New York

Carson, R. (1955) *The Edge of the Sea*, Houghton Mifflin, Boston, MA

Carson, R. (1962) *Silent Spring*, Houghton Mifflin, Boston, MA

Eiseley, L. (1970) *The Invisible Pyramid*, University of Nebraska Press, Lincoln, NB

Eiseley, L. (1978) *The Star Thrower*, Harcourt Brace and Company, New York

Elder, J. (1985) *Imagining the Earth*, University of Illinois Press, Chicago, IL

Elder, J. (1998) *Reading the Mountains of Home*, Harvard University Press, Cambridge, MA

Elder, J. (2006) *Pilgrimage to Vallombrosa*, University of Virginia Press, Charlottesville, VA

Engel, J. R. (2002) 'The Earth Charter as a new covenant for democracy', in P. Miller and L. Westra (eds) *Just Ecological Integrity*, Rowman and Littlefield, Lanham, MD

Engel, J. R. (2007a) 'The covenant of life', in S. Meshack (ed) *Mission with the Marginalized*, Christava Sahitya Samithi (CSS Books), Tiruvalla, India

Engel, J. R. (2007b) 'A covenant of covenants', in C. Soskolne (ed) *Sustaining Life on Earth*, Lexington Books, Lanham, MD

Frost, R. (1923) 'Stopping by Woods on a Snowy Evening', in *New Hampshire*, Henry Holt and Co., New York

Havel, V. (1996) *Disturbing the Peace*, Vintage, New York

Hawken, P. (2007) 'To remake the world', *Orion*, May/June

Holdgate, M. (1999) *The Green Web*, Earthscan, London

Jeffers, R. (1938) 'The answer', in *The Collected Poetry of Robinson Jeffers*, Stanford University Press, Palo Alto, CA

Jensen, D. (2006) *Endgame*, Seven Stories Press, New York

Leopold, A. (1949) *A Sand County Almanac*, Oxford University Press, New York

Meine, C. (1988) *Aldo Leopold*, University of Wisconsin, Madison, WI

Meland, B. (1947) *Seeds of Redemption*, The Macmillan Company, New York

Mumford, L. (1946) *Values for Survival*, Harcourt, Brace and Company, New York

Newton, J. L. (2006) *Aldo Leopold's Odyssey*, Island Press, Washington, DC

Osborn, F. (1947) *Our Plundered Planet*, Little, Brown and Company, Boston, MA

Rockefeller, S. and Elder, J. (1992) *Spirit and Nature*, Beacon Press, Boston, MA

Stern, N. (2007) *The Economics of Climate Change*, University of Cambridge Press, Cambridge, UK

Sturm, D. (2000) 'Identity and alterity', *Journal of Liberal Religion: An Online Theological Journal*, http://meadville.edu/journal/2000_sturm_1_2.pdf, accessed 15 November 2007

UNEP (United Nations Environment Programme) (2007) *Global Environment Outlook 4*, United Nations Publications, New York

Vinciguerra, T. (2007) 'At 90, an environmentalist from the 70s still has hope', *New York Times*, June 19, pD2

Westra, L. (1994) *An Environmental Proposal for Ethics*, Rowman and Littlefield, Lanham, MD

17

Confounding Integrity: Humanity as Dissipative Structure

William E. Rees

INTRODUCTION: THE TRUE NATURE OF 'PRODUCTION'

Modern humans think of themselves as imaginative, creative and resourceful. Certainly no other species on Earth comes close to *Homo sapiens'* seeming mastery of matter and ability to shape the physical world to its own purposes. The accelerating proliferation of laptops, cell-phones, iPods and other electronic gadgetry alone, much of it unheard of only a few years ago, is ample testament to the inventiveness of the modern human mind. Meanwhile our houses get bigger and grander, our cars sleeker and faster and, at least in high-income countries, hardly anyone is concerned about where his next meal is coming from. Little wonder that we think of the economic process mostly in terms of production, wealth creation and general progress in improving the lot of humankind.

But there is something missing from this vision. It is at best a partial picture, like a crime-scene viewed through a keyhole that blinds the observer to the bodies on the floor. In effect, humanity's economic and technological hubris has become a form of unintentional self-delusion. The purpose of this chapter, therefore, is to open the door a crack, to broaden our perspective on techno-economic progress. In particular, I want to draw attention to a simple fact: from a biophysical perspective, virtually every form of economic activity is more consumption than production. While the purported goal of the economy is to maximize human satisfaction (utility) through the efficient production of goods and services, these things actually constitute only a small part of total material output. The major product by mass or volume is degraded energy/matter. Indeed, it is becoming apparent that waste in every conceivable form is the most significant cumulative product of economic activity.

Consider the material waste load dissipated into the ecosphere from the economies of some of the world's most efficient countries. This ranges from 11 metric tonnes per person per year in Japan to 25 metric tonnes per person per year in the US. When so-called 'hidden flows' are included – flows resulting from economic activity but which do not actually enter the production process, such as soil erosion, mining overburden and earth moved during construction – total annual material output increases to 21 metric tonnes per person in Japan and 86 metric tonnes per person in the US (WRI, 2000). Ironically, the burgeoning economy that the world hopes will eradicate poverty and improve wellbeing for all implies an accelerating increase in global entropy – the destructive disordering of the very ecosystems upon which the entire human enterprise depends.

The second law as governing factor

This contradiction is, in part, a direct consequence of the second law of thermodynamics. The second law is fundamental to all real processes involving energy and material transformation. The second law is therefore arguably the ultimate governor of human ecological/economic processes, *yet it is still ignored completely by conventional economists and mainstream economic models.*[1]

In its simplest form, the second law states that any spontaneous change in an isolated system – one that can exchange neither energy nor matter with its environment – increases the 'entropy' (randomness) of that system and the system moves closer to thermodynamic equilibrium. This is a state of maximum entropy in which nothing further can happen. With each successive event, an isolated system becomes increasingly degraded and unstructured in its inexorable slide towards equilibrium. Available energy dissipates, concentrations disperse and gradients disappear.

Early formulations of the second law referred strictly to simple isolated systems close to equilibrium. We now recognize, however, that *all* systems, whether isolated or not, near equilibrium or not, are subject to the forces of entropic decay. Thus *any* differentiated system has a natural tendency to erode, unravel and disperse. Why, then, don't complex systems like our bodies, ecosystems and the economy spontaneously crumble and decay? For much of history philosophers and other analysts argued that living organisms and social organizations were exempt from the second law precisely because they do *not* run down and dissipate. Indeed, 'from the earliest times of human thought, some special non-physical or supernatural force (*vis viva*, entelechy) was claimed to be operative in the organism, and in some quarters is still claimed' (Schrödinger 1945). Far from 'tending toward equilibrium', biological systems, from individual foetuses to the entire ecosphere, generally *gain* in mass and organizational complexity over time.

Only in the past few decades has this seeming paradox been reconciled with the second law (Schneider and Kay, 1994a, b, 1995). Systems scientists now recognize that complex self-producing systems exist as loose nested hierarchies, each component system being contained by the next level up and itself comprising a chain of linked subsystems at lower levels. Kay and Regier (2000) refer to this nested pyramid of quasi-independent subsystems, or 'holons', as a 'self-organizing holarchic open' (SOHO) systems hierarchy. (Consider the following SOHO hierarchy: organelle, cell, organ, organism, population, ecosystem, ecosphere.) At each level in the hierarchy, the relevant subsystem maintains itself and grows by 'importing' available energy and material (essergy or negentropy) from its host system one level up and by exporting degraded energy and material wastes (entropy) back into its host. Because living and other self-organizing systems survive, maintain themselves and grow by continuously degrading and dissipating available energy and matter, they are called 'dissipative structures' (Prigogine, 1997).

How then does a living organism or system avoid decay? In Schrödinger's words, 'The obvious answer is by eating, drinking, breathing and (in the case of plants) assimilating [solar energy].' A living organism normally 'continually increases its entropy – or, as you may say, produces positive entropy – and thus tends to approach the dangerous state of maximum entropy, which is of death. It can only keep aloof from it, i.e. alive, by continually drawing from its environment negative entropy' (Schrödinger, 1945). The living organism also discharges its waste, 'positive entropy', into its immediate environment (in other words into its host ecosystem in the SOHO systems hierarchy).

In a normal ecosystemic steady state, the rates of resource imports and waste discharge by any subsystem (for example a species population) are maintained by negative feedback within a range that is compatible with the rates of production and assimilation by its host system. The systems hierarchy, therefore, retains its long-term functional integrity despite its contribution to a continuous increase in 'global' entropy (in other words the solar and chemical energy necessarily degraded to maintain the entire hierarchy is literally dissipated off the Earth as low-grade infrared radiation). However, the hierarchical relationship between subsystems and their hosts contains the seed of potential pathology. If any subsystem (for example the human enterprise) demands more than its host can produce, or discharges more waste than its host can assimilate sustainably, then the development and growth of that subsystem will necessarily be at the expense of the structural and functional integrity (increased entropy) at higher levels in the systems hierarchy (see Schneider and Kay, 1994a, b). If this situation persists, it may eventually result in the collapse and restructuring of the entire system.

Everyone recognizes that the uncontrolled growth of cells and tissues is the hallmark of cancer and ultimately destroys the integrity of the 'host' organism. It is less well understood that the ever-growing economy and the non-growing ecosphere exist in a similar nested hierarchical relationship. Of course, both the ecosphere and the economy are far-from-equilibrium dissipative structures. However, while the ecosphere evolves and accumulates by dissipating incoming solar radiation – an *extra-terrestrial* source of essergy – the economy, as a subsystem of the ecosphere, develops and grows by dissipating energy and material gradients in the ecosphere itself. In short, the human enterprise is thermodynamically positioned to consume the ecosphere from within (Rees, 1995 and 1999).

In this light, think of productive forests, grasslands, marine estuaries, salt marshes and coral reefs; and of crystalline air and water, mineral deposits, petroleum, natural gas and coal. These forms of 'natural capital' are either highly ordered self-producing ecosystems or accumulations of energy/matter with great human use potential (negentropy). Now think of forest clear-cuts, eroding farmlands, depleted fisheries, marine 'dead zones', and of anthropogenic greenhouse gases, acid rain, poisonous mine tailings and synthetic toxicants. All these things represent degraded systems or dissipated energy/matter with little use potential (high entropy). A moment's reflection reveals that the main thing connecting these two system conditions is the human economic activity operating under the second law. Table 17.1 contrasts the properties of human-less and human-dominated ecosystems.

Critics might argue that economic activity is not only dissipative but that it also creates order in the form of sophisticated consumer goods and useful services. This is true, but misses two points: first, the creation of products and processes by the human enterprise requires the transformation of available energy and matter extracted from the ecosphere. Since economic production involves thermodynamic processes that are always less than 100 per cent efficient, the manufactured order of the human enterprise (for example the accumulation of manufactured capital) never fully compensates thermodynamically for the degradation of the ecosphere (the consumption and dissipation of natural income and natural capital). In short, negentropy production in the economy is always less than the negentropy drawn from the ecosphere, so the net entropy of the global system increases. Second, as noted, the human enterprise is a subsystem and is thus *dependent* on the continued functioning of ecosphere. To the extent that the growth of manufactured capital stocks is derived from the depletion and dissipation of natural capital stocks, economic growth destroys the material basis of its own existence. (And, optimists' claims notwithstanding, the accumulated manufactured capital cannot substitute functionally for the degraded/dissipated natural capital.)

Table 17.1 *Comparing human-less and human-dominated ecosystems*

Human-less ecosystems	Human-dominated ecosystems
Develop by degrading and dissipating solar energy (increases entropy of the solar system)	Grow by degrading and dissipating resource gradients including supportive ecosystems (increases entropy of ecosphere)
Anabolism exceeds catabolism	Catabolism exceeds anabolism
Production dominates	Consumption dominates
Net accumulation	Net depletion

Second law analysis thus provides two basic criteria for sustainability:

1   consumption by the economy cannot persistently exceed production by its host ecosystems; and
2   waste generation by the economy cannot persistently exceed the assimilative capacity of its host ecosystems.

When either condition is violated, the economy has exceeded long-term carrying capacity and is in a state of overshoot.[2] At this point, further growth of the material economy is necessarily derived, in part, from the depletion of natural capital stocks (forests, fish stocks, hydrocarbon deposits and so on), rather than from current natural income (sustainable bio-production). As long as this situation obtains, the economy is undermining life-support systems, eroding long-term carrying capacity and jeopardizing its own future.

ECO-INTEGRITY AND THE SECOND LAW

Virtually any so-called environmental problem can be interpreted in light of the second law. Consider the accumulation of greenhouse gases and resultant anthropogenic climate change. These phenomena result from the fact that industrial economies 'produce themselves' by consuming and dissipating, as water vapour and carbon dioxide, the massive 'gradient' of available energy represented by carboniferous fossil fuels (ancient solar energy). Even the most high-tech industrial economies are carbon-based. Astonishingly, 'when bulky flows like water, soil erosion and earth-moving are excluded, carbon dioxide accounts, on average, for 80 per cent by weight of material waste in the five study countries [high-efficiency economies]'. Indeed, the atmosphere is by far the biggest dumping ground for industrial wastes (WRI, 2000). Shifting climate is an indirect result of the entropy law.

But the story does not end there. The negentropy represented by fossil fuels has enabled humans to extend the scope and intensity of their exploitation of the ecosphere, to increase their 'harvest' of everything from fish and logs to groundwater and petroleum itself. In short, fossil fuels are the principal means by which humans obtained everything else needed to sustain the recent explosion of the human population and all its material baggage. During the 20th century, energy use increased 16-fold (and CO_2 emissions 17-fold), the human population almost quadrupled to 6.4 billion, industrial production exploded more than 40-fold and water use increased by a factor of nine (Arrow et al, 2004).

One consequence is that humans are now the dominant consumer organism in virtually all the major ecosystem types on Earth. For example, in terms of bioenergy and material flows, *Homo sapiens* is actually the most ecologically significant predator in the world's oceans. In the past 100 years, fossil energy and modern technology have enabled the global fishing fleet to expand the catch by a factor of 35. Fishing now appropriates seafood for humans representing 25–35 per cent of net marine primary productivity from shallow coastal shelves and estuaries, that 10 per cent of the oceans that produces 96 per cent of the catchable fish (Pauly and Christensen, 1995). Despite diminishing returns on fishing effort, the collapse of several major fisheries and the unambiguous warnings of fisheries scientists, there is no evidence that the pattern of exploitation is changing. Christensen et al (2003) and Myers and Worm (2003) report that after only 50 years of industrial fishing, the large predatory fish biomass of the world's oceans has been reduced to about 10 per cent of pre-industrial levels – 90 per cent of the targeted biomass has been removed from the sea.

Similarly, humans are the principal consumer in most of the world's significant terrestrial habitats, diverting from grasslands and forests at least 40 per cent of the products of photosynthesis for direct and indirect human use (Vitousek et al, 1986; Haberl, 1997). Of course, the biomass humans consume and dissipate is irreversibly unavailable for consumption by other species, and when people take over habitat for food production or settlement they permanently displace other organisms. Consequently, by 1988, 11 per cent of the 4400 extant mammal species were endangered or critically endangered, and a quarter of all mammal species were on a path of decline which, if not halted, is likely to end in extinction (Tuxill, 1998). McKee et al (2004) suggest that human population growth alone will increase the number of threatened species in the average nation by 7 per cent by 2020 and 14 per cent by 2050. All these data underscore the fact that on a finite planet, the continuous growth of humanity, just one component of the SOHO hierarchy of living subsystems, is necessarily at the expense of other species that share the limited photosynthetic bounty of the ecosphere. Maintaining eco-integrity becomes an impossibility.

Meanwhile, increasing human populations and rising consumption levels impose a steadily increasing dissipative pressure even on long-settled landscapes. Arable lands and productive soils represent concentrated stocks (in other words steep gradients) of the nutrients and organic matter essential for food production. The vital components in soil have accumulated over thousands of years of negentropic interaction among parent soil material, climate and thousands of species of bacteria, fungi, plants and animals, both below and above ground. However, since the dawn of farming 8000–10,000 years ago, agricultural practices have tended to degrade the basis of farming itself. Depending on the climate and agricultural practices, topsoil is being 'dissipated' 16 to 300 times as fast as it is regenerated. Diamond (1987) refers to agriculture as the 'worst mistake in the history of the human race'.

The more allegedly 'sophisticated' and 'productive' our agricultural technology, the more intense the forces of entropic decay. Agriculture-induced erosion, water-logging, acidification, and salination of soils, combined with the leaching and global dissipation of nutrients (removed with the harvest) and organic matter (the oxidation of agricultural soils is a major source of anthropogenic atmospheric carbon dioxide), have seriously compromised the productivity of large areas of cropland around the world. By 1990, 562 million hectares (38 per cent) of the roughly 1.5 billion hectares in cropland had become eroded or otherwise degraded, some so severely as to be taken out of production. Since then, 5 million to 7 million hectares have been lost to production annually (SDIS, 2004). According to the UN Food and Agriculture Organization, a cumulative 300 million hectares (21 per cent) of cultivated land – enough to feed almost all of Europe – has been so severely degraded 'as to destroy its productive functions' (FAO, 2000). Only 35 per cent of global arable land is free from degradation and more land is coming out of production today because of degradation than is being brought into production.

Ominously, to keep pace with the UN's medium population growth projections, food production will have to increase by 57 per cent by 2050. Improving the diets of billions of people could push the needed increase towards 100 per cent. However, the foregoing data suggest that future increases in agricultural output will depend largely on further intensification of irrigation, chemical inputs and mechanization, in other words ever-greater reliance on remaining fossil energy stocks. This, in turn, implies increased entropic damage to soils, ground and surface waters, and the atmosphere (Conforti and Giampetro, 1997).[3] Whither eco-integrity?

CONCLUSION: ECO-INTEGRITY MEANS THE END OF GROWTH

The biophysical perspective advanced in this chapter recognizes that *Homo sapiens* is only a secondary producer. All economic activity requires the consumption of low entropy energy/matter first produced by nature. Beyond a certain point, the operation of the second law ensures that growth of the human enterprise will drive the entropic dissipation of the ecosphere.

For this reason, biophysical analysis more correctly defines the so-called 'environmental crisis' as a problem of 'human ecological dysfunction' (Rees, 2002). Indeed, W. M. Hern likens our species to a kind of planetary disease – the sum of human activities over time 'exhibits all four major characteristics of a malignant process: rapid uncontrolled growth; invasion and destruction of adjacent tissues (ecosystems in this case); metastasis (colonization and urbanization); and dedifferentiation (loss of distinctiveness in individual components)' (Hern, 1997). Within a century, the 11 billion people that might conceivably be sharing the planet will have encroached on the last vestiges of untouched nature, rendering most attempts at habitat rescue futile.[4] Any remaining wildlife preserves will be heavily human-influenced. Already a distinct species of plant or animal disappears every 20 minutes and half of all bird and mammal species may be lost within 200–300 years (University of Texas, 2002).

To reiterate, there is an essential lesson here for those who would work to restore and maintain the structural and functional integrity of ecosystems and global life-support functions. The rate at which natural systems can produce both themselves and the goods and services they provide to humans is tightly limited by the solar flux and various intrinsic biological factors. It follows that to ensure eco-integrity, the scale of the human enterprise cannot exceed the point at which its dissipative powers exceed the cumulative forces of the ecosphere.

This is the unspeakable elephant in the sustainability parlour. The simple thermodynamic fact of the matter is that continuous population and material growth run foul of the second law of thermodynamics – and there are no exemptions from the second law. If we want to conserve ecological integrity and achieve general sustainability, techno-industrial society will have to abandon the theory of perpetual economic growth. Although it was not his intent, no one has made this point more eloquently than Sir Arthur Eddington:

> [Thermodynamics] holds the supreme position among the laws of nature. ... If your theory is found to be against the second law of thermodynamics, I can give you no hope; there is nothing for it but to collapse in deepest humiliation. (Eddington, 1928)

NOTES

1   Nicholas Georgescu-Roegen (1971 and 1991) famously pioneered the application of thermodynamic concepts to the modern economy, largely to no avail.
2   For most of human history – certainly until the widespread adoption of agriculture – our species lived in various states of 'undershoot' in which we appropriated less of nature's goods and services than might have been sustainably possible. Any state of human undershoot represents a sustainable state in which more net primary production is available to support non-human consumer organisms. That is, undershoot is good for biodiversity.
3   Fossil energy supplies themselves may be problematic. Petroleum reserves are finite, global consumption of oil has exceeded discovery annually since the early 1980s and various experts suggest that 'peak oil' (the point at which global production/extraction of fossil fuels reaches a maximum and begins its inexorable decline) is upon us.
4   There is a good chance, however, that climate change, resource scarcity, systems collapses and geo-political chaos will intervene well before the human population reaches such heady heights.

REFERENCES

Arrow, K., Dasgupta, P., Goulder, L., Daily, G., Ehrlich, P., Heal, G., Levin, S., Mäler, K-G., Schneider, S., Starrett, D. and Walker, B. (2004) 'Are we consuming too much?', *Journal of Economic Perspectives*, vol 18, no 3, pp147–172

Christensen, V., Guénette, S., Heymans, J., Walters, C., Watson, R., Zeller, D. and Pauly, D. (2003) 'Hundred-year decline of North Atlantic predatory fishes', *Fish and Fisheries*, vol 4, pp1–24

Conforti, P. and Giampietro, M. (1997) 'Fossil energy use in agriculture: An international comparison', *Agriculture, Ecosystems and Environment*, vol 65, pp231–243

Diamond, J. (1987) 'The worst mistake in the history of the human race', *Discover Magazine*, May, pp64–66

Eddington, A. S. (1928) *The Nature of the Physical World*, Cambridge University Press, Cambridge, UK

FAO (2000) *Land Resource Potential and Constraints at Regional and Country Levels*, Land and Water Development Division, Food and Agriculture Organization of the United Nations, Rome

Georgescu-Roegan, N. (1971) 'The entropy law and the economic problem', Distinguished Lecture Series No 1, Department of Economics, University of Alabama, Tuscaloosa, AL

Georgescu-Roegen, N. (1991) *The Entropy Law and the Economic Process*, Harvard University Press, Cambridge, MA

Haberl, H. (1997) 'Human appropriation of net primary production as an environmental indicator: Implications for sustainable development', *Ambio*, vol 26, pp143–146

Hern, W. M. (1997) 'Is human culture oncogenic for uncontrolled population growth and ecological destruction?', *Human Evolution*, vols 1–2, pp97–105

Kay, J. and Regier, H. (2000) 'Uncertainty, complexity and ecological integrity', in P. Crabbé, A. Holland, L. Ryszkowski and L. Westra (eds) *Implementing Ecological Integrity: Restoring Regional and Global Environment and Human Health*, NATO Science Series IV: Earth and Environmental Sciences, volume 1, Kluwer Academic Publishers, Dortrecht, The Netherlands, pp121–156

McKee, J. K., Sciulli, P. W., Fooce, C. D. and Waite, T. A. (2004) 'Forecasting global biodiversity threats associated with human population growth', *Biological Conservation*, vol 115, no 1, pp161–164

Myers, R. A. and Worm, B. (2003) 'Rapid worldwide depletion of predatory fish communities', *Nature*, vol 423, pp280–283

Palmer, M., Bernhardt, E., Chornesky, E., Collins, S., Dobson, A., Duke, C., Gold, B., Jacobson, R., Kingsland, S., Kranz, R., Mappin, M., Martinez, M. L., Micheli, F., Morse, J., Pace, M., Pascual, M., Palumbi, S., Reichman, O. J., Simons, A., Townsend, A. and Turner, M. (2004) 'Ecology for a crowded planet', *Science*, vol 304, no 5675, pp1251–1252

Pauly, D. and Christensen, V. (1995) 'Primary production required to sustain global fisheries', *Nature*, vol 374, pp255–257

Prigogine, I. (1997) *The End of Certainty: Time, Chaos and the New Laws of Nature*, The Free Press, New York

Rees, W. E. (1995) 'Achieving sustainability: Reform or transformation?', *Journal of Planning Literature*, vol 9, no 4, pp343–361

Rees, W. E. (1999) 'Consuming the Earth: The biophysics of sustainability', *Ecological Economics*, vol 29, pp23–27

Rees, W. E. (2002) 'Globalization and sustainability: Conflict or convergence?', *Bulletin of Science, Technology and Society*, vol 22, no 4, pp249–268

Schneider, E. and Kay, J. (1994a) 'Life as a manifestation of the second law of thermodynamics', *Mathematical and Computer Modelling*, vol 19, nos 6–8, pp25–48

Schneider, E. D. and Kay, J. J. (1994b) 'Complexity and thermodynamics: Toward a new ecology, *Futures*, vol 26, nos 626–647, pp364–365

Schneider, E. D. and Kay, J. J. (1995) 'Order from disorder: The thermodynamics of complexity in biology', in M. P. Murphy and L. A. J. O'Neill (eds) *What is Life: The Next Fifty Years, Reflections on the Future of Biology*, Cambridge University Press, Cambridge, UK

Schrödinger, E. (1945) *What is Life: The Physical Aspect of the Living Cell*, Cambridge University Press, Cambridge, UK

SDIS (2004) *Disappearing Land: Soil Degradation*, Sustainable Development Information Service, Global Trends, World Resources Institute, Washington, DC

Tuxill, J. (1998) 'Losing strands in the web of life: Vertebrate declines and the conservation of biological diversity', Worldwatch Paper 141, The Worldwatch Institute, Washington, DC

University of Texas (2002) 'Extinction rate across the globe reaches historic proportions', press release, University of Texas, Austin, TX, www.sciencedaily.com/releases/2002/01/020109074801.htm, accessed 10 January 2002

Vitousek, P., Ehrlich, P. R., Ehrlich, A. H. and Matson, P. (1986) 'Human appropriation of the products of photosynthesis', *BioScience*, vol 36, pp368–374

WRI (2000) *The Weight of Nations*, World Resources Institute, Washington, DC, http://pdf.wri.org/weight_of_nations.pdf

18

Socio-material Communication in Eco-sustainable Societies of the Future

Richard Westra

INTRODUCTION

The Global Ecological Integrity Group (GEIG) utilizes the concept of integrity to calibrate the degree of sustainability in the interfacing of human beings and nature. Succinctly put, integrity captures the properties of autopoiesis and reciprocal articulation of natural processes characteristic of wild ecosystems: to live in integrity demands that human beings organize their society in ways which simulate reproductive modalities of wild ecosystems and that lead to the combined sustainability of the eco/social system as a whole (Westra et al, 2000). While actually achieving a pristine integrity outcome is a stated goal for the future, GEIG nevertheless believes that efforts can be made in the here and now to begin the process of achieving integrity goals. This chapter accepts with GEIG that seeking to synchronize human activity with eco-sustainability and re-embed economic life in nature is a pressing concern for human society. However, it focuses on the way the debate over integrity, and eco-sustainability more broadly, proceeds in the absence of careful consideration of the exigencies of human material reproductive viability and how human material life is to be institutionally configured to effectuate a symbiosis between economic viability and eco-sustainability. To paraphrase Karl Marx (as so many have): human beings *do* make their own world, but they do *not* make it just as they please. The choices among viable modes of organizing the economic life of human societies are not unlimited. And the potential transformability of a viable mode of material reproduction is not open-ended. Further, particular modes of economy embody tendencies inimical to eco-sustainability that institutional re-jigging will never eviscerate within the material reproductive contours of those modes.

Argumentation over the political economic change necessary to ensure the eco-sustainability of human society tends to swirl around questions of human rationality. The culprit, as treated in an instructive review of the literature (Little, 2000), is alleged to be the instrumental, benefit-maximizing 'rational' economic agent referred to in neoclassical economics textbooks. It is this *Homo economicus* that is purportedly responsible for ravaging and depleting the biospheric commons. Of proposed means to deal with the proclivities of *Homo economicus*, the radical remaking of human subjectivity and replacing of *Homo economicus* with an ascetic *Homo ecologicus*, as clamoured for in green social theory, is oppugned over the potential authoritarian political outcome of inculcating the new ecological subjectivity, and the extent of social regression entailed in green visions of self-sufficient micro-communities. A second alternative, predicated upon the writings of Jurgen Habermas, seeks to promote a culture of 'communicative rationality' (the notion that at a fundamental level people tend to convey ideas to each other free of subterfuge), which, if able to permeate the public sphere, would offer a forum for human interaction untrammelled by powerful sectional interests such as those promoting neoclassical models of human behaviour as the 'end of history'. However, as critics note, while this view offers a pathway towards informing mass publics of the supposed collective environmentally degrading consequences of individual benefit-maximizing agency, it is less forthcoming on the discursive principles of an environmental counter-project. A third position, drawing upon the writings of Andre Gorz, fills in the blank page on the question of a unifying principle for such a counter-project. What is advanced is the notion of an 'eco-social' rationality which, if articulated in a discursively democratic public sphere, will serve to circumscribe instrumental rationality and tether it where required to long-term goals of eco-sustainability. Presumably, a concept such as integrity could function as the cornerstone of that. In short, these views arrive at a conclusion where the ultimate thwarting of *Homo economicus* 'is at the democratic behest of the meeting of *Homo ecologicus* and *Homo civicus*' (Little, 2000, p130).

Why, despite much theoretical huffing and puffing, the question of potential institutional vehicles upon which an eco-sustainable, economically viable social order might be fashioned is never broached relates to the ideological coup engineered by neoclassical economics. Karl Polanyi dubs this the 'economistic fallacy' (1977, pp10ff). Quite simply, this fallacy refers to the dual senses in which the term 'economic' is used and how one notion of economics currently substitutes for both. We, of course, in common parlance, talk about 'economic interests' as those relating to our needs as human beings for material sustenance and its provisioning. Put differently, the foregoing amounts to little more than the rather banal recognition that economic life is a necessary feature of every human society in history. Neoclassical economics, which in fact studies the capitalist, or, in its own terms, 'market economy', refers to its field as 'economics', and the economic interests of human beings as 'rational', in a fashion that does not distinguish between the particular modalities of material existence and expression of economic interests holding under capitalism and those existing as the substantive foundation of all human life. And it is neoclassical economics, substituting of its notion of 'economic' for economic per se, which in perpetuity forestalls those steeped in its tradition from grappling with the historical peculiarity of capitalism in a way that allows them to genuinely make sense of the world in which we live today, or think creatively about our planet's eco-sustainable transfiguration.

The 'culprit', in other words, is not *Homo economicus*, 'rationally' (how could it be otherwise?) expressing their instrumental interest in material survival. Nor do there exist trans-historical modalities of 'economy', as supposedly captured by neoclassical economics, that confront human beings as an immutable natural order and limit human choice regarding how to deal with an environmental morass of mammoth proportions to (a) simply adapting (as humans do to natural forces like hurricanes), as neoclassical economics suggests, with a spurious physics-like, so-called 'cost–benefit' analysis; (b) better elucidating the anti-ecological thrust of these purported 'forces' through increased civic engagement, and then 'regulating' them; or (c) inculcating humans with a counter-ecorationality to those alleged trans-historical 'economic' modalities. Rather, the culprit is the socially and historically constituted principles of economy under the force of which human material reproduction unfolds and the motivations of human economic agency are circumscribed. It is the interrogation of these variant principles that forms the subject matter of this chapter. What I refer to as modes of *socio-material communication* (Westra, 2007a, b and c) are the means by which human beings communicate to reproduce their material existence – personal/face to face, impersonal/abstract, language based, symbol based, signal based, etc – characteristic of historical forms of economy. Implications of these modes of socio-material communication will be explored in this chapter to precisely elucidate the political economic and institutional roots of current environmental degradation. Modes of socio-material communication will then be identified which may be utilized both singly and in combination to fashion an economically viable eco-sustainable society for our human future.

The economic viability and eco-sustainability of capitalism

Sweeping historical research by economic historian Karl Polanyi (1977) identifies three basic modes of economy, or what I have referred to as modes of socio-material communication characterizing human history (See Figure 18.1). These are *reciprocity*, characteristic of early, largely pre-agrarian, societies, and predicated upon face-to-face human interactions leading to the rudimentary satisfaction of group, clan and so forth needs; *redistribution*, involving interpersonal relations of domination and subordination characteristic of both Asiatic and Western feudalism; and *markets*, as in the impersonal *society-wide self-regulating* market characteristic of capitalism. Polanyi distinguishes this market from what we might call the small-m market involving face-to-face 'exchange', akin to barter, which has existed as an adjunct mode of socio-material communication across human history.

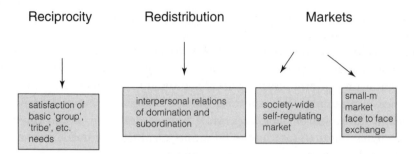

Figure 18.1   *Karl Polanyi and modes of economy*

This research by Polanyi corresponds in an instructive fashion with earlier work by Karl Marx. For Marx, human history is characterized by the existence of modes of production each marked by a governing principle of economic reproduction (reflected in a mode of socio-material communication as outlined above), this then set within a system of social class relations. Marx named these modes of production *primitive communism* (this reflecting the existence of a division of labour and status distinctions in early societies but no social class divisions), *slavery* (referring to the great slave labour-based societies of Europe and the Near East), *feudalism* (with its European and Asian variants), *capitalism* (or so-called market society), and *communism/socialism* (exemplars of which, of course, never materialized in Marx's lifetime). I find it felicitous to sketch out the correspondence between the work of Marx and Polanyi, where reciprocity corresponds to primitive communism, redistribution to slavery, feudalism and the Soviet-style experiments with socialism (which Marx never witnessed), and markets correspond to capitalism with the welfare state social democracies mixing markets with redistribution, though where redistributive state policies are formulated democratically (See Figure 18.2).

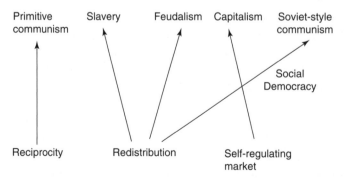

Figure 18.2   *Polanyi correspondence with Karl Marx's modes of production*

What this exercise accomplishes, first, is to reinforce the fact that, contra neoclassical economics with its axiom of the supra-historic individual, economic life across the span of human history has assumed several discrete forms which condition human material reproductive agency in divergent ways. Second, spotlighting the different principles of economy upon which the viability of human existence is predicated is a way of turning the discussion onto the historical peculiarity of capitalism. For also noted by Polanyi in his research on human economic history (1977, p55) is the fact that in societies antedating capitalism to even *think* about the economy as an entity distinct or *dis-embedded* from other sets of social relations – thaumaturgy, religion, culture, politics and so forth – was inconceivable. Marx, whose work precedes that of Polanyi by half a century, similarly recognized the historical peculiarity of capitalism that springs from the tendency of capitalist economic life to dis-embed from other realms of the social. Marx well understood that this formed the very ontological condition for economic theory, given how for the very first time in human history economic life is rendered 'transparent' in capitalist society for theory to explore (Westra, 1999). However, for Marx, economic life in capitalist society does not simply dis-embed from other social practices: through its organization in society-wide integrated systems of self-regulating markets it takes on 'a life of its own', wielding other realms of the social for its own self-aggrandizement – the augmentation of value (or profit-making). Marx refers to capitalism, as such, as an 'upside down' or 'fetishistic' society. The most precise concept to capture this socio-economic condition of capitalism, where socially and historically constituted relations of production confront human beings as an 'extra-human' power, is that of *reification*.[1]

Reification is the key to capitalist economic viability, capitalist 'efficiency' as a *production-centred* society and its innate anti-environmental thrust. Developing Marx's work further, Japanese political economist Kozo Uno (1980) argues that whatever principle of economy or mode of socio-material communication, or combination of these, marking an economy, to ensure the material reproductive viability of the society, the principles have to satisfy the 'general norms of economic life'. The key norm is that social demand for basic goods must be met with a minimal waste of resources. If resources are chronically misallocated (for example, the supply of available labour power is continuously devoted to producing iron while people are clamouring for grain) the respective society will die out. And human history is replete with examples of societies that could not pass this essential test. What particularly challenged Uno then was to demonstrate how it is possible for capitalism to satisfy the general norms of economic life, given the way it dissolves the face-to-face interpersonal economic relations of the past, replacing them with the impersonal operation of systems of society-wide self-regulating markets. To explain the economic viability of capitalism, under conditions of reification where the economy appeared to take on a 'life of its own', requires exploring the phenomenon of what economists refer to as the market reaching a state of equilibrium.

When economists praise the efficiency of capitalist markets over alternative institutional arrangements for an economy, what they are adverting to is the 'cost-less' transmitting of economic information by markets in the form of market prices. From the perspective of business actors, prices act as signals indicating where profitable investment opportunities exist. The ability of capitalism to rapidly shift to the production of *any* good as per changing patterns of social demand and possibilities for profit-making is rooted in the existence of a class of 'free labourers' uprooted from ties to the land and available in the market for businesses to purchase as but another input into the production process. To arrive at an equilibrium where demand for both means of production and means of consumption is supplied at prices that ensure profits are made and goods purchased by both the workers that made them and business investors, the market must perform a series of abstract calculations based upon a *quantitative* value/price criterion.

This mode of socio-material communication predicated upon an abstract quantitative criterion is what makes capitalism the most suitable form of economy for the standardized mass-producing of material goods. Put differently, capitalism is the production-centred society *par excellence*. As a historically constituted mode of economic life, capitalism comes into being at a particular level of development of human material wants and productive technique. It demonstrates a measure of transformability with market operations obtaining key institutional supports.[2] However, and this has nothing to do with its revolutionary overthrow as conventional Marxism asserts, capitalism reaches its limitations as technologies and energy sources that are not capitalistically operable emerge on the horizon and as human wants spill out beyond the range of those which capitalism is able to satisfy (see Figure 18.3). That is, capitalism comes into being at the twilight of agricultural economies as changing human

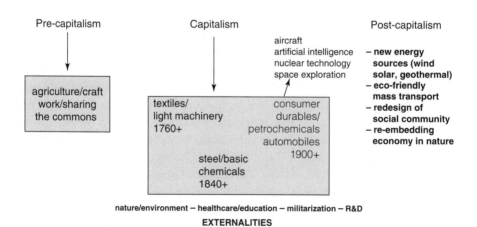

Figure 18.3   *The historical specificity of capitalism*

wants for its mass-produced consumer goods and the technologies available for their production emerge on the horizon. The reconfiguration of mass production from light goods to heavy industrial mass-produced products to consumer durables exemplifies the transformability of capitalism. Yet, with the dawning of the 21st century, there exist a changing array of human wants capitalism is unable to satisfy and a host of new technologies beckoning humanity which are simply not operable on a capitalist basis.

In fact, if we examine the employment profile of the most advanced capitalist countries, we can see quite clearly that the component of total work time devoted to the production of material goods has considerably diminished. In fact, on this basis alone we can question even whether we continue to live in a capitalist society, despite what the hegemonic economic theory tells us. Looked at from another angle, we can see that the social demand for those mass-produced goods characteristic of the capitalist era is satisfied with a minimum of our labour resources, potentially liberating human beings to assume other tasks. Yet conventional wisdom based on antiquated economic theories continues to blind us to the changes which have occurred right before our eyes (see Figure 18.4).

Neoclassical economics never interrogates its own historicity as a discipline. If it did, it would see that its policy implications are tailored to a society in which reproduction of human material existence is predicated upon abstract quantitative criteria, and where human economic life is reproduced as a by-product of value-augmentation or profit-making. Because value-augmentation is an *abstract-quantitative* goal, we can say that at the most fundamental level capitalism is destined to conflict with *concrete-qualitative* human goals to the extent that the latter necessitate respect for the Earth and the life-world within which long-term human existence is necessarily embedded. Such is illustrated so

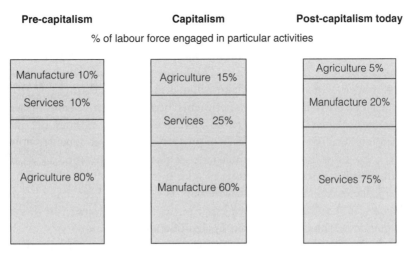

Figure 18.4 *The waning of production-centred society*

vividly by the historical record of capitalism, which displays how value-augmentation can proceed extremely successfully through the production of noxious goods as well as those with the potential to destroy life itself. Paradoxically, therefore, while an unimpeded procedure of abstract-quantitative market calculation is the basis of capital's ability to constitute a viable economic order, it is also the root of capitalism's profaning of the human life-world and the Earth.

RETHINKING ECONOMIC VIABILITY AND ECO-SUSTAINABILITY IN NON-CAPITALIST ECONOMIES

If the mode of socio-material communication of integrated systems of self-regulating markets no longer guarantees human economic viability and is inimical to eco-sustainability, are there modes of socio-material communication which we can deploy to build an economically viable eco-sustainable future for humanity?

Without entering the debate over what kind of economy the Soviet-style system was, the oft-referred-to 'economics of shortage' of its cumbersome centralized state-planning apparatus never met the test of economic viability. It not only failed to meet the demand for basic goods, but chronically misallocated resources, generating a huge 'parallel economy' that helped to support human material existence by a welter of extra-planning means. And, with its disintegration, the disgraceful environmental record of the Soviet Union has been vividly exposed. Thus we can immediately discount the society-wide centralized planning variant of the redistribution mode of social-material communication as the guarantor of an eco-sustainable future.

Notions of so-called market socialism, or 'socializing' the market, have also been put forward as non-capitalist alternatives. However, if these models seek to base material reproduction upon the mode of socio-material communication of society-wide systems of self-regulating markets, it is not clear how economic outcomes will differ from capitalism. The fact is that the efficiency gains sought in these models, which socialists claim will make market socialism more attractive than the fallen centrally planned experiments, necessarily derive from the abstract quantitative calculation procedure of market allocation. Besides the issue of maintaining the aforementioned class of property-less 'free labourers' to optimally capture these gains, interfering with society-wide market operation by socializing both distributive outcomes and costs of addressing externalities (those aspects of economic life in capitalist society which markets have never been able to manage – see Figure 18.3) will face the same clash of interests experienced in the world's social democracies recently overrun by neo-liberalism.

Though discredited in its Soviet-style form, economic planning has been resurrected in models purporting to surmount the two main deficiencies of their predecessor – authoritarian centralism and allocation inefficiency. To begin with the latter point, these demonstrate how computers may be utilized to perform market calculations and obtain equilibrium solutions combined with redistributive social outcomes. Paralleling this work are models confirming that the information relied upon to arrive at equilibrium allocations of social resources need not emanate from a central plan but could be channelled through decentralized participatory micro, meso and macro democratically elected planning bodies. While this work demonstrates that redistribution as a mode of socio-material communication for industrial as opposed to agricultural societies can be institutionally varied to ensure economic viability, where participatory planning models miscarry is in their conception of planning as a *society-wide* endeavour of simulating abstract quantitative equilibrium calculations of the capitalist market. This reduces the possibility of socialism to an abstract technical question and imports into socialism or an otherwise-named possible future society a mechanism of the capitalist economy at the root of capitalist insensitivity to qualitative human concerns over the sanctity and sustainability of the life-world and nature.

We have already touched upon critics' oppugning of the so-called 'small-is-beautiful' model at the heart of green theory. What may be added here is that there is no inexorability in reduced scale per se engendering sound environmental outcomes; green writing has been vague on how communities might coordinate eco-policy to ensure that the results of potentially unsound activities are not blithely passed along from one small-is-beautiful community to another. Of the greatest import from the point of view of this chapter is the question of economic viability. As captured in Marx's dictum paraphrased earlier, modes of economy cannot simply be generated *ex nihilo*. And economically viable forms of human society require at their core an operative principle or set of these to ensure that the general norms of economic life are met. In eschewing both markets and planning as economic principles, it is incumbent upon green theory to elaborate a replacement. That they have not been forthcoming with one is a gaping lacuna in their work.

Economic viability and eco-sustainability in future societies

What this section of the chapter proposes is a way of combining modes of socio-material communication in a fashion which takes advantage of their benefits and overcomes their limitations with respect to both economic viability and eco-sustainability. It is predicated upon the important distinction between those sorts of goods the production of which either markets or forms of planning as modes of socio-material communication are most propitious given the economy of scale and quantitative exigencies of their production and those where these considerations are far less important. These categories of goods and their economic sectors will be simply labelled *quantitative* and *qualitative*:

- **Qualitative goods:** agriculture/food, furniture, light consumer goods, building materials, apparel, toys, household sundries, etc.
- **Quantitative goods:** heavy building materials, transportation equipment, infrastructure goods, etc.

Building upon earlier work (Sekine, 1990 and 2004; Westra, 2002, 2004, 2007a and 2007b) on the breaking down of economies into sectors, communities and modes of socio-material communication, the proposed economy will include communal reciprocity, local small-m markets and sector-delimited economic planning. First, a qualitative goods sector community might be formed around rural areas and small towns, and with potentially arable lands and boroughs adjacent to major urban centres. Its production focus, depending on local resources, would be goods such as foodstuffs, furniture, apparel, household sundries and so forth. However, while such qualitative goods-producing communities replicate geo-spatial aspects of the small-is-beautiful model, on questions of economic reproduction they follow Marx and Polanyi. As the historical studies of Marx and Polanyi make abundantly clear, markets for face-to-face personal exchange or barter of goods existed as benign supplements to the varying dominant principles of economic life marking pre-capitalist modes of production. Similarly, types of markets such as local exchange and trading systems (LETS), 'need exchanges', community barter, and reciprocity for goods and services, all based on a local community currency, may be adopted as benign instruments for viably organizing future economic life, given socializing of property ownership and extension of direct economic and political democracy.

Second, a quantitative goods or state sector would assume responsibility for producing heavy goods, both producer and consumer, as well as environmentally sound forms of mass transportation, energy delivery and social infrastructure, all forms of use-value production carrying economy of scale requirements transcending capacities of qualitative communities to manage. The potential range of ownership choices for the socialist state sector are quite varied; however, a scheme of shareholding predicated on that of contemporary corporations, with shares held by qualitative goods communities linked to the state sector and state sector workers themselves, might be adopted. The mode of socio-material communication of this sector would duplicate aspects of the aforementioned iterative participatory planning schemes. However, the requirement of a society-wide equilibrium outcome would be dropped, in part because demand for basic goods is met by more face-to-face exchanges in qualitative communities. Like corporations today in transportation and producer goods and many consumer durable sectors, economic programming and planning has already replaced markets in allocating resources. The quantitative goods state sector would have its own currency, exchangeable both with the local currencies of the communities with which it interfaces and with the currencies of other 'states', though the issue of whether the construction of an eco-sustainable commonwealth of states would utilize the configuring of current states as a template is something that must be dealt with in practice.

Third, an administrative sector, interlinked with local communities and quantitative goods sectors through ownership and shared currency may, for the near future, remain the site of governance. Of course, the distinction between these categories is not firm and will necessarily vary according to the local and regional geo-spatial conditions and structures of the pre-socialist economy. The force of this tri-sector Utopia (see Figure 18.5) is intended as a means of disrupting capitalist production and distribution chains shaped by quantitative considerations and placing the focus of economic life on qualitative considerations. The absence of a heavy goods and administrative sector in green models is a major weakness of the approach as it is through such sectors that elements of cosmopolitan society can be salvaged from capitalism and the material means to clean up capital's rampage across our biosphere ensured.

In applying the metric for eco-sustainability, the prospective dumping of eco-problems on others inhering in small-is-beautiful districts will be averted by the fact that, though collectively owned and largely politically independent, qualitative goods communities are linked to each other through ownership relations with the quantitative state and administrative urban sectors, thus promoting a broader collective interest in the eco-sanctity of lived environments. Further, and I revisit this issue below, procedures must be established for

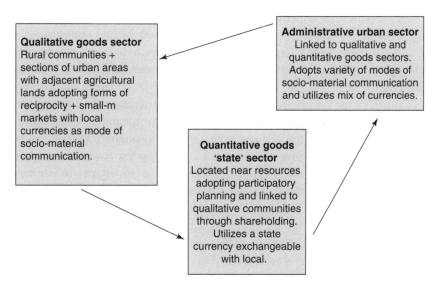

Figure 18.5 *Economy of a tri-sector Utopia*

democratic rotation of working families through each sector. This will offer an incentive to promote eco-sustainability through the entire system of communities. Moreover, with participatory planning in the quantitative goods sector involving both state enterprise stakeholding workers and shareholders from qualitative communities, not only will capitalism's bias towards polluting industrial environments distanced from suburban homes of business owners be reduced, but eco-sustainable communities will be empowered to radically transform the energy profile and production process from that under the abstract rule of capitalism. Also, the adopting of different modes of socio-material communication to satisfy the material requirements of society moves qualitative human needs and the sanctity of the human life-world and nature in which material life is embedded to the centre of attention. Finally, the eco-pedigree of each community and sector, as well as the patterns of interconnections among them, may then be regularly assessed according to techniques of 'ecological footprinting' (Wackernagel and Rees, 1996; Chambers et al, 2000), where the environmental carrying capacity of regions are measured and deficits democratically addressed.

In applying a test for economic viability to the tri-sector Utopia, it is evident that with the severing and rehabilitation of local community economic life from the ravages of global markets, geo-spatial reconnecting of production and consumption, instituting of collective ownership, and adopting of varying forms of economic reciprocity and LETS markets as core economic principles, the demand for basic goods within qualitative use-value sectors will be met with minimal difficulty and misallocation of social resources. Surpluses may then be traded for both services and quantitative sector use-values. In the quantitative state sector, socialist enterprises may effectively transmit economic information through iterative participatory plans and compete as do successful publicly owned companies today. Demand for basic goods will be met in both the state and administrative sectors by qualitative sector supply and potential auxiliary production established in those sectors as with guerrilla gardening in urban settings today.

In much of the developed highly urbanized industrial world, the sectors will not be separated geo-spatially, but rather the tri-sector format will create vehicles for the instatement of forms of direct political empowerment of publics as well as for the optimal functioning of modes of socio-material communication best geared to the requirements of producing the different categories of use values. In less developed economies and less urbanized areas of developed states, the tri-sector format offers a benchmark for revitalizing community economic life torn asunder by globalization's siphoning-off of resources (including the very livelihood of communities themselves) towards its urban sprawls and slums. The democratic rotation of working/owning families will contribute to the multidimensionality of human beings in their work lives and erode divides between mental and manual labour and town and country. Regularizing cooperative relations among sectors will contribute to a 'withering away' of the bureaucratic state. Such a system could be extended within a wider commonwealth, facilitating open emigration and immigration in efforts to overcome the apartheids, political, economic and environmental, that mark the current global era.

CONCLUSION

What precise name we give to this eco-sustainable, economically viable, tri-sector Utopian society is not important. We may call it socialism or give it another name, given the way the former conjures up images of the failed experiments of the past. What is more important is to comprehend how the making of an eco-sustainable future for humanity is inexorably bound up with one further consideration. Remember, when capitalism faced off against its antecedents and later Soviet-style competitors, it emerged the victor given the advancement of human freedom it entailed. That is, in the great redistributive societies where humanity experienced its economic existence ensnared in interpersonal relations of domination and subordination, the motivation or compulsion for work was always *extra-economic*. Capitalism liberates human beings from this as it replaces, at least paradigmatically, extra-economic coercion with impersonal *economic* motivation for work. It is true, as touched upon above, that the self-seeking economic proclivities of individuals in capitalist society are nevertheless tethered to the 'collective' chrematistic operation of capitalism which reproduces human economic life as a by-product of augmenting value or profit-making, but this does not change the fundamental economic compulsion for work experienced by each individual. Where the Soviet-style experiments most glaringly miscarried was in the fact that they attempted to reinstate forms of extra-economic compulsion for work. However, capitalism already offered a clear historical advancement over this. To provide a genuine advancement over capitalism, our eco-sustainable society of the future must enshrine *self-motivation* as the compulsion for work. Self-motivation will be facilitated by the transfigured economic, ownership and institutional structures of the new society. Self-motivation is also the key to the reinstatement of the qualitative considerations of economic reproduction necessary to maintain respect for the life-world and Earth.

NOTES

1   The argument as to precisely what constitutes capitalist reification requires elaboration which exceeds the bounds of this chapter. Readers interested in pursuing this are directed to Westra (1999), Albritton (1999, Chapter 2) and, for those bent upon deeply delving into the inner workings of the capitalist economy, Sekine (1997).

2   Issues of the transformability of capitalism and the fashion in which markets are supported across capitalist history and capitalist 'externalities' managed by a matrix of extra-market institutional props is most felicitously addressed within the context of the study agenda of *phases of capitalist development*. On this, see Albritton et al (2001) and Westra (2006).

REFERENCES

Albritton, R. (1999) *Dialectics and Deconstruction in Political Economy*, Macmillan Press, Basingstoke, UK

Albritton, R., Itoh, M., Westra, R. and Zuege, A. (eds) (2001) *Phases of Capitalist Development: Booms, Crises and Globalizations*, Palgrave, Basingstoke, UK

Chambers, N., Simmons, C. and Wackernagel, M. (2000) *Sharing Nature's Interest: Ecological Footprints as an Indicator of Sustainability*, Earthscan, London

Little, A. (2000) 'Environmental and eco-social rationality: Challenges for political economy in late modernity', *New Political Economy*, vol 5, no 1

Polanyi, K. (1977) *The Livelihood of Man*, Academic Press, New York

Sekine, T. (1990) 'Socialism as a living idea', in H. Flakierski and T. Sekine (eds) *Socialist Dilemmas, East and West*, M. E. Sharp, New York

Sekine, T. (1997) *An Outline of the Dialectic of Capital* (two volumes), Macmillan, Basingstoke, UK

Sekine, T. (2004) 'Socialism beyond market and productivism', in R. Albritton, S. Bell, J. Bell and R. Westra (eds) *New Socialisms: Futures Beyond Globalization*, Innis Centenary Series: Governance and Change in the Global Era, Routledge, London

Uno, K. (1980) *Principles of Political Economy*, Humanities Press, Atlantic Highlands, NJ

Wackernagel, M. and Rees, W. (1996) *Our Ecological Footprint: Reducing Human Impact on Earth*, New Society Publishers, Gabriola Island, Canada

Westra, R. (1999) 'A Japanese contribution to the critique of rational choice Marxism', *Social Theory and Practice*, vol 25, no 3

Westra, R. (2002) 'Marxian economic theory and an ontology of socialism: A Japanese intervention', *Capital and Class*, vol 78

Westra, R. (2004) 'The "impasse" debate and socialist development', in R. Albritton, S. Bell, J. Bell and R. Westra (eds) *New Socialisms: Futures Beyond Globalization*, Innis Centenary Series: Governance and Change in the Global Era, Routledge, London

Westra, R. (2006) 'The capitalist stage of consumerism and South Korean development', *Journal of Contemporary Asia*, vol 36, no 1

Westra, R. (2007a) 'Socio-material communication, community and eco-sustainability in the global era', in C. A. Maida (ed) *Sustainability and Communities of Place*, Environmental Anthropology Series edited by Roy Ellen, Berghahn Books, Oxford, UK, and New York

Westra, R. (2007b) '*Green* Marxism and the institutional structure of a global socialist future', in R. Albritton, R. Jessop and R. Westra (eds) *Political Economy and Global Capitalism: The 21st Century Present and Future*, Anthem, London

Westra, R. (2007c) 'Market society and ecological integrity: Theory and practice', in C. Soskolne (ed) *Sustaining Life on Earth: Environmental and Human Health Through Global Governance*, Lexington Books, Lanham, MD

Westra, L., Miller, P., Karr, J. R., Rees, W. and Ulanowitz, R. E. (2000) 'Ecological integrity and the aims of the Global Integrity Project', in D. Pimentel, L. Westra and R. F. Noss (eds) *Ecological Integrity: Integrating Environment, Conservation and Health*, Island Press, Washington, DC

19

The Way Forward: Governance for Ecological Integrity

Klaus Bosselmann

A human being is a part of a whole, called by us 'universe', a part limited in time and space. He experiences himself, his thoughts and feelings as something separated from the rest ... a kind of optical delusion of his consciousness. This delusion is a kind of prison for us, restricting us to our personal desires and to affection for a few persons nearest to us. Our task must be to free ourselves from this prison by widening our circle of compassion to embrace all living creatures and the whole of nature in its beauty. (Albert Einstein)

This quotation reminds us of the delusion of our consciousness. Despite overwhelming evidence to the contrary, our dominant consciousness still assumes a separation of humans from nature. Over the last 15 years, the Global Ecological Integrity Group (GEIG) has aimed at freeing ourselves from this prison: humans are an integral part of the whole of nature. If we are losing sight of this basic truth, we are destroying the integrity of the Earth's ecological systems and ultimately our own.

It has been the contention of this book to place ecological integrity squarely into our way of thinking about the environment. The environment is not separated from us, it is not 'the other' and not a mere assembly of natural resources. The environment is an ecological system with humans included, a community of life. It makes no sense, therefore, to protect the environment in an altruistic or compassionate manner like giving to charity. There isn't much morality involved when looking after your own needs.

One of the enduring themes of this book has been to consider care for ecological integrity not as a moral option, but as a matter of compelling human rationality in all its inter-related forms, scientific, ethical, political and legal, philosophical and theological. So beyond all ethical reasons, the case for ecological integrity is based on good science and sound argument. The chapters by Beumer, Huynen and Martens, Soskolne, Rees and others provide the evidence that the concept of integrity best describes health and wellbeing. The chapters by L. Westra, Mackey, Taylor and Engel all demonstrate the central importance of the concept for the development of public policy and governance. As a measurable parameter, ecological integrity is equally important for economics, as the chapters by Crabbé and Manno, Pimentel, Miller and R. Westra have shown. It is also used in the work of many professions. Fundamentally, it reflects common sense. Most people assume stability and reliability if a structure, system or a person is said to have integrity. Moreover, we think of integrity as an ethical quality. A person of integrity is dependable, responsible and clear in their judgement of good and bad.

Ecological integrity reasoning has been so fruitful because of its interdisciplinary and integrative characteristics (see, for example, Pimentel et al, 2000; Manuel-Navarrete et al, 2007). When health experts, environmental scientists, philosophers, theologians, lawyers and economists have no difficulty agreeing on the validity of the same concept, surely that is an encouraging sign!

Caring for ecological integrity is the adequate response to the crisis of human existence. This is the book's title, content and conclusion. In the following I will outline some ideas about governance as a next logical step. As we become aware of the fact that human existence is threatened by the disintegration and collapse of ecosystems, we also become aware of the need to restore their integrity. There is a direct link between the experience of disintegration and the need for re-integration. Consequently, restoring and protecting the integrity of the Earth's ecological systems is the most pressing issue for human governance.

HOW CAN WE ENVISAGE GOVERNANCE FOR ECOLOGICAL INTEGRITY?

Again, the book's title gives us an important clue. If human existence is threatened, the notion of human existence deserves full attention. This notion involves the conditions under which human life is possible, but also the individual human condition. In fact, reconciling human existence with ecological integrity is foremost a personal challenge. It is hard to imagine governance for ecological integrity if we are not clear about the kind of individual consciousness that is required here. We have to first leave our personal prison 'by widening our circles of compassion to embrace all living creatures and the whole of nature in its beauty'.

Such holism is alien to governance models and political ideologies that have shaped modernity. Liberalism has overexposed the individual, overlooking the common good, and socialism has overexposed the common good, overlooking the individual. Both have ignored the reality of social interdependencies. Worse, and truly alarming for our time, they have also ignored the reality of ecological interdependencies. In the Western traditions of anthropocentrism and dualism, liberalism and socialism, by focusing on the social context of human existence, had no sensitivity for its ecological context.

The new model of governance can no longer be Western; it must be global. And its subject can no longer be human communities, excluding life communities. This model of truly global governance has found its best expression in the Earth Charter.

The Earth Charter has been described as having potential to 'play a vital role in advancing the global governance structures, instruments and processes needed to secure a more just, sustainable and peaceful world' (Mackey, this volume, p62). The emphasis is on potential and the significance of the role; it can only function as a signpost towards new governance.

Remarkably, the Charter addresses states, business and civil society alike. It assumes the legitimacy of the existing United Nations system and international law. There is no speculation about a world without states, a world republic or some other kind of new world order. In this sense, the Charter takes a realistic, political approach. However, by pronouncing the new principles of the community of life and ecological integrity, the Earth Charter expects states and other institutions of governance to reconsider anthropocentrism and dualism. In this sense, it takes a revolutionary approach.

The Preamble of the Earth Charter starts with a vision 'to bring forth a sustainable global society founded on respect for nature, universal human rights, economic justice and a culture of peace'. These four commitments form the structure of the Charter itself, with its 77 principles around four main themes: 'respect and care for the community of life' (Principles 1–4), 'ecological integrity' (5–8), 'social and economic justice' (9–12) and 'democracy, nonviolence and peace' (13–16).

The first two themes contain the ecological principles, the other two themes contain the social and economic principles of a sustainable global society. To this end, we can say that the Earth Charter is reflective of the concept of sustainable development with its three components of environmental, social and economic equity. The three-components model is commonly accepted by states, expressed in many soft law documents (for example the 1992 Rio Declaration and the 2002 Johannesburg Declaration) and popular among business. Known as the 'three-pillar' model (OECD Glossary, 2005), it is consistent with the current structures of global capitalism and international law.

However, the Earth Charter organizes the three components in a different way. It not only defines them in great detail – a novelty in itself! – but also clarifies their relationship to each other. The ecological system is not merely the resource base for human consumption and not just one of three equally important systems. It is the basis of all life, including human social and economic systems. The Earth Charter strongly rejects the three-pillar model as inadequate for sustainable development. The more accurate model has two pillars, with ecological integrity as its fundament.

We might picture this model as the façade of a temple with two pillars (social and economic welfare), a foundation (ecological integrity) and a roof (symbolizing cultural identity). Such a 'temple of life' surely is more sustainable than three pillars lacking fundament and roof.

The two models represent profoundly different rationalities. The three-pillar model follows economic rationality,[1] the temple of life ecological rationality.[2] And while current economic practice has not even given equal importance to social and environmental concerns, the popular three-pillar model would still follow economic rationality, even though it could be perceived as 'enlightened' economic rationality. The concept of sustainable development is stretching the old paradigm, but so far has not replaced it.

At an ethical level, the three-pillar model represents anthropocentrism. By contrast, the Earth Charter promotes a shift from a narrow human-centred to a broader life-centred perspective. This shift marks the difference between the current business-as-usual approach and the future approach of governance for ecological integrity.

A COVENANT FOR THE COMMUNITY OF LIFE

The morality underpinning the new governance model is spelled out in the Earth Charter's Preamble: 'It is imperative that we, the peoples of Earth, declare our responsibility to one another, to the greater community of life, and to future generations.' Stating the need for responsibility to one another as 'imperative' recalls Kant's categorical imperative, and the inclusion of the community of life and future generations fits Jonas's 'imperative of responsibility' (Jonas, 1984).

The Preamble's notion of universal responsibility is reflective of the principle of sustainability (Bosselmann, 2008) and cannot be confused with shallow versions of sustainable development. The indispensable element of the new categorical imperative is responsibility for the community of life. Whether such deviation represents an anti-Kantian or post-Kantian perspective may be a matter of debate (Ott, this volume), but its political importance cannot be in any doubt. If translated to political theory, responsibility for all life requires a total rethinking of law and governance.

An important link between ethical reasoning and changing our behaviour is to (publicly) declare the intent. This is the Preamble's imperative. Responsibility for the community of life must be 'declared', not just accepted. Only a declaration in the sense of a genuine commitment brings that responsibility. Depending on its socio-political context, a declaration can be a very powerful manifestation of changed awareness and morality. What then would qualify for a powerful declaration?

As individuals we can declare our responsibility in the form of a promise. A promise may be highly significant in a moral sense, but not normally in a legal sense. A promise cannot be enforced and there are no direct consequences in the event of its being breached. As a collective we can declare our responsibility in a variety of ways, for example as a code of conduct, statute, policy, act, constitution or international agreement (soft law, treaty and so on). All of these different declarations possess legal quality and can be enforced, albeit to varying degrees.

A covenant, on the other hand, is not legally binding and not even a legal document in a strict sense. Expressing a deeply felt commitment to one another, a covenant escapes the usual classification of social contracts. Yet it represents the most profound and powerful social bond we know. It takes its authorization not from a legal sovereign, but from a 'higher' sovereign understood as God, nature or universal order. We are all born into covenants, for example those of a family or local community. Any coherent group rests on some form of a covenant constituted by 'individuals-in-community' (Engel, 2007, p30) and serving as a 'matrix' (Elazar, 1998). The functioning of relationships depends on covenantal bonds and no community can exist without them. Considering the importance that the Earth Charter's values and principles have for humanity as whole, we can describe them as expressing covenantal global responsibilities. The Earth Charter, then, is a document that shows us how a covenant for the community of life might look. As such it may be defined as a 'universal covenant' (Engel, 2007, p35). However, a covenantal quality cannot be 'declared' or 'adopted', it must be created. The intensity and validity of a covenant will be determined by the process of individual commitments and the general realization of responsibilities involved. Arguably, this process has only just begun.

As the covenant underlies any form of social organization, it also underlies human governance. Fundamentally, governance is a set of rules and instruments that people need so they can organize their affairs effectively. A useful definition might be 'Governance is the framework of social and economic systems and legal and political structures through which humanity manages itself' (WHAT, 2000, p7). Declaring responsibility for the community of life and ecological integrity would then mean incorporating it into the 'framework of social and economic systems and legal and political structures'. Again, such incorporation is not possible through a single act. A covenantal responsibility of this nature is too fundamental (being non-anthropocentric) and too far-reaching (reflecting ecological rationality) to allow a simple act of incorporation, for example by a showing of hands or a rewriting of statutes. It can only emerge through a process.

During the 15 years of its existence, GEIG, a group itself bound by a covenant, has initiated and described the process towards governance for ecological integrity. Members and friends of GEIG have written widely about it, not least in this book. Thus, it may be possible to summarize where this process stands today.

REDEFINING THE PURPOSE OF GOVERNANCE

First, what is wrong with the dominant model of governance? The short answer is its ecological blindness. By overlooking the ecological dimension of human existence, conventional governance models are purely concerned with human welfare following economic rationality. This narrow anthropocentric view led to 'economic governance' on the one hand and 'environmental governance' on the other. The work of GEIG has contributed to the understanding of such limitations and, at the same time, raised the profile of ecological integrity as a common reference for both forms of governance.

Governance for ecological integrity is fundamentally different from environmental governance. In most societies environmental governance has never been more than a minor concern, an add-on, a minimalist, shallow programme designed to avoid litigation and voter disquiet. It is the poor cousin of economic governance as a motor for ongoing growth in productivity, profit and material output at the expense of social and environmental inequality. While governance for ecological integrity has its origins in holistic awareness, benign empowerment, social equality and profound care for the community of life, the current domination of economic governance is the product of personal distress and oppression. Its defensive, reactive, expert-based, problem-solving focus contrasts with our need for imaginative, proactive design and redesign approaches to personal, social and ecological health and wellbeing.

Second, throughout its conferences and publications GEIG has aimed at re-conceptualizing the nature and purpose of governance. Given the failures of governance systems so far, we need to decide whether we are correct in continuing to govern so as to maximize human freedom to use the Earth, intervening only when that use threatens or undermines the rights of other humans. The purpose must be to govern ourselves so that we function as productive members of a community of life that exists within a larger universal order.

The ethical implications of such a purpose description may not be entirely clear to everyone. Some would argue that anthropocentrism can be enlightened enough to embrace ecological integrity, while others consider this possible only on the basis of non-anthropocentrism. GEIG has treated the relationship between ecological integrity and human values with much care (Brown et al, 2000, pp398–400), but always highlighted the need to conceptualize governance for ecological integrity in non-anthropocentric terms (Westra, 1994, 1998 and 2006).

At a practical level, making the shift from anthropocentrism to ecocentrism may be more evolutionary. Most changes in society occur gradually, less abrupt than perhaps experienced at a personal level. As we look at the laws guiding our present governance systems, we can detect some trends that may not be dramatic in themselves, but taken together point into a new direction of governance.

For example, in a national legal system, the purpose of an act may be reflected in the long title or objects, and typically this is translated into practice by requiring the persons to whom the act gives decision-making powers to be guided by this purpose. The protection and restoration of ecological integrity could easily be described as a main purpose. Legislation may also stipulate that certain principles must be applied in making a particular decision. To this end, sustainability could be established as the key principle. Further, legislation commonly refers to decisions that must be taken for the public good or national interest. These notions could be understood to include the 'whole community' of present and future generations and non-human species. Similarly, it might be appropriate to require land-use planning decisions to be based on an ecological assessment. This would include the 'whole community' rather than an assessment of narrowly defined 'needs and desirability' as is so often the case in planning decisions. The list goes on.

There are many examples of advanced legislation of this kind. Early developments include the 1972 Great Lakes Water Quality Agreement mentioned by Laura Westra and Jack Manno in this book and various amendments towards biocentrism in the German Federal Nature Conservation Act. In 1991 New Zealand adopted the world's first general environmental code based on sustainability principles (Bosselmann, 1995, pp129–135). In 1992 the Canada Forest Accord was signed (Miller and Ehnes, 2000), and during the 1990s a number of countries, including the US, countries in Europe, Australia and New Zealand, increasingly adopted ecosystem approaches to environmental legislation (Brooks et al, 2002). More recent trends include the move towards integrated environmental management (Kotzé, 2007) and a general greening of constitutions with environmental rights and state obligations towards sustainable development (Bosselmann, 2008).

At the international level, sustainable development is now being considered as a principle of international law (Tladi, 2007, p112). And while international environmental law is still a long way from developing a coherent sustainability approach, soft law documents (for example Agenda 21), voluntary codes (Wood, 2006) and the Earth Charter are promoting integration and integrity.

All these trends may not amount to a complete turnaround, but seem to indicate a greater interest in integrative, more effective governance. What may be needed now is a clear vision of what the new form of governance might look like.

The community of life approach to governance is not intended to be a lofty, transcendental theory. It must be, literally and metaphorically, down to Earth, and grounded in our experience of the natural world. At every turn we must look at laws and aspects of existing governance systems and ask ourselves 'How would this look from the perspective of the whole Earth community?' What might a particular law look like if the subjects of it were not only human and we really acted as if the flourishing of the whole Earth community was our primary concern? For example, how can participation in decision-making ensure that humans are not the only affected parties to be considered? Do we have adequate techniques and methodologies for 'consulting' and ascertaining the current and future interests of rivers, lakes and soils? If not, how might they be developed?

The Earth Charter is not prescriptive in this respect and mainstream legal theory has only begun to consider the implications of ecological ethics for governance and law. But the emerging areas of ecological legal theory (Schröter, 1999), Earth jurisprudence (Cullinan, 2002, p143) and ecological jurisprudence have stimulated the legal debate. Clearly, support for Earth governance models, ecological justice and ecological human rights has grown in recent times.

In the following, we take a closer look at two of the most fundamental concepts in law – justice and human rights. If we realize, for example, how the Earth Charter promotes a broader concept of justice and linkages between human rights and responsibilities, the case for redefining justice and human rights becomes strong and convincing.

Reconceptualizing Justice and Human Rights

Traditionally, legal relationships – including those of justice – are perceived as relationships purely between people: humans have no legal obligations towards nature, and nature has no rights towards humans. Environmental law and governance are deeply moulded in this anthropocentric tradition. However, since the early 1970s, this anthropocentric perception has been challenged from an environmental ethical point of view (Stone, 1996). The differences between anthropocentric and ecocentric positions continue to be debated, but a consensus already exists that the success or failure of environmental law depends on sound ethical fundaments (Kiss and Shelton, 2000, pp11–27).

In recent times, environmental ethics have stimulated new theories of justice (Bosselmann, 2006). There are two broad approaches. One is to maintain a categorical separation between ethics and justice; the other is to utilize ethical principles for the legal concept of justice. While each approach can be associated with either an anthropocentric or ecocentric perspective, it is important to note that the current justice debate does not entirely follow this divide. There are various attempts to accommodate some form of ecocentrism within the Rawlsian conception of justice. One of the important issues with respect to governance is whether responsibilities towards the community of life can be addressed by extending the liberal idea of justice. While there is some common ground between liberalism and ecologism, for example the idea of guardianship for non-human and future interests (Baxter, 2004) or the concept of 'restraint' (Wissenburg, 1999, p193), liberal extensionism insists on individual autonomy in a paradigmatic way (Gillroy, 2000, p12), thus seeing responsibilities as categorically distinct from rights. So far, liberal theorists have rejected any attempt to redefine property in the light of ecological restraints. As Prue Taylor has argued (Chapter 6 of this volume), ecological integrity requires us to create a much closer relationship between rights and responsibilities than political liberalism would allow for.

For a theory of ecological justice it is not enough to merely consider environmental ethics; unless we see all the various conceptions of justice as reflections of ethics, we will not be able to transform them. But even if we agree that 'all claims of justice are rooted in certain values other than justice itself' (Heller, 1987), the problem of reaching sufficient commonality of values remains. Can a commonality of values simply be assumed or could it only emerge from a public discourse? This question leads us to the problem of how ethical norms can be incorporated in ways that are consistent with democratic process. As has been suggested by Konrad Ott (Chapter 3 of this volume), ecocentrism does not have to be either imposed or purely hoped for as a matter of course. Just as discourse ethics can be influenced by new ideas, new ideas can also directly influence the political and legal system. If the legal system provides for sufficient resonances, it can absorb ecocentrism. While public debate is necessary, progress can also be made through such 'self-reflection of law' (Bosselmann, 1995, p234).

A decisive cue in favour of eco-justice is the principle of ecological integrity, as it includes respect and care for the community of life. The intrinsic values of 'non-human others' can be expressed in legal concepts, not least in the idea of justice (Westra, 2006, Chapter 6).

Both liberal and ecological approaches to eco-justice aim to integrate the non-human world in environmental decision-making. Principally, the integration can be pursued either through ethical discourse or through justice discourse. It would not matter if both discourses would equally lead to better decision-making. But do they? According to Rawls (1993), justice is based on a commonly agreed discourse and, therefore, facilitated by institutions, in other words law and governance. Ethics, on the other hand, reflects comprehensive ideals that cannot per se be communicated through institutions. Ethics may inform justice, but cannot guide decision-making in ways that the institutions of justice are offering.

The categorical distinction between justice and morality determines all liberal conceptions of justice. The inherent assumption is that issues of justice are different from, and superior to, moral values. Justice represents the values of an assumed public rationality that disassociates itself from a morality of compassion and empathy. No matter how important the non-human world may be regarded by humans, it has to stay 'outside the scope of the theory of justice' (Rawls, 1993, p448). Attempts for an extension of justice can be made, of course, but they can hardly be presented as a 'green twist' (Wissenburg, 1999, p173) of Rawls's original position. Why should Rawls or any other liberal theorist throw the baby out with the bathwater? Their anthropocentric bias prevents them from expanding justice to include the community of life.

From an ecological point of view, ethics ought to be understood as informing *any* idea of justice. Having one set of (legal) justice principles for humans and another set of (moral) justice principles with respect to non-humans makes no sense. Nothing captures the ecological complexities better than the term 'ecological integrity'. It reflects the view that all living beings, including humans, depend on the integrity of the Earth's ecological systems. Thus, to correct the lopsided idea of justice favouring humans over other species, we need to consider 'interspecies justice' (Almond, 1995, p32). Ecological justice, therefore, is a three-fold concept containing the elements of intragenerational, intergenerational and interspecies justice (Bosselmann, 2006, p150).

Broadening the concept of justice in this manner would have profound consequences for the legal discourse in general and the design of environment-related laws in particular. The three elements of eco-justice can be used to interpret existing laws, to critically assess them and to guide the design of future laws. I have shown elsewhere how this can work in practice (Bosselmann, 2006, pp156–163). The New Zealand Resource Management Act 1991, for example, contains these three elements of justice, albeit in a rudimentary form. Courts have interpreted the Act in ways that clearly reveal applications of ecological justice. It became possible, therefore, to identify the Act's strengths and weaknesses, allowing a more informed discussion about improvements. Another example is the development of ecosystem regimes and management in North America and elsewhere. Most of the principles guiding them are, in some way or other, concerned with issues of ecological justice. To better understand and apply these principles, it would be useful to expressively relate them to the fundamental principle of ecological justice. This would, for example, give the precautionary principle a clearer direction and wider scope.[3]

At the international level, some soft and hard law documents take an ecosystem approach and are also reflective of global and ecological justice. Examples include the 1982 World Charter for Nature and the Earth Charter, and to some extent the 1992 Convention on Biological Diversity and the 1991 Protocol on Environmental Protection amending the 1959 Antarctic Treaty. The implementation of these and other agreements could be greatly improved if supported by a defined concept of ecological justice.

The reasoning for an ethically reflected concept of justice also applies to human rights. Just as there is no justice without some underpinning morality, there are no human rights without ethical assumptions. For example, whether or not property rights should be defined to include ecological limitations is not a matter of the 'law', but of ethical considerations underpinning it. Most constitutions define private property as a combination of individual entitlement and social responsibility. Property cannot be protected in the abstract, but only in a social context. It can, therefore, be reasoned that human rights are limited not solely by their social context, but also by their ecological context (Taylor, Chapter 6 of this volume). Individual freedom is determined not just by laws of society, but also by laws of nature. The ecological approach to human rights has influenced human rights theory and constitutional development, for example in Germany and Brazil (Bosselmann, 2001), as well as international law (Taylor, 1998).

Comparing the justice debate to the rights debate, we find that the objections against a concept of ecological justice are the same as those against ecological human rights.

Central to the liberal idea of justice has been the liberal conception of rights. And although only a few liberal theorists of justice have argued for the possibility of extending rights to animals and plants, it would be possible to do so, at least structurally. From a purely legal perspective, rights can be attributed to all sorts of entities, like, for example, companies and states. There is no legal reason to confine rights to the sphere of human beings. The crucial issue to be addressed is what should be gained with rights for nature?

Rights for nature have been advocated since ancient times (the Stoic School) and include such names as Spinoza, Leipniz, Goethe, Fichte, Schopenhauer, Bentham and, in our times, Jonas, Meyer-Abich and, with respect to animals, Singer. All of these were or are philosophers, but it took a lawyer, Christopher Stone (1996), to trigger a wider debate on rights and social change. To a degree, this debate can be seen as settled now. Adding nature's rights to the catalogue of human rights would not make much difference so long as the rights interpretation of liberalism and individualism prevails. What matters is ecological awareness. If we realize individual freedom is determined not only by social, but also by ecological relations, the interpretation of human rights may indeed change. And only then will it be possible to temper rights with responsibilities ('ecological human rights').

CONCLUSION

It is appropriate that our search for responsible governance should end with human rights and responsibilities. But the search must also begin here. It is the most fundamental level of governance for ecological integrity.

Because human beings as individuals, in community and in humanity are meant to follow a universal order of human rights, they are related to one another. This inter-relationship has created a bond, or covenant we might say, based on freedom, respect and equity. This is the theory of current global governance.

The practice is the opposite. In reality economic wants continue to trump human needs. They seek first to realize basic economic rights. Where political oppression reigns, they seek first to realize political rights. Every bit of progress in one area of life, however, causes the structure of life to get out of balance. The obsession with economic growth in industrial nations has pushed the political, social and personal balance of human beings to the edge of destruction. And the hegemony of the rich is pushing the poor over the edge.

If this practice is bad enough and calling loudly for global economic justice, the call for global ecological justice must be even louder. The human race has pushed itself to the edge of destruction. Economic wants have trumped ecological needs, so much so that our present form of governance finds care for ecological integrity too costly.

To reverse this logic of self-destruction, humanity has to restrain itself. Our idea of governance needs to include an appreciation for the entire community of life. At the heart of this attempt is ecological citizenship (Bosselmann, 2007, p14) changing 'the role of *Homo sapiens* from conqueror of the land-community to plain member and citizen of it' (Leopold, 1949, p204). If we see ourselves as citizens of social and ecological communities, we become aware of the incredible power of connectedness and responsibility. We will need to mobilize all this power to make the transition from *Homo economicus* to *Homo ecologicus*, to eventually justify the name *Homo sapiens*.

NOTES

1   For an illustration see John Emerson's description: 'The problem with economic man is not that he is an imaginary theoretical fiction, but that there are too many of him. Economic rationality, which is supposedly a purely formal assumption, has bled out into the community and has become a foundation for ethics.' ('What does economic rationality do?', www.idiocentrism.com/economic%20rationality.htm).
2   See for an overview Bosselmann (1995). One key aspect differentiating ecological from economic rationality is the concept of individual freedom; it cannot be perceived in isolation from its social and ecological context; see, for example, Chaudhury (2004).
3   Following this approach, members of GEIG have recently assisted in drafting the International Union for the Conservation of Nature (IUCN) 'Guidelines for Applying the Precautionary Principle for Biodiversity Conservation and Natural Resource Management' (www.iucn.org/themes/law/pdfdocuments/LN250507_PP Guidelines.pdf).

REFERENCES

Almond, B. (1995) 'Rights and justice in the environmental debate', in D. Cooper and J. Palmer (eds) *Just Environments: Intergenerational, International and Interspecies Issues*, Routledge, London

Baxter, B. H. (2004) *A Theory of Ecological Justice*, Routledge, London

Bosselmann, K. (1992) *Im Namen der Natur*, Scherz Publishing, Munich, Germany

Bosselmann, K. (1995) *When Two Worlds Collide: Society and Ecology*, RSVP, Auckland

Bosselmann, K. (2001) 'Human rights and the environment: Redefining fundamental principles?', in B. Gleeson and N. Low (eds) *Governance for the Environment*, Palgrave, London, pp118–134

Bosselmann, K. (2006) 'Ecological justice and law', in B. J. Richardson and S. Wood (eds), *Environmental Law for Sustainability*, Hart Publishing, Oxford, UK, pp129–163

Bosselmann, K. (2007) 'Institutions of global governance', in C. Soskolne (ed) *Sustaining Life on Earth*, Lexington Books, Lanham, MD, pp9–25

Bosselmann, K. (2008) *The Principle of Sustainability: Governance and Law*, Ashgate, Aldershot, UK

Brooks, R. O., Jones, R. and Virginia, R. A. (2002) *Law and Ecology: The Rise of the Ecosystem Regime*, Ashgate, Aldershot, UK

Brown, D., Manno, J., Westra, L., Pimentel. D. and Crabbé, P. (2000) 'Implementing global ecological integrity: A synthesis', in D. Pimentel, L. Westra and R. F. Noss (eds) *Ecological Integrity*, Island Press, Washington, DC, pp385–405

Chaudhury, M. (2004) *Bounds of Freedom: Popper, Liberty and Ecological Rationality*, Rodopi, New York

Cooper, D. and Palmer, J. (eds) (1995) *Just Environments: Intergenerational, International and Interspecies Issues*, Routledge, London

Cullinan, C. (2002) *Wild Law: Governing People for Earth*, Siber Ink, Claremont, South Africa

Elazar, D. J. (1998) *The Covenant Tradition in Politics* (four volumes), Transaction Publishers, New Brunswick, NJ

Engel, J. R. (2007) 'A covenant of covenants', in C. Soskolne (ed) *Sustaining Life on Earth*, Lexington Books, Lanham, MD, pp27–40

Gillroy, J. M. (2000) *Justice and Nature*, Georgetown University Press, Washington, DC

Heller, A. (1987) *Beyond Justice*, Basil Blackwell, Oxford, UK

Jonas, H. (1984) *The Imperative of Responsibility*, University of Chicago Press, Chicago, IL

Kiss, A. and Shelton, D. (2000) *International Environmental Law* (second edition), Transnational Publishers, Ardsley, NJ

Kotzé, L. J. (2007) 'Toward sustainable governance in South Africa', in C. Soskolne (ed) *Sustaining Life on Earth*, Lexington Books, Lanham, MD, pp155–169

Leopold, A. (1949) *A Sand County Almanac*, Oxford University Press, New York

Manuel-Navarrete, D., Kay, J. K. and Dolderman, D. (2007) 'Evolution of the ecological integrity debate', in C. Soskolne (ed) *Sustaining Life on Earth*, Lexington Books, Lanham, MD, pp127–153

Miller, P. and Ehnes, J. W. (2000), 'Can Canadian approaches to forest management maintain ecological integrity?', in D. Pimentel, L. Westra and R. F. Noss (eds) *Ecological Integrity*, Island Press, Washington, DC, pp157–175

OECD Glossary of Statistical Terms (2005) 'Three-pillar approach to sustainable development', http://stats.oecd.org/glossary/detail.asp?ID=6591

Pimentel, D., Westra, L. and Noss, R. F. (eds) (2000) *Ecological Integrity*, Island Press, Washington, DC

Rawls, J. (1993) *A Theory of Justice*, Oxford University Press, Oxford, UK

Schröter, M. (1999), *Mensch, Erde Recht: Grundfragen ökologischer Rechtstheorie*, Nomos, Baden-Baden, Germany

Stone, C. D. (1996) *Should Trees Have Standing?* (25th Anniversary Edition), Oxford University Press, Oxford, UK

Taylor, P. (1998) 'From environmental to ecological human rights: A new dynamic in international law?', *Georgetown International Environmental Law Review*, vol 10, pp309–397

Tladi, D. (2007) *Sustainable Development in International Law*, Pretoria University Law Press, Pretoria, South Africa

Westra, L. (1994) *An Environmental Proposal for Ethics: The Principle of Ecological Integrity*, Rowman and Littlefield, Lanham, MD

Westra, L. (1998) *Living in Integrity: A Global Ethic to Restore a Fragmented Earth*, Rowman and Littlefield, Lanham, MD

Westra, L. (2006) *Environmental Justice and the Rights of Unborn and Future Generations*, Earthscan, London

WHAT (2000) 'Governance for a sustainable future', report by the World Humanity Action Trust, London

Wissenburg, M. (1999) 'An extension of the Rawlsian savings principle to liberal theories of justice in general', in A. Dobson (ed) *Fairness and Futurity*, Oxford University Press, Oxford, UK, pp173–194

Wood, S. (2006) 'Voluntary environmental codes and sustainability', in B. J. Richardson and S. Wood (eds) *Environmental Law for Sustainability*, Hart Publishing, Oxford, UK, pp229–276

List of Contributors

Carijn Beumer is a junior researcher and a teacher at the International Centre for Integrated assessment and Sustainable development (ICIS). She holds a MA diploma in Arts and Science Studies at the Faculty of Arts and Culture of Maastricht University, the Netherlands. After graduating in 2005 she studied Psychology at the Open University Netherlands and started her own platform for consultancy in Quality of Life. In 2007 she started working at ICIS. Her researech interests are ethics, cultural values, perspectives on nature, the art of living, biodiversity in a changing climate, global complexities and sustainability science. She is preparing a PhD trajectory on the effects of climate change on the perspectives of biodiversity conservation.

Klaus Bosselmann, PhD, is Professor of Law and Director of the New Zealand Centre for Environmental Law at the University of Auckland. He has previously taught at the Freie Universität Berlin and was co-founder of Germany's first Institute for Environmental Law in Bremen (1987). He has been a visiting professor at various universities in the US, Brazil, Sweden, Italy and Germany. A co-founder of the Greens in Germany (1980) and New Zealand (1990), he has strong interests in political ecology and social change. He is currently Co-Chair of the Ethics Specialist Group in the World Conservation Union (IUCN). The latest of his fifteen books in the area of environmental law is *The Principle of Sustainability: Transforming Law and Governance* (2008).

Donald A. Brown is Associate Professor of Environmental Ethics, Science, and Law at Penn State University, where he teaches interdisciplinary courses on climate change and sustainable development. He is also director of the Pennsylvania Environmental Research Consortium, an organization comprised of 56 Pennsylvania universities and the Pennsylvania Departments of Environmental Protection and Conservation and Natural Resources. He has written about and lectured extensively on climate change issues over the last 20 years. His career interest has been the need to integrate environmental science, economic, and law in environmental policymaking. His latest book is *American Heat: Ethical Problems with the US Response to Global Warming.*

Helmut Burkhardt was born in Romania, educated in Germany, and lives in Canada. He has a doctorate in physics from the Faculty of Natural Sciences at the University of Stuttgart in Germany. His early research was on thermonuclear fusion and on magneto-hydrodynamic energy conversion, which he studied at the University of Stuttgart, the Institute for Mathematical Sciences, New York University, and at the University of Quebec. Later in his career he got interested in a full spectrum, wide-angle scientific view of the world and in scientific ethics. He is life member and past president of Science for Peace Canada, member of the International Network of Engineers and Scientists for Global Responsibility, and member of the Canadian Pugwash Group.

Simon Counsell directs the Rainforest Foundation UK, www.rainforestfoundationuk.org, the non-governmental organization working for the rights of local and indigenous peoples in tropical rainforest areas of the world.

Philippe Crabbé is Professor Emeritus of Environmental and Natural Resources Economics at the University of Ottawa and has been teaching in the areas of sustainable development and complex systems for over twenty years. He was the co-editor of one of the first books on the economics of natural resources and the environment in Canada and, more recently, of a multidisciplinary book devoted to ecological integrity, published in the NATO Science Series. He is a past President of the Société Canadienne de Sciences Économiques. He was Lead Author for the IPCC Third and Fourth Assessment Report (WG III). He has also been serving on the Advisory Committee for the Environmental Commissioner of Ontario.

Joseph W. Dellapenna is Professor of Law at Villanova University, in Pennsylvania. He has taught at law schools in the US and abroad for 38 years, during which time he has practised, taught and written about water, both in the US and internationally. He teaches a course on managing the water environment, as well as courses on admiralty, Chinese law, comparative law, and transnational litigation. He has been a member of the faculty of the University of Cincinnati and of Willamette University. He has been a Fulbright Senior Professor in the Republic of China, the People's Republic of China, and Portugal.

Ron Engel is Professor Emeritus at Meadville/Lombard Theological School (University of Chicago affiliate), and Senior Research Consultant, with primary responsibilities for the Program on North American Global Responsibilities, at the Center for Humans and Nature (New York and Chicago). In 2007 he served as Senior Research Fellow at Martin Marty Center for Religion and Public Life, Divinity School, University of Chicago. He founded and led the Ethics Working Group in the World Conservation Union (IUCN) for twenty years and served on the core drafting committee for the Earth Charter. He is a member of the steering committee for the Global Ecological Integrity Group.

Robert Goodland, an environmental scientist, served as the environmental adviser to the World Bank from 1978 to 2001, where he wrote most of their social and environmental policies. He catalysed the creation of the World Commission on Dams, and was technical director of the independent Extractive Industry Review. He is helping the Catholic Bishops Conference with a sectoral assessment of the impacts of mining on Indigenous Peoples and rice production in the Philippines.

Maud Huynen holds Masters degrees in Environmental Health Science (2001) and Epidemiology (2003) and a PhD in Global Health (2008). She conducted her PhD research on 'Future health in a globalising world' at the International Centre for Integrated Assessment and Sustainable Development (ICIS), Maastricht University. She currently works at ICIS as a researcher on topics related to global and environmental health, and she teaches in several courses at Maastricht University on topics related to sustainable development, global health, globalization, and integrated assessment. She is also a member of the editorial board of the international journal *Globalization and Health*.

James R. Karr was born in the US, where a fascination with nature led to his career in ecology and environmental policy. After completing his education at the University of Illinois, he held postdoctoral appointments at Princeton University and the Smithsonian Tropical Research Institute, Panama (where he later became deputy and acting director), and faculty positions at several US universities: Purdue, Illinois, Virginia Tech, and Washington. Over time, his research expanded from basic ecology to environmental policy and from natural ecosystems to human environmental impacts. He developed the first ecological multimetric index to evaluate the effects of human actions on the health of living systems. His present concern is how to incorporate biological information into societal decision-making.

Brendan Mackey is a Professor of Environmental Science at The Australian National University, Canberra. His teaching and research are in the field of ecological conservation (with particular interest in forest ecosystems), along with environmental ethics and associated public policy concerns. He currently serves as co-chair of the Earth Charter International Council, and is a member of the IUCN Ethics Specialist Group.

Jack P. Manno is Associate Professor of Environmental Studies at the State University College of Environmental Science and Forestry in Syracuse, New York, USA. His research and writing focuses on sustainability theory, in particular the translation of ecological concepts and principles into economic policy and governance practice. He is the author of *Privileged Goods: Commoditization and Its Impacts on Environment and Society*, and has been active in the Global Integrity Project since the early 1990s.

Pim Martens is Professor of Sustainable Development and the Director of the International Centre for Integrated assessment and Sustainable development (ICIS) at Maastricht University. Professor Martens has been a Fulbright New Century Scholar and winner of the Friedrich Wilhelm Bessel-Forschungspreis. In recent years, Martens has been a visiting professor at the London School of Hygiene and Tropical Medicine (UK), Harvard University (USA), Heidelberg University (Germany) and ETH Zurich (Switzerland). Martens has published 5 books and many articles in refereed journals on globalization and sustainable development.

Peter Miller is a Senior Scholar in Philosophy at the Centre for Forest Interdisciplinary Research at the University of Winnipeg, publishing in environmental ethics, forest and energy policy, and public values and participation. With Laura Westra, he co-edited *Just Ecological Integrity: The Ethics of Maintaining Planetary Life* (Rowman and Littlefield, 2002). He is active in several ENGOs and resource advisory processes and has led a number of regulatory interventions. Dr Miller is a former President of the Canadian Society for the Study of Practical Ethics.

Bradford W. Morse is a barrister and solicitor, and a Professor of Law at the University of Ottawa, where he has served as Vice-Dean and Director of Graduate Studies. He has taught a wide variety of courses including Canadian and comparative Indigenous law issues, labour, trusts, property and other subjects. He has also served as legal adviser to many First Nations as well as national and regional Aboriginal organizations in Canada,

Australia and New Zealand since 1974. Professor Morse was the Director of Research for the Aboriginal Justice Inquiry in Manitoba, the Chief of Staff to the Minister of Indian Affairs and Northern Development as well as a Fulbright Senior Scholar and a visiting scholar to a number of law schools over his career in Australia, Hong Kong, New Zealand and the US. He has authored over 100 books, articles, book chapters and commission reports.

Professor Dr **Konrad Ott**, fighting entropy since 1959, studied philosophy and history at the University of Frankfurt. In 1989, he did his PhD under the supervision of Jürgen Habermas about the origins and the discursive logic of scientific history. In the 1990s he worked at the universities of Tübingen and Zürich. His ongoing fields of research are discourse ethics, environmental ethics, theories of sustainability, ethical aspects of climate change, history of nature conservation. He has published in these fields. Since 2000 he has been a member of the German Environmental Advisory Council, which advises the German Government in environmental affairs. He is also a member of the German UNESCO commission and the Board for Sustainable Development of the Protestant Church of Germany.

David Pimentel is a professor of ecology and agricultural sciences at Cornell University, Ithaca, New York. His research spans the fields of energy, ecological and economic aspects of pest control, biological control, biotechnology, sustainable agriculture, land and water conservation, and environmental policy. Pimentel has published more than 600 scientific papers and 27 books and has served on many national and government committees, including the National Academy of Sciences, President's Science Advisory Council, US Department of Agriculture, US Department of Energy, US Department of Health, Education and Welfare, Office of Technology Assessment of the US Congress and the US State Department.

Having received his PhD in philosophy from Harvard, **Thomas Pogge** writes and teaches on moral and political philosophy, and Immanuel Kant. He is Professor of Philosophy and International Affairs at Yale University, Professorial Fellow at the ANU Centre for Applied Philosophy and Public Ethics (CAPPE), and Research Director at the Oslo University Centre for the Study of Mind in Nature (CSMN). He is editor for social and political philosophy for the Stanford Encyclopedia of Philosophy and a member of the Norwegian Academy of Science. With support from the Australian Research Council, the UK-based BUPA Foundation and the European Commission, he currently heads a team effort towards developing a complement to the pharmaceutical patent regime that would improve access to advanced medicines for the poor worldwide (www.patent2.org).

William Rees is a human ecologist, ecological economist, Professor and former Director of the University of British Columbia's School of Community and Regional Planning (SCARP) in Vancouver, Canada. He is currently Director of the School's Centre for Human Settlements where his research and teaching focus on planning for global ecological change and creating the necessary conditions for sustainable development. He is a founding member and past President of the Canadian Society for Ecological Economics. He is perhaps best known in 'ecol econ' as the originator and co-developer of ecological footprint analysis; his book on eco-footprinting, with Mathis Wackernagel, has been translated into eight languages, including Chinese. He has also authored more that 120 peer reviewed papers and book chapters and numerous popular articles on humanity's (un)sustainability conundrum.

Colin Soskolne was born and raised in South Africa. He has been with the University of Alberta, Canada, since 1985. Educated at the University of the Witwatersrand in Johannesburg, he trained initially in applied mathematics. He first worked as a statistician in education research and then moved into biostatistics, focusing on occupational cancer, both in toxicological and human studies. After his PhD in epidemiology from the University of Pennsylvania in 1982, he moved to Canada. His research interests soon expanded from the occupational environment to include the broader environment, as well as on ethics. He is currently concerned, as a transdisciplinary researcher, about expanding the methods of epidemiology to measure health impacts from global change to better inform policy for the sustainability of life on Earth. Having contributed some 300 published works, he is most recently senior editor of *Sustaining Life on Earth: Environmental and Human Health through Global Governance* (Lexington Books, 2008).

Prue Taylor LLB, LLM (Hons), LLM (Envt'l & Energy) received her legal qualifications from Victoria University, New Zealand and Tulane University, US. She has been teaching law at the University of Auckland since 1995. She currently teaches environmental and planning law to graduate and undergraduate students. She became the Deputy Director of the New Zealand Centre for Environmental Law in 2003, and has been a long-standing member of the IUCN Commission of Environmental Law and its Ethics Specialist Group. Her specialist interests are in the areas of climate change, human rights, biotechnology, environmental governance, ocean law and policy, and environmental ethics. In 2007 she received an outstanding achievement award from the World Conservation Union in recognition of her contribution, as a world pioneer on law, ethics and climate change.

Laura Westra is Professor Emerita (Philosophy), University of Windsor, PhD in Law, Osgoode Hall Law School and Adjunct Professor of Social Science, York University, Canada. After her first PhD in philosophy she taught at several universities in Canada and the US, specializing in environmental ethics and environmental justice. In 1992 she founded the Global Ecological Integrity Group, and over the following 7 years she was funded by Canadian sources to initiate and continue the work of the group. She returned to school in 2000 to pursue a second PhD in Jurisprudence. She is the author of 18 books, including *Environmental Justice and the Rights of Unborn and Future Generations* (Earthscan, 2006) and *Environmental Justice and the Rights of Indigenous Peoples* (Earthscan, 2007), and has contributed articles and chapters to over 80 journals and books.

Richard Westra has taught at universities and colleges around the world, including The Royal Military College of Canada, Queen's University, Kingston, the International Study Centre, East Sussex, UK and the College of the Bahamas, Nassau. He is currently Assistant Professor in the Division of International and Area Studies, Pukyong National

University, Pusan, South Korea. His work has been published in numerous international journals, and he has co-edited and contributed to several books, including *Marxist Perspectives on South Korea in the Global Economy* (Ashgate, 2007) and *Political Economy and Global Capitalism: The 21st Century, Present and Future* (Anthem, 2007).

Index

The Transformation of Agri-Food Systems
Globalization, Supply Chains and Smallholder Farmers
Ellen B. McCullough, Prabhu L. Pingali and Kostas G. Stamoulis

The driving forces of income growth, demographic shifts, globalization and technical change have led to a reorganization of food systems from farm to plate. The characteristics of supply chains – particularly the role of supermarkets – linking farmers have changed, from consumption and retail to wholesale, processing, procurement and production.

This has had a dramatic effect on smallholder farmers, particularly in developing countries. This book presents a comprehensive framework for assessing the impacts of changing agri-food systems on smallholder farmers, recognizing the importance of heterogeneity between developing countries as well as within them.

The book includes a number of case studies from Asia, Africa, Latin America and Eastern Europe, which are used to illustrate differences in food systems' characteristics and trends. The country case studies explore impacts on the small farm sector across different countries, local contexts, and farm types. Published with FAO.

Paperback £39.95 • 416 pages • 978-1-84407-569-0 • 2008

The Future Control of Food
A Guide to International Negotiations and Rules
on Intellectual Property, Biodiversity and Food Security
Geoff Tansey and Tasmin Rajotte

'This is the best single summary of the political choices facing food and agriculture policymakers that has been written in this decade.'
Pat Mooney, Executive Director, the ETC Group

This book is the first wide-ranging guide to the key issues of intellectual property and ownership, genetics, biodiversity and food security. Proceeding from an introduction and overview of the issues, comprehensive chapters cover negotiations and instruments in the World Trade Organization, Convention on Biological Diversity, UN Food and Agriculture Organization, World Intellectual Property Organization, the International Union for the Protection of New Varieties of Plants and various other international bodies.

The final part discusses the responses of civil society groups to the changing global rules, how these changes affect the direction of research and development, the nature of global negotiation processes and various alternative futures. Published with IDRC and QIAP.

Paperback • £19.99 • 224 pages • 978-1-84407-429-7 • 2008

For more details and a full listing of Earthscan titles visit:
www.earthscan.co.uk

publishing for a sustainable future

A History of World Agriculture
From the Neolithic Age to the Current Crisis
Marcel Mazoyer and Laurence Roudart

'A magnificent book, by far the best ever produced on the subject.'
Samir Amin

A History of World Agriculture begins with the emergence of agriculture after thousands of years in which human societies had depended on hunting and gathering.

It shows how agricultural techniques developed in the different regions of the world, and how this extraordinary wealth of knowledge, tradition, and natural variety is endangered today by global capitalism, as it forces the unequal agrarian heritages of the world to conform to the norms of profit.

During the twentieth century, mechanization, motorization, and specialization have brought to a halt the pattern of cultural and environmental responses that characterized the global history of agriculture until then. Today, a small number of corporations have the capacity to impose on the planet the farming methods that they find most profitable. Mazoyer and Roudart propose an alternative global strategy that can safeguard the economies of the poor countries, reinvigorate the global economy, and create a livable future for all.

Paperback £22.95 • 512 pages • 978-1-84407-399-3 • 2006

Hunger and Health
World Hunger Series 2007
United Nations World Food Programme

'We are deeply in debt to those who have written and contributed to Hunger and Health. Let this report... serve as the roadmap that we must all follow.'
Paul Farmer, MD, Harvard Medical School and Partners in Health

Hunger and Health explores the multiple relationships between hunger and poor health, and how they affect the growth of individuals, physiologically and psychologically, constraining the development of nations both socially and economically.

Examining the profound effect that hunger has on health, including disease prevention and treatment, it gives special attention to access to quality food and healthcare, in particular for the marginalized and poor. It also identifies critical junctures in the human life cycle when the benefits of reducing hunger and improving poor health have a profound impact. It demonstrates how aligning of hunger and health interventions can offer proven solutions that reach those most in need, and contains compelling evidence which confirms that hunger and poor health are solvable problems today. Essential reading for anyone concerned about eliminating hunger.

Paperback • £18.99 • 192 pages • 978-1-84407-546-1 • 2007

For more details and a full listing of Earthscan titles visit:
www.earthscan.co.uk

publishing for a sustainable future

The New Peasantries

Struggles for Autonomy and Sustainability in an Era of Empire and Globalization
By Jan Douwe van der Ploeg

'Jan Douwe van der Ploeg combines long engagement in the empirical study of farming and farmers, and of alternative agricultures, in very different parts of the world, with a sophisticated analytical acumen and capacity to provoke in fruitful ways.' Henry Bernstein, School of Oriental and African Studies, University of London, UK

'This book makes a timely and original contribution. The author revitalizes our interest in peasant societies through an in-depth examination of how rural populations in state systems respond to neo-liberal globalization.' Robert E. Rhoades, University of Georgia, USA

This book demonstrates that the peasantries of this world are far from waning. Instead, both industrialized and developing countries are witnessing complex and richly chequered processes of 'repeasantization'. These arguments are based on three longitudinal studies (in Peru, Italy and The Netherlands) that span 30 years and which provide original and thought-provoking insights into rural and agrarian development processes. The book combines and integrates different bodies of literature: the rich traditions of peasant studies, development sociology, rural sociology, neo-institutional economics and the recently emerging debates on Empire.

Hardback £65.00 · 384 pages · 9781844075584

Human Health and Forests

A Global Overview of Issues, Practice and Policy
Edited by Carol J. Pierce Colfer

Hundreds of millions of people live and work in forests across the world. One vital aspect of their lives, yet largely unexamined, is the challenge of protecting and enhancing the unique relationship between the health of forests and the health of people. This book, written for a broad audience, is the first comprehensive introduction to the issues surrounding the health of people living in and around forests, particularly in Asia, South America and Africa.

This book is a vital addition to the knowledge base of all professionals, academics and students working on forests, natural resources management, health and development worldwide.

Part I is a set of synthesis chapters, addressing policy, public health, environmental conservation and ecological perspectives on health and forests (including women and child health, medicinal plants and viral diseases such as Ebola, SARS and Nipah Encephalitis).

Part II takes a multi-lens approach, featuring case studies from around the world that cover important issues such as the links between HIV/AIDS and the forest sector, and between diet and health.

Part III looks at the specific challenges to health care delivery in forested areas, including remoteness and the integration of traditional medicine with modern health care. It concludes with a synthesis designed for use by practitioners and policymakers to work with forest dwellers to improve their health and their ecosystems.

Published with CIFOR and People and Plants International

Hardback £65.00 · 400 pages · 9781844075324

publishing for a sustainable future

Public and Private in Natural Resource Governance
A False Dichotomy?
Thomas Sikor

'The book is excellent for courses in governance and public policy in any resource and environmental field.' *Jeff Romm, professor for resource policy, University of California at Berkeley, US*

Bringing together a group of internationally respected researchers, this book provides a new perspective on prominent issues in resource governance, including the state, NGOs, civil society, communities, participation, devolution, privatization and hybrid institutions, highlighting the three-dimensional nature of relations between 'public' and 'private'.

It builds on empirical analyses from six fields of natural resource governance – agri-environment, biodiversity, bioenergy, food quality and safety, forestry and rural water – and employs a comparative approach that goes beyond the specifi cities of individual policy fields, recognizing shared elements and allowing for a greater understanding of the dynamics underlying governance processes. Introductions to the volume and to each section summarize the key debates and highlight linkages between chapters.

This is essential reading for academics, students and policy experts in natural resource governance, development and environmental policy.

Hardback £70.00 · 256 pages · 978-1-84407-525-6 · 2008

The School Food Revolution
Public Food and the Challenge of Sustainable Development
Kevin Morgan and Roberta Sonnino

Drawing on new empirical data collected in urban and rural areas of Europe, North America and Africa, this book makes an innovative contribution to both political and academic efforts to promote sustainable food systems through creative public procurement strategies.

The starting point of the book is that school meal systems can provide significant payoffs, including lower food miles, the creation of markets for local producers and effective food education initiatives that empower consumers by nurturing their capacity to eat healthily.

To assess this potential, the book compares a variety of sites involved in the school food revolution - from rural communities committed to the values of 'the local' to global cities such as London, New York and Rome that feed millions of ethnically diverse young people daily. The book also examines the developing country school feeding programme of the United Nations, which sees nutritious food as an end in itself as well as a means to meeting the Millennium Development Goals and raising the quality of life of the poorest of the poor.

Ultimately the book provides a critical look at the worlds of theory, policy and practice and it is a guide to the design and delivery of sustainable school food systems.

Hardback · £45.00 · 240 pages · 978-1-84407-482-2 · October 2008

For more details and a full listing of Earthscan titles visit:
www.earthscan.co.uk

publishing for a sustainable future

Ethical Sourcing in the Global Food System

Stephanie Barrientos, University of Sussex, UK
Catherine Dolan, Northeastern University, USA

Ethical sourcing, both through fair trade and ethical trade, is increasingly entering the mainstream of food retailing. Large supermarkets have come under pressure to improve the returns to small producers and conditions of employment within their supply chains.

But how effective is ethical sourcing? Can it genuinely address the problems facing workers and producers in the global food system? Is it a new form of northern protectionism or can southern initiatives be developed to create a more sustainable approach to ethical sourcing? How can the rights and participation of workers and small producers be enhanced, given the power and dominance of large supermarkets within the

global food chain? What role can civil society and multistakeholder initiatives play in ensuring the effectiveness of ethical sourcing? This book brings together a range of academics and practitioners working on issues of ethical sourcing in the global food system. It critically explores the opportunities and challenges in the ethical sourcing of food by combining analysis and case studies that examine a range of approaches. It explores whether ethical sourcing is a cosmetic northern initiative, or can genuinely help to improve the conditions of small producers and workers in the current global food system.

Paperback £22.95 • 224 pages • 978-1-84407-199-9 • 2006

Sharing Power
A Global Guide to Collaborative Management of Natural Resources

Grazia Borrini-Feyerabend, Michel Pimbert, M. Taghi Farvar, Ashish Kothari and Yves Renard
with Hanna Jaireth, Marshall Murphree, Vicki Pattemore, Ricardo Ramírez
and Patrizio Warren

'Sharing Power brings together an incredible range of experience from diverse communities and countries... a "must read" for all who care about the future of Earth's wonderful natural resources.'
Mark Poffenberger, executive director of Community Forestry International

This book is designed for professionals and people involved in practical co-management processes, and distils a wealth of experience and innovative approaches 'learned by doing'. It begins by offering a variety of vistas, from historical analyses to a clear grasp of key concepts.

Illustrated in detail is the understanding accumulated in recent decades on starting points for co-management, conditions and methods for successful negotiations, ideas to manage conflicts and types of agreements and co-management institutions emerging from the negotiation tables. Simple tools, such as checklists distilled from different situations and contexts, are offered throughout. Examples and insights from experience highlight the importance of participatory democracy - the enabling contexts where 'sharing power' is ultimately possible and successful.

Paperback • £49.95 • 502 pages • 978-1-84407-497-6 • 2007

For more details and a full listing of Earthscan titles visit:
www.earthscan**.co.uk**

publishing for a sustainable future

Earthscan E-Alerts

Sign up today!

Keep up to date with Earthscan's new titles in all aspects of sustainable development.

Sign up today to be reminded of new publications, forthcoming events and details of exclusive special offers.

E-alerts also include links for inspection and review copy requests.

Visit **www.earthscan.co.uk** to sign up for our monthly e-newsletter and subject-specific book e-alerts in the following subjects:

- Agriculture, Food and Water
- Architecture and Construction
- Business and Environmental Management
- Cities and Infrastructure
- Climate and Climate Change
- Design
- Development
- Ecology, Biodiversity and Conservation
- Economics
- Energy
- Environmental and Sustainability Assessment
- Forests
- Health and Population
- Natural Resource Management
- Politics, Governance and Law
- Risk, Science and Technology
- Sustainable Development
- Tourism

Once you have registered you can log in using your email address and password, and you can manage your e-alert preferences on your member's page. If you have any queries about your membership or anything else, don't hesitate to email us at **earthinfo@earthscan.co.uk** or give us a call on **+44(0)20 7841 1930**.

www.earthscan.co.uk